Teaching Translation

C000271243

Teaching Translation is the most comprehensive and theoretically informed overview of current translation teaching. Contributions from leading figures in translation studies are preceded by a substantial introduction by Lawrence Venuti, in which he presents a view of translation as the ultimate humanistic task—an interpretive act that varies the form, meaning, and effect of the source text. Twenty-six incisive chapters are divided into four parts, covering:

- certificate and degree programs
- teaching translation practices
- studying translation theory, history, and practice
- surveys of translation pedagogies and key textbooks

The chapters describe long-standing programs and courses in the US, Canada, the UK, and Spain, and each one presents an exemplary model for teaching that can be replicated or adapted in other institutions. Each contributor responds to fundamental questions at the core of any translation course—for example, how is translation defined? What qualifies students for admission to the course? What impact does the institutional site have upon the course or pedagogy?

Teaching Translation will be relevant for all those working and teaching in the areas of translation and translation studies. Additional resources for Translation and Interpreting Studies are available on the Routledge Translation Studies Portal: http://cw.routledge.com/textbooks/translationstudies.

Lawrence Venuti, Professor of English at Temple University, USA, is one of the world's leading translation theorists and a prolific literary translator. His recent publications include *Translation Changes Everything: Theory and Practice* (Routledge, 2013) and *The Translation Studies Reader* (3rd edn, Routledge, 2012).

Teaching Translation
Programs, Courses, Pedagogies

Edited by Lawrence Venuti

LONDON AND NEW YORK

First published 2017
by Routledge
2 Park Square, Milton Park, Abingdon, Oxon OX14 4RN

and by Routledge
711 Third Avenue, New York, NY 10017

Routledge is an imprint of the Taylor & Francis Group, an informa business

British Library Cataloguing in Publication Data
A catalogue record for this book is available from the British Library

Library of Congress Cataloging-in-Publication Data
A catalog record for this book has been requested

ISBN: 978-1-138-65460-0 (hbk)
ISBN: 978-1-138-65461-7 (pbk)
ISBN: 978-1-3156-2313-9 (ebk)

Typeset in Times New Roman
by Apex CoVantage, LLC

Printed and bound by CPI Group (UK) Ltd, Croydon, CR0 4YY

Contents

Acknowledgments

The seed for this book was sown at the conference, "Pedagogies of Translation: Current Methods and Future Prospects," held at Barnard College on May 4–5 of 2012. My thanks to Peter Connor for his willingness to sponsor the event through the Center for Translation Studies and for his help in co-organizing it with me. The book itself would not have been initiated without the encouragement and support of Margit Longbrake, formerly senior acquisitions editor in the Office of Publications at the Modern Language Association and currently senior editor at the Historic New Orleans Collection. It emerged through conversations with Margit, as well as my own work on different MLA committees, including Texts and Translations and the Publications Committee (2005–2012), where the need for such a volume became apparent. Unfortunately, the MLA publications process proved to be less supportive of the project. Louisa Semlyen, my editor at Routledge, also saw the need for it and helped to bring it to fruition. Chris Rundle, one of the appreciative readers for the press, made some useful suggestions for revision.

The call for papers attracted 164 proposals from twenty-four countries, which inevitably led to disappointing many committed teachers of translation who had devised courses and programs worthy of inclusion. This groundswell of interest demonstrated, nonetheless, that the project was timely and could potentially appeal to an international audience. I am grateful, in particular, to a number of faculty who shared information about their teaching, their syllabi, and their programs: Rosemary Arrojo, Kathryn Batchelor, Thomas O. Beebee, Susan Bernofsky, Carol Bove, Susanna Braund, Diego Burgos, Odile Cisneros, Eva Espasa, Ola Furmanek, Maysa Abou-Youssef Hayward, Elizabeth Lowe, Carol Maier, Elizabeth Marcus, Christi Merrill, Marcella Munson, Yopie Prins, Jamie Richards, Myriam Ruthenberg, Jordan Stump, Lorena Terando, Alyson Waters, Bethany Wiggin, and B. Christopher Wood. Corinne Scheiner provided helpful information about translation in Comparative Literature departments and programs. Trevor Margraf performed some essential research.

L.V.
New York City
January 2016

Notes on Contributors

Brian James Baer is Professor of Russian and Translation Studies at Kent State University. He is the author of *Translation and the Making of Modern Russian Literature* (2015) and the editor of *Contexts, Subtexts, and Pretexts: Literary Translation in Eastern Europe and Russia* (2011) and *Russian Writers on Translation. An Anthology* (2013). He is also the founding editor of the journal, *Translation and Interpreting Studies*, general editor of the Kent State Monograph Series in Translation Studies, and co-editor of the Bloomsbury series, "Literatures, Cultures, Translation."

Sonia Colina is Professor of Hispanic Linguistics in the Department of Spanish and Portuguese at the University of Arizona. She is the author of *Teaching Translation: From Research to the Classroom* (2003), *Spanish Phonology* (2009), and *Fundamentals of Translation* (2015). Her work has been published in such journals as *Babel*, *Target*, and *The Translator*. She is the Vice President of the American Translation and Interpreting Studies Association and serves on the editorial boards of *Translation and Interpreting Studies* and *The Interpreter and Translator Trainer*.

Sean Cotter is Associate Professor of Literature and Translation Studies affiliated with the Center for Translation Studies at the University of Texas at Dallas. He is the author of *Literary Translation and the Idea of a Minor Romania* (2014) and the co-editor of *The Man Between: Michael Henry Heim and a Life in Translation* (2014). His translations from Romanian include Nichita Danilov's *Second-Hand Souls: Selected Writings* (2003), Liliana Ursu's *Lightwall: Poems* (2009), Nichita Stănescu's *Wheel with a Single Spoke and Other Poems* (2012), and Mircea Cărtărescu's novel, *Blinding* (2013).

Karen Emmerich, formerly of the Department of Comparative Literature at the University of Oregon, is currently Assistant Professor of Comparative Literature at Princeton University. She is the author of *Translation and the Making of Originals* (forthcoming). Her articles on modern Greek literature and translation have appeared in such journals as *Arion*, *Journal of Modern Greek Studies*, *Translation Studies*, and *Word & Image*. Her translations include Miltos Sachtouris's *Poems: 1945–1971* (2006), Amanda Michalopoulou's stories, *I'd Like* (2008), Margarita Karapanou's novel, *The Sleepwalker* (2010), and a collection of Eleni Vakalo's poetry, *Beyond Lyricism* (2015).

Peter Filkins is Professor in the Division of Languages and Literature of Bard College at Simon's Rock, where he coordinates the Poetry and Fiction Series. He is the author of four books of poems, including *Augustine's Vision* (2010) and *The View We're Granted* (2012). Among his translations from German are *Songs in Flight: The Collected Poems of Ingeborg Bachmann* (1994), Alois Hotschnig's novel *Leonardo's Hands* (1999), Bernd Stiegler's *Traveling in Place: A History of Armchair Travel* (2013), and several novels by H. G. Adler, including *The Wall* (2014). The recipient of awards from the American Literary Translators Association and the Austrian government, he has held fellowships at the American Academy in Berlin and the Leon Levy Center of Biography at the CUNY Graduate Center.

Luise von Flotow is Professor of Translation Studies in the University of Ottawa's School of Translation and Interpretation, which she currently directs. She is the author of *Translation and Gender: Translation in the "Era of Feminism"* (1997) and the editor of *Translating Women* (2011). She has also co-edited several volumes, including *The Third Shore: Women's Fiction from East Central Europe* (2006) and *Translation Effects: The Shaping of Modern Canadian Culture* (2014). Among the novels she has translated from German and Québécois French are Emine Sevgi Özdamar's *Life Is a Caravanserai* (2000), France Théoret's *Girls Closed In* (2005), and Christa Wolf's *They Divided the Sky* (2013).

Reginald Gibbons is Frances Hooper Chair in the Arts and Humanities and Professor of English, Classics, Spanish, and Portuguese at Northwestern University, where he directs the Center for the Writing Arts. He is the author of ten books of poems, including *Creatures of a Day* (2008) and *Last Lake* (2016). He has also published a novel, *Sweetbitter* (1995), and a critical work, *How Poems Think* (2015). He is the translator of *Guillén on Guillén: The Poetry and the Poet* (1979), *Selected Poems of Luis Cernuda* (1999), and Sophocles' *Selected Poems: Odes and Fragments* (2008). With Charles Segal, he translated Euripides' *Bakkhai* (2001) and Sophocles' *Antigone* (2003).

Maria González-Davies is Senior Lecturer in the Department of Foreign Languages in the Faculty of Psychology, Education, and Sports Sciences at the Universitat Ramon Llull in Barcelona. She is the author of *Multiple Voices in the Translation Classroom* (2004), the coauthor of *Medical Translation Step by Step: Learning by Drafting* (2007), and the editor of *Secuencias. Tareas para el aprendizaje de la traducción especializada* (2003). She is on the editorial boards of *The Interpreter and Translator Trainer* and *Translation and Translanguaging in Multilingual Contexts*. Her articles have appeared in such journals as *Meta: Translators' Journal* and *Quaderns: Revista de Traducció*.

Lee Haring is Professor Emeritus of English at Brooklyn College of the City University of New York. He is the author of *Malagasy Tale Index* (1982), *Collecting Folklore in Mauritius* (1992), *Verbal Arts in Madagascar: Performance in Historical Perspective* (1992), and *Stars and Keys: Folktales and*

Creolization in the Indian Ocean (2007). His research in East African oral literatures also yielded the translation, *How to Read a Folktale: The Ibonia Epic from Madagascar* (2013). A Guggenheim Fellow, he received a Lifetime Scholarly Achievement Award from the American Folklore Society.

Michelle Hartman is Associate Professor of Arabic Literature in the Institute of Islamic Studies at McGill University. She is the author of *Joseph, Jesus, and Job: Readings of Intertextual Rescriptings of Religious Figures in Lebanese Women's Fiction* (2002) and *Native Tongue, Stranger Talk: Voices from the Arabic and French Literary Landscapes of Lebanon* (2014). Her articles on Arabic literature and translation have appeared in such journals as *Feminist Studies*, *Tulsa Studies in Women's Literature*, and *International Journal of Middle East Studies*, as well as in several edited volumes, including the MLA's *Approaches to Teaching Naguib Mahfouz* (2011). Among her translations of Arabic novels are Iman Humaydan Younes's *Wild Mulberries* (2008) and *Other Lives* (2014) and Alexandra Chreiteh's *Always Coca-Cola* (2012).

Jan Walsh Hokenson, Professor Emerita of Comparative Literature at Florida Atlantic University, currently lives in Vermont. She is the author of *Japan, France, and East-West Aesthetics: French Literature 1867–2000* (2004), *The Idea of Comedy: History, Theory, Critique* (2006), and, with Marcella Munson, *The Bilingual Text: History and Theory of Literary Self-Translation* (2007). Her recent work on translation includes "Comedies of Errors: Bergson's *Laughter* in Modernist Contexts" in *Understanding Bergson, Understanding Modernism* (2013), edited by Paul Ardoin, S. E. Gontarski, and Laci Mattison.

Michael D. Hubert is Associate Professor of Spanish in the Department of Foreign Languages and Cultures at Washington State University. His research interests include second language acquisition, second and foreign-language writing, Spanish phonetics and phonology, and the teaching of translation. His articles have appeared in such journals as *Electronic Journal of Foreign Language Teaching*, *Foreign Language Annals*, *International Journal of Applied Linguistics*, and *Journal of Education and Training Studies*.

Ignacio Infante is Associate Professor of Comparative Literature and Spanish at Washington University in St. Louis. He is the author of *After Translation: The Transfer and Circulation of Modern Poetics Across the Atlantic* (2013). His articles have appeared in such journals as *Journal of Spanish Cultural Studies*, *Revista Híspanica Moderna*, *Revista Estudios Hispánicos*, and *Variaciones Borges*. He has also written Spanish translations of John Ashbery's *A Wave* (2003) and Will Self's *How the Dead Live* (2003).

Bill Johnston is Henry Remak Professor of Comparative Literature at Indiana University. He is the author of *Values in English Language Teaching* (2002) and *The First Year at University: Students in Transition* (2010). Among his many translations of Polish fiction and poetry are Andrzej Szczypiorski's *Self-Portrait with Woman* (1997), Witold Gombrowicz's *Bacacay* (2004), Magdalena

Tulli's *In Red* (2011), and Tomasz Różycki's *Twelve Stations* (2015). His translation of Wiesław Myśliwski's *Stone upon Stone* (2010) won several awards,
including the PEN Translation Prize. The recipient of fellowships from the
NEA, the NEH, and the Guggenheim Foundation, he was awarded the 2014
Transatlantyk Prize for his work on behalf of Polish culture.

David Johnston is Professor of Hispanic Studies at Queen's University, Belfast,
where he leads the research group in translation and cultural encounter. He is
the author of *Federico García Lorca* (1998) and the editor of *Stages of Translation: Interviews and Essays on Translating for the Stage* (1996). He has co-
edited *Betwixt and Between: Place and Cultural Translation* (2007) and *The
Spanish Golden Age in English: Perspectives on Performance* (2007). Among
his drama translations are Lorca's *Blood Wedding* (1989), Edgar Chías's *On
Insomnia and Midnight: A Tale to Frighten Chambermaids* (2006), and Lope
de Vega's *Lady Boba: A Woman of Little Sense* (2013). His translations have
been staged by the BBC, the Gate, the Royal Court, and the Royal Shakespeare
Company, among many other venues.

Paul Losensky is Associate Professor in the Departments of Central Eurasian
Studies and Comparative Literature at Indiana University. He is the author of
*Welcoming Fighāni: Imitation and Poetic Individuality in the Safavid-Mughal
Ghazal* (1998). His translations from Persian include Farid ad-Din 'Attar's
Memorial of God's Friends: Lives and Sayings of the Sufis (1998) and, with
Sunil Sharma, *In the Bazaar of Love: Selected Poetry of Amir Khusrau* (2013).
A former fellow at the National Humanities Center, he has published in such
journals as *Iranian Studies* and is a frequent contributor to the *Encyclopedia of
Islam* and the *Encyclopaedia Iranica*.

Sarah Maitland is Senior Lecturer in Translation Studies at Goldsmiths, University of London, where she directs the master's program in translation. She is
the author of *What Is Cultural Translation?* (2016). Her articles have appeared
in such journals as *The International Journal of the Humanities*, *Bulletin of
the Comediantes*, *Translation Studies*, *Perspectives: Studies in Translatology*,
and *Quaderns: Revista de Traducció*. She has translated Spanish drama for the
Theatre Royal Bath, the Unicorn and New Diorama theaters in London, and
the Rose Bruford College of Theatre and Performance. Her drama translations
include Ernesto Caballero's *On the Rock* (2005), José Ramon Fernandez's
Nina (2007), and Lourdes Ortiz's *Mad King Ludwig* (2008).

Anne Malena is Professor of French in the Department Modern Languages
and Cultural Studies at the University of Alberta. She is the author of *The
Negotiated Self: The Dynamics of Identity in Francophone Caribbean Narrative* (1999) as well as the editor of *Les Antilles en traduction/The Caribbean
in Translation* (2000) and *Traduction et (im)migration/Translation and
(Im)migration* (2003). Her articles on Francophone writing and translation
have appeared in such journals as *TTR: Traduction, Terminologie, Rédaction*,
Journal of West Indian Literature, and *Translation Studies*. She has translated
from English to French two novels by the Icelandic-Canadian writer Kristjana
Gunnars, *La maraude* (1995) and *Degré zéro* (1998).

Françoise Massardier-Kenney is Professor of Modern and Classical Language Studies at Kent State University, where she currently directs the Institute for Applied Linguistics. She is the author of *Gender in the Fiction of George Sand* (2000). She has co-edited several volumes, including *Translating Slavery 1: Gender and Race in French Women's Writing, 1783–1823* (2009), *Translating Slavery 2: Ourika and its Progeny* (2010), and *Literature in Translation: Teaching Issues and Reading Practices* (2010). Among her translations from French are George Sand's novel, *Valvèdre* (2007) and Antoine Berman's *Toward a Translation Criticism: John Donne* (2009). She is the general editor of the American Translators Association Scholarly Monograph Series and the co-editor in chief of *George Sand Studies*.

Jane O. Newman is Professor of Comparative Literature and European Studies at the University of California at Irvine. She is the author of *Pastoral Conventions: Poetry, Language, and Thought in Seventeenth-Century Nuremberg* (1990), *The Intervention of Philology: Gender, Learning, and Power in Lohenstein's Roman Plays* (2000), and *Benjamin's Library: Modernity, Nation, and the Baroque* (2011). She has translated *Time, History, and Literature. Selected Essays of Erich Auerbach* (2014), which received the MLA's Scaglione Prize for a Translation of a Scholarly Study of Literature. A Guggenheim and Humboldt fellow, as well as a Fulbright Senior Scholar in Berlin, she held the M. H. Abrams Fellowship at the National Humanities Center.

Markus Nornes is Professor of Asian Cinema in the Department of Screen Arts and Cultures and the Department of Asian Languages and Cultures at the University of Michigan. He is the author of *Japanese Documentary Film: The Meiji Era Through Hiroshima* (2003), *Forest of Pressure: Ogawa Shinsuke and Postwar Japanese Documentary* (2007), and *Cinema Babel: Translating Global Cinema* (2007). He has written the English subtitles for a number of Japanese films, including Sato Makoto's documentary, *Artists in Wonderland* (1998). The recipient of fellowships from the Fulbright Program, the Japan Foundation, and the Taiwan Ministry of Education, he has held visiting professorships at Harvard University and Fudan University (Shanghai).

Lynn Penrod is Professor of French in the Department of Modern Languages and Cultural Studies at the University of Alberta, where she is also Lecturer in Law. She is the author of *Hélène Cixous* (1996) and the co-author of *Mise en pratique: Manuel de lecture, vocabulaire, grammaire et expression écrite* (2009). Her articles on French women's writing, literary translation, and the interrelationships between literature and the law have appeared in a number of edited volumes, including the MLA's *Approaches to Teaching George Sand's Indiana* (2015).

Joshua Price is Professor in the Department of Sociology and in the Translation Research and Instruction Program at the State University of New York at Binghamton. He is the author of *Structural Violence: Hidden Brutality in the Lives of Women* (2012) and *Prison and Social Death: The Abyssal Divide* (2016). His articles on translation have appeared in *Mutatis Mutandis*, *Target*, and

Translation Perspectives. He is the co-translator of Rodolfo Kusch's study, *Indigenous and Popular Thinking in América* (2010), and José Pablo Feinmann's novel, *Heidegger's Shadow* (2015).

Roger Sedarat is Associate Professor of English at Queens College of the City University of New York. He is the author of *New England Landscape History in American Poetry: A Lacanian View* (2011) and two collections of poetry, *Dear Regime: Letters to the Islamic Republic* (2007), which won the Ohio University Press's Hollis Summers Prize, and *Ghazal Games* (2011). His translations from Persian have appeared in such magazines as *Arroyo*, *Ezra*, *Guernica*, and *World Literature Today*. In 2015, he won the Willis Barnstone Translation Prize.

Shaden M. Tageldin is Associate Professor of Cultural Studies and Comparative Literature and Director of the African Studies Initiative at the University of Minnesota, where she is currently Director of Graduate Studies. She is the author of *Disarming Words: Empire and the Seductions of Translation in Egypt* (2011), which received an Honorable Mention for the Harry Levin Prize of the American Comparative Literature Association. Her articles on comparative literature and postcolonial theory have appeared in such journals as *Comparative Literature Studies*, *International Journal of Middle East Studies*, *Journal of Arabic Literature, Journal of Historical Sociology*, and *PMLA*.

Sevinç Türkkan, formerly Visiting Assistant Professor at the State University of New York at Brockport, is currently Assistant Professor of Comparative Literature and Translation Studies at the State University of New York at Binghamton. She co-edited the MLA volume, *Approaches to Teaching the Works of Orhan Pamuk* (forthcoming). Her articles on translation, Turkish literature, and Bulgarian and Turkish film have appeared in several edited volumes, including Mehnaz Afridi and David Buyze's *Global Perspectives on Orhan Pamuk's Literature* (2012). Her translations from German and Turkish have appeared in the Dalkey Archive Press annual, *Best European Fiction*.

Karen Van Dyck is Kimon A. Doukas Professor of Modern Greek Literature in the Classics Department at Columbia University, where she directs the Program in Hellenic Studies. She is the author of *Kassandra and the Censors: Greek Poetry since 1967* (1998) and the editor and translator of *The Rehearsal of Misunderstanding: Three Collections by Contemporary Greek Women Poets* (1998) and *The Scattered Papers of Penelope: New and Selected Poems by Katerina Anghelaki-Rooke* (2009). She also edited and contributed translations to *A Century of Greek Poetry* (2004), *The Greek Poets: Homer to the Present* (2009), and *Austerity Measures: The New Greek Poetry* (2016).

Ben Van Wyke is Assistant Professor of Spanish and Translation Studies at Indiana University-Purdue University at Indianapolis. He is the author of *Delectable Bodies and their Clothes: Plato, Nietzsche, and the Translation of Latin America* (2010). His articles have appeared in *Translation Studies* and *The Translator* and in such edited volumes as Yves Gambier and Luc van

Doorslaer's *Handbook of Translation Studies* (2010). His literary translations from Spanish have been published in several magazines, including *Absinthe*, *Massachusetts Review*, and *Rattapallax*.

Lawrence Venuti is Professor of English at Temple University. He is the author of *The Translator's Invisibility: A History of Translation* (2nd ed., 2008), *The Scandals of Translation: Towards an Ethics of Difference* (1998), and *Translation Changes Everything: Theory and Practice* (2013), as well as the editor of *Re-thinking Translation: Discourse, Subjectivity, Ideology* (1992) and *The Translation Studies Reader* (3rd ed., 2012). His translations from Italian include Antonia Pozzi's *Breath: Poems and Letters* (2002), Massimo Carlotto's *The Goodbye Kiss* (2006), and I.U Tarchetti's *Fantastic Tales* (2014). His version of Catalan poet Ernest Farrés's collection, *Edward Hopper* (2009), won the Robert Fagles Translation Prize. The recipient of awards from the PEN American Center, the NEA, the NEH, and the Guggenheim Foundation, he held a Fulbright Senior Lectureship at the Universitat de Vic (Catalonia).

Introduction

Translation, Interpretation, and the Humanities

Lawrence Venuti

Teaching Translation Studies

Over the past half-century, translation studies has emerged decisively as an academic field around the world, and in recent years programs devoted to the teaching of translation have proliferated. Surveys indicate more than 350 programs worldwide (for a list periodically updated by the European Society for Translation Studies, see http://www.est-translationstudies.org/resources/tti/tti.htm). They offer a variety of certificates and degrees, undergraduate and graduate, emphasizing either practice or research or combining both, training not only professional translators but also scholar-teachers of translation and of foreign languages and literatures. The number of programs has risen not only with the expansion of the field but also with the steady increase of international organizations, the continual eruption of political and military conflicts, and the consequent displacement of mass populations, all of which create the urgent need for translators and interpreters. In multi- and bilingual cultures, meanwhile, translator training has long been a necessity insofar as translation is a fact of daily life.

The emergence of the field has coincided with the gradual development of a fairly standard curriculum for teaching translation studies, especially at the master's level, where students are trained to enter the job market as translators or to proceed to doctoral research and academic careers. In the current configuration, mandatory courses (i.e., term-long units or modules in a program) focus on theory and practice, joining the study of theoretical concepts and research methods with the acquisition of practical skills in translating and interpreting. The concepts tend to be derived from varieties of linguistics, from literary and cultural studies, and from sociology; the skills are often taught in relation to specific genres or text types (legal, medical, commercial, literary, and so forth) and according to language pairs (i.e., an assortment of source and translating languages that often reflect the location of the institution). Optional courses might provide instruction in more specialized areas, such as audiovisual translation and computer-assisted translation tools, and sometimes in other, related fields, such as literary history and international politics. The variety of course offerings, as a rule, depends on the expertise of the instructors who staff the program. Translation studies now consists of a recognizable body of knowledge that is codified in a curriculum and presented in a significant number of widely adopted textbooks in various languages, although English remains the lingua franca in the field. Alongside this development, a scholarly literature on translation pedagogy has accumulated through research monographs, journals, and conference proceedings that explore different teaching methods.

Foremost among the aims of this book is to take stock of how translation studies is taught at the present time. It seeks to document a variety of programs, courses, and pedagogies situated in various kinds of institutions. In so doing, it seeks to display possibilities for curricular and pedagogical innovation in a field where a certain degree of consolidation has now occurred. It implicitly asks how the teaching of translation research and practice can improve—and how improvement can be measured—when the field, like every academic specialization, has achieved such stability as might resist change in order to maintain a viable institutional position.

Questions about improvement can be given different answers, no doubt, which might vary according to the methodological terms, cultural situations, and historical moments in which they are posed. Taking the translation market as the main criterion for the effectiveness of a program or course, developing pedagogies in accordance with changing market conditions and demands is likely to rank high in assessing teaching, and so it should, especially for genres and text types in pragmatic and technical fields where functionality is inextricably linked to economic value. Yet market-driven assessments of teaching limit or even preempt the sort of critical examination—whether of translation or of the market—that can stimulate other kinds of innovation and improvement. With the market as the main or sole standard of pedagogy, translation ultimately serves quantitative thinking that aims merely to reduce or overcome linguistic and cultural differences and thereby neglects the values, beliefs, and representations that constitute those differences and of which translation itself is the vehicle and support.

This book takes a rather unusual approach to questions of improvement by focusing on a place where the teaching of translation studies is undergoing a sophisticated yet markedly uneven development that has yet to solidify into a standard or model: North America, especially the United States. Here the field is beginning to grow, finally, after decades of being restricted to relatively few academic institutions. The chapters that follow show how instructors make use of translation research, textbooks, and pedagogies originating in places where the field is more consolidated. They also reveal the cross-fertilization from neighboring fields that at once enables and constrains the creation of programs and courses in translation studies. They offer an opportunity to learn from a situation characterized by extreme diversity, if not sheer disarray, fostering the experimentation and inventiveness that can occur when a field is at a rudimentary stage of growth. But they are also intended to advance translation pedagogies beyond this stage while elevating the status of translation studies as a distinct academic field. With these aims in mind, specific chapters document practices in such other countries as Canada, the United Kingdom, and Spain, where translation studies has achieved a firm institutional basis.

In the United States, the number of programs has traditionally been small, even if it has grown considerably, and their emphases have generally been divided between pragmatic and technical translation, on the one hand, and literary translation, on the other. The 1950s saw the creation of what is currently the Middlebury Institute for International Studies at Monterey, which developed a master's curriculum in translator training with a focus on pragmatic and technical texts as well as conference interpreting. In the 1960s, workshops in literary translation began to be offered in graduate creative writing programs at the University of Iowa, Columbia University, and elsewhere. In the 1970s, the Translation Research and Instruction Program was established at the State University of New York at Binghamton to offer graduate certificates in translation practice to supplement degrees in humanistic disciplines. In the 1980s, the Department of Modern Languages and the Institute for Applied Linguistics at Kent State University initiated a master's program in translation that trains students to become professional translators, again primarily of pragmatic and technical texts. These programs metamorphosed over the years as changes occurred in the translation market, in the field of translation studies, and in the institutions where the programs are housed. Today they remain among the main sites where translation research and practice can be studied in the United States.

Over the past two decades, they have been joined by various other developments that indicate the increasing academic presence of translation. Foreign-language departments continue to be deeply committed to the direct communicative method of language teaching, a pedagogy that has been extremely effective in producing students with native proficiency because, in part, it minimizes or excludes English-language translation. Yet recently these departments have created more opportunities to study translating and interpreting into and out of English, including programs on both the undergraduate and graduate levels designed to train students for careers as translators (e.g. the Department of Languages and Cultural Studies at the University of North Carolina at Charlotte, the Department of Spanish and Portuguese at Rutgers University, and the Department of Romance Languages at Wake Forest University). Some programs in creative writing, both undergraduate and graduate, have broadened their traditional emphasis on poetry and fiction to offer not just translation workshops but seminars in translation topics; they have also begun to allow students to submit a book-length translation as a senior or master's thesis (e.g. Princeton University and Queens College in the City University of New York). Princeton has initiated a pioneering undergraduate program in translation and intercultural communication, in effect devising a model that is likely to be adopted at other institutions. In what is perhaps the most exciting trend, reflecting recent debates provoked by the revival of the notion of "world" literature, departments and programs of comparative literature have developed courses and certificates that allow students to explore the history of translation theory and practice, to translate literary texts, and to consider the problem of teaching foreign-language texts in translation (e.g. Colorado College, the University of Oregon, and Washington University in St. Louis).

Institutional Antinomies

These developments have brought with them complications for the institutional sites where they have occurred as well as for the profession of languages and literatures at large, since it is mainly in this profession that translation studies has emerged in the United States. The complications might be formulated as a set of antinomies that currently beset the establishment of the field there. I will mention three so as to sketch in a more detailed way the situation from which this book derives and into which it aims to intervene with greatest consequence.

First, *although the creation of translation courses and programs should be welcomed as a sign of progress, there has been a tendency to staff them with instructors, including senior faculty, who neither translate nor conduct research in translation.*

This tendency runs counter to what is perhaps the most hallowed principle defining the identity of the scholar-teacher: only instructors who are professionally current in a field, who are not only conversant with its trends and methods but conduct research in it and participate in its debates, should be assigned to teach courses in that field. The fact is that the faculty from various languages and literatures, periods and areas who are sometimes assigned courses in translation studies would never condone the assignment of courses in their specialties to teachers who lack a professional credential as well as currency in those specialties. To be sure, a faculty member's retooling in translation studies can lead to effective teaching, and one aim of this book is to encourage an immersion in translation theory and history as a productive way for faculty to develop courses and to improve pedagogical strategies. Yet in translation studies, as in any academic field, retooling cannot replace ongoing research and publication as a credential or qualification that underpins committed, innovative, and responsible teaching. The antinomy seems to point to a lingering attitude that may well be unconscious but that in any case needs to be abandoned if we truly acknowledge that translation studies can make a unique contribution to the study of languages, literatures, and cultures. I would describe that attitude as a reluctance to recognize translation studies as an academic field in its own right, with its own body of scholarship, its own debates, trends, and methods, its own traditions of theory and commentary, practice and pedagogy, its own conferences, journals, and presses with lists or series in the area.

Here a second, related antinomy appears: *Although in 2011 the Modern Language Association of America (MLA) adopted guidelines for evaluating translations in hiring and in reviews for tenure, promotion, and merit raises, a decision to dedicate one's research and scholarship to translation in any form continues to be tantamount to jeopardizing one's academic career.*

Scholars in classical and modern languages have long included translation as part of their work, but a stigma came to be attached to the practice during the twentieth century. As a result, the production of a translation *per se*, especially in the absence of commentary, has been considered ancillary to scholarship and finally inadequate. It is hardly surprising, then, that, in the United States, an expertise in translation studies is only beginning to be listed as a qualification for an appointment in a department or program of English, a foreign language, or comparative literature. The rarity of such an advertisement became apparent in 2011, when the Department of Comparative Literature at the University of Oregon took the unique step of advertising for "a tenure-track assistant professor in Translation Studies" to teach courses and to develop programs where translation theory, history, and practice are central. A related indication of the professional stigma that still attaches to translation is the paucity of doctoral dissertations that take as their object of study not the work of a canonical author, not a theme, genre, practice, or medium that has achieved professional recognition, but rather the work of a translator or a body of translations, especially those produced by translators who are not canonical authors.

In many departments of languages and literatures, students are discouraged from studying translation merely by the curriculum. Courses in translation studies are not widely or frequently offered, although the increasing appeal of such courses to both undergraduate and graduate students is demonstrated by current enrollments in departments and programs that routinely offer them. To take one striking example, the undergraduate course titled "Introduction to Translation Studies," an elective offered in the Comparative Literature Program at Barnard College, has been attracting over 100 students from the Barnard and Columbia communities every fall since 2012. Nonetheless, a trawl through United States college and university websites indicates that only about 25 percent of the more than 180 schools currently offering comparative literature in some form include translation studies in their course inventories. This figure seems quite low for a field that could not exist without the extensive use of translations, especially on the undergraduate level. The situation seems not to have significantly changed since 2005, when a report on the undergraduate curriculum in comparative literature showed that 76.2 percent of the forty schools responding required courses on world literature in translation, but only 14.3 percent required courses in translation theory and practice (Association of Departments and Programs of Comparative Literature 2006: 181).

The two antinomies I have described suggest that the profession of languages and literatures lacks a consensus as to the very nature of translation, that competing ideas of what it is and does contribute to its continuing marginality by provoking an uncertainty about its value. Prevalent notions of translatability conceive of translation as a one-to-one correspondence with the source text, reducing it to a process of mechanical substitution. Prevalent notions of untranslatability conceive of translation as an inevitable loss of source-text features, reducing it to a representation that is incomplete, distorted, inauthentic. Today, translatability rests on concepts of equivalence, often formulated on the basis of discourse analysis, systemic-functional linguistics, and pragmatics, leading to the development and application of compensatory translation strategies, whereas untranslatability rests on concepts of indeterminacy, often formulated on the basis of poststructuralist theories of language and textuality, leading to the identification and interrogation of mistranslations (for an example of the former, see Baker 2011; for the latter, see Cassin 2004).

Both notions constitute implicit arguments against thinking of translation as scholarship or as art, as a kind of writing that should be valued for its learning or its creativity, or that might be learned and creative at the same time. Yet both notions, despite the dichotomy they seem to represent, actually assume the same model or paradigm of translation, what I shall call the instrumental model, in which translation is seen as the reproduction or transfer of an invariant that is contained in or caused by the source text, whether its form, its meaning, or its effect. Hence either translation can be easily done or it can never be done: these views are inversions of one another. Jacques Derrida's now famous paradox—"nothing is translatable; nothing is untranslatable"—encapsulates the instrumental model of translation, although without decisively breaking with it (Derrida 1999: 178).

This kind of thinking reveals a third antinomy: *Although George Steiner's widely read book* After Babel *(1975a) propagated the very different model of translation as an interpretive act, although this model has long been assumed in the German and French traditions of hermeneutics as well as in poststructuralism and therefore can be said to belong to the current critical orthodoxy in literary and cultural studies, the instrumental model of translation remains so entrenched in academic institutions that a hermeneutic approach has yet to be developed and widely applied in all its conceptual and practical ramifications.*

This antinomy can be glimpsed in various academic practices that are widespread enough to be considered routine, if they have not simply become conventional. Research monographs that display formidable theoretical and critical self-awareness quote from and comment on translations without any recognition of their status as translations, let alone an acknowledgement that the translation has inscribed an interpretation in the source text that might support or be consistent with the interpretation advanced in the monograph. Translators' names are omitted from bibliographies that otherwise provide the requisite data about works cited. Reviews of translated scholarship similarly make no mention of the translation or restrict any mention to an assessment of its readability or accuracy—yet without any recognition that the translation has interpreted the source text so as to affect the reviewer's comprehension and evaluation of it. Such practices all make the instrumentalist assumption that translation can and should reproduce a stable form and meaning inherent in the source text without hindrance or without the interposition of any difference worth remarking. For these scholarly intents and purposes, the translation is effectively the source text.

We can agree that a translation is capable of maintaining a semantic correspondence to the source text, even that it can approximate the formal features characteristic of that text, so that summaries of plots and arguments, accounts of characters and conceptual terms, analyses of style, figure, and discourse may all be intelligibly and convincingly grounded on the textual evidence presented by the translation. Nevertheless, a text is a complex linguistic and cultural artifact that supports meanings, values, and functions specific to its originary situation. Not only is any text much more than the correspondences and approximations established by a translation, but they can never preempt the decisive transformation entailed by rewriting a text in a different language for circulation in a different culture. The transformation can be viewed as decisive, however, only if we assume that translation is an interpretive act whereby the translated text comes to support meanings, values, and functions specific to the receiving situation.

If scholarly research has not yet been able to free itself from a deep-seated instrumentalism in understanding and using translations, we might wonder how this model has affected teaching. Consider the MLA series, *Approaches to Teaching World Literature*. The MLA's rigorous guidelines and evaluative procedures ensure that each volume reflects professional norms as embodied in prevalent teaching practices: the process begins with a membership-wide call for papers and a survey of instructors who specialize in the specific author, genre, or period addressed in the volume, while the essays themselves offer diverse accounts of courses and pedagogies, sampling a broad spectrum of classroom practices and experiences. There can be no doubt about the enormous usefulness of these volumes as guides to teaching; those that are recent or updated can also serve as helpful indicators of current research trends. The series as a whole displays considerable sophistication, mirroring developments in literary theory and criticism that have informed the profession since the mid-1980s, when the books began to appear.

Yet since almost half of them, roughly forty thus far, are dedicated to the teaching of non-Anglophone texts, we must wonder whether these volumes are addressed solely to instructors who can work with the foreign languages in which the texts were originally written. For the comments on English translations *as translations* are limited to assessments of their accuracy in communicating the foreign-language text and placed in an introductory section; when a translation is quoted in the essays, it is generally presented without comment and therefore assumed to be an untroubled communication of the foreign-language text. In both instances, the formal and semantic features of that text, including its tropes and styles, plots and genres, narrators and characters, discourses and themes, are treated as invariants that are either transferred intact or misrepresented by the translation. The volumes rarely include essays that consider the teaching of English translations as texts that are relatively autonomous from the foreign-language texts they translate precisely because translations inscribe interpretations that necessarily transform their source texts (the omission was noticed in Venuti 1998: 91–2). These interpretations deserve to be articulated and studied in the receiving contexts in which they were produced, especially since they inevitably inflect the teaching of translations in Anglophone classrooms. But they will become intelligible only if we abandon instrumentalism and adopt a hermeneutic model in our understanding of translation.

Recent volumes in the series, reflecting the emergence of translation studies in the profession, have begun to include essays that address the challenge of teaching English-language translations. In Waïl Hassan and Susan Muaddi Darraj's *Approaches to Teaching the Works of Naguib Mahfouz* (2012), for instance, Maysa Abou-Youssef Hayward's chapter, "Teaching Mahfouz: Style in Translation," discusses how she engages Anglophone students in an illuminating analysis of Trevor Le Gassick's 1975 version of Mahfouz's novel, *Midaq Alley* (1947). Focusing

on formal features such as style and register, narrative point of view and dialogue, Hayward locates points where Le Gassick's translation both approximates
and shifts away from the Arabic text, although she does not treat the translation
dismissively. On the contrary, she acknowledges that the structural differences
between Arabic and English as well as different linguistic and cultural norms
make the translation no more than one possible interpretation of Mahfouz's novel.
"An effective translation," she observes, "like Trevor Le Gassick's, highlights
key elements of the original and interprets as well as transmits the text" (Hayward
2012: 130). Hence in the classroom she turns the approximations and shifts to
account, using them to teach United States-based students about the novel and the
translation, about Arabic and English, and about Egyptian culture and their own.

A Humanistic Practice

The hermeneutic model of translation underlies the contributions to the present
volume. Here translation is understood as an interpretive act that varies the form,
meaning, and effect of the source text according to the intelligibilities and interests of the translating culture. The variation is inevitable, driven in the first place
by the structural differences between languages and by the differences in values,
beliefs, and representations between cultures. Translation works by detaching
the source text from the set of contexts—linguistic and cultural, institutional and
social—that constitute it as a signifying process and by building another set of
contexts that constitute the translated text so as to permit it to signify in another
language and culture. The process involves, on the one hand, a loss of intricate
relations between source-language features and source-culture contexts and, on
the other hand, a gain of comparable relations between translating-language features and translating-culture contexts. These two movements are simultaneous,
and although they are related, usually motivated by a mimetic impulse on the
translator's part, they result in the inscription of an interpretation in the source text
that answers to the receiving situation.

The translator inscribes an interpretation by applying a category that mediates
between the source language and culture and the translating language and culture,
a method of transforming the source text into the translation. This category consists of interpretants, which may be either formal or thematic (my use of the term
"interpretant" develops Umberto Eco's commentary on Charles Peirce's semiotics: see 1976a; Eco 1976b: 69–71; 1979: chap. 7). Formal interpretants include a
concept of equivalence, such as a semantic correspondence based on dictionary
definitions (in other words, a lexicographical equivalence), or a concept of style,
a distinctive lexicon and syntax related to a genre or discourse. Thematic interpretants are codes: they might include specific values, beliefs and representations;
a discourse in the sense of a relatively coherent body of concepts, problems, and
arguments; or a particular interpretation of the source text that has been articulated independently in commentary. Interpretants are fundamentally intertextual,
rooted primarily in the receiving situation even if in some cases they may incorporate source cultural materials. It is the translator's application of interpretants

that recontextualizes the source text, replacing source intertextual relations with a receiving intertext, with relations to the translating language and culture which are built into the translation.

The hermeneutic model can be seen as offering an account of the translation process that is both comprehensive and incisive. In displaying the interpretive force of the translator's verbal choices, it aims to expose the various determinations that make possible a translation by focusing the attention of both translator and reader on the application of interpretants in a particular cultural situation at a particular historical moment. At once a conceptual category and an analytical tool, the interpretant lays bare not only the diverse conditions that figure in the production of a translation, of its formal and thematic features, but their relations to the hierarchy of cultural values and social institutions in the receiving situation where the translation both originates and circulates.

Hence the notion of translation as an interpretive act must not be viewed as licensing an arbitrary or indiscriminate treatment of the source text. Not only does the hermeneutic model allow for the translator's application of varying concepts of equivalence, but the range and selection of interpretants are both enabled and constrained by the situation in which the translation is produced, by the hierarchical arrangement of linguistic usage, literary forms, cultural values, and social positions in that situation. Moreover, a translation is an interpretive act regardless of the genre or text type of the source text. Whether the translator is working with pragmatic, technical, or humanistic texts, a museum brochure, a scientific article, or a novel, verbal choices constitute interpretive moves made through the application of formal and thematic interpretants. The interpretants applied in translating a scientific article would include a lexicographical equivalence that combines the current standard dialect of the translating language with the standardized terminology used in the particular scientific field that gave rise to the source text. The translator's choices are enabled and constrained by the text type as well as by the function that the source text is designed to serve, but they nonetheless inscribe an interpretation that might differ with a change of genre or function, such as when a technical text is incorporated into a novel.

The hermeneutic model brings the awareness that no text is ever available in some unmediated form. A text is indistinguishable from the prior interpretive act that Derrida calls an "inscription": "the written origin: traced and henceforth *inscribed in* a system, in a figure which it no longer governs" (Derrida 1978: 115; his italics). The source text is always already mediated, whether read in the source language or translated into a receiving language, and that mediation consists of an interpretation that is itself determined by a network of signification beyond the control and often the awareness of author and translator, whether in the source or the receiving culture. The source text can never be viewed as strictly original, then, because the inescapable inscription "brings[s] the origin or a priori principles in relation to what exceeds them" (Gasché 1986: 161). By the same token, no translation can be described, explained, or evaluated without an inscription, the interposition of interpretants that serve as analytical tools and evaluative principles. Thus any analysis or evaluation of a translation that proceeds simply on the basis of a comparison to the source text conceals, in effect, a crucial third category: a prior inscription or application of interpretants that makes possible and limits the analysis or evaluation.

This point shows that the hermeneutic model can avoid the mystification that results from the instrumentalism assumed by any theory, commentary, or evaluation that imagines translation as the unmediated reproduction or transfer of an invariant. The instrumental model renders a translation invisible by assuming that it can and should reproduce the source text. Yet this model also renders invisible the necessary application of interpretants, which include a particular reading of the source text that fixes its form and meaning as well as a particular concept of equivalence that depends on that reading to determine whether a translation contains linguistic errors or is free of them. For the fact remains that a noticeable or material shift from the source text—an omission or insertion of words and phrases, for example, or a change in verb tense or mood—cannot in itself be considered an error: it can be branded an error only according to a concept of equivalence applied by the evaluator, but it may well be treated as equivalent according to another such concept. A shift, moreover, might have been deliberate on the translator's part, intended as an interpretive move. It will, in any case, have an interpretive force for the reader who does not have access to the source text, and so it cannot be simply dismissed as erroneous. What particularly recommends the hermeneutic model, then, is the critical self-consciousness that it requires of the reader of translations as well as the translator, the awareness of the unavoidable mediation or inscription through the application of interpretants that intervene between the source text and the translation as well as between the translation and the uses to which it is put.

In arguing for the idea of translation as an interpretive act, I also aim to evoke the origins of translation pedagogy in antiquity. Translation as a form of interpretation was central to humanistic education in ancient Rome, what Cicero called "the study of the humanities and of literature" (Zetzel 2009: 174; "studiis humanitatis ac litterarum": Clark 1911: 2) in his defense of the Greek poet Archias (62 BCE). Roman education was bilingual; students were taught Greek as well as Latin, and translation exercises were routinely performed in the two main subjects: grammar, which focused on language, poetry, and pronunciation, and rhetoric, which focused on invention, style, organization, memory, and delivery—that is, the skills of the orator (McElduff 2013: 21–2, 116–17). In his later commentary on the ideal orator (46 BCE), Cicero famously linked different kinds of translation to the teachers of each subject: the grammarian, whom he called an "interpres," translated closely, describing and explaining a poetic text word by word and line by line (Kaster 1988: 12), whereas the orator translated freely, even paraphrastically, so as to invent a compelling Latin text that displaced but was nonetheless based on a typically Greek source (Copeland 1991: 30; McElduff 2013: 111–15). Although commentators like Cicero and Quintilian reserved the term "interpretatio" for the grammarian's translation, every kind of Roman translation constituted an interpretation inscribed through interpretants—even though their commentary was mired in instrumentalism (Venuti 2012a). These commentators valued the orator's translations over the grammarian's because they found that the latter's interpretations reflected a limited education and hence possessed "insufficient intellectual imagination" to achieve the orator's goal of manipulating the source text in order to fashion his own voice (McElduff 2013: 109).

Translation remained extremely important to humanistic study in later periods even as the very nature and function of the humanities underwent redefinition. Today, despite the marginal position occupied by the study and practice of translation in academic institutions, humanistic disciplines from anthropology, literature, and history to philosophy, religion, and sociology could not conduct their research and teaching without translated texts and various kinds of translation, whether the conventional, interlingual variety or the cultural, intralingual translating that we all do when we interpret and teach. Translation is in fact basic to human cognition, active in the pursuit of intelligibility and in the negotiation of linguistic and cultural differences. It can facilitate or obstruct communication, sometimes both simultaneously. Yet insofar as issues of cosmopolitanism, globalization, and transnationalism have become persistent themes in humanistic study, the urgency to recognize translation as a key practice of intercultural communication has never been greater. Cicero defended the Greek-born Archais against the charge that he was not a Roman citizen, not simply by citing Archais' long residence in Rome, but by appealing to the jury's investment in "all the areas of learning that contribute to our humanity" (Zetzel 2009: 174; "omnes artes quae ad humanitatem pertinent": Clark 1911: 1)—although Cicero's argument finally stoked their chauvinism by pointing to the propagandistic value of poetry, and his notion of humanity applied only to the Roman elite. Still, might not translation be studied and practiced in ways that advocate a democratic humanism, cognizant of differences in languages and cultures without devolving into questionable notions of untranslatability and the impossibility of translation? Might not humanistic translation be rethought as a qualification for a yet-to-emerge form of global citizenship which recognizes but resists the asymmetries that structure international relations, whether cultural or political, economic or legal, military or ideological?

The chapters gathered in this book bring these questions into the classroom by demonstrating how the instructor's assumption of a hermeneutic model can guide the teaching of translation practice and research. Although kinds of translation might be distinguished broadly as humanistic, pragmatic, or technical according to the fields in which it is performed, translation is regarded throughout as a fundamentally humanistic activity because it is a form of interpretation.

In the nine chapters that describe courses devoted to translation practice (chapters six to fourteen), translation is not taught as the reproduction of a source invariant which then becomes the absolute standard by which student work is evaluated. Instead students learn that the interpretation offered by a translation can vary with clients and institutions, disciplinary debates and cultural developments, even while establishing a semantic correspondence and a stylistic approximation to the source text, so that their work can be evaluated only in relation to a set of changing conditions. Students apply concepts of equivalence and discursive strategies as they are linked to genres or text types, moving from word to text as the unit of translation, figuring in features like tone, register, and style in connection with the function that the translation is intended to serve and the audience for which it is produced. The teaching proceeds, in other words, from formal interpretants that focus on language and textuality to thematic interpretants that focus on differences between the source and receiving cultures as they in turn affect the translator's verbal choices and interpretive moves. Chapters thirteen and fourteen in particular describe courses in which students begin by analyzing the discursive strategies in literary translations in relation to translation theory and critical commentary on an author's work or on a literary tradition, including issues of gender and sexuality, diaspora, cultural minority, and postcoloniality. The teaching explores how such thematic interpretants can inform equivalence and strategy, not only in professional translations but in the students' own translations for the course.

In the ten chapters that describe courses in translation research (chapters fifteen to twenty-four), the spectrum of formal and thematic factors expands to encompass basic practices such as how to read and teach translations as translated texts, various media that include the audiovisual and the digital as well as the linguistic, and a diverse and timely group of cultural and social issues such as world literature, bilingualism, disciplinary divisions, immigration, and human rights. Students learn about the centrality of translation practices to their own cultures, whether they examine translations and translation theories, conduct research in humanistic disciplines and current events, or participate in community service. In every case, they confront and implement the interpretive act that is translation.

The Project

The approach I have taken in editing this volume is methodological rather than linguistic or national. Although the chapters cover a wide range of source languages, kinds of translation, and cultural traditions, the overall aim is to describe the teaching of translation research and practice so as to help initiate or improve it. Written translation is emphasized over interpreting (or oral translation), which might more effectively be covered separately, given the different conditions under which interpreters work. The focus also falls squarely on translation into English. Apart from the merely practical consideration that more than one translating language could not be treated thoroughly in a single book, this decision acknowledges not only the location of most of the contributors, the United States, where English remains the main language of instruction in tertiary institutions, but also the fact that English has become the lingua franca of the international community of translation scholars.

The decision carries pedagogical implications too. It assumes not that effective translation can be performed only into the translator's mother tongue but rather that learning to translate into a second language has been a form of foreign-language instruction, not necessarily translator training, and these two tasks should be sharply distinguished—regardless of the fact that no translation can occur without prior or even ongoing instruction in a foreign language. Most importantly, a translator must have a broad and deep familiarity with linguistic patterns, literary traditions, and cultural values in the receiving situation, not just in the culture where the source text originates. Hence the focus on English allows the chapters to build an informed and nuanced sense of the factors that play into Anglophone translation.

The kinds of translation discussed here include pragmatic and technical as well as humanistic texts, emphasizing literature but also encompassing drama, film, and such other disciplines in the human sciences as anthropology, history, philosophy, and sociology. The first section contains descriptions of existing and in some cases long-standing translation programs, both undergraduate and graduate, offering degrees or certificates. Curricula and courses designed to train translators are distinguished from those designed to train translation scholars. In the second and third sections, a broad gamut of courses is considered, including translation workshops, surveys of translation theory and commentary, historical approaches to translations from particular languages and cultures, and thematic investigations relating to current trends and debates in literary and cultural studies. Course descriptions outline syllabi, discuss pedagogical strategies, and explain activities and assignments. The fourth section contains chapters in which scholarship on pedagogies of translation practice as well as various types of translation textbooks are submitted to critical discussion.

The institutional sites of the programs and courses are extremely varied, including translator training programs, creative writing programs, departments of foreign languages and literatures, and departments and programs of comparative literature. I sought to maintain coherence amid such variety by insuring that the contributors framed their chapters so as to respond to certain basic questions:

- Does the program or course have any eligibility requirements or prerequisites? How do students' linguistic backgrounds or preparation affect the learning outcomes?
- How is translation defined or conceived in the program or course? Are different kinds of translation taught? Is translation distinguished from adaptation and other kinds of second-order practices?
- What requirements, whether a sequence of courses or a set of readings and assignments, have been developed to realize the conception of translation underpinning the program or course?
- How does the institutional site shape the curriculum, course, and pedagogy?
- What impact does the program or course have on students' careers as they continue in the academic institution and after they graduate? Do students pursue other, related degrees? Do they work in the translation industry? Do they publish translation research or translations?

As a result of the answers provided to these questions, the chapters can be seen as presenting exemplary models that can be replicated or adapted in other institutions.

Although each of the sections is devoted to a particular topic related to teaching, the chapters they contain offer many points of intersection that not only highlight the differences among the descriptions but also increase their useful-ness in developing programs and courses. The courses in translation practice and research described in the second and third sections might be regarded as supple-ments to the program descriptions in the first section, courses that might conceiv-ably be taught in those programs, thus broadening or enhancing their offerings. The course inventory for the MFA in literary translation (chapter four), for exam-ple, could well include the translation workshops in poetry, in poetry and prose, and in drama (chapters nine, ten, and eleven). Similarly, the graduate certificate in translation studies (chapter two), especially since it is housed in a department of comparative literature, could conceivably offer research-oriented courses that focus on world literature, postcolonial translation, and bilingual authorship (chap-ters nineteen, twenty-one, and twenty-two). These sorts of connections are more explicit in the case of the two chapters written by faculty at Kent State University: an account of their master's program in translator training is further developed by a discussion of a course on translating text types that is regularly taught in the program (chapters three and seven).

Another useful point of intersection emerges from the comments on which course materials are assigned and how they are employed in class discussions and activities. The same textbooks and readings might be put to different uses, theoretical, historical, or practical, depending on the course and program as well as the department or field. The very notion of what constitutes translation theory is redefined in the movement between sections. The assigned readings include not only practice-oriented commentary with a basis in linguistics or in profes-sional experience, typified by the so-called craft essay, but also philosophically oriented commentary that encompasses such other discourses as literary theory, psychoanalysis, and poststructuralism. And just as the instructor new to the field can profit from the chapters on translating particular genres and text types, so can any instructor profit from the chapters that show how to address the translated status of a translation in the classroom.

The project of describing current practices in teaching translation studies, although designed primarily to advance them, enables this volume to perform a number of other functions. It can help faculty learn about traditions of trans-lation theory and commentary as well as recent developments in translation research. It outlines and illustrates various kinds of pedagogies to teach transla-tion theory, history, and practice. It presents a body of knowledge and experi-ence that can be useful not only in devising translation-oriented programs and courses but also in conducting job searches to staff them. Ultimately, it demon-strates the scholarly integrity of translation studies as well as the necessity for translators, teachers of translation, and teachers of translated texts to be deeply immersed in the field.

Part I

Certificate and Degree Programs

1   An Undergraduate Certificate in Translation Studies

Ben Van Wyke

The Program

The undergraduate certificate in translation studies at Indiana University-Purdue University, Indianapolis (IUPUI), is housed in the Department of World Languages and Cultures. It is offered primarily in French, German, Spanish, and American Sign Language, although students can arrange independently to work with other languages taught in the department such as Arabic, Chinese, and Japanese. The program emphasizes the intersection between theory and practice as the key factor in educating effective and responsible translators. The certificate helps students to overcome age-old clichés about translation that novices often bring to the classroom: they come to question the notion that translation is a mechanical task and see it instead as an intellectual activity requiring reflection, research, and meticulous writing skills.

Most certificate students come from the School of Liberal Arts, primarily from the Department of World Languages and Cultures, English, and the Latino Studies Program. Others come from the Schools of Engineering, Law, Medicine, and Science. To be eligible, students must be at least sophomores in good academic standing and have completed two English writing courses, one in elementary composition, the other in argumentative writing, as well as an introductory-level composition course in their source language. Prior to admission, students must demonstrate a minimum level of bilingual skills by successfully completing the introductory translation workshop, one of the required courses for the certificate.

Once admitted, students are required to take nine courses distributed over three categories: core, translation, and a final project. The core includes advanced professional writing (business, administrative, creative, or editing), advanced grammar or linguistics in the source language, and an upper-level course in the source culture. The courses in translation include an introduction to translation studies and interpreting, two translation workshops (introductory and advanced), an introduction to computers and translation, and a course in terminology that is not only specific to a source language but to a field (business, medicine, or law). After fulfilling these requirements, students demonstrate their translation competence by completing a substantial project, which may be either a sixty-hour internship or an independent study in which they produce a translation. Every course involving translation or interpreting requires students to write reflective essays that evolve progressively in length and scope, building on material from previous courses.

The Workshops

Most students gain their first exposure to translation through the introductory workshop, which enables them to discover whether they are truly interested in this practical application of their language skills to continue with the certificate. The translation workshops use real-life texts that are selected to raise important theoretical and practical concerns and to stimulate class discussion. Students learn that texts can be translated in multiple ways, that translating means active participation in creating new texts, and that translators need to be able to defend the choices they make. A wide gamut of text types is covered, from medical and legal texts to journalism and literature. Students translate mostly into their native tongue, although occasionally into their source language as well, since they can learn a great deal when required to translate bi-directionally. Translations are done in and out of class, assignments are put through revisions, and students submit half-page to page-long commentaries that discuss their translation process, strategies, difficult problems, and the solutions they developed. In-class activities allow them to draw on each other's creative energy by working in groups, translating catchy advertisement slogans, for example, or rhyming children's literature.

Students' written commentaries on their work raise theoretical issues that are addressed partly in readings. With Spanish translators, Kelly Washbourne's manual (2010a) is quite useful since it offers an undogmatic engagement with translation theory that is helpful to instructors as well as students and can be assigned in both the introductory and advanced workshops. Readings in Washbourne are paired directly with translation assignments. The students' exposure to theory, however, comes mostly from class discussions regarding the texts they translate. Guided by the instructor, students tackle such issues as how to handle culture-specific references, how to translate seemingly untranslatable source texts, how to translate for particular target audiences, and how to address asymmetrical power relations in language pairs. Classes focus heavily on effectively utilizing research tools from both traditional and online sources (monolingual and bilingual dictionaries, thesauri, web forums such as ProZ.com, corpuses like Linguee.com, and search engines like Google) while stressing their benefits and limitations and the importance of employing them together.

Interpreting is also introduced in the workshops. After translating a medical text, students learn about interpreting norms and practice consecutive interpreting in a medical context with a group of three students switching roles among interpreter, doctor, and patient. A similar exercise is performed after translating a legal text with a situation that involves an interpreter, a lawyer, and a client. Students interested in continuing their work with interpreting later take the courses in field-specific terminologies and medical interpreting.

The most challenging and rewarding activity in both workshops is the service learning component, particularly in the Spanish courses. Since many nonprofit organizations increasingly deal with Spanish-speaking clients, the demand for translators is great, and productive working relationships can easily be established with community partners. Students have translated brochures, forms, and webpages for a local food bank, a women's shelter, a fire department, an autism awareness association, the YMCA, a cancer support group, the National Alliance on Mental Illness, and a transportation agency for seniors.

This work is collaborative. Students are divided into groups and assigned a section of a document to be translated, although they must each draft a complete version of the section before the group meets to decide on the translation to send to the class for editing. The class then discusses each group's translation, considering the function of the document, the target audience, and the impact of these factors on their verbal choices. After each group revises their text, a representative from the community partner visits the class, and students learn more about the organization, seek answers for pending questions, and practice client education. As the experts in the target language and culture, students, much to their surprise, often enlighten the community partner about its audience or constituency. They also realize that access to a client who is presumably familiar with the operation does not solve all of their translation problems, and they must still make their own decisions. They learn that translation is an interpretive act based on the translator's assessment of the source text in relation to the context where it will circulate. They write an essay in the form of a report to the organization that sponsored the project, detailing their approach, highlighting problems (e.g. a confusing or poorly written source text, technical terms and names of official programs, cultural elements that are particularly difficult to convey) and describing solutions with the help of the theoretical concepts they have encountered. Students tend to find the service learning projects the most enriching activities of the course because of the sustained work they do and their awareness that the translation will be published and used in the community.

In evaluating student translations, the greatest emphasis is placed on the interrelationship between accuracy and the functional coherence of their writing in the target text. Accuracy is assessed on the basis of their comprehension of the source text and the manner in which they effectively construct a linguistically coherent translation that can function according to the aim of the assignment. Here students' reflections become key documents: they form the site where students provide a rationale for their choices, including any that deviate from the instructor's notion of an ideal translation. The reflections allow students to enact the kind of exchange they might have with clients regarding their work. In the classroom setting, the instructor assumes the role of the client, although one who is likely to be more generous to students' opinions than the clients they might encounter in the professional world and with whom they can negotiate their choices. In the end, the expectation is that students will produce translations that are not only meticulously written texts but also usable in relation to the function they are intended to perform.

Courses in Translation Studies

The workshops complicate the novice's simplified vision of translation, although primarily through translation practice. The introduction to translation studies and interpreting, in contrast, uses critical reading and writing to focus directly on issues that have dominated Western translation discourse for two millennia. With readings from various anthologies (Gambier and van Doorslaer 2010; Robinson 1997b; Venuti 2012b), the course surveys theory from antiquity to the present, and students learn various approaches to the study and practice of translation while critiquing traditional views about equivalence, authorial intention, and the secondary status of translation. Emphasis is placed on acquiring the ability to synthesize the readings in clear, coherent writing. In weekly assignments students select a passage from the readings and expound upon it for a half-page to a page, ideally relating it to other readings. They then revise and expand three of these assignments.

The course begins with material that does not seem to be overtly about translation: videos of United States Supreme Court Justices Antonin Scalia and Stephen Breyer who have expressed different opinions about how the United States Constitution should be interpreted. If constitutional scholars on the highest court, we ask, are reading the same document in the same language, how could they be at such odds regarding its meaning? How can we expect translation between languages to communicate a clear, univocal meaning when it does not seem possible in just one language?

Because the Bible has been so important for the formation of Western thinking about translation, we first consider readings by and about Bible translators in different periods, providing a range of views regarding the treatment of sacred texts. These readings include accounts of the Septuagint (Aristeas and Philo Judaeus), defenses of translation practices (Jerome and Martin Luther), commentary on biblical poetics (Meschonnic 2003), as well as prefaces to modern translations such as the *New American Bible* (1970). Since these readings are all concerned with maintaining a certain equivalence to the source text, they are useful in demonstrating that translation is simultaneously and inextricably linguistic and cultural, so that any meaning to be found in the Bible is necessarily historically and culturally bound.

We also consider authors' differing opinions regarding their relationship to those who recreate their texts in other languages (e.g. Cunningham 2010; Kundera 1992). A productive conversation emerges among these views as students examine the consecration of authorship in our culture, the hierarchy established between authorial originality and derivative works like translations, the sometimes unreasonable and rather naïve demands that certain authors make on translators, and the extent to which these demands, as well as the cultural and legal conditions on which they rest, can be negotiated.

The controversial issue of how much the source text should be assimilated to the receiving culture is given due attention. Nicolas Perrot d'Ablancourt's advocacy of assimilation is juxtaposed to German Romantics such as Johann Gottfried Herder, who championed translation that accommodates the source text. Students read contemporary scholarship on domestication and foreignization that has developed and redefined these terms (Venuti 1995: 1–32). To provide a metaphor to imagine these viewpoints, the class considers contemporary press that provides very different ideas about how immigrants should be translated or assimilated into United States culture. Students immediately connect the theoretical arguments to a range of related and timely questions. Should immigrants maintain a certain foreignness? Is there any validity to the common expectation that immigrants assimilate into a host culture actually composed of a myriad of diverse cultural identities despite the dominance of one? How is the polyglossia of the United States obscured by a hierarchy of languages that privileges a standard dialect?

These questions lead to an exploration of the late twentieth-century shift away from essentialist views of translation to an explicit questioning of the stability of meaning that characterizes most of the texts discussed early in the course. Students consider the emergence of new thinking that foregrounds the power dynamics pervading language and translation. Assigned readings include feminist approaches that expose and search for alternatives to the patriarchal structures embedded in translation theories and practices (Chamberlain 1988; Simon 1996; von Flotow 2010) and postcolonial approaches that scrutinize and challenge the hierarchical relations that have existed between cultures and languages (Bandia 2010; Bassnett and Trivedi 1999; Merrill 2013).

The professions of translation and interpreting are never far away from the discussions as students want tangible examples of how these broader theoretical concepts matter for actual translation practice. To understand expectations from professional organizations, codes of ethics such as those by the American Translators Association are read with contemporary accounts of interpreting (Chen 2006; Pöchhacker 2010; Wadensjö 2009) as well as critiques that complicate the sometimes utopian or unrealistic expectations contained in these codes (Apter 2009; Arrojo 2005 and 2012).

As computer-assisted tools are now essential in the translation profession, students are required to take a course that introduces them to the uses, applications, and evaluation of translation technologies. This course covers translation memory systems (primarily Wordfast and Trados), terminology management, and the practice of creating digital glossaries. Assignments ask students to compare translations from automatic programs such as Google Translate, Systran, and BabelFish and identify what the computers have done well and where they are lacking in the human knowledge that can produce a usable translation. Because of the variety of languages among students, they usually select their own texts within specific parameters from their source language and translate them into English. The course also provides an introduction to localization and internationalization, especially the adaptation of websites to other linguistic and cultural environments. Additionally, students must become proficient with a variety of other computer programs (electronic dictionaries, concordancers) that are important for professional translators today and effectively use them in project management and workflow.

The courses in terminology were developed to equip students with a strong background in specific fields that interest them. The main course offerings focus on medicine, law, and business. In all three courses, students are required to shadow an approved professional in the field for six hours. Many of the students who take the course in medical terminology, for example, observe the work of professional medical interpreters at a local hospital. Students who take the course in legal terminology typically observe interpreters in the state courthouse. The contact personnel play an integral role by explaining, often as they move from one patient or case to another, the ins and outs of the field and by answering questions about the processes students have witnessed. Students who take the course in business terminology may observe a bilingual employee of a company that has international accounts. If Spanish is the students' source language, they may also attend a meeting of the local Spanish chamber of commerce.

The course in medical terminology begins with anatomical terms and moves to systems, illnesses and diseases, and medications. Vocabulary is learned not by memorizing lists but by reading medical texts in which students are required to research specific words. Using bilingual medical dictionaries, they must build their own glossaries. In addition, special modules address medical specialties like pediatrics or general tasks like taking medical histories in both source and target languages. Students who plan on pursuing a career as interpreters in health care are encouraged to register for the course in medical interpreting after studying terminology. Here they receive intensive interpreting practice. The textbook is Holly Mikkelson's class manual (1994), which provides exercises for training medical interpreters.

The course in legal terminology begins with a module that presents an anatomy of the legal system. Students must become familiar with the court room, distinguishing between and identifying the duties of judges, bailiffs, clerks, prosecutors, and public defenders. At the end of the course, students are given a topic and must give a ten-minute presentation to the class, proposing pertinent questions for discussion that often appear on the final exam.

The course in business terminology requires students to complete two participatory projects. Students who work with Spanish, for example, must visit a Spanish-speaking business such as a market and write up an observation report on the product placement and cash register system, including the way the meat counter is arranged, whether the meat is pre-packaged or freshly distributed, and so forth. This report becomes the basis for a six-page essay on the differences in business models between so-called typical markets and Hispanic markets in the United States. In groups of three to five, students also create a fictitious business that includes a name, logo, business cards, letterhead, and a plan as to how they will market it, deciding, for example, whether to use Anglophone or Spanish marketing with a Hispanic population. They then develop a sales pitch for their business that they present to the class.

The Final Project

Whether students choose an internship or a directed translation as their final project, they must write a fifteen-page essay detailing their experience, drawing from the whole of their work in the program to show that they are able both to put theory into practice and to theorize their practice. This essay becomes the basis for their oral presentation before their capstone committee, which consists of three faculty members who assign a grade to the project.

Students who decide to undertake a translation must find a source text that will yield twenty double-spaced pages. Projects have involved literary texts in different genres as well as nonliterary texts that are specific to such other areas of study as biology and engineering, resulting in translations that will ultimately benefit students in the careers they pursue. In the case of literary texts, students are asked to translate previously untranslated works. In this way, they do not have the benefit of consulting the strategies and solutions of other translators. More importantly, the requirement allows them to submit their translations for publication. They are required to show drafts of their work to their instructors, with whom they discuss their goals, their process, and the problems they are encountering. Recent projects have included short stories by the young Spanish writer Mercedes Cebrián and by the Costa Rican scholar Fernando Durán Ayanegui. In their essays, which act as a kind of translator's foreword, students often examine the differing poetics between the source and target cultures, defend their decisions with respect to a foreignizing or domesticating approach, describe how they dealt with culture-specific terms and how they struggled with power differentials between languages, and consider what expectations might be brought to their translations by publishers and readers in view of the book market in the United States today.

The nonliterary texts that students have chosen for translation have tended to be scientific or medical. A biology major who planned to pursue a specialization in oncology translated a Spanish document about alternative cancer treatments. In his accompanying essay, he reflected on the fact that, because this document was a report based on clinical studies, the target audience would be mostly composed of doctors. However, he also thought that, given our scientific-minded medical community, patients and family members might be the main consumers of this material. Thus he described how he sought to maintain a balance between the two readerships and how he approached the difficulty of finding an adequate terminology for terms that had not come into widespread use in the United States.

The sixty-hour internship has been by far the most popular choice for the final project. Because the Department of World Languages and Cultures has a strong history of service learning, many community partners are willing to provide internships for students. Students who decide to undertake an internship are usually paired with an organization that matches to some extent what they would like to do with translation. The positions have involved work in the Indiana State House, hospitals, low-income medical and legal clinics, and businesses. In the state house, for example, students have worked in Hispanic outreach as translators and interpreters, and they have helped both to write and to record emergency messages played during drills and actual emergencies. In the medical and legal clinics, students might answer phone calls from non-English-proficient speakers, help patients or clients with intake procedures such as filling out forms, guide them to departments and offices in the building, and act as an interpreter during interviews with doctors or lawyers. Students are always placed in settings where native speakers of the target language who have experience with translation can oversee their work and give feedback on their performance.

Given the diversity of possible internships, the students' essays will vary greatly, but certain issues do recur. Many share observations about the importance of translation and interpreting in institutions, about the social realities they confronted in dealing with the situations of immigrants, and about the difficulty of following certain prescribed codes of objectivity and impartiality when patients and clients are so happy to meet somebody who speaks their language. In addition, beyond the linguistic aspects, most students say that the experience made them reconsider not only the plight of immigrants, but people in the United States generally who have struggled with health care and legal costs.

Student Outcomes

Students who complete our certificate branch out in diverse directions. Some fully immerse themselves in the practice or study of translation while others use translation as a complement to another degree. Several students have opened their own translation agencies, while others have become bilingual workers, interpreters or employees of international companies where they use translation together with their expertise in such areas as engineering. Many nursing and pre-med students complete the certificate, and although they learn the importance of using certified interpreters, they affirm that their experience in the program provides them with the skills to interact positively with patients—not just those patients who speak the language they studied, but all non-English-speaking immigrants. Students who pursue graduate degrees have gone on to specialize in anthropology, comparative literature, linguistics, and translation studies.

In their final reflections most students mention how, after devoting so much thought to the fundamental role translation plays in shaping world affairs, they view differently such things as anthropology, history, national and international politics, even thinking in general. They realize the importance not only of foreign-language study but also of reflecting on the relationships forged between languages and the cultures that use them. This sort of impact is truly one of our primary goals with all students who enter the translation certificate program, regardless of the professions they later enter.

2 A Graduate Certificate in Translation Studies

Bill Johnston and Paul Losensky

The Department of Comparative Literature at Indiana University offers a graduate certificate that aims to provide a solid foundation in the practice and scholarship of literary translation. Although based in Comparative Literature, the program is designed as a supplementary qualification for master's and doctoral degrees in any humanities-related discipline. Students have recently come from such departments and programs as Creative Writing, French and Italian, Musicology, Near Eastern Languages and Cultures, and Slavic Languages and Literatures. Instruction is based on the faculty's conviction that literary translation is a creative and interpretative decision-making process. The goals are to show students the range of linguistic, aesthetic, and cultural choices that translators make, to understand the principles and values at stake in making these choices, and to provide controlled opportunities for students to practice making them on their own. The focus throughout is translation into English.

There are no eligibility requirements other than matriculation in a graduate program. Students, especially those in the humanities, demonstrate advanced reading proficiency in a foreign language in their departments. To earn the certificate, students must take a total of six courses—three core courses and three electives—and complete a capstone translation project. The three core courses are "History and Theory of Translation," "Workshop in Literary Translation," and "Advanced Workshop in Literary Translation." Although the titles of these courses suggest a distinction between translation theory and practice, we maintain that theory and practice should ideally inform one another—indeed, that the theory/practice dichotomy is deeply problematic. Hence we do not require our students to take the courses in any particular sequence, however interesting it might be to investigate empirically whether studying theory before practice (or vice versa) results in a significant impact on learning outcomes. In any case, while the instructors of the courses share syllabuses and ideas, there is no conscious attempt to align or coordinate the two—each is designed as a free-standing course, largely because there are also numerous students who are not pursuing the certificate and who take one course without the other.

"History and Theory of Translation" puts equal emphasis on both parts of its title. During the first half of the course, the focus is on history. As an initial disciplinary orientation, the course first examines the changing place of translation studies within the field of comparative literature, reading a series of polemical statements by André Lefevere (1995), Susan Bassnett (1993: 138–61), and Emily Apter (2006: 243–51), who all argue in various ways for the centrality of translation in the comparative enterprise. We next consider the place of comparative literature within the broader field of translation studies, if only as a reminder of the vast range of important nonliterary areas of translation that lie outside the scope of the class. The examination of the history of translation concentrates on the English tradition since this is the common language of all students. The chapters on "Historical Development" in Peter France's guide to literary translation (2000) provide the basic framework for this portion of the class, accompanied by an examination of some representative translations from each period. For the Middle Ages through the Enlightenment, the class analyzes multiple translations of two odes by Horace (by John Dryden, Ben Jonson, Alexander Pope, and several modern poets, selected from Carne-Ross and Haynes [1996] and McClatchy [2002]). In considering the history of the translation of sacred texts, the class examines several versions of Psalm 137, a passage from Paul's *Letter to the Corinthians*, and *sura* 101 from the Qur'an (including versions by George Sale [1734], A. J. Arberry [1955], Michael Sells [1999], and M.A.S. Abdel Haleem [2004]). Edward FitzGerald's *Rubaiyat of Omar Khayyam* and a comparative reading of two translations (by F. W. Newman and Matthew Arnold) of short passages from Homer serve to represent Victorian translation practices, and a substantial selection from Ezra Pound's translations bring us into the twentieth century. Early conceptual statements on translation are also integrated into this historical survey, by writers and translators such as Jerome, Miles Smith, John Dryden, Goethe, Matthew Arnold, Jorge Luis Borges, and Pound (Borges 1935; Pound 1929). Polysystem theory, especially the concept of translation norms expounded by Theo Hermans (France 2000: 10–15), provides a conceptual grounding for this portion of the course. There are two major goals in introducing students to translation from a historical perspective. The first is to demonstrate the central importance of translation to the global circulation of texts, cross-cultural exchange, and the formation and development of national literatures. The second is to decenter and broaden the concept of translation itself, to show the wide variety of writing practices that have been accepted under the rubric of translation and to show its relationship to other forms of rewriting and textual transcreation.

The second, more strictly theoretical component of the course begins with a consideration of the concept of theory itself. George Steiner's skepticism toward theory based on the model of the hard sciences is set against Rosemary Arrojo's more humanistic, historically contingent concept of theory (Arrojo 1998; Steiner 1975a: 236–95). By viewing theory as a framework for understanding, students are encouraged to evaluate the claims of competing theorists not against some unattainable, scientific ideal, but as responses to a limited set of problems from a particular perspective with specific goals. To bring this point home, we look at the bitter contention between Vladimir Nabokov (1955) and Douglas Hofstadter (1997: 255–78) over the translation of Pushkin's *Eugene Onegin*. The course then surveys translation theory since the 1960s with the help of the third edition of

The Translation Studies Reader, supplemented by other articles included in the second edition, as well as extended selections from works by Haroldo de Campos (2007: 312–26), Jacques Derrida (1985), Douglas Robinson (1991: 127–93; 2001: 141–79), Gideon Toury (1995: 129–65), Lawrence Venuti (1995: 1–35), and Kevin West (2010). In discussing these readings, the class considers the sort of issues each theory is best equipped to deal with and how issues in translation touch on broader developments in literary criticism and cultural studies, such as deconstructionism, ideological analysis, language philosophy, postcolonialism, and gender studies. In examining major trends in translation theory, students are encouraged to consult the Mona Baker and Gabriela Saldanha's encyclopedia of translation studies (2002) for further references.

This course is conducted as a seminar and has two requirements: a final research paper and a translation journal. Each student presents a project proposal orally to the class near midterm and then submits it in written form. Students have proven remarkably adept at carefully critiquing one another's work, quickly spotting problems with the feasibility of the project or its conceptualization and suggesting revisions or further lines of development. Projects examining the translation history of a particular work or set of works are encouraged, but students have ample latitude to pursue their own interests. Because students bring to the course linguistic backgrounds as diverse as French and Swahili, Japanese and Yiddish, and Wolof and Polish, they are compelled to frame and present their analyses in ways that are accessible to any educated reader, a necessary skill as they look ahead to working in the broader scholarly and academic communities. Although the course is not rigorously coordinated with the workshops, many of the research papers have been directly related to the student's workshop and certificate project. The topics of some recent projects have included: Elie Wiesel as a self-translator, the psychodynamics of Constance Garnett's translation of Chekhov's short story "The Black Monk," translations of Omar Khayyam into Arabic verse and popular song, German and Spanish versions of Jules Verne's *Voyage au centre de la terre*, and the intersections of performance theory and translation theory.

The second requirement, the translation journal, offers students an opportunity to try out some of the theoretical ideas on a short stretch of text. Students select a brief text of no more than 200–400 words to work on over the course of the semester. The goal here, unlike the workshops, is not to produce a finished translation but rather to manipulate the text in as many ways as possible into English and to have some fun doing so. These experiments are usually based on a particular question: What does it mean to translate "by the letter"? Is a phonetic translation possible? What are the limits of domestication or foreignization? Can a verbal text be translated into other media? One student even attempted a translation into odor, a "sense-for-scents translation," as she called it. The journal is meant to be a playground but also calls into question the deeply ingrained sacralization of the source text as an inviolable, self-sufficient whole.

The "Workshop in Literary Translation" is conceived as an introduction to the practice of literary translation. No experience is required, though many students have done some nonliterary translation before, and some have tried their hand at translating literature. Students taking the course typically come from a wide range of departments—a recent class comprised thirteen students from no fewer than nine different departments and programs, the languages represented ranging from French, Italian, Spanish, and Portuguese to Greek, Hebrew, Arabic, and Uyghur.

The course comprises two parallel components. The first consists of a close examination of multiple translations of key works of literature. In each case, we read five or six renderings of the same excerpt from the work. For example, we look at different versions (of the many more available) of the first tablet of *Gilgamesh*, Canto I of Dante's *Inferno*, the opening chapter of Cervantes' *Don Quixote*, and that of Tolstoy's *War and Peace*. To the extent that we are able, given the language expertise of instructor and students, we incorporate a discussion of the source text. The translations under consideration are chosen to represent a range of translation approaches. When looking at Dante, for example, we examine translations responding variously to the question of rhyme and meter, as well as diction and paratextual apparatus. In most cases, the aim is not primarily to identify "good" and "bad" translations but to consider the effect of particular macro- and micro-level translation choices on the experience of reading the translation. In considering the various translations of *Beowulf*, at the macro level we discuss the effect of rendering the text in prose or of sticking closely or loosely to a modern English version of the Anglo-Saxon alliterative line with its caesura; micro-level choices include particular instances of word choice, sentence structure, and enjambment. In examining different versions of a scene from Chekhov's *The Cherry Orchard*, among other things we discuss how character and relation can be more or less effectively conveyed through language, for example, in rendering one character as pretentious, another disdainful towards the first.

The second component of the course asks the students to produce three short translations in three genres—poetry, prose, and drama. In each case they are asked to select a previously untranslated piece of literature. Each translation is to be about two to five pages in length—thus, typically, a few lyric poems, a short story, and a microdrama or a scene from a longer play. Each translation is submitted in multiple drafts, and throughout the semester students workshop their translations in class, sharing an early draft of their work. In each case, after an introduction of the author and work in question, we begin by discussing particularly thorny translation problems identified by the translator him- or herself (in this respect the format differs from that used in many creative writing courses, where the author of the workshopped piece is asked to listen to feedback but not respond, initially at least). Only after we have addressed the issues presented by the translator do we open the floor to comments and suggestions from other students; since time is short, these comments are often given to the presenting student in the form of written notes. Throughout, the instructor serves as moderator of the discussion as well as contributor. While most students work from a single language for all three assignments, some choose to work from more than one language.

A crucial dimension of the course is an emphasis on the professional facets of literary translation, an important part of which is the ability to present an author and her work to a nonspecialist audience (something that students who focus on literary scholarship often find particularly challenging). This dimension is emphasized in two ways in the written work required for the course. First, for each of the three translation projects the student is asked to provide a one-page, nonspecialist introduction to the writer and the work. Second, a final fourth requirement is to prepare one of the three projects for submission to a literary journal. With guidance, students select an appropriate journal, write a one-page cover letter, and revise one of their translations, formatting it as required by that journal. While students are not required to actually send their work to the journal, many in fact do, and numerous students have had work from the course accepted for publication. At the end of the semester, all drafts of all four assignments are assembled in a portfolio that is used as the basis for the final grade.

The portfolio is assessed according to four criteria. The first is evidence of mindful revision through successive drafts of the translation with a particular focus on the complex relationship between the source text and its original context, on the one hand, and the translated text and its place in the receiving culture on the other. Students are encouraged to consider how the translated text relates not just to the source text but also to the new literary, linguistic, and cultural context in which it must take its place, Anglophone literature of the early twenty-first century. The second criterion is evidence of lucid reflection on the practice of translation, as displayed in the students' short written commentaries on the translation process. These commentaries may focus on a variety of points, from the rendering of particularly problematic cultural concepts to broader questions concerning, for instance, English-language possibilities for conveying relations between characters that are indicated in the source language by the use of formal and informal second-person pronouns. The third criterion is the ability to present a foreign author clearly and effectively to a nonspecialist general readership. And the fourth is the quality of the final draft of the translations, evaluated according to consistency of tone or voice, resourcefulness, idiomaticity, and other appropriate aspects often derived from the student's own presentation of the work and its particular qualities.

The "Advanced Workshop" offers a continuation of the translation work in the introductory course. In this course each student selects an extensive translation project—usually though not always one that will fulfill the project requirement of the certificate—and works on it throughout the semester, periodically submitting extracts in draft and then in revision and workshopping their work in rotation during class meetings. As with the introductory workshop, the grade is awarded primarily on the basis of a portfolio, evaluated as described above; this time, however, the components of the portfolio are multiple drafts of successive extracts from a single long project. Students often send submissions to literary journals, and many have succeeded in placing their work in this fashion; in addition, at least two book-length publications and one dissertation have resulted in part from the advanced workshop in recent years.

Concerning the electives, as with the core courses, our overarching goal is to nurture mindful, competent, well-informed practice in literary translation. With this aim in mind, we have found it best to be flexible regarding what other courses can count toward the certificate. These may include some combination of: graduate coursework in which literature in the language of the project is read in the original; advanced language coursework; further graduate classes in translation; additional workshops; and project credits.

The capstone project is a substantial original translation into English. We are flexible on the meaning of "substantial," depending on the level of difficulty of the source text, but typically this will mean about twenty-five to thirty pages of lyric poetry or thirty to fifty pages of prose. The translation itself is accompanied by an essay of about ten to twenty pages outlining certain translation issues raised by the translation, though there is considerable leeway here—some students focus more narrowly on the conventional kinds of translation problems presented by particular words, phrases, or cultural concepts in the source; some frame their translation conceptually in a way that relates it, and the process by which it was produced, to aspects of translation theory; others still find it most interesting and relevant to address contextual issues of history, reception, and so on. For example, a recent project involving contemporary Japanese poetry took the first approach, focusing on linguistic and cultural differences between English and Japanese pronoun systems, verb mood, and the significance of the use of *kanji* versus *hiragana* and *katakana* in the Japanese writing system. In each case, the final project is submitted to a committee comprising two members of the Department of Comparative Literature's Translation Committee (frequently the authors of this chapter) and one expert in the literature from which the translation comes.

In recent projects, the languages represented have been French, Hebrew, Japanese, Polish, Slovak, and Swahili. To take four representative cases: an MFA student in Creative Writing completed a translation of a selection of twenty-five poems comprising a cross-section of the work of twentieth century Japanese poet Yoshihiro Ishihara. A doctoral student in Slavic Languages and Literatures presented a translation of the first seven chapters of Slovak author Pavol Rankov's (2008) novel *It Happened on the First of September (or Some Other Time)*. An MA student in French Literature produced a translation of a set of fantastic tales by contemporary French writer Nathalie Dau. And a doctoral candidate in Comparative Literature submitted several chapters from the late twentieth-century novel *Divide* by Swahili-language novelist Said Ahmed Mohamed.

A considerable number of translations generated through the certificate and its required courses have seen publication. Short translations have been published in a broad range of literary journals, including *Absinthe*, *The Dirty Goat*, *The New England Review*, *Words Without Borders*, and *No Man's Land*. At least two book-length publications have resulted in part from the advanced workshop: Mira Rosenthal's (2007) translation of Tomasz Różycki's lyric poetry, *The Forgotten Keys*, and Luke Hankins' (2011) rendering of Stella Vinitchi Radulescu's *I Was Afraid of Vowels Their Paleness*.

One project, the novel by Pavol Rankov, has become the first translation project to be accepted at Indiana University as a doctoral dissertation project. (It will be accompanied by an extensive commentary.) In the Department of Comparative Literature, a translation project, also with accompanying commentary, can be used to fulfil the master's thesis requirement; a recent example of such a project was translation of a novella by nineteenth-century Brazilian author Machado de Assis, "The Blue Orchid."

Several articles have also been published from the "History and Theory" course. These include a piece by Elizabeth Geballe on Constance Garnett's translations of stories by Anton Chekhov in *Literature and Medicine* (2013), Wendeline Hardenberg's essay on self-translation in the work of Samuel Beckett, Ngũgĩ wa Thiong'o, and Vladimir Nabokov in the journal *Metamorphoses* (2009), and Mira Rosenthal's essay on Czesław Miłosz's translations of Anna Świrszczyńska in *Canadian Slavic Papers* (2010).

Lastly, graduates of the program have also become active in other aspects of literary translation. Rosenthal writes a column on poetry in translation in the highly regarded literary magazine *American Poetry Review*. Others have become active in the conferences and activities of the American Literary Translators Association.

3 An MA in Translation

Françoise Massardier-Kenney

The MA in translation offered by the Institute for Applied Linguistics at Kent State University prepares students to embark on professional careers as translators, terminologists, and language project managers, although some graduates do pursue advanced degrees in a foreign language or literature or in linguistics. The program focuses on English translation from six languages: Arabic, French, German, Japanese, Russian, and Spanish. It assumes that translation is a multifaceted act of linguistic and cultural interpretation while emphasizing the materials and skills that are currently necessary for working translators. Just as what constitutes reading and writing has been redefined by technological advances and globalization, so translation has evolved from a solitary craft to an industrial sector, from an in-house activity to outsourced work, and it now forms part of a complex cycle of multilingual documentation. Today translators are also responsible for desktop publishing, proofreading, and editing.

These changes are reflected in a curriculum in which coursework falls into one of three categories: principles, guided practice, and tools. Courses require students to link these categories while creating a shared body of knowledge. The principles introduced in a survey of translation theory, for example, are applied in language-specific workshops in which students practice specialized translation in such fields as business and law, science and medicine, literature and culture. In these practical courses, meanwhile, students use the tools introduced in courses on technology, including translation memory software, research databases, and corpora of machine-read texts.

At the start of the program, students are required to take three fundamental courses. The first, intended to develop their skills in writing and research, rests on two premises: good translation requires good writing, and translators must develop systematic methods of finding information in the various fields in which they may undertake a translation. The text type that students practice writing combines the expository or argumentative essay with the research paper. Assignments are based on a topic or document, and students address a question or set of questions that necessitate extensive research. They might be asked, for example, whether reading scholarship on a particular author would be helpful to a prospective translator of that author's work. Whether they argue for or against the usefulness of such reading, they learn how to present a coherent argument with sufficient documentation, how to use such resources as bibliographies, databases, reference works, and journals, and how to identify trends, debates, and methodologies in commentary on the author's work. Alternatively, they might be given a document, like an NGO report on water management or a review article on surgical technology, and tasked with discovering how knowledge is organized and disseminated in the field, whether it requires the use of a standardized terminology, how the importance of field-specific documents can be accurately gauged, and how parallel texts (i.e., texts of the same type performing the same function) can be identified in English.

Beginning students also take a course in translation theory that aims to establish the relevance of theory to practice. This course enables students to communicate theoretical concepts in a synthesized, persuasive manner, to analyze and apply different theories, to make more informed and effective decisions in their own translations, and to employ a conceptual vocabulary in discussing translation and the academic field of translation studies. Readings consist of primary texts in anthologies of theory and commentary that encompass foundational materials as well as more recent developments in the field. Students may also read expositions of theory such as Jeremy Munday's introductory text (2016), whereby they become acquainted with a wide range of approaches from different periods and traditions. Among the topics considered are equivalence, translation strategies, functionalist approaches, and ethics (Chesterman 2001; Emery 2004; Gil Bardají 2009; Nord 2005). A typical assignment might ask students to examine the impact of different concepts of equivalence on the translating they are doing in the language-specific practical courses. This sort of examination would require them to assess the value of the concepts on the basis of specific examples from their own work.

The third fundamental course focuses on documents in multilingual contexts and introduces students to technological tools available to translators. Among the many challenges facing translators today is the preponderance of source texts that are written not in Word but rather in markup languages that are used on the Web and in technical documents, notably HTML and XML. These markup languages annotate text and image, indicating how they should be displayed and identifying what kind of data is presented. Since students planning to work in the translation industry must become familiar with these languages, the course emphasizes the language of coding, the major tags used to create markup documents. Students are also taught the basic principles of computer-assisted translation, learning about such tools as electronic dictionaries, concordancers, and terminology databases. By the end of the course students have created their own webpages and are capable of using a wide range of tools to handle texts in a variety of formats.

The language-specific workshops emphasize the need for self-reflection, discussion, and feedback with translation practice. Students translate texts that belong to different genres or text types but do not require specialized knowledge, ranging from recipes, movie reviews, and prose fiction to political speeches, advertisements, and commercial websites. They accompany their draft translation with a commentary or log that documents the translation process by identifying problems, describing what strategies were deployed, and explaining why verbal choices were made. The workshops require students to justify their selection of parallel texts that informed their verbal choices and to assess the selections made by other students. The goal is to increase their awareness of the complex decision-making process involved in translation and to enable them to describe it more precisely in order to improve their practice. Hence their descriptions might rely on various terminologies for strategies (Delisle, Lee-Jahnke, and Cormier 1999; Vinay and Darbelnet 1995). They might discuss the "skopos" or purpose of a translation in evaluating it (Nord 2005; Vermeer 1989). Or they might use poly-system theory to situate a translation in a larger cultural context, considering how its position in the target-cultural system might affect the adoption of strategies and solutions (Even-Zohar 1978).

Students sometimes use software that records the computer-screen activity during their production of a translation. This software allows them to submit their process to close scrutiny after the fact, providing information useful for improvement. Extensive pauses in on-screen activity may reveal difficulties of which the student is usually unaware. Screen recording can likewise document the textual unit on which the student concentrated while translating, whether the word, the phrase, or the sentence, often showing that the smaller the unit, the more problematic the translation may prove to be. Most importantly, the record displays patterns in problem-solving that students can formulate independently of the translation process.

From the language-specific workshops students acquire a number of competences that are directly linked to the research methods and theoretical discourses they have been learning (cf. Pym 2003). Target-language competence combines an awareness of, as well as an ability to reproduce, various styles and registers in the translating language. Textual competence consists of familiarity with, as well as the ability to translate, various nonspecialized genres and text types. Contrastive competence entails the identification of problems encountered in translation—semantic and syntactic, stylistic and discursive, cultural and social. Transfer competence consists of the effective application of cognitive strategies and problem-solving techniques. Students develop quality-control competence by learning how to assess the adequacy of translations, whether their own or those of their peers, as well as to check and edit their work. Professional competence requires students to demonstrate a certain ethical responsibility in following instructions, meeting deadlines, and working independently and collaboratively.

The program requires three specialized courses in translation practice that are divided into distinct fields, each with their own genres and text types and their specific kinds of terminologies. The fields are literary and cultural; legal, diplomatic, and commercial; and scientific, medical, and technical. The courses do not so much equip students with sufficient expertise to translate in these specialties as give them further opportunities to develop their writing and research skills and to advance their manifold competences while translating specialized texts. In these courses students also embark on a longer project in which they produce not only a translation but a sustained critical analysis of it.

A few exemplary projects can illustrate the learning outcomes. One involved a translation of a French medical article on treatments for breast cancer, another a translation of a German report on solar energy, and yet another a translation of a Spanish short story to be included in a secondary school textbook. In each case, students constructed a terminology database using computer-assisted tools, analyzed the stylistic characteristics of the text type, located appropriate parallel texts in English, and described the translation difficulties they encountered as well as the strategies they deployed, taking into consideration both the function of the translation and the audience that it was designed to serve.

The specialized translation courses include readings related to the field of the source text, addressing such topics as patent writing, the anatomy of a financial report, and cultural differences in health care. The course in literary and cultural translation, in particular, pairs exercises with theoretical readings so that students can integrate principles into practices. After reading Friedrich Schleiermacher's (1813a) lecture on the different methods of translating, students may be asked to produce two versions of the same source text in accordance with his distinction between translations that either bring the source author to the reader or bring the reader to the source author. Students discuss which strategies each approach requires and in what context one approach might be more justified than the other. If the source text is a poem deeply anchored in a specific cultural context, they may be asked to reflect on the usefulness of Eugene Nida's distinction (1964) between formal and dynamic equivalence, that is, between close adherence to source-text form and meaning and free rendering that aims to reproduce the effect of the source-text on the target-language reader. Unlike the other specialized courses, the course in literary and cultural translation includes more speculative readings that consider the very concept of what a translation is, as well as the differences between literary and other kinds of translation. Examples include Walter Benjamin's "The Translator's Task" (1923b) and Roman Jakobson's "On Linguistic Aspects of Translation" (1959). These readings do not provide models for specific translations but rather abstract conceptual parameters with which a translator may formulate and potentially solve problems.

Students are also required to take two further courses in translation technology that are more specialized in their approach and content. The first provides a systematic introduction to computer-assisted translation, including the design of terminology databases, the documentation of terms and concepts in multilingual contexts, term extraction, and translation memories that store segments of source texts and their translations for retrieval. Configured around long-term learning as opposed to simple tools training, the course emphasizes the evolution and comparative features of tools and their use in the language industry. Students learn how to evaluate tools for user friendliness, efficiency, and compatibility with other tools. Assignments include the creation of terminology databases and translation memories that cover carefully selected subfields of knowledge. The faculty who staff the technology courses maintain close contact with tools developers throughout the industry so as to keep abreast of new developments and to maintain the currency of the tools deployed in the computer labs at the university.

The second required course in technology addresses software localization and internationalization. Localization extends beyond the translation of text to encompass the adaptation of nontextual materials such as icons, colors, and graphics, among other aspects of digital texts. Internationalization refers to the process of authoring digital materials to facilitate subsequent translation and localization without the need for redesign or re-engineering. After acquiring a firm theoretical grounding in these concepts, students learn to apply what they have learned by localizing authentic materials, by identifying and critically analyzing localization and internationalization problems, and by recognizing best practices that can expedite the translation and localization of software, websites, graphics, and documents. In the more specialized technology courses, students read a variety of theoretical and descriptive texts, as well as many pragmatic documents that bear on industry procedures and standards (Bowker 2002; Dunne and Dunne 2011; Esselink 2000). They further their technological skills through the completion of a rigorous sequence of projects based on industry practice while reflecting on their process and evaluating the product.

Students take two electives from a growing list of offerings. Some are language-specific, like medical interpreting into Spanish, while others might be helpful to translators working with any languages, such as editing and project management. These courses allow students to develop additional competencies in subfields in which their interests coincide with market demand. The elective in Spanish medical interpreting fills a gap created by the federally mandated requirement that health care personnel provide culturally and linguistically accessible services to patients with limited English proficiency. The course fosters competencies in areas that are not only specific but crucial to interpreting: linguistic and cognitive, interpersonal and professional, setting-specific and sociocultural. Students learn not only how to perform various forms of interpreting (consecutive, simultaneous, in person, or by telephone) but also how to analyze the interpreting needs of different health care environments, to identify the legal and ethical implications of interpreters' decision making including compliance with current legislation, to assess interpreting performance based on objective criteria, and to integrate acquired skills. The course links theoretical and practical considerations so that students are not only able to interpret but to understand the cultural, institutional, and social implications of interpreting.

An elective in editing was developed to meet the increasing demand from language providers that translators and project managers be able to copyedit, proofread, and fact-check human translations as well as post-edit machine translations. Building on the writing and research skills that students begin to acquire from the start of the program, the course combines readings in standard manuals, ranging from the *Chicago Manual of Style* to Amy Einsohn's *The Copyeditor's Handbook* (2006) to Brian Mossop's *Revising and Editing for Translators* (2014), with the editing of actual documents such as machine-translated text and chapters from books that have recently been translated but not yet published.

Project management is the focus of another specialized elective for students who wish to gain a better understanding of the translation industry and to be more competitive in the global marketplace. This course shows students how to be effective service providers so that they can broaden their career opportunities beyond the traditional roles of translator, editor, and proofreader by working as project managers in language companies or in the language departments of private and public-sector organizations. Working individually and in groups, students learn project management concepts and processes as they specifically apply to translation. They then apply this knowledge in authentic learning activities, including project scope definition; the creation of a work breakdown structure; the estimation of task duration, resource requirements, and cost in relation to the schedule and budget; the creation of a risk management plan; and a procedure for quality control. As in the other courses, students learn to submit data, processes, and their own decision making to critical analysis.

The general focus of the program on the integration of learning across the various facets of translation culminates in the case study, a substantial project that is the equivalent of a thesis, requiring at least a semester to complete and involving an oral defense. In this capstone project, students demonstrate their ability to apply the concepts and skills they have learned in their courses by working independently with a longer text, typically in the range of 5,000 words. The case study includes a translation, a critical analysis, and a term base in which students show their understanding of key concepts in terminology management. Students are required to keep a journal during the entire process so that they can collect material for the critical analysis and refer back to specific decisions they made at different points. In consultation with an advisor, students choose a source text. Using the conceptual vocabulary in translation studies, they define a brief or set of instructions for their translation such as might be given by a client. Then they carry out their pre-translation research, analyze the characteristics of the source text and its text type, select an approach appropriate to the brief, apply translation strategies to solve difficulties posed by the text, and produce their translation, revising and editing it as necessary. When students defend their case studies, they are examined by a committee (the advisor who directed their project, one faculty member who works with the same language pair, and one with expertise in the subject area). The type and amount of questioning that each student faces are an indication of the acceptability of her work.

The topics of the case studies vary greatly. Recently a few students have selected a literary or a cultural text. One translated into French the first chapter from British writer Jim Crace's (2013) novel, *Harvest*, while another translated into English an excerpt from Japanese writer Kenichi Yamamoto's 2008 novel, *The Secret of the Tea Master*. Some students have developed projects in localization, choosing to work on a Russian anti-Putin website or a website dedicated to French Canadian immigration. Others have translated specialized documents, such as a medical article on cervical malformations, a report on the treatment of gays in Russia, and a government white paper from Venezuela about forestry. Students do not necessarily choose a topic or a text type with which they are already familiar. On the contrary, since the case study is the final opportunity to benefit from the feedback of experts, the key to gaining expertise, they often select a text that will challenge them.

The MA in translation attracts students from a variety of academic backgrounds. The majority come from the humanities, with undergraduate majors or minors in such fields as art history, English, foreign languages, linguistics, and the teaching of English as a second language. Some have concentrations in business, cognitive science, computer science, and law. A few applicants have already gained significant professional experience as translators but seek comprehensive formal training. However, students are expected not to have previously studied translation but to display an intellectual curiosity in their application materials. Before entering the program, they must submit oral and written samples that demonstrate they have achieved advanced proficiency in a foreign language, as defined by the American Council on the Teaching of Foreign Languages, or in English if they are international applicants. These samples, which are assessed by faculty members in pertinent language pairs, have proved to be more accurate reflections of students' proficiency than such traditional measures as transcripts and test scores, especially in the case of international students.

The program enrolls approximately fifty full-time students. About 40 percent are international, natives of countries in Europe, South America, Africa, the Middle East, and Asia. For each of the six language pairs, teaching assistantships are available (two to four per language per year) in order to attract the most promising applicants. Assistants teach the equivalent of three courses per year, usually serving as discussion leaders, graders, or instructors of record in lower-division language courses. Ninety percent of the students graduate in two years and find employment in the translation and language industries.

Ten full-time tenure-track faculty members staff the curriculum. Because the Institute for Applied Linguistics is committed to translation as a discipline, the faculty are in most cases scholar-translators engaged in translation research and practice, and any outsourcing of instruction is avoided, except in unusual situations (faculty leaves are covered by professional practitioners who teach part-time). Although faculty have language-specific expertise as well as a specialized area of research, they are expected to develop courses as needed in secondary areas. A faculty member who works with gender issues, for instance, may teach not only literary and cultural translation but also research methods or legal, diplomatic, and commercial translation. Another whose body of research is in terminology may teach a course in German literary translation, while yet another whose research focuses on cognition may teach a course in Spanish medical translation. Most faculty were trained in foreign languages or in comparative literature, but some come from adjacent disciplines where translation is particularly relevant, such as psychology of language and intercultural communication. Future hires are likely to come directly from translation studies, since the last decade has seen the development of full-fledged doctoral programs in the field. Whatever their individual specialization, faculty must be flexible, willing to gain new expertise, to develop courses in new areas, and to direct case studies in a wide range of topics. Although faculty are expected to have experience as practitioners, the only translations that are currently considered scholarship for the purpose of tenure and promotion are those accompanied by an apparatus or paratexts such as introductions and afterwords. Translation that falls into the copyright category of "work for hire" is not considered in the evaluation of one's scholarship.

4 An MFA in Literary Translation

Roger Sedarat

Founded in 2007, the MFA program in literary translation at Queens College of the City University of New York operates on the assumption that better writers make better translators. Hence, in addition to intensive instruction in translating texts from various languages into English, students take creative writing courses in the genres in which they translate. Translation students benefit from sustained interaction with peers and faculty working in fiction, poetry, and drama. Conversely, many students in creative writing enroll in translation courses, experimenting with translation in their respective genres.

Admission remains highly selective, based on a transcript showing evidence of an applicant's advanced reading proficiency in a language other than English, recommendations from academic specialists in foreign languages and literatures, and a sample literary translation into English that demonstrates significant ability to translate. Applicants tend to come from foreign-language departments and comparative literature departments and programs. Many already work full-time as professional translators prior to admission. Students to date have translated from the following languages: Arabic, Chinese, Czech, French, German, Gujarati, Hebrew, Hindi, Italian, Jamaican Patois, Japanese, Korean, Latin, Modern Greek, Portuguese, Russian, Scots, Spanish, and Urdu.

Although faculty teaching translation know Bosnian, French, Hebrew, Persian, and Spanish, they cannot possibly accommodate the range of student languages. Anticipating the need to educate developing translators with only two instructors, the program makes use of the resources in the English Department in which it is housed as well as in the college and in the university system. Other faculty in the department are fluent in such languages as Haitian Creole, German, Swahili, and Turkish. A few publish translations along with their scholarship. These instructors evaluate admission applications, teach required MA courses, and serve as second readers of theses. Additionally, language departments in the college include published translators whose linguistic backgrounds qualify them to teach and serve as second readers. Translation students also take courses throughout the university system, seeking out literature faculty in the languages from which they translate.

The curriculum, completed in two or three years, is designed to advance translation practice with a special focus on developing a command of the rhetorical skills needed for the genres in which students translate. Students are required to take four writing workshops (two in translation and two in another literary genre), two craft courses (which center on issues raised by the formal features of literary texts), one course in literary theory and criticism, and three courses in literature, whether in English or in a foreign language. Students are required to submit a thesis, typically a book-length translation, and to take a workshop designed to support the composition of this final project by creating a venue for presenting it as a work in progress. The thesis is defended before a faculty committee.

The curriculum allows for the comprehensive study of translation in theory and practice while accommodating various languages, traditions, and genres. The required course in literary theory and criticism, for example, begins to provide students with the necessary conceptual tools to analyze source texts, their own translations, and those of their peers. Presenting a survey of the philosophy of language that includes poststructuralist concepts of textuality, this course is typically offered to students early in their study to ensure that discussions in workshops and craft courses move beyond belleletristic assumptions in the critique of translations. The literature courses allow students to enrich their knowledge of a literary period and genre. Seminars in English literature support the search for rhetorical models comparable to those deployed in the source text, while seminars in foreign literatures lead to a closer examination of literary influences upon source authors.

The translation workshops and craft courses form the core of the curriculum in translation. The workshops are modeled on those offered in creative writing programs: students submit their translations each week for critical discussion by the class. While the students' translations remain the principal texts for this course, published translations as well as translation theory and commentary are also assigned. Required readings in the workshops range from Dick Davis's practical account of translation problems, "On Not Translating Hafiz" (2004), which prompts students to interrogate the idea of untranslatability in a short reflective paper on their own translations, to Walter Benjamin's speculative introduction to his Baudelaire translation, "The Translator's Task" (1923b), which acts as the basis of an assignment that asks students to consider how their own translation might be seen as undergoing an "afterlife." Other commentary on translation has included two edited volumes, Eliot Weinberger and Octavio Paz's *19 Ways of Looking at Wang Wei* (1987), which models comparative analysis of translations before we begin workshopping student submissions, and Esther Allen and Susan Bernofsky's mix of theoretical and practical reflections, *In Translation* (2013). Willis Barnstone's study, *The Poetics of Translation* (1993), has also been assigned. Students are often asked to submit response papers that relate arguments deriving from such readings to their own translation practice.

Workshops introduce rhetorical exercises like homophonic translation and imitation to encourage creative play during the translation process. Both to build a more student-centered workshop and to encourage translating beyond conventional practices, collaborative translation is often required. Other exercises include the translation of a well-known poem from a language with which students have little or no knowledge, an exercise that forces the class to rely on the same set of trots and notes provided by the instructor. Completed drafts in turn lead to a detailed comparison of linguistic choices, and we deepen this analysis by turning to seminal publications on the source text. Since students work from a variety of languages in each workshop, translation assignments require formal analysis of the source text through relatively detailed translator's notes. Developed over the course of the semester, these notes involve extensive research into the source author's biography, literary influences, and culture. In an effort to broaden the context of the workshop discussions, students also present previous versions of the same text or other translations of the same author.

The workshop treats the translation of a literary text as a creative work in its own right. Discussion begins with the translator reading aloud a section of his or her project, first in the source language, then in the English version. When a dramatic translation has been submitted, parts are assigned to be read by the class. Students evaluate the translator's linguistic choices, ensuring that the translator has maintained a semantic correspondence to the source text, but they also consider the literary effects of those choices, drawing upon their experiences in poetry, fiction, and drama workshops. Although grouping translators with such disparate language backgrounds necessarily limits the attention to the source text, translators working from the same Romance languages do frequently enroll in the same workshop. The sole Greek or Japanese translator might lack a comparable partner, but he or she benefits from teaching the class about the literary tradition as well as the language of the source text. Workshops require a final project consisting of a revised draft of the student's translation as well as a process paper that gathers and develops the translator's notes submitted throughout the semester.

Craft courses reinforce and extend the instruction in the workshops. In their emphasis on form, they localize key aspects of the translation process and foreground problems that translators commonly confront, enlisting the class in troubleshooting and the development of strategic solutions. As in the workshops, competing published translations from such classic texts as the Bible or the poems of Ovid are often assigned to immerse students in the process of discriminating among linguistic choices and literary effects. Although craft courses vary according to the instructor and perceived student need, all tend to isolate specific approaches in rendering literature into English regardless of individual text choice. A craft unit on biographical approaches to source texts, for example, paired a discussion of John Felstiner's *Translating Neruda* (1980) with an exercise that asks students to track the life of the foreign author they are translating in relation to his or her developing body of work.

Craft courses, much more than workshops, teach students how to deploy a critical discourse in their commentary about translation. John Dryden's distinctions between "Metaphrase," "Paraphrase," and "Imitation" and Roman Jakobson's classification of "intralingual," "interlingual," and "intersemiotic" translation expand students' conceptual vocabulary in discussing their craft (Jakobson 1959: 127). To consider recurring questions of equivalence, Barnstone's distinction between the "servile translator" bent on "mechanical replication" and the "new author" aiming for "originality" in "imitation" provides a useful spectrum that moves between identification and interpretation (Barnstone 1993: 94). In subsequent discussions as well as in a short writing assignment, students practice positioning their translations along this spectrum. Given the ubiquity of metaphors in translation studies, students have been tasked with locating and analyzing the metaphorical formulations used by various writers in anthologies like Lawrence Venuti's *The Translation Studies Reader* and Rainer Schulte and John Biguenet's *Theories of Translation*. After such preliminary investigative work, students are then asked to devise their own extended metaphor of the translation process.

Craft courses in particular adopt interdisciplinary approaches to engage, in both theory and practice, what proves difficult to translate. Ellen Bryant Voigt's analysis of tone in *The Flexible Lyric* (1999) is linked to an assignment that asks students to explicate the interaction of discursive with nondiscursive elements in their own translated texts. Students attempt to isolate the sound or music of their prose, poetry, or drama, independent of meaning, juxtaposing it with such elements as diction and syntax.

Because all students in this program are both creative writers and translators, craft classes emphasize the interplay between critical reflection and translation. Various translators' notes are discussed, ranging from the annual translation issue of *Poetry* to Seamus Heaney's introduction to his version of *Beowulf* (2001), and students are asked in turn to experiment with extended commentary on their own process. In response to a reading of Paschalis Nikolaou's essay, "Notes on Translating the Self," which advocates a more expansive exploration of "what is a person and a literary consciousness as much as a translator" (Nikolaou 2006: 31), students track their translation process in subjective as well as objective terms. For example, a student translating a collection of Japanese *zuihitsu*, prose texts in which an author responds to his surroundings, included the usual detailed explanations required in a translator's note: in this case, bio-critical summaries of the source authors that appeared in the collection, an account of the genre, and a comment on diction. In addition, however, the student offered brief journal entries about how the subject matter proved to be personally evocative for him. He responded to a list of objects that one source author had lost by recalling the losses in his own life in a journal entry. He was in effect writing in the zuihitsu form, and in his note he critically examined how the style of such a poem, a list, structured his own recollected emotion.

The workshops enable students to develop simultaneously as translators and as writers. These courses involve original compositions in poetry, fiction, and drama. Since creative writing faculty know some of the frequently represented languages, including French, Italian, and Japanese, they sometimes assign translation exercises related to their genre. The sustained feedback offered in the workshops through the revision process helps to enhance the translator's skill in constructing sentences and honing dramatic dialogue. This sort of instruction can be continued if translation students elect the additional option of taking a craft course in their preferred genre. "Poetic Closure" is an especially popular course that has proven helpful in teaching translators how to tighten concluding lines and stanzas. Using a range of both Western and Eastern poems in different forms, some of which have been translated into English, students analyze various endings with the help of Barbara Herrnstein Smith's *Poetic Closure* (1968). Students are given the opportunity to practice in their own poetry and translations various topics covered in the course, such as paratactic, sequential, and dialectic structure.

To prepare for their thesis, students in translation, like those in creative writing, take a specially designed thesis workshop before their intensive one-on-one work with their advisor. Designed as a capstone course for the degree, the thesis workshop offers sustained attention to every student's project, regardless of the track or genre. Over the course of the semester, students regularly submit parts of their theses to workshop for subsequent revision. Typically students receive more in-depth feedback here than in a traditional workshop, and they are often referred to other texts in order to develop the thesis further. To accommodate translation students, faculty always include translated texts as well as texts about the art of translation alongside other craft-oriented readings.

A curriculum that combines translation with creative writing often leads students to create hybrid theses that combine translations with original compositions. Conversely, translation students who demonstrate sufficient mastery of original composition at times choose to include some of their own work alongside their translations. The attention to craft that follows upon sustained application to original compositions seems to improve rather than impede their own translation choices.

The length of a translation thesis varies with the genre and the source text. If the latter has previously appeared in English, the student needs to substantiate why the text warrants retranslation and what makes his or her version distinctive relative to previously published versions. Students working in poetry must submit twenty-five to thirty pages, while fiction students must submit at least seventy-five pages. A dramatic translation involves a full-length play. Typically the translation concentrates on a single work or body of work by the same writer, although with reasonable justification a student can obtain permission to anthologize different writers from the same tradition to highlight comparable features of disparate texts.

Every thesis must include a process paper, at least ten pages long, which both critically and theoretically contextualizes the project. The translator uses the paper to address what reasoning led to the selection of the source text, what concept of equivalence was applied during the translation process, and how that concept is connected to the translator's interpretation of the source text. While process papers by students in poetry, fiction, or drama might read their work against key influences that have come to inform it, translation students track influences upon the form and theme of the source material and consider analogous English-language models that have shaped their translations. Their theoretical approaches to translation reflect the concepts of language and textuality studied in the required course on literary theory and criticism as well as the translation theory and commentary in the anthologies used in the workshops and craft courses. During the student's last semester, a complete draft of the thesis is submitted to a primary advisor and a second reader, who provide suggestions for further revision before final approval.

Readers assess the thesis holistically based on a variety of criteria. In the process paper, they evaluate the translator's critical reflection upon the English rendering, examining how translation difficulties unique to the chosen text have been identified and resolved. Graders also consider how effectively the translator has situated the source-language author and text in the context of the source literary tradition while responding to the history of previous English renderings. The translator must describe and implement a definitively different approach to the source text, providing a compelling rationale as to why a new translation seems warranted. Even when offering a first-ever English translation, the translator must track trends in the translation of comparable literary works from the source language, articulating how his or her translation engages with these trends. Translations are read both for a semantic correspondence as well as deliberately creative choices that construct an effective analogy to the tone and rhetorical functioning of the source text. Stylistic choices are examined for consistency relative to the genre, period, and tradition of the source text.

Near the end of the last semester, the student completes a one-hour oral exam. Modeled on a doctoral defense, the exam is based on the thesis as well a reading list consisting of theoretical texts, published translations, and works in the student's chosen genre. The program compiles a master list of readings divided into four genres—poetry, drama, nonfiction, and translation—each of which includes a section of pertinent criticism. Students use the master list to select thirty texts tailored to their interests: fifteen in their genre of focus, five in another genre, five in criticism, and, with their advisor's approval, five texts that do not appear on the list. A student translating the poetry of André Breton, for instance, might choose previous translations of Breton's poetry by Jean-Pierre Cauvin and Mary Ann Caws (2006), the work of such other surrealist or surrealist-influenced poets as Aimé Césaire, Philip Lamantia, and Dean Young, Breton's novel, *Nadja*, critical works like George Steiner's *After Babel* as well as Schulte and Biguenet's *The Craft of Translation*, and George Melly and Michael Wood's personal history of the movement, *Paris and the Surrealists* (1991). The list of criticism might be wide-ranging, including not only fundamental works like Aristotle's *Poetics* and T. S. Eliot's essay, "Tradition and Individual Talent" but also historical documents like David Gascoigne's *A Short Survey of Surrealism* (1935). At the defense, the student must respond to the questions in a way that is not simply articulate but learned, demonstrating enough theoretical, critical, and literary sophistication to explain the significance of the project.

The program offers students various opportunities to become acquainted with the profession of literary translation. It runs a lecture series called "Trends in Translation" that has brought to campus distinguished writer-translators like Marilyn Hacker and Charles Martin to discuss their work and to confer with students. *Ozone Park*, a national publication of creative writing and literary translation founded and staffed by MFA students, includes a student editor to handle translation submissions. Faculty encourage attendance at the annual conference of the American Literary Translators Association (ALTA) and sometimes participate on panels with students. The college has been the site of national translation conferences facilitated in large measure by MFA students who joined in the planning and moderated panels as well as assisted with such other tasks as publicity and book sales.

Graduating students and alumni compete each year for the "Loose Translation Prize," awarded to the most outstanding translation thesis in any genre. Faculty nominate candidates whose work is then voted upon by the editors of Hanging Loose Press, a noted small press based in Brooklyn. The prize is publication with national distribution. Thus far the award has gone to three students: Anne Posten for her translation of Tankred Dorst and Ursula Ehler's German novella, *This Beautiful Place* (2012), Ilaria Papini for her translation of Fausto Paravidino's postmodern Italian play, *Still Life in Ditch* (2013), and Yves Henri Cloarec for his translation of Guillaume de Fonclare's French memoir, *Inside My Own Skin* (2014). Other students have gone on to publish translations with Rizzoli, Haus Publishing, Frisch & Co., and O/R Books.

Students take advantage of the professional support offered by a number of institutions in the New York City area. This support tends to be genre-specific. Drama translators can have their plays performed in staged readings by professional actors at the Flea Theatre in Lower Manhattan. Poetry translators can benefit from a partnership with the Poetry Society of America, which brings nationally acclaimed poets to campus for readings and class visits. Each fall students participate in the Turnstile Reading Series, an event organized by the consortium of creative writing programs in the university system. Additionally, the program maintains affiliations with several publishers and writers' organizations where students can serve as interns, including New Directions, the PEN American Center, and the Asian Writers' Workshop.

Students in translation have received grants from the National Endowment for the Arts and the PEN American Center, a Fulbright award, ALTA travel fellowships, and fellowships to the Vermont Studio Center. Graduates go on to doctoral programs in foreign languages as well as comparative literature. Others teach as adjuncts in foreign-language departments or continue to work as professional translators for institutions such as the United Nations or as freelance contractors for various companies and presses.

5 A Doctoral Program in Translation Studies

Luise von Flotow

A Brief History

The School of Translation and Interpretation at the University of Ottawa has offered a doctorate in translation studies since 1997. It was designed to meet the need, created by Canada's official bilingualism, to train those who train the many translators and interpreters that work in federal and provincial parliaments and ministries, in international missions, in legal institutions, in research agencies and government think tanks, and in the translation services that support the requirements of the Canadian policy. The initial impetus for the doctorate is perhaps easier to understand if one keeps in mind how ubiquitous translation is in Canada, where not only parliamentary debates but also street signs, computer manuals, even cereal boxes are bilingual, drawing attention to the two official languages on a daily basis and offering exercises in comparative linguistics or translation criticism to anyone who might be interested. Translation, quite simply, permeates daily life in Canada.

The doctoral program initially had two important goals. It focused specifically on translation pedagogy, that is, research on how to train those who would train translators. This goal was enhanced by related specializations in lexicology, terminology, and translation technologies such as corpus analysis tools and memory systems. The other, more general goal was to train scholar-teachers whose work would develop translation studies in its many different facets. This goal was served by a humanities-based segment that explored the history of translation and the study of humanistic translations (anthropological, literary, historical, philosophical, religious) and their diverse impact on receiving cultures. The Canadian situation ensured that, at this initial stage, the main languages of faculty and students were English and French.

The program has since widened its scope to move beyond its origins in Canadian bilingualism. Ten years after its founding, it underwent a rigorous restructuring that defined two major fields of study and two distinct curricula, with a substantial increase in requirements: humanities-based translation studies, on the one hand, and terminology and translation technologies, on the other. Furthermore, marked changes in the applicant pool, as well as the international growth of translation studies as a field, led to a proliferation of language combinations and research topics, so that neither Canadian French and English nor the Canadian cultural and social situation can be viewed as norms. The description that follows is concerned with the program in its *current* state, providing a look at its goals as well as admissions requirements and the student body.

An International Focus

The program rests on the premise that doctoral work in translation studies trains future scholar-teachers of translation research and practice. It sees translation as an important factor not only in human interactions in the past but also in globalization today. The global political economy increases the need for translators and interpreters and hence for translation research. It embeds social institutions in ever-expanding networks that are fundamentally *translational* because they are interlingual and intercultural, thus supporting and promoting the study of translation. The aim of the doctoral program, as a result, is to produce graduates who possess professional currency as defined by the international community of translation scholars.

Applicants must demonstrate an academic interest in studying linguistic and cultural transfers in the broadest sense. They submit a research proposal that details this interest and sketches out a possible research project. All of them have completed master's degrees, predominantly in the humanities, in such fields as communications, cultural studies, history, literature, philosophy, and translation studies. Some have worked in the more technical or applied areas of language studies, such as computational linguistics, corpus linguistics, lexicology, and terminology, or in fields related to translation technologies, such as software localization and language engineering. All of them have had some experience with the practice of translation. While this experience is not an absolute requirement for admission, it enormously enhances students' work in the program, deepening their engagement with the courses that precede the examinations and with their dissertation research.

The student body is bilingual and bicultural, more often multilingual. Recent admissions have hailed from countries as diverse as China, Colombia, France, India, Mexico, Romania, and Syria. To a large extent, these international students work with language combinations that reflect their cultural origins, using English as the lingua franca. However, given the bilingual mandate of the University of Ottawa as well as the cultural background of the faculty who also train undergraduates and master's students for the Canadian translation market, French is another much-appreciated lingua franca. For Hispanophone students, in fact, French is often the language of choice for research and writing, while Asian and Middle Eastern students largely use English.

Coursework

The curriculum consists of two electives taken in the first semester and two mandatory courses in the second. Some students may be required to take additional courses if, during the admissions process, they are deemed to have gaps in trans-lation theory and in computer applications, the two fields that form the basis of the program. Incoming students choose from a number of electives, among them translation history, discourse analysis, linguistics, translation pedagogy, and ter-minology and documentation. They can also study independently with individual faculty to hone a specialization they wish to develop, such as audiovisual trans-lation or translation memory systems. Overall, the courses in translation theory, translation history, and discourse analysis prove to be the most popular in the first semester, since most students come from humanistic disciplines. However, because terminology and technologies play an increasingly important role in the translation industries worldwide, these areas have recently seen considerable development.

The course in theory explores the diverse theoretical discourses that have been formulated to think about translation. These discourses come largely from Euro-pean, British, and American traditions of literature, philosophy, and religion. At the beginning of the course, the centuries-old dichotomy between translating the word and translating the sense is studied through such authors as Walter Benjamin (1923a), Antoine Berman (1984), and Jean-René Ladmiral (1994), whose coin-age "sourcier vs. cibliste" (source-text oriented vs. target-text oriented) succinctly seeks to denote the two sides of this historic argument. Subsequently, more recent ways of thinking about translation are brought to the fore: descriptive approaches, manipulation, interventionist or politicized translation practices and research, and functionalist ideas or perspectives on translation as a purposeful activity (Brisset 2010; Hermans 1985; Nord 1997; Steiner 1975a; Toury 1995; Vermeer 1996; von Flotow 1997). The concept of equivalence to the source text, the staple of much popular writing about translation, underlies discussions, and students are expected to engage with it constantly. Contemporary texts on translation ethics and socio-logical approaches are touched upon briefly but covered in greater depth in the mandatory course offered in the second semester (Chesterman 2001; Pym 2012; Wolf 2001). Students produce critical summaries of key texts, present a particular author or text in class, and write a final paper in which they apply a set of theoreti-cal concepts in the analysis of a specific instance of translation practice.

The course in translation history assumes that every translation is a reading of another text. Students trace the movements of translated texts as artifacts that present evidence of reading, studying different translations of the same source text—say, Thomas More's *Utopia* in several different French incarnations. In the process, they learn how relative such readings are, how they evolve over time, and how the study of translations reveals this evolution. The focus here is the historic-ity of reading as found in translations, in the prefaces to translations, and in the ways in which translations are disseminated and received. Texts by such authors as Leonardo Bruni (2008), Clara Foz (1998), and Marc de Launay (2006) serve as resources that demonstrate how such studies might proceed and what theoretical and historiographical underpinnings they might require. Students are encouraged to make use of the University of Ottawa's growing collection of rare books (which specializes in translated artifacts) and study the object itself, the translated book, its presentation, annotation, and history as an object. Assignments include critical readings of translators' prefaces as statements of intention that require interpretation and assessment in historical contexts as well as comparison with the translation strategies visible in the text.

The course in discourse analysis and its applications in translation studies assumes that all translation involves contexts and no text exists or is produced or received without the complexities and tensions of contextual meaning. This course examines the extent to which terms like language, discourse, text, and context enter into and provide help in understanding the production, use, and function of translated materials. Jan Renkema's introduction (2004) serves as a basic text, developing ideas and methods from critical discourse analysis (Fairclough 2005), a useful tool in analyzing and comparing translations. The course also examines discourse as a vehicle of ideologies in translation (Baker 2006; Munday 2007), as well as the discourses of the field of translation studies itself (Chamberlain 1988; Hermans 2004; Shreve 2012). Students are required to produce analytical work (critical summaries and essays, in addition to class presentations) that links theoretical concepts with practical issues.

The course in linguistics is divided into three distinct sections. It first studies the interface between structural linguistics and translation (Catford 1965; Jakobson 1959; Nida and Taber 1969) that sought context-transcendent universals in translated texts. It then considers the systemic-functional linguistics that underlie descriptive approaches to translation (Mason 2012; Reiss 1981). Finally, it takes up the contribution of corpus linguistics, contemporary studies in the machine-driven analysis of huge corpora of translated texts (Olohan 2004; Tognini-Bonelli 2001). Students are confronted here with the various attempts—theoretical, descriptive, and technical—to theorize and identify levels of identity between translated texts and the translator's decision-making.

The course in translation pedagogy sets out from the fact that the School of Translation and Interpretation is in the business of producing professional translators. This course addresses the need for teachers to identify competencies in translating and interpreting, in revising and in research, and in the use of terminology. Supported by readings in educational theory (Anderson and Krathwohl 2001), students choose a translation-oriented course they would like to teach, pinpoint the skills that should be acquired by the end of it, develop assessment tools to determine the degree of acquisition, and design real-world learning and teaching activities. They weigh the pros and cons of assessments that refer either to norms or to criteria, to linguistic and cultural values, or to the application of client specifications. They consider how these approaches are manifested in professional translator certification and quality-control models and formulate their own criteria, performance indicators, and alphanumeric grading systems.

The course in computer applications, often required of incoming students with humanities backgrounds, provides an overview of advanced computational aids for human translation as well as some hands-on experience. The applications include terminology management, desktop publishing, and corpus analysis. The course also offers students a survey of computer-aided and machine translation, along with the opportunity to analyze machine translation output. By the end, students understand the underlying approaches used in various computer-aided and machine translation tools. They can compare and evaluate a selection of these tools and grasp the basics of research.

After this immersion in computers, students often proceed to the course in terminology and documentation, which provides a more in-depth introduction to the theories and practices of using corpus analysis and developing corpora as a translation resource. Exploring the use of corpus linguistics for translation (Baker 1996; Bowker 2000) and the construction and use of all manner of databases, lexica, electronic and traditional dictionaries, the course exposes students not only to the technologies of data management in and for translation but also the theoretical and cultural, even political questions that arise in the area. Student assignments include designing corpora for a specific project, comparing and assessing various forms of specialized dictionaries and glossaries, reflecting on the resources used for corpora and terminology needs, comparing the use of databases by terminologists and by translators, and producing collaborative translations.

The foregoing seven courses, all electives, constitute the core of the curriculum. Students do have other options as well. They may choose a workshop in literary translation, where the emphasis falls on reading the source text in detail before a translation is undertaken and where students are required to pursue publication of their final piece of work. Or they may select a course in adaptation, which currently centers on the many types of audiovisual translation (voice-over, subtitling, dubbing, audio description, videogame translation) as well as the ideological and technical aspects underlying their production and dissemination. This course involves work with various Montreal-based companies involved in such translation. Students are also encouraged to look beyond the School of Translation and Interpretation to take at least one course in other areas that can broaden and deepen their work in translation studies. Examples include business management, Canadian studies, history, law, and literary theory.

The two mandatory courses examine contemporary developments in research, one in translation studies, the other in terminology and technology. The content can vary according to the faculty assigned to teach them. Most recently, the course in translation studies has paid most attention to the crisis of representation that anthropology underwent in the 1970s and the political and sociological approaches to translation research that developed from that moment. Theoretical and methodological readings focus on the work of Pierre Bourdieu (2002) and Bruno Latour (1996). Considerable emphasis is given to Niklas Luhmann's systems theory (2013) and its applications to translation. Students are required to submit a final paper in which they devise, justify, and apply a theoretical framework to the dissertation project they are preparing.

The course in terminology and technology similarly explores advanced research in the area, familiarizing students with current trends and debates. They study various approaches to terminology that have evolved since the early days of the field in the first half of the twentieth century—communicative, sociocognitive, socioterminological, and textual-lexico-semantic. The final assignment is a research paper and conference presentation that must address the principal themes of the course. Students benefit from the approval that the university ethics committee has given for projects involving questionnaires, surveys, and interviews—with translators, for example, for whom the question of "terminometrics" is no small one, as they are increasingly subject to a considerable volume of terminologies and technologies in their work (Bowker 2006).

Examinations, Dissertation, and Professionalization

This coursework forms the bulk of each cohort's group experience. As they move through the program, students quickly find their own different projects and paths. The first doctoral exam, however, which takes place in the third semester, keeps them together for a short time longer. This exam is based on an annually updated list of readings that consists of two main areas: translation as product and as process, along with a few more specialized categories. The list contains roughly one hundred titles, ranging from James Holmes's essay, "The Name and Nature of Translation Studies" (1972), which is often seen as a roadmap for the field, to histories of translation in different parts of the world (Ballard 1992; Bandia 2005; Berman 1984; Cheung 2002; Trivedi 2006) to process-oriented work (pragmatics, functionalism, terminology, computer-aided translation, software localization) and product-oriented studies (Buzelin 2005; Casanova 2002; Hermans 1999; Meschonnic 1999). A final segment focuses on the translating subject (Simeoni 1998; Simon 1996) and ethics (Bermann and Wood 2005; Venuti 1998). Two essay questions make up the exam, which tests general knowledge in the two fields of the program as well as students' abilities to analyze, synthesize, and write. A typical question might cite a scholar's view of translation as mediating between cultures, asking students to elaborate on and update this citation with special emphasis on their own research topic. A question in the area of translation technology might address claims made for recent technological developments, requiring students to evaluate the accuracy of such claims. Students also submit a longer assignment in their chosen area of specialization.

The second exam, normally scheduled for the end of the fourth semester, consists of a thirty-page presentation and defense of the dissertation project. As can be imagined in such an interdisciplinary field of study, the projects are quite varied, representing all the areas explored in the curriculum. Recent dissertations have examined the role of translation in the Westernization of eighteenth-century Russia, sociological aspects of translating philosophical texts in twentieth-century Mexico, the history and politics of translation in the Russian Orthodox church, the translation of sound in text, and best practices for managing terminology in an integrated "Translation Environment Tool," a comprehensive software application designed to simplify the translator's work. A dissertation that consisted of a literary translation accompanied by a lengthy commentary was accepted in a joint effort with the Spanish Department. To accommodate the multilingual student body and its diverse interests, the School of Translation and Interpretation engages in numerous collaborations, sometimes with universities in France, more often with co-supervisors from different disciplines within the University of Ottawa or from other North American universities. These collaborations in themselves require a labor of translation.

The program puts considerable emphasis on the professionalization of its doctoral students. To this end, students gather at regularly scheduled seminars to present and provide feedback on research papers or in preparation for conference participation. Many students benefit from four years of research or teaching assistantships as part of their admissions package. They gain valuable research experience by working for an individual professor or in larger projects funded by Canadian federal grants. This kind of experience can lead to publications such as the recent monograph on Luhmann's work by alumnus Sergei Tyulenev (2012). As teaching assistants, doctoral students participate in course development, bibliographical work, and text management, and they assist with exercises in undergraduate courses and technology labs. Those who have French and English, as well as an excellent command of their native language, often become full-fledged part-time teachers, taking on responsibility for their own undergraduate course.

All doctoral students receive financial support from the School of Translation and Interpretation, the Graduate Student Association, and the university to attend and present their work at national and international conferences. They regularly participate in the annual meetings of the Canadian Association of Translation Studies and the Association francophone pour le savoir in Canada, at the biennial conferences of the American Translating and Interpreting Studies Association, and at the triennial conferences of the International Association for Translation and Intercultural Studies. With the number of such meetings on the rise, students travel widely—from Asia to Africa, from Europe to Latin America. They also find employment in wide-ranging places, in academia, government, and the private sector. Most recently graduates have found positions at Boston University, the University of Durham, the Monterey Institute of International Studies, various Canadian universities and government ministries, and in the burgeoning language industries.

Part II
Teaching Translation Practices

6 Teaching Translation to Foreign-Language Majors

Michael D. Hubert

Teaching Translation in a Foreign-Language Department

The teaching of translation in a university-level foreign-language department presents a series of challenges that originate with deeply heterogeneous levels of foreign-language proficiency across student populations as well as with instructor beliefs concerning effective teaching practices. Although foreign-language students often attain only modest levels of proficiency even after years of study, such is not always the case. Due to various personal and institutional factors that include differences in the time when language learning occurs, called "critical period" effects (Han 2004), and a wide range of previous language learning experiences, students often come to the classroom with very disparate levels of proficiency, some much more fluent and capable of producing the language than others. In an institutional environment that heavily encourages teaching methodologies intended to develop spoken communicative competence (Cook 2003), some instructors may find it difficult to understand or accept the teaching of a course that does not take as its main goal an immersive target language experience. However, as high levels of speaking proficiency are not required for translating, a course focused primarily on the decoding of the foreign language and the production of written English-language translations can fit well within the goals and outcomes of a foreign-language department.

This chapter describes a Spanish-to-English translation course that is guided by two main goals: (1) to provide students with a basic introduction to translation theory and strategies and (2) to provide practice in translating a variety of text types. Most of the theoretical material is taken from Kelly Washbourne's *Manual of Spanish-English Translation*, as are many of the activities I use throughout the semester. Organized according to the information presented in this textbook, the course is designed to give students experience in applying translation theories to a series of concrete activities and assignments. It also relies heavily on computer-assisted translation tools.

The main constituency is native Anglophone students who are concentrating in Spanish in a department of foreign languages and cultures. The course is offered as part of a "Spanish for the Professions" series of third-year courses. All students are required to complete the equivalent of two years of university-level foreign-language study before registering for the course, although some will have

completed considerably more. Students have therefore attained Spanish proficiency levels that range from novice up to advanced on the scale devised by the
American Council on the Teaching of Foreign Languages, although most seem to
fall within the intermediate level. None of the students has previously completed
a course in translation studies, and most have had little to no training in Spanish
literature or in linguistics.

Approaches, Tools, Activities

Although most Spanish intermediate courses at the university level are taught
in Spanish, I generally conduct the theoretical explanations in English because
the textbook is written in English and the author urges its use as the language
of instruction. Washbourne asserts that "striving for an 'immersion' environment
in a translation class sends the message that language acquisition is the primary
goal, which it is not" (Washbourne 2010b: 11). Unlike other foreign-language
courses, which seek to build language proficiency and spoken communicative
competence, students in this course use their reading knowledge of Spanish to
create a written product in English. Consequently, a great deal of class discussion
involves the acceptability and naturalness of the translation choices *in English*,
making the translating language a strategic vehicle for this discussion.

I initially approach the act of translation from a purely linguistic standpoint and
then quickly transition to a more culturally oriented approach. I begin by introducing students to a set of tools and strategies that help them to move from the
very common tendency of translating in an extremely literal, often word-for-word
manner to a more accurate and interpretive approach to the production of a written
translation. I stress proper dictionary use early on, placing strong emphasis on the
careful negotiation of word denotation and connotation. For example, one class
activity teaches students how to use context to determine correct word choice
by focusing on several common Spanish words like *madre* (mother) and *padre*
(father). Although these words do denote the concepts of "mother" and "father"
in the same way that they do in English, they can also carry additional, vastly different connotations: *madre* as a swear word and *padre* as a positive descriptive
adjective. I also teach that translation is an act of creation resulting in the production of a new text and not simply a transfer of sense from one language to another.
Almost all students seem completely unaware of this crucial point. Washbourne
states that "language is too chimerical, too changing, and too connotative for a
single rendering to capture every facet of a source text" (2010a: 15), and although
there are many possible valid interpretations of a single text, not all translations
are equally valid.

A good translation is therefore the product of both interpretive and creative
processes, a communicative tool that not only maintains a strong semantic correspondence to the source text but also creates a product that is both natural-sounding
and easy for the target audience to read. Meeting the needs of one's audience
becomes paramount. I help students to recognize where their translations are
stilted or otherwise difficult to understand for a monolingual English speaker and

to move past the stage of awkward translationese towards the production of easily readable, idiomatic English. Translationese, according to Washbourne (2010a: 126–7), is language that is "stuck in interlanguage": it is often manifested in jarringly incorrect target-language syntax based directly on source-language word order. To solidify this concept, students complete various fix-it activities in which they improve on poorly translated texts, always taken from real-life examples.

As students begin to produce their own translations, I introduce them to a series of computer-assisted tools that they are required to make use of, and report on, to complete all future assignments. I heavily discourage the use of machine translators such as Google Translate and instead teach students to differentiate between them and computer-assisted tools: whereas machine translators create a completely automatic translation by taking all decisions out of the translator's hands, computer-assisted tools do not try to replace the translator. They rather give the translator powerful means by which to make those decisions on his or her own by providing access to additional information from a variety of authentic sources. These sources include online translation forums, online linguistic corpora, and search engines used to locate appropriate terms, collocations, idioms, and parallel texts.

I first show students the online translation forum at www.wordreference.com. Although wordreference functions as a traditional dictionary resource, the site also offers a threaded discussion forum board that can be accessed from the bottom of any dictionary entry page. Translators needing help post a question on a word, term, or phrase, providing enough context to make an interpretation possible. Other forum users, native speakers of both source and target languages, then produce translations of the requested items, often giving explanations or asking additional questions for clarification. I teach students to use wordreference to search for key terms and phrases not readily available in a standard dictionary and to verify their translation choices in English. I require the entire class to register for free wordreference accounts that allow them to pose their own questions.

I also introduce students to the *Corpus of Contemporary American English*, an enormous database comprised of authentic language samples that are correlated and made searchable by keyword. Students first complete a textbook activity in which they learn about collocations, predictable co-occurrences of words in a language that are made acceptable through usage but that do not follow any identifiable rule. Then they are given a list of adjectives to match with a list of nouns with which each adjective most typically collocates. The adjectives include words like "confirmed," "knee-jerk," and "blithering," followed by nouns like "bachelor," "reactionary," and "idiot." I then instruct them to use the Corpus of Contemporary American English to verify their matching choices of "confirmed bachelor," "knee-jerk reactionary," and "blithering idiot," all typical collocations in English, many of which these young students are generally unaware of.

Lastly I introduce them to the concept of the parallel text, a document written by a native speaker of the target language in the same field as the text being translated. A parallel text represents "[a boon] to the translator, [. . .] one of the main resources for creating authentic target texts" (Washbourne 2010a: 91). Parallel texts, located with the help of search engines, can be used to verify translation choices involving tone, register, and term selection. I draw on a variety of activities to reinforce this concept. For example, in one activity taken from the textbook, students prepare to translate a text on wine-making, a topic with which almost all are completely unfamiliar. To produce the translation, they create a bilingual glossary of twenty to twenty-five words searching the internet to find English parallel texts on this topic.

Maintaining the appropriate tone and register in translation constitutes an important grading criterion. Tone, indicative of attitudes toward the subject matter and the audience, is expressed through a particular linguistic register, or degree of formality and informality. Students learn to consider the function of the source text as well as its projected audience in order to establish a suitable tone in their translations through a corresponding register. They complete a number of exercises in which they identify tone and register in Spanish texts and analyze these features in English translations, improving them where necessary. In a translation of an advertisement for a Mexican resort, for instance, students initially translated the phrase *ubicado al pie de la majestuosa Sierra Tarahumara* as the register-inappropriate "located at the foot of the majestic Sierra Tarahumara." After discussion and revision, the more appropriate "nestled in the foothills of the majestic Tarahumara Mountains" was chosen.

I devote another course module, following the textbook, to dealing with figurative language, including idioms, metaphor, and humor. My students are always surprised to learn that the translation of figurative language often involves a complete departure from the discrete lexical items used in the source text, including the wholesale replacement of a source-language idiom with an equivalent target-language idiom. A pertinent classroom activity asks students to use computer-assisted tools to match a list of Spanish-language idioms with their English-language equivalents. Students quickly come to realize that equivalent idioms between two languages often contain none of the same words, and that successful translation often requires very careful close reading of the source text. Examples include *pan comido* (literally translated as "eaten bread"), for which the equivalent idiom is "easy as pie," and *papar moscas* (literally translated as "to swallow flies"), meaning "to gawk."

As students are exposed to a wider variety of texts, specifically texts on cultural and consumer-oriented translation, I teach that quality translation not only requires managing isolated linguistic elements but also that the translator is both a purveyor of information and a cultural broker. In one textbook activity, students prepare to translate Spanish-language marketing materials on Machu Picchu for an audience of well-educated but monolingual American tourists. The students first brainstorm on special tasks and considerations that are involved in tourism and hospitality translation. They then search for parallel texts on the topic, using words and phrases from a list of possibilities provided in the textbook. This activity can be effective in sharpening their sense of how their translations might be received, since some of the words and phrases are culturally appropriate for this audience and some are not.

To help students translate effectively for different audiences, I introduce a variety of basic techniques that require them to consider cultural and social issues.

These techniques include explicitation (inserting an explanation to increase intelligibility), substitution (replacing an unfamiliar cultural reference with a familiar one), and compensation (offsetting the loss of source-text meaning with a different form in the translation). Students complete a variety of exercises to practice using these techniques. For example, students view a scene from the English-language film *Shrek* (Adamson and Jenson 2001) in which the nursery rhyme "The Muffin Man" is used as a plot device. As this rhyme does not exist in Spanish, translators substituted the well-known children's song *Pin Pon*, which fit well for dubbing purposes but which had no semantic correspondence to the English text.

Assignments

To encourage students to come to class prepared, I devote the first ten minutes of most class meetings to a short graded quiz. The material consists of the pages in the textbook we are scheduled to cover in a particular class as indicated in the syllabus. Students are not assigned a separate participation grade, as these quizzes are intended to ensure that they actively take part in classroom discussions.

During the semester, I administer two written exams in which students first define terms from the textbook and provide short answers to theoretical and methodological questions. Typical questions include the following: "What are corpora? Explain in detail the proper way to use a corpus in translation"; "Discuss the unique considerations the translator must keep in mind when translating marketing materials"; "Explain what makes literary translation especially challenging and different from all other types of translation." Next students choose among one of several short passages on different topics to translate individually. Since they are allowed to produce the translation with the use of electronic dictionaries and any other computer-assisted resources, they must complete and submit the first section of the exam before they can begin to work on the second. This procedure prevents them from using smartphones or laptops for the definitions and short answers they should have memorized.

During the first four weeks of instruction, I assign a series of four online forum discussions in which students deploy theoretical concepts presented in class by both answering an initial question prompt and by responding to each other's posts. They are asked to share experiences and opinions regarding each topic and to provide concrete examples to illustrate and strengthen their points. These discussions address the purpose and effectiveness of different translations, the differences between true, false, and partial cognates, the use of corpora, register and tone, and parallel texts. For example, students locate a short Spanish text that strongly conveys a certain tone and post the source text and their translation to the forum. They also cite five items from their translation that illustrate how they maintained tone and register. Then they discuss their choices with their peers, receiving and responding to constructive criticism on their choices.

I assign eight group translation projects throughout the semester, starting in the fifth week of instruction. I consider these assignments to be the backbone of the course, as they require learners to apply the theories and strategies they learned in class to produce a concrete translated product out of class and to take as much time as they need to do so. The criteria for grading the projects become familiar through repeated application: accuracy, appropriate register and tone, and consideration of audience. Students must also submit a formal report explaining and providing concrete examples of how they used computer-assisted tools to complete their translations and how a minimum of five theoretical points or strategies presented in the textbook influenced their work. These points or strategies should be not only linguistic but cultural, should take into account not only features like denotation and connotation but also strategies aimed to reach particular audiences like compensation.

The first of the group projects tasks students with fixing a poor commercial translation currently in use on the website of a South American ski resort. Students are sent to a specific portion of www.chileanski.com and directed to find ten different text sections that are badly translated from Spanish into English and to suggest alternative, improved translations of each. Each group is also required to prepare a detailed report on their alternative (as described in the previous paragraph) and explain how textbook theories on internet marketing and consumer-oriented translation informed their work. Past semesters have included similar assignments on different texts. For example, I give students a manual and recipe book for a Swedish bread mixer that contains a number of poor translations, including the lack of conversions for such terms as decaliters into United States measures. Students are asked to examine a copy of the translation, locate questionable renderings, and suggest improved versions.

The second group project tasks students with translating two rather generic texts, each approximately 400 words in length. The texts address topics that are extremely familiar to the students, allowing them to practice their newly acquired translation skills on texts of comparatively low difficulty and complexity. The first is a newspaper article reporting on research with bilingual Spanish-Guaraní children in Argentina; the second is a short blog post on environmentalism. The remaining group projects ask students to translate texts on topics related to each textbook chapter, covering a range of fields and text types: commercial and financial, legal and political, medical and scientific, technical and literary.

I assign a full-length translation to be submitted at the end of the course. I feel that this assignment provides students the opportunity to produce their very best work by taking advantage of what they have learned through the semester. In preparation, I use one of the group projects to encourage students to start on the final translation early, and I require them to complete a report that describes their use of computer-assisted tools as well as the theories and strategies they have gleaned from the textbook.

I give students a set of guidelines for selecting a text for translation. The source text must meet a minimum standard of written quality and be approximately 500 words in length. It must be an original composition produced by a native speaker of Spanish, not a Spanish translation of a text originally written in a language other than Spanish. It cannot have been previously translated into English. Following second language reading research that strongly suggests higher levels of topic familiarity lead to reading comprehension and retention (Carrell 1987; Kintsch

1998; Pritchard 1990), I also strongly encourage students to select a source text on a topic that interest them or with which they have at least some, if not great, familiarity. Students are required to meet individually with me by mid-term in order to determine the acceptability of their chosen source texts.

The final translation project is completed in a multidraft process in which I provide students with feedback. The first draft is useful in locating problem areas according to the basic evaluative criteria we have been using in the course. Students are asked to address these areas in a second draft and to use, where necessary, additional computer-assisted tools to decide how to make the revisions. Students are informed that their translations are expected to be professional in quality. I tell them, quite simply, that if they are unable to fool me into believing that I am reading a document originally written in English, I do not give full marks on any of the drafts. I have taught this course on three separate occasions and have found each time that almost all my students are capable of producing an effective, easily readable English translation, although only if they are willing to put forth the effort necessary.

Conclusions

Student reaction to the course has been extremely positive. Aside from being the only departmental course that directly addresses translation studies, students have expressed a great deal of satisfaction with the concrete, real-world applicability of the translation skills they acquire in only one semester. They are also pleased with having an increased awareness of the requirements of and challenges inherent in the production of a quality translation. And some have reported that they continue to use the concepts and strategies upon graduation.

Inevitably, student reaction has included criticisms. The course design has received complaints: some students have found it difficult to meet outside of class time to complete the group translation projects, while others have raised concerns regarding the fairness of assigning the same grade to every member of the group, regardless of individual effort. The textbook has not pleased every student, although the responses have varied, with some finding it difficult because of the concepts and others finding the presentation dry. Heritage speakers do not always regard the course as meeting their needs as well as it does the needs of native English-speaking students. These criticisms clearly reflect the backgrounds that individual students bring to the course. They might well be mitigated if the course were offered in a translation studies curriculum or supported by other translation-oriented courses. Although their nature and frequency vary from one iteration to the next and from one class to the next, I try to preempt them by encouraging an equal effort in group work, by using the textbook in more student-friendly ways, and by helping heritage speakers to see how thinking about and practicing translation can deepen their awareness of both Spanish and English.

Perhaps the most compelling aspect of the classroom environment fostered by the textbook is its task-based approach to the production of translations that can function in the real world. As Washbourne himself points out, long experience in the classroom has demonstrated that translation students need not only to be passive receptors of knowledge concerning translation studies but also to be active in producing their own translations. This call for students to take ownership of the translation process (Savery and Duffy 1996) is mirrored by similar calls from other educators for students to take on additional responsibility for their own learning (Conzemius and O'Neill 2001; Lee and Van Patten 2003). Although many foreign-language instructors do not appear to view the act of translation as compatible with the teaching of language and the development of proficiency, they do tend to look favorably upon the use of task-based instructional activities that result in the creation of a tangible product that can then be assessed for quality and for evidence of language learning. Translation courses, especially those that employ computer-assisted tools to enhance student access to authentic language sources, provide an excellent means of allowing students to put their foreign-language skills to use. Additionally, these courses promote language acquisition by increasing learner skills in using both source and target languages and by deepening student knowledge of the cultures in which these languages are spoken.

Finally, an approach that allows such high levels of achievement can provide students profound motivation. Although these Spanish majors and minors are not transformed into industry-ready professionals by the end of the course, a few each semester produce final projects that are extremely effective and nearly flawless in terms of accuracy, register-appropriateness, tone, and naturalness. This course truly demonstrates that even intermediate foreign language students can be taught to produce effective translations, even though none of them is able to speak the source language at a level even approaching native-like proficiency.

7 Teaching Translation Through Text Types

Brian James Baer

I've often conjectured that it would be much easier to teach an introductory course in translation, whether at the undergraduate or master's level, if the students entered the classroom *tabula rasa*, that is, without any preconceived notions about what translation is or ought to be. Instead, most students, at least in the United States, bring with them the notion of translation as a kind of linguistic matching game—"merely 'transcoding' a source text, merely 'transposing' it into another language," as Hans Vermeer puts it (1989: 192)—which can be successfully completed with the help of a large bilingual dictionary. The natural result, perhaps, of their experience in foreign-language classes, where translation is still often used as a grammar or vocabulary check, or of the hype surrounding popular machine translation tools, such as BabelFish and Google Translate, this view supports a literalist approach to translation, characterized by an almost exclusive focus on small, subsentential units, namely words and phrases, which results in translations that are awkward and unnatural-sounding—in a word, *translationese.* (Of course, the literalness of the novice translator should not be confused with literalness as a conscious and purposeful approach taken by an expert translator based on his or her evaluation of the translation *skopos* or aim, a point made repeatedly by Vermeer.)

The novice's focus on words and phrases is reflected in the overuse and misuse of bilingual dictionaries—*overuse* in the sense that bilingual dictionaries are often used to the exclusion of other research tools, such as parallel texts, and *misuse* in the sense that novice translators typically choose the first definition listed in the dictionary and fail to check that definition against the context. This focus on words and phrases is also reflected in a tendency to ignore global textual features, such as cohesion and coherence. And so one of the primary goals of any introductory course in translation must be, in addition to introducing a variety of strategies and tools, to initiate a profound rethinking of translation that would bring novice translators from a view of translation as mere transcoding, characterized by a focus on words and phrases and a blind fidelity to the source text, to an appreciation of translation as what the Czech theoretician Jiří Levý (1967) described as a complex decision-making process, which presumes the unit of translation to be the text as a whole and acknowledges the important role of extra-linguistic factors, such as the intentions of the author or client and the expectations of the end users of the translation.

The implications of such a rethinking should not be underestimated insofar as they have the potential to alter the ways students conceive of certain fundamental questions related to translation quality, the translator's role, and, as a consequence, translation ethics. This rethinking may alter students' perception of translation quality to the extent that equivalence is no longer viewed in terms of words and phrases but as distributed more broadly throughout the text and even beyond the text—in relationship to what Neubert and Shreve (1992: 1) describe as the text's "environment," that is, the communicative or social context of its reception. At an even more profound level, this rethinking has the potential to affect students' self-image as translators by altering the way they perceive the translator's role—no longer as a neutral conduit of information, a transcoder, but as a co-constructor of meaning, a decision maker, and, as Vermeer puts it, "an expert in intercultural communication" (1989: 192). This leads, in turn, to a redefining of translator ethics less in terms of blind fidelity to the source text and more in terms of responsibility, or "loyalty," to use Christiane Nord's term (1997: 125), to both the author, or client, and to the end users of the translation. The objective is to liberate novice translators from what Alan Duff referred to as the "tyranny of the source language" (1981: 113–18) or, to use Vermeer's more colorful phrase, to release them "from the corset of an enforced—and hence often meaningless— literalness" (1989: 201), transforming transcoders into experts, capable of making and defending conscious and purposeful decisions based on the communicative environment in which they are translating.

In order to achieve such a productive rethinking and to make students aware of its implications for their practice and for their professional identity, the introductory course I describe below combines theoretical readings with guided practice. The goal, however, is not to privilege theoretical discussion over practice. The course is designed under the assumption that the relationship between theory and practice is a two-way street, that is, thoroughly dialectical, and so, while altering someone's thinking about translation may affect his or her practice, altering one's practice may also initiate a re-thinking of translation and the translator's role. Therefore, the effective pairing of theoretical texts with guided practice is of paramount importance. That being said, I have found the theoretical texts to be of particular importance in refocusing the novice translators' attention from the level of the word and phrase to the level of the text and beyond.

I should mention here that this introductory course on translation practice is the first that students take in our master's program in translator training and is typically the first translation-related course that most of these students have ever taken. It is meant to prepare them for subsequent courses that deal with the translation of specialized texts, i.e., scientific/technical/medical, legal/commercial/diplomatic, and literary/cultural translation. The introductory Russian>English workshop course is taught in conjunction with an introductory course on translation theory for all the first-year students, taught in English across the language groups. The practice course is organized around the translation of six texts, representing different text types (sometimes called "text varieties" or "genres" in the literature). The approach I describe can easily be adapted for upper-level undergraduates.

The texts selected for translation are representative samples of various pragmatic text types, ranging from recipes to instruction manuals and museum guides. What is important here is that texts of this kind are rather formulaic, although never entirely so. The production of such texts, therefore, is not wholly free but rather is based on fairly prescribed scripts and frames, which may differ across cultures. Moreover, text types can be more or less prescriptive. Patents and contracts, for example, are two very prescriptive text types, while museum guides are less so.

From Word to Text

The classroom and at-home activities related to the translation of these text types are designed to spiral upward, that is, to encourage students to move from a consideration of translation choices at the level of word and phrase to the level of the text as a whole and even beyond the text to the overall cultural context of the text's reception. The activities are divided into three categories: pre-translation (comparative textual analysis), translation (presenting and defending translation decisions), and posttranslation (reflection and revision). The pre-translation analysis begins with a determination of the purpose or purposes of the source text, based on Katharina Reiss's three text types: informative, expressive, and operative, with the understanding that few texts belong exclusively to one of these categories but are often hybrid (Reiss 1981). A recipe is a good example of a hybrid text type in that, while its primary function is—if it appears in a cookbook, for example— informative, instructing the reader on how to make a certain dish, many recipes also include expressive elements meant to sell a lifestyle to the reader, as well as operative elements insofar as the ultimate goal of the recipe is to encourage the reader to actually make the dish.

Once the text type of the source text has been determined, students are then asked to collect a variety of parallel texts, that is, texts belonging to the same text variety—the recipe—but written originally in English for an English-speaking audience. Students are also instructed to make sure that the parallel texts they have chosen are not themselves translations. They are asked to defend their selection of parallel texts by relying on the reputation and authority of the venues in which they appeared. At this point, the students are placed in small groups and asked to do a comparative analysis of the source text and their parallel texts based on the categories given by Derek Offord (1996). Moving from the level of the word to the level of the sentence, Offord analyzes the various registers of modern standard Russian according to vocabulary (presence of technical terms, professional jargon, slang, etc.), phraseology (set phrases and collocations), grammatical forms, and syntax (use of active or passive voice, inversion, complex sentences). Reading through Offord's analysis of sample texts in modern standard Russian is a very helpful preparation for the students' comparative analysis of the source and parallel texts.

The students then share their findings with the rest of the class. In their analysis of the vocabulary in the source and parallel texts, students typically note that

English has a wide variety of verbs to describe specific forms of cutting, such as chopping, dicing, mincing, while Russian tends to use a general verb "to cut" accompanied by prefixes and adverbs to indicate how the cutting should be done. In their analysis of grammatical forms in Russian recipes, students typically note the Russian preference for infinitive rather than imperative forms when giving commands in this text type. When focusing on syntax, students remark that Russian sentences are often very long, consisting of multiple subordinate clauses, whereas the sentences in English recipes tend to be short and simple, typically containing a single command or instruction. Already this discussion of subsentential features of the source and target texts has complicated any simple notion of equivalence in the student's mind. At this point, we break to discuss the theoretical reading that I pair with this translation exercise. This reading is designed to turn the students' attention to considerations of the text as a whole.

From Text to Beyond

The text is Shoshana Blum-Kulka's "Shifts of Cohesion and Coherence in Translation" (1986), which I have found to be very useful in broadening the novice translator's perspective from an exclusive focus on isolated words and phrases to include textual features, that is, features that are dispersed across sentences and paragraph boundaries, throughout a text, and even beyond the boundaries of the text proper. In order to understand the implications of Blum-Kulka's findings and to devise strategies to deal with the difference in norms, I have students read the sixth and seventh chapters in Mona Baker's *In Other Words* (1992) for a clear discussion of the concepts of cohesion and coherence. Students should be able to distinguish between coherence, as the ideational structure of a text, and cohesion, as the reflection of that structure on the surface of the text. In the chapter on cohesion, Baker offers a comparative overview of the varieties of cohesive devices across languages, including referencing, substitution, ellipsis, and lexical cohesion. Now students are prepared to read Blum-Kulka's article and to evaluate the argument she makes, namely that shifts in cohesion and coherence occur almost inevitably in translated texts due to the "different norms governing the use of cohesive devices in the source and target languages" (Blum-Kulka 1986: 300).

After considering the many ways that cohesion is achieved in texts and discussing Blum-Kulka's findings, the students conduct a comparative analysis of the cohesive patterns and coherence structures of the source and parallel texts. When asked to compare the cohesive devices in these texts, students often focus on pronominal referencing, which is typically used more frequently in Russian texts. We then address why this should be so, considering the fact that in a language with grammatical gender, like Russian—Russian has a masculine, feminine, and neuter gender—it is easier to trace the referent of a pronoun, whereas in English careless use of "it" and "they" can easily lead to ambiguity. It is also the case that Russian stylistics discourages the frequent repetition of words, as a rule, whereas English texts tend to tolerate a greater degree of repetition, especially in texts where clarity is an important consideration.

Discussion of the difference in coherence between the source and target texts often leads students to see a difference between the strictly chronological order of the instructions in English recipes—one can follow the recipe step by step, without having read it through to the end first—and the Russian recipes, which are not strictly chronological. This is perhaps most evident in the fact that English recipes that involve baking will almost invariably begin with "Preheat oven to X," whereas no such information appears anywhere in Russian recipes. A truly functional English translation of a Russian recipe, then, might reorder the directions to meet the expectations of the users of the translated recipe. At this point, the students begin to understand how they might justify making changes above the sentence level, in this case, reordering the information as presented in the source text and, perhaps, using different cohesive devices in order to align the translated texts with target text norms.

In order to explain why shifts in coherence and cohesion might be inevitable in translated texts, Blum-Kulka introduces the concepts of *implicitation* and *explicitation*. They move the attention of novice translators beyond the level of the text itself to the relationship between the text and its readers. The concepts are relatively simple, but they carry significant implications for translators. Discussion should lead students to an understanding that the level of explicit information in a text is directly related to the amount of shared knowledge between the author and the readers of that text. The greater the shared knowledge, the more the author can rely on implicitation, or implied meanings, confidant that the intended readers will understand because they are capable of filling in the blanks. When there is less shared knowledge between the author and the audience, then the author must explicitate, that is, spell things out, so that the intended readers will understand. A discussion of implicitation now leads the student to look beyond the text itself and to consider their decision making in relation to the needs of the intended readers of the translation. We then contemplate how a consideration of our audience's background knowledge might affect our translation decisions: How might we translate a text differently for an audience of experts as opposed to an audience of lay people? How might we translate a text differently for an audience of children as opposed to an audience of adults? In fact, it is often productive to have the students complete two or more translations of a single source text, each one designed for a specific audience.

An effective way to connect Blum-Kulka's theoretical account with the assignment is to begin the discussion with culture-specific items insofar as they may require various forms of explicitation. For example, I often assign a recipe for an Easter cake, which in Russian is called *paskha*, the Russian word for Easter (and Passover). Discussion of possible translations of the word immediately complicates any simple act of transcoding. The literal translation, "easter," would be ridiculous. The students typically propose various forms of explicitation, such as "Easter cake" or "Paskha cake." One of the main ingredients in the recipe is a culture-specific item, *tvorog*, which in English is close to what is referred to as farmer's cheese, but *tvorog* plays a far more prominent role in Russian cuisine than does its English counterpart in United States cooking, so farmer's cheese might be hard to find in a store in the United States. The term often elicits a rather lively discussion of possible translations. Some Russian cookbooks written originally in English for an English-language audience provide directions for how to make *tvorog* from cottage cheese. Classroom discussion also invariably turns to the question of whether or not to translate measurements from the metric system into the English system and how this might be done so as not to end up with bizarre quantities, i.e., 2.1 ounces.

When comparing the source text to the parallel texts in terms of implicitation, students typically find that the English recipes contain far more detailed and specific instructions, explaining every step in the process and leaving few choices. Russian recipes, in contrast, contain more implicitation and offer less precise directions, such as "Bake at 325–350 degrees." Such a temperature range does not typically appear in English recipes, which emphasize precision. Russian recipes tend to assume the reader can do simple preparatory procedures, such as hard-boiling eggs, whereas those procedures may be spelled out in an English-language recipe—or the reader may be referred to those instructions elsewhere in the cookbook.

Students are encouraged to analyze these differences in terms of implicitation and explicitation, and they typically arrive at the conclusion that Russian users of recipes have a greater degree of background knowledge than their counterparts in the United States, so they do not require such detailed instructions. A discussion of cooking in the two cultures can lead to interesting insights into many aspects of daily life. For example, the fact that during the Soviet period Russians did not have access to fast food and frozen foods to the same extent as Americans and that Russians lived with their parents until they married, typically in small apartments, meant that a culture of cooking was handed down from generation to generation in a more or less unbroken fashion. This was not true of the United States after the Second World War, and so one cannot assume that American readers of recipes have the basic culinary knowledge possessed by the average Russian. In this way, students are led to see these texts as shaped by their cultural context. Individual students or groups of students can be assigned to give a presentation on the culture of cooking in Russia to instigate awareness of these cultural differences. It is important for these discussions to take place before the students begin the actual translation, so that when they translate they are already sensitized to how deeply cultural beliefs and practices shape the source text and consequently how they might play a role in shaping the target text.

This spiraling up to a discussion of the cultural context of the source text is also quite productive in relation to the assignment involving a museum guide. The text I use is an excerpt from a guide for a World War II museum in the city of Tver'. A discussion of the Russian name for this war—the Great Fatherland War—can in itself lead to some important insights into Russian history as well as to the place of the historical event in the Russian cultural imagination today (few Russian texts refer to it as World War II; the name references Russia's 1814 war with Napoleon, known as the Fatherland War). The importance of the war to Russians is evident throughout the text in the repeated use of "us" and "we" and "our country."

Yet none of the text types makes the cultural environment more decisive than the last one we discuss, advertisements, where the dominant functional mode shifts from informational to persuasive. A rather extensive literature now exists on the translation of advertising texts, which are often radically adapted to meet the persuasive function of the genre. Geneviève Quillard's 2006 study of North American advertisements translated for a French Canadian readership, for example, provides striking examples of how different cultural dispositions shape advertisements in English and French and how a sensitivity to such differences might influence a translator's decision making at various levels. The selection of texts for translation is therefore crucial in ensuring an illuminating discussion of the cultural context of reception.

Workshopping and Reflecting

Following an in-class analysis of the source text in comparison to English parallel texts, the students workshop their translations under the guidance of their instructor. Students are expected not only to provide possible solutions but also to defend those solutions to the class, based on research and on their overall approach to the translation (consistency). In the workshopping sessions, students are encouraged to rely on their parallel texts to defend translation shifts at the level of text, such as inserting "Preheat oven" at the beginning of the recipe or including directions on how to make *tvorog* from cottage cheese. Even with the parallel texts, the students are reluctant to make such changes, a reflection of the unconscious literalness of novice translators. Empowering novice translators to make such shifts, supported by research and authoritative parallel texts, is an ongoing struggle throughout this introductory course but one that is essential to producing experts out of transcoders.

Reflection is also an important part of the learning process. Students are asked to keep a log in which they document specific challenges they encountered and defend their decisions as well as their decision-making process. The keeping of the log, along with teacher feedback on the log, is a crucial component in developing the students' sense of responsibility for their translation choices. Over the course of the semester, the logs reflect the students' growing awareness that they have a responsibility to defend their decisions with something more than "That's what I found in the dictionary." The ability to defend their decision-making process effectively, by referring to parallel texts and other reliable sources, enhances the workshopping sessions. This skill is also important in the professional world, where many clients continue to entertain the notion of translation as transcoding. Because feedback is such an important part of training experts, I provide regular and extensive feedback on translations and logs and give the students an opportunity to turn in a revised translation.

The translations themselves are assessed using a holistic rubric that includes four categories: content; register, vocabulary, terminology; translation brief and orientation to target text type; and written expression (Robinson, Rodríguez, and Sánchez 2008). The categories spiral up from consideration of more or less discrete points in the translation to more global concerns at the textual level. Moreover, either the instructor assigns or the students choose a specific publication venue for the translation and therefore a more or less defined audience, providing the necessary parameters for assessing the students' decision-making. Thus the category of content addresses not only whether any relevant content was omitted in the translation process but also whether the content aligns with the background knowledge of the assumed readers of the target text. Has the student translator adequately adjusted the target text, I ask, to meet the target readers' capacity for grasping implicitation? The second category groups register, vocabulary, and terminology together in order to frame questions of word choice not in terms of semantics proper but in terms of appropriateness, which is based, again, on the needs of the target audience (experts or laypeople, children or adults, and so on). The third category assesses whether the student's translation has been effectively resituated in the target culture, that is, adjusted at the level of discourse organization to align with norms of the target text type, again taking into account audience, venue, and any specific client demands stipulated in the brief. The final category addresses the stylistic peculiarities of persuasive, informative, and operational writing across cultures: Has the student employed the stylistic resources of the target language to support the purpose(s) of the translation?

In a sense, ontogeny recapitulates phylogeny in the introductory translation classroom insofar as the evolution of every student's thinking about translation reproduces, to some degree, the evolution of thinking in translation studies from the post-World War II period onward. On the one hand, the field witnessed "the shrinking role of linguistics as [its] intellectual basis" (Neubert and Shreve 1992: 9), where "linguistics" is understood as the study of abstract language systems; on the other hand, interest grew in texts and in the social and cultural contexts in which texts function. Hence I judge this course a success if my students come to understand that translation, as Jeremy Munday states, "is a practice-based activity that centers on texts" (2014: 69), although with the important caveat that we can no more comprehend words outside the context of the text than we can comprehend texts outside the cultural environment in which they circulate.

8   A Collaborative Pedagogy for Translation

Maria González-Davies

This chapter describes an undergraduate course in translation where the source languages are Catalan and Spanish and the translating language is English. The language combination is not central, however, as the knowledge, skills, and tasks presented here can be transferred to different institutional sites in different linguistic communities. In accordance with the three levels of instructional organization suggested by Richards and Rodgers (adapted from Richards and Rodgers 2001: chap. 2), I will first present the theoretical framework that underlies the nature of learning and translation in the course (approach), followed by a description of classroom dynamics based on a syllabus (design), and, finally, some examples of activities, tasks, and projects carried out by the students (procedures).

The Approach: Collaborating in a Community of Practice

The pedagogy that drives the course is based on social constructivist assumptions (Kiraly 2000; Vygotsky 1978; 1981). Learning is viewed mainly as a social act that helps to construct knowledge and takes the form of a collaborative exploration of the translation process and product. The classroom becomes a working environment in which students, guided by the teacher, work together, forming a community of practice that shares responsibility for the learning process and its outcome. Collaborative learning abandons the teacher-centered approach whereby the teacher transmits knowledge, the student memorizes and regurgitates it, and interaction—when allowed to occur—is limited to discussions among relatively few students and the teacher. Instead, collaboration underlines three pedagogical principles (adapted from Van Lier 1996): learner *autonomy*, that is, the centrality of the learner's role in decision-making to produce a valid product, in our case, an effective translation; *awareness*, achieved through reflection and interaction while accessing appropriate resources and materials; and *authenticity*, achieved through first-hand situated experiences that include simulations as well as translation projects such as might actually be commissioned.

The primary objective of fostering collaboration is to reconcile theory and practice through the interaction of individual and group work that favors the acquisition of translation skills. Teamwork helps students resolve both translational and social issues, supporting those who feel more confident if allowed to voice their opinion in small groups. Collaborative experiences also seek to reproduce professional contexts that include specific assistance or "scaffolding" to reduce the gap between what students actually know and the goals to be attained, what Vygotsky calls the "zone of proximal development" (1978: 86). Yet the emphasis on collaboration does not shift the responsibility for learning solely or mostly onto the students' shoulders. Rather, learning opportunities are triggered and then guided explicitly by the teacher, who must be flexible enough to heed the students' suggestions and needs while maintaining a focus on the aims of the procedures.

Translation is understood here as "a dynamic process of communication" (Hatim and Mason 1990: 223) that strives to convey the source message and to create the desired effect on a target audience. This definition is combined with Nord's functionalist notion of translation, which stresses compliance with the aim assigned to the project by its initiator, thus providing a clear reference to guide decision-making (Nord 1997: 20). As a result, students learn to move away from a literalist approach to translation towards an approach that encourages creative, motivated choices informed by a specific translation assignment.

Collaborative learning typically involves the production of authentic translations where external agents or clients assess and accept a translation as publishable. This process can also be simulated through role-playing among students and teachers. Students can thus feel supported by the teacher while experiencing the risk of making decisions and justifying their work with a real or simulated client. Collaborating while translating implies that planned learning input, or translation models to be followed, shares ground with unplanned learning opportunities that spring from the students' actual contributions and needs while they are translating.

In this course, reflection is encouraged with discussions and practical work grounded on readings from four texts recommended at suitable key stages: Baker's *In Other Words* (1992), González-Davies and Scott-Tennent's "A Problem-Solving and Student-Centred Approach" (2005), Haywood, Thompson, and Hervey's *Thinking Spanish Translation* (2009), and Kiraly's "Project-based Learning" (2005).

The Design: Building a Syllabus

The main components of the syllabus include relevant translation competences, specific aims or expected outcomes, procedures assigned to the students (activities, tasks, and projects), and bibliography. The syllabus also incorporates a grading scale that takes into account the learning process and the product.

Kelly defines translation competence as "A combination of skills, knowledge, aptitude and attitudes [. . .] including disposition to learn as well as know-how" (2005: 157). Her proposal comprises areas of competence that are listed in our syllabus: communicative and textual, cultural and intercultural, subject-specific, professional and functional, attitudinal or psycho-physiological, interpersonal, and strategic (2005: 32). These competences are assessable in that they relate directly to the learning outcomes at the end of the course. We expect the students to be able to translate narrative, descriptive, and persuasive texts; to edit translated texts and to justify their modifications; to spot translation problems, to solve them appropriately by applying translation strategies or techniques, and thereby to show their capacity for decision-making; to produce translations that conform to specific assignments, adapting to the initiator's specifications; to be familiar with basic translation tools and to be capable of dealing with new technological challenges; to be able to understand and communicate information, ideas, problems, and solutions to both specialists and nonspecialists; to show a professional sense of responsibility, a concern for quality, and a respect for the ethical codes of the profession; and, finally, to work effectively, individually and in teams, and to be able to reach agreements through negotiation.

At the first class meeting, the students receive a copy of the complete syllabus as well as the guidelines to carry out the procedures. Before reading the syllabus together, they are asked to form groups to discuss and note down their expectations regarding the subject. These expectations, which may vary according to each group of students, are then examined against the syllabus to ensure that the perspectives of the teacher and institution and that of the students converge as much as possible. Next the guidelines for the procedures are read. These guidelines explain that students will carry out activities to help them with specific linguistic, stylistic, or translation-related questions, along with tasks and an authentic group project. Every two or three weeks they will also submit an individual translation of a text related to the topic under study. Finally, they are given the grading scale, where, in our case, 10 is the top mark and 5 is passing. The scale includes the marking criteria. The highest grade, for example, indicates that the translation transmits the source message using appropriate solutions, conforms to target-language conventions, keeps to the assignment, and would be accepted for publication with few or no changes. The students then translate and peer-evaluate a brief text (100–150 words) to become familiar with the scale and the challenges of marking a translation.

This approach implies that the classroom becomes a discussion forum and hands-on workshop where the teacher alternates her role as guide and expert with that of project coordinator. She must be open to treating spontaneous contributions as learning opportunities rather than time-wasting deviations from a predetermined syllabus that stresses idealized and enforced exercises. Students are expected to become active participants in their community of practice, sharing their knowledge and know-how explicitly and collaboratively.

The Procedures: From Soloing to Jamming and Back Again

The translation-oriented procedures that will make our approach and design visible are *activities* or brief, concrete exercises that help students practice specific points, *tasks* or chains of activities with the same global aim, and *projects* or multicompetence assignments that enable students to engage in pedagogical and professional activities and tasks while working together on an authentic end product. Materials to develop these procedures are incorporated in an open-ended dossier that can be adapted to the needs of the group as the course develops.

The dossier is organized around topics such as tourism, food and drink, or films and literature, and it contains a variety of text types for the students to translate, including instructions, recipes, tourist leaflets, and film soundtracks. Some texts in the dossier also deal with subjects that support discussions related to translation, such as critical articles, new translation releases, and the translation market.

More tightly structured than a project and more controlled by the teacher, a task usually takes several class sessions to complete. Because tourism is an important industry worldwide, this topic can serve as a convenient illustration. Students are given a week to locate and take photographs of touristic texts that contain mistranslations. At the first class meeting devoted to the task, we discuss the translation of consumer-oriented texts from Haywood, Thompson, and Hervey's textbook (2009: chap. 14). Particular emphasis is placed on the different text types used in tourism, the effect that the texts might produce on the target reader, and the need to know about the accepted linguistic and pragmatic conventions of each community. The students then work in small groups, pooling their mistranslations and selecting three per group. The selected mistranslations are distributed among the students, who form new three-member groups to perform a number of activities with their assigned mistranslations: they are asked to spot the problems, to name them, to suggest appropriate translation strategies to solve the mistranslations, and to justify their final choices.

At this stage, the students usually need help to become familiar with the concept of translation strategy, defined here as an informed decision to solve translation problems using specific translation options. The discussions of strategies included in Haywood, Thompson, and Hervey (2009: chaps. 2 and 5) increase the students' awareness of the possibilities available to them. They learn about "cultural transplantation," for example, "in which culture-specific elements in the [source text] are replaced in the [target text] by elements that are specific to the [target language] culture" (1995: 80). Baker's book, which approaches translation problems through systemic-functional linguistics and pragmatics, is also extremely useful, especially the sections that deal with appropriate strategies to solve "non-equivalence" at and above word level (2011: 20–43, 46–77) as well as to cope with textual cohesion and coherence (2011: 119–215). To these strategies can be added the teacher's and students' proposals.

An effective way to help students organize their work is to use a written protocol (as described in González-Davies and Scott-Tennent 2005: 23), essentially a grid with four columns. Students are asked to insert a mistranslation in the first column (e.g. "Liquidation by Close," photographed in a shop window near Barcelona). In a second column, they suggest the possible source text (e.g. "Liquidación por cierre"), describe the problem (calque, or a literal translation that resembles the language in the source text, word for word), and pinpoint a plausible target audience for their translation (potential shoppers). In a third column, they note down a strategy to solve the problem (idiomatic translation), and then, in a fourth column, they offer a translation that uses an appropriate solution ("Clearance Sale").

Once the students become familiar with this technique, they also hand in a written protocol with their individual assignments. These protocols contribute to an explicit reflection on problem spotting and solving that triggers in-class discussions and much debate at individual tutorials. They clearly help students to evolve in their critical thinking about their translation choices and their self-image as translators. Relevant sources, creative solutions, and informed decisions are shared in the groups and then in the class as a whole so that students learn to voice and to justify their options with increasing confidence as the course progresses.

Activities that involve simulations can be useful in helping students to expand the repertoire of strategies by which they translate cultural references. In a simulation set in a tourist information office, they tackle oral translation and peer-edit their written and oral translations. They work in pairs in which each student has half of a Catalan conversation on a sheet of paper and a bilingual glossary that corresponds to the other student's text. They each translate their own text into English and then together correct both translations, using the glossaries and other sources such as online dictionaries. Next they prepare three scenarios, loosely based on the translated conversation, in which a tourist arrives in town and asks for directions to a hotel. They take turns playing three different roles: a tourist who can speak only the foreign language (in this case, English), a local resident who speaks only the language of the locale (Catalan), and an interpreter who speaks both languages. They note down any problems without interrupting the role-play and then discuss their problems and solutions together and with the rest of the class, drawing from their growing list of strategies.

Strategies to translate cultural references are introduced through Haywood, Thompson, and Hervey (2009: chap. 5), to which others are added as they arise. The authors suggest the following range of strategies depending on whether the translator leaves the source-text elements in their original form or replaces them with elements from the target-language culture: exoticism, cultural borrowing, calque, communicative translation, deletion, and cultural transplantation. The teacher first introduces examples of cultural references that the students analyze in context. The students then gather examples of their own to share with the class. In small groups they practice applying different strategies to the same text and finally compare them with the published translation, which is not necessarily always a more suitable rendering than theirs.

For instance, a sentence in the simulated encounter in the tourist information office reads: "Després continueu tot dret fins arribar al Circ Romà." This sentence can be translated as "Then continue straight ahead until you reach the Roman Circus," in which case the translator is relying on a communicative translation of "Circ Romà," i.e., a translation in line with the customary way of conveying the message in the target language. Or the reference can be left as "Circ Romà," in which case the translator is resorting to exoticism, i.e., a translation that retains the source-language reference. Each choice may be justifiable since the first makes it easy for the tourist to understand the expression, whereas the second makes it easy for the person to follow the road signs to the site.

Other examples can be found in leaflets at museums or art exhibitions where the choice of strategies is not always consistent and different choices can raise social and political issues. In a leaflet for an exhibition on the Majorcan painter

Miquel Barceló, the Catalan reference to the "capella de Sant Pere" was translated into Spanish as "capilla de San Pedro" (communicative translation) but into English as "chapel of San Pedro" (exoticism). The English version, however, insofar as it uses the Spanish form of "Sant Pere," favors the majority language in Spain, Spanish or Castilian, since the original name of the chapel is in Catalan, not Spanish.

Students can increase their inventiveness with activities that require them to develop translation strategies for more rhetorically complicated texts. For instance, they are given a real-life advertisement for a department store where each letter of the alphabet corresponds to a department or service. The students form groups in which the letters are shared out among the members, and each group translates the ad, aiming to preserve the layout, message, and rhetorical effect, which is primarily persuasive but may have such other dimensions as humor. Almost as soon as they start, they usually find that they cannot maintain the correspondence between the letters and department names in the target language, and so they have to devise creative solutions. "Boutiques Internacionales" ("International Boutiques"), for example, is translated as "Bookshop" to keep the initial "B." The groups then present their translations, noting whether there is any overlapping due to similar solutions. Finally, they compare their work with the published translation and discuss similarities and differences. This activity triggers intense discussions around several conceptual categories: the unit of translation (the word or phrase had to be abandoned, and the whole text adopted, as the unit), degrees of fidelity (adhering closely to the source or to the target language, moving on a scale from literal to free translation), and translation as re-creation or the creation of a text that is relatively autonomous from the source text. The activity winds up provoking a visible change in the students' views on translation.

Once a task chain has been completed, each student hands in an individual translation of a text related to the topic (250–300 words). The assigned text poses challenges that cover specific points studied when the task was performed. The students receive the text at the outset of the task so that they can work on it and improve it gradually as the task develops. They also hand in a written protocol that records the main problems they encountered in the text and their reasoned solutions. The problems are not determined beforehand by the teacher as they may be different for each student.

Project Work: Some Guidelines and Examples

As part of the course, the students carry out an authentic translation project that usually takes up about 30 percent of the class meetings. The development of a project ideally involves an external agent or client who decides whether the end product is publishable. A real-life context is replicated as closely as possible, with students adopting different roles: editor, coordinator, terminologist, and so on. The class is divided into small groups, each with a coordinator who liaises with other group coordinators and the teacher to make sure that the work in progress is developing adequately. During class meetings, the teacher circulates among the students, offering suggestions and moderating the discussions.

A virtual class site is set up so that the class and teacher gain easy access to the work in progress. Shared folders are used to pool sources, to display the agreed distribution of pages to be translated for all to consult, and to set up a specific glossary which expands as the work advances. In the first session dedicated to the project, the students all read the text to be translated and identify potential problems. At this stage, they also share out the work among the members of the team, distribute roles, and set dates for online meetings and deadlines to hand in their translations. The client's deadline is recorded as immovable. In the second session, we discuss project work and provide a rationale for the procedure by reflecting on how authentic practice accompanied by scaffolded teacher and peer support can foster expertise and reinforce their self-reliance as translators (Kiraly 2005). In my experience, the students themselves ask for extra tutorials outside the allocated class sessions once the project gets under way. These meetings mainly revolve around discussions regarding the glossary for the project (e.g. agreeing on the inclusion of specific terms) or web searches and technological problems (e.g. translation software).

The sequencing of contact hours within the classroom corresponds with the stages of planning, doing, and revising the work (Kolb 1984: 21–2). The students keep to the deadlines as closely as possible. Each group's final draft translations are published on the virtual platform for all the groups to read, whereupon they send comments to the coordinators and teacher. Authentic text-editing guidelines by a well-known publisher are used for editing, thus underlining the professional standpoint of this approach. The teacher meets with the coordinators to discuss the translations of all the texts, and each group revises the translations according to the comments, using previously discussed readings from the textbooks to solve translation problems. Finally, they hand in the translation on the assigned deadline to be evaluated by both the client and the teacher.

The projects that have been carried out in my classes have been both wide-ranging and ambitious. NGOs have occasionally provided material for translation, such as a perpetual calendar crafted by a group of children in Guatemala in order to raise funds to build a school. Students have translated entire books which would not have otherwise been translated, sometimes in tandem with another group of students at the same or another educational institution. One class translated Catalan children's books for a European Picture Book Collection, a project of the National Center for Research in Children's Literature at the University of Roehampton. Another class translated the university website in collaboration with the computer skills teacher, the webmaster, and his team. Students receive some kind of tangible acknowledgement for their work, either a certificate or the inclusion of their names in the ensuing publication.

Some Conclusions

The open-ended and collaborative nature of activities, tasks, and projects results in the advancement of the students' aptitudes and attitudes as translators, enabling them to take a step from novices toward experts. The students always complete a questionnaire that records their comments on the instructional framework, and the teacher keeps a class diary to note critical incidents and to compare results. The students quite consistently reveal that they develop their professional know-how by learning to network, that they make increased and informed use of parallel texts, web sources, dictionaries, and other material, and that they apply creative and critical thinking to solve real problems. They also see the point of reading about translation and translation skills as they realize that they need to know as much as possible to justify their decisions to potential clients and to each other. Significantly, the exchange of focused information with each other and the teacher, as well as the interaction with a client, are highly appreciated. Peer correction is regarded as especially useful for improving their translation skills. Needless to say, unexpected linguistic, cultural, and translational challenges surface as their work progresses, triggering discussions and further developing their negotiating skills.

The global results of the questionnaires show that the students perceive activities, tasks, and project work as stimulating learning tools that connect their learning experiences, thus helping them improve their translation skills. The teacher's diary entries reflect how the interpretations of the text are much more to the point and professional. The students usually acknowledge that they "really learnt" during the first four weeks, before delivering the first partial translation. According to them, they had to learn many new things, from managing a virtual environment collaboratively to evaluating and being evaluated.

It is possible to create an instructional framework where the students improve their skills and knowledge with the support of a community of practice consisting of peers, the teacher, and a client. Within this framework, unplanned learning opportunities optimize a planned syllabus by adjusting its goals to the real needs of the students. Students learn to manage uncertainty and to make informed decisions, thus furthering their own translator competence through collaborative social practices.

9   Teaching the Translation of Poetry

Reginald Gibbons

What might the desired outcome be for an undergraduate course on the translation of poetry? Students may enter the course thinking of translation as a process of understanding the poem word by word, interpreting it accordingly, and reconstituting it in translation by semantic correspondence and by analogical replacement of source-language idioms by target-language ones. During our studies and translation practice, however, they will considerably refine and complicate such a view.

My goals are simple, but achieving them is a process of generating interactive, interrelated, simultaneous trains of study. The first goal is to bring the students to a much higher competence in reading poetry and in recognizing qualities of language beyond the semantic, especially those meaning-making elements that poetry exploits. These elements, to which poets are so intensely attentive, include not only the expected poetic devices (the use of sound and rhythm, registers of diction, etymological resonances, plays on word morphology, figures of speech and structure), but also grammatical and syntactic effects and the relationship between the very nature and texture of a language—how a given language characteristically thinks—and the specifically poetic thinking that has been done in the source language and in the individual poem that we translate from it. By "poetic thinking" I mean how and why a poem moves the way it does from one image or stage of thought and feeling to the next, and the next—how a poem enacts a poetic mode of thought rather than a discursive one.

My second goal is for students to experience how the practice of literary translation enhances our grasp of several kinds of difference: between languages, between literary traditions, and between the functions and uses of poetry in distinct cultures and historical moments. To achieve such goals I set students the dual tasks of translating a few short poems that I select and reading essays in translation theory and practice. At the end of our ten-week academic quarter they produce significantly revised translations of the set poems and an eight-to-twelve-page paper that reflects on translation issues.

The course is a combination of seminar and workshop in which we all discuss both the students' draft translations and the readings; I sequence the three or four specimen poems in such a way as to highlight contrasts between the problems each translation will try to solve. Everyone translates the same three or four poems. Every few weeks we begin a new one, analyzing it and then workshopping the students' draft translations. Meanwhile and in between the poems, our readings include both theorizations of translation and practical accounts by literary translators. I assign readings from three collections of such essays: Rainer Schulte and John Biguenet's *The Craft of Translation* and *Theories of Translation* and Lawrence Venuti's *The Translation Studies Reader*. On a course website, I also provide students with copies of a few additional essays that address various problems relating to the translation of poetry. Examples include pieces by translators like Dick Davis (2002) and Haroldo de Campos (2007), commenting on translation history or their practice, and by theorists like Robert Eaglestone (2005) on translation ethics and Jan Mukarovský (1964) on poetic language.

During the first six weeks of the quarter, I require students to post weekly responses to any two of the essays assigned for the week, summarizing arguments, comparing similarities or pointing out contrasts, and adding questions of their own. In class discussions of the readings, we compare conceptual tools that are relevant to translation practice as well as translation practices that imply or use theoretical stances. Thus, by the end of the quarter, especially if students have read each other's posts, they should have discovered which of the readings most interest them. The last few meetings of the course are devoted to oral presentations on the students' papers, with critique and suggestions from the group as a whole. My hope is always that the practical experience of translating a few poems will inflect the students' reading of the theoretical and practical essays and vice versa.

To focus the end-of-term paper, students may choose among three possibilities. I require that no matter which of these three the student chooses, he or she will need an argument and must cite at least three of the assigned readings. I give students three choices of focus for the papers:

1   To address a theoretical issue, problem, or method (linguistic, critical, cultural, political, ethical, historical) and argue for or against the adequacy of particular positions in the essays they cite.
2   To critique both theoretically and practically an existing published translation of a short poem, considering the specifics of the translator's decisions and arguing for or against them (as exemplified by Margaret Sayers Peden's 1989 essay on translating Sor Juana Inés de la Cruz). Such an argument will be based not only on how the translator lives up to what Hans Vermeer calls the "commission" (1989: 191–202) but also on how the translation relates to the theoretical arguments that the student has found to be most useful or persuasive in evaluating a published translation. I also stipulate that by an "existing published translation" I mean a literary translation, rather than a "translation" into a different medium, such as film or dance. (I have made a few exceptions for projects that include a musical setting of a source poem as an additional "translation" to be compared, for what it implies about how the poem may be interpreted with literary translations.)

3   To write about the practice of translation, discussing some of the prob-
     lems and issues raised in the student's own translation of one short poem
     (or excerpt from a longer poem) of the student's own choice (not one of
     the poems that we have translated together). Such problems and issues will
     engage both the source and target languages and cultures. Thus the student
     must discuss the source text, reasons for choosing it, and decisions (and rea-
     sons for them) in translating it. Such a paper might be somewhat like an essay
     in Schulte and Biguenet's *The Craft of Translation*. And in addition to the
     languages of our source poems, students will often bring another language
     into their papers. One paper of a few years ago addressed the problems raised
     by translating source texts in slang—in this case, the ingenious French argot
     called "verlan."

Our theoretical readings broaden our understanding of linguistic, aesthetic,
philosophical, cultural, and ethical issues involved in translating; the practical
essays give us some models of how to do translation and how to talk about the
process and problems of literary translating. I group the readings in four categories: **language**; **methods**; **poetics**; and **culture and ethics**. (Any one essay might
make points in more than one category.) We read through the categories in this
order. The practical essays raise some of the same issues but mostly do so only
in passing.

More than in merely reading a poem carefully, the process of translating a poem
and studying approaches to translation itself makes aspects of literary cultures—
source and target—more apparent. Difference produces contrast, and contrast
produces more clarity. These issues would include broader cultural and historical
realities, ideas about the social functions or uses of poetry, differences in whole
traditions or schools of poetic practice and poetic thinking, and also questions
about the ethics of translation, whether of a single poem or of a whole body or
tradition of poems.

The contrast in linguistic qualities and characteristics and in poetic practices
and possibilities when one looks at two languages and two literary histories is
always interesting, and in the midst of translating, this contrast always raises
more questions than anyone can answer. Translating from one literary history into
another can make more legible the ways in which the semantics, poetics, structure
and movement of a poem in one language may be built not only upon cultural and
historical realities but also upon the aggregate of artistic choices over time that
have come to define distinct differences between one poetic tradition and another.
Such traditions may have a lot to do with the distinct qualities of usage and life-
world. But the tradition may also have been narrowed or intensified by those
historically accumulated choices in poetic practice over time that are influenced
by cultural change more than by inherent aspects of language. To illustrate this
engaging issue, I ask students to read the characterization of such differences by
Yves Bonnefoy, the French poet and translator, in his description of the difficulties
of translating English, specifically Shakespeare, into French (Bonnefoy 2004).

In the introduction to the book in which this essay appears, John Naughton quotes Bonnefoy on such contrast:

> Readers familiar with his work know that for Bonnefoy translating from English to French has meant "the 'testing' of one way of thinking by another," since for Bonnefoy an "opposing metaphysics" governs the French and English languages. [. . .] And so French *excludes* rather than describes, is fascinated by the idea or the essence of things rather than with things themselves. French poetry is thus inherently Platonic, while Shakespeare's reflects "a sort of passionate Aristotelianism."
>
> (Bonnefoy 2004: x)

In this undergraduate course these are issues, problems, and questions that I want to raise for their own sake, not because we can find answers, solutions, or theoretical clarity. I want to excite students about a form of slow reading that will make all their subsequent literary study (or other studies) more competent and more rewarding. I don't call it "close reading" because in the context of literary studies over the last thirty years that phrase has come to imply that reading poetry (and of course reading prose) is about semantic values—defining, decoding, historically situating, and even psychoanalyzing them. Confirming possibilities of meaning in dictionaries and getting a sense of them in their historical and cultural context, parsing the sentences or fragments, and tracking down referents and allusions can in fact displace our sense of how poetic meaning is proliferated by extra-semantic aspects of language. That is, it's easy to spot extra-semantic aspects in some poetry of all eras—not only in avant-garde poetry, from the mid-nineteenth century to our own day. Extra-semantic aspects are integral to poetics and so must be addressed when translating. I should put this the other way around: the meaning-making of a poem is often only secondarily semantic. An awareness of this is what I try to increase in students by means of the translation of poetry.

In fact, it's my own memory of first becoming aware in this way that led me to invent the course, which exceeds the usual disciplinary boundaries. It is jointly offered by two academic units—the English Department and the Program in Comparative Literary Studies. I began teaching it some time ago because I remembered the great pleasure that I myself, as a graduate student at Stanford, enjoyed in a seminar on poetry translation led by Donald Davie. I was then at work on a PhD in comparative literature, translating a book-length selection of poems by the Spanish poet Luis Cernuda, and writing a lengthy essay on his work and life. Davie, whose Spanish may have been only his French plus a Spanish-English dictionary, was nevertheless not at all easy to impress, for he regarded any translation as inadequate if it was dull. Subsequently, completing my volume of Cernuda and translating another of Jorge Guillén early in my writing life, I learned much more about poetic thinking from the problems of translation than what I had learned only by reading poems. This is what kept me at it, translating many individual poems by a number of Romance language poets, then working from ancient Greek, initially with a great scholar as my co-translator, then most recently from Russian, with a co-translator whose own poetry in Russian is tremendously skilled and rich in sound, word-sense, and thought. My learning process, over the years, has led me to create for undergraduates a structure, a sequence, of learning that will deepen their understanding of poetry and of language and the literary—just as the practice of translation has deepened my own.

Northwestern University has a very strong and demanding undergraduate creative writing program, and for students trained in it, poetic translation can substantially supplement their literary education: they learn more of poetic technique, grow in expressive capability, and understand that there are different modes of poetic thinking. It's not surprising that those students, as well as students in Comparative Literary Studies and in language departments, would seek out such a course. What continues to surprise and please me is that even in this small seminar, most of the students come from other disciplines entirely. In search of something thoroughly literary in the midst of other studies, and having a reading knowledge or even a speaking fluency or native ability in a language other than English, these students too take to the riddles and rewards of translating. They have come from such disciplines as engineering, economics, pre-med, philosophy, American studies, international affairs, history, political science, music performance, and theater.

And they have brought with them—whether from studies, formative residence abroad, immigrant communities or the cultural legacies of their own families—linguistic competence in ancient Greek, Arabic, Chinese, French, German, Korean, Latin, modern Hebrew, Polish, Portuguese, Russian, Spanish, Swedish, and Urdu. However, no matter the linguistic range of any cohort, everyone will end up having to work on at least one poem, and perhaps two or three, in a language she or he does not know. (For the occasional non-native, not fully bilingual, speaker of English, our target language too may present challenges to writing idiomatically.)

On the basis of the linguistic competence in the seminar I decide on which languages will provide us with our source poems. Here are two sets of poems I have recently chosen: (1) a sonnet in Spanish by Argentine poet Alfonsina Storni, a ghazal in Urdu by Ghalib, a poem in Polish by Wisława Szymborska; (2) a poem in Spanish by Cecilia Vicuña that the poet was prohibited from publishing for decades during and even after the dictatorship in Chile, a poem in modern Hebrew by Yehuda Amichai, and two short poems in Portuguese by Brazilian poet Carlos Drummond de Andrade. I always include one poem in an ancient language or a contemporary non-Western language. When we begin to read and discuss each poem, I bring in a guest informant—a literary native speaker or a literary scholar from among my university colleagues—who will introduce us to the poem in every way possible in an hour and twenty minutes and to whom I can send more questions. On a few occasions I have been able to host the author as informant—as when we translated a poem by a colleague, the Russian poet Ilya Kutik; when Nigerian-born writer (now also a colleague) Chris Abani brought us one of his poems in Igbo; and recently when we translated a poem by the Chilean poet Cecilia Vicuña.

I always begin with a contemporary poem in Spanish (for which I can serve as informant). On the very first day, we start our work. That is, I provide no preliminary mapping of the history of literary translation or theories thereof, nor of the source and target poetic contexts. We grapple from the first with the poem itself—a contemporary one, since it will allow us to feel we have a more immediate access to it, even though it will also gradually reveal its distance from us. Such a poem might even seem quite easy to translate, at first, because everyone starts from the assumption that translation means transferring semantic values from one language to another. But soon our discussion begins to turn up ambiguities, puzzles, grammatical elements, words too polysemous in too characteristic Spanish, or phrases too idiomatic, to have analogues in English, and then we begin to see how Spanish and English taxonomic vocabularies differ (creatures and plants, tools, everyday particularities). We look at etymologies and definitions in a large source-language (not bilingual) dictionary, for the sake of collecting connotations, and we begin to identify grammatical necessities versus grammatical options. As we study the poem, I introduce basic elements of poetics, including phonetic figures, marked versus unmarked language, prosody and varieties of free verse, and poetic structures, both in the sense of the use of stanzas and traditional poem-forms and in the sense of the structure of thought and feeling that the poem achieves—that is, its movement through stages of one kind or another, which can be noticed in (shifts in) imagery, tropes, diction, point of view, addressee, typography, affect and tone of voice, and so on. (For students who come from outside literary studies, and even for some within, this practical primer on poetics is likely to be mostly unfamiliar.) I choose short poems because they allow me to urge students to revise each translation more than once during the term. In the second week of the quarter, we start working through our readings and relating them to the practical translation problems we are encountering.

Occasionally a publishable translation may emerge from one or more students in any given group, and one student may later produce a brilliant undergraduate honors thesis on translation. But I do not regard the purpose of the course as being to produce definitive translations, but rather a productive and exciting engagement with the practice and theory of translation, and with poetry and poetics.

As class members work together on the same poems, in sequence, analyzing, and then presenting in workshop-style meetings their individual first drafts of their translations, we engage in a group process of interpretation that finally yields a variety of concrete results in the form of the individual students' revised translations. These revisions show not only different responses to different poetic elements in the source poem but also different choices about the sort of gesture the poem makes as a whole. I urge students to go beyond the usually semantic focus of their first drafts. Together we attain an awareness of not only what poems *say* but also of what poems *do*, of how they make meaning, and of how the poem as a whole may be a complex verbal gesture (made of a sequence of smaller gestures).

Among our class readings is my 1985 essay "Poetic Form and the Translator," which gives us a conceptual tool for comparing the importance of one poetic element versus another. The task of translation highlights precisely such necessary comparisons. Readers may differ, of course, in what they take the hierarchy of poetic values to be in any particular poem, and translations too may differ, especially if they begin with different purposes. Also, in our discussions around differing draft translations, as aspects of the source poem are clarified because of the questions that arise from different ways of translating this line or that, this poetic element or that, even an apparently simple line may come to seem rather more difficult to translate as we look past what it says and consider what its effect is as a moment in the train of thought and feeling in the poem. And we try to think through the implications, for the translation of the poem as a whole, of this or that particular local decision.

Everyone may take anything from anyone else's translation. Any particular find of an apt word in English, a felicity of phrase, a particular word order (which English makes such discriminative use of), or an interpretive decision becomes common property at this stage of our process. We never arrive at a single consensual version, however, because the students eventually make individual decisions about their translations and take responsibility for them. In fact, different purposes, different commissions in Vermeer's sense, produce different *kinds* of translations. Students too follow different theoretical approaches or practical methods. After all, we would not expect Walter Benjamin, Vladimir Nabokov, Kwame Anthony Appiah, and Margaret Sayers Peden, for instance, to produce similar translations. One student translator's ear, or imagination, may be better or worse than another's. The proof is in the quality of the engagement, for I can't expect everyone to be literary.

I assess students' work according to how deeply their translations and essays engage with the theoretical and practical issues we have been exploring in our discussions. My goal is to lead them to use translation as a way to think about poetics, about poetic forms, practices, and traditions, both as these elements are realized in the source texts and as they might inform their own translations. Hence I also evaluate their ability to critique a published translation and to comment on aspects of each other's draft translations in our workshop sessions. They demonstrate this critical ability by measuring their grasp of source-text poetics against translations and by developing solutions for the problems raised by poetic elements. For these solutions I expect them to deploy the techniques that I try to help them acquire and with which they can refine their own translations.

How *do* our readings come into play in the midst of the practical issues of translating a poem? From some, we get conceptual tools that clarify how to achieve an adequate (adequate in response to which purpose?) representation in our target language: we ponder the difference between what a poem *says* and what it *does*. The full range of possibilities in the finished student translations may range from a close version to a playful spin-off (for example, homophonic, or drawn from an Oulipo technique) that supplements rather than represents the source poem. Also, I take from George Steiner's "fourfold hermeneutic motion of translation" (1975b: 156) the case for making, with a translation, some gesture of restoration or restitution to the source poem and even to the literary tradition or situation in which it was created. A real translation, Steiner says, gives evidence that "the source-text possesses potentialities, elemental reserves as yet unrealized by itself" (1975a: 160). This would be true, also, of the whole tradition within which, or even against which, the source poem was written. Perhaps every literary translator feels that this is exactly what literary translation is for, and yet translations of poetry seem to me not to achieve this often enough, even at the first level of the adequacy of the translation to what the source poem does, much less at the level of suggesting the potentialities and reserves that have not been brought over. Our era and our English seem to me to require ethically that we try to create such restitution in translations, since the English language itself is effectively pushing into obscurity, in terribly difficult times and places, what needs to be brought to light in as many places as possible, if it is to survive in a wider regard.

10 A Multilingual Workshop in Poetry and Prose Translation

Peter Filkins

In order to help students realize the importance of thinking about translation as a kind of performance, rather than a simple and direct representation, the very first day of my undergraduate Translation Workshop at Bard College begins with a piece of music. Though I could imagine many pieces working well, the one I choose is Brahms Op. 78, No. 1, his first sonata for piano and violin, as played by Isabelle van Keulen and Ronald Brautigam. Playing just the first minute of the first movement, I ask them simply to listen and think about what the music makes them think of or feel. I then play the same segment again, this time asking them to write down what kind of mood, setting, even narrative they might possibly come up with. It is uncanny how similar their accounts often are. Students see something about childhood, memory, sunlight pouring through a parlor window, loss, regret, tenderness, and romance, all of which connects to circumstances of Brahms' life that inform the music, though they do not know this when they first listen.

Only after sharing some of these writings aloud in class do I give them more facts relating to the music. The piece is dedicated to Felix Schumann, Brahms' godson and the son of Robert and Clara Schumann, the latter Brahms' life-long, unrequited love, to whom he sent the score on Felix's death from tuberculosis at age 25 in 1879. With this information in hand, I then play the same opening segment again, asking the students to write a new version of what they hear in the music. Indeed, longing might now be seen as regret or melancholy, or sunlight might now be understood as hope for future redemption, or Felix's having passed on to a better world. Reading these second versions, we discuss such changes in perception, as well as extensions of their initial perceptions, all the while noting differences in interpretation on the part of each student. Sometimes students even see the music in dramatically different ways than when they began, or even feel that only with more information in hand do they truly come to understand the proper mood and intent of the music.

Then I play a trick on them. Saying that now I would like them to listen to an altogether different piece of music and write about it, I play the same Brahms sonata and the same opening segment, but this time recorded by Anne-Sophie Mutter and Alexis Weissenberg. It takes only a few seconds for a couple of heads to rise and smile with understanding, but what is astonishing is how the students actually carry on writing yet another version of their response to the piece, everyone in the class realizing that while the first performance felt lyrical, romantic, even at times schmaltzy, the Anne-Sophie Mutter version is wrenching, elegiac, and much more the song of a mother grieving for the loss of her son. Reading a few of these responses aloud, we then talk about the differences between the two performances. To develop this lesson further, I quickly play a third version of the same piece, this one by Itzhak Perlman and Vladimir Ashkenazy. Slow, regal, stately, and poised, it is much more the effort to maintain dignity and composure in the face of loss, the students seeing immediately that the three different pieces are distinct and almost autonomous artistic acts.

At this point, I welcome them to Translation Workshop, even saying that, in some ways, they have just done their first translation. Though their work will focus on the four texts they choose to translate from whatever language they know, as well as revisions to two of those translations along the way, the act of interpreting the Brahms sonata and then each performance is their own kind of rendering of the music in another medium, namely that of language. This translation is of course not interlingual, but intersemiotic, moving between two different sign systems. And yet the feel of shifting from one medium to another is crucial to ready themselves for the realization that, indeed, different languages are different mediums, and different levels of language *within* a single language function as different mediums as well.

Understanding how language serves as a medium *through which* meaning is expressed, rather than as a direct and obvious statement of ideas, is a crucial lesson to students not only of translation but also of world languages and literature, for the appreciation of nuance and tone is central to any interpretive understanding. The need to understand, maneuver, and perform this shift is also the first crucial step in *any* undergraduate writing workshop. In a poetry or fiction workshop, undergraduates almost always enter thinking they are entirely in charge of the language they use, its sources, and the effects it will have upon their reader. However, the question is, can they shape it? Can they control syntax and diction and tone, even anticipate a reader's response to both, or better yet, recognize the change in a poem or story if they re-write and thus re-perform it in an effort to get at the even better poem or story that may be lurking within their first draft? Such engagement also helps writing students appreciate more fully the multilayered operations of metaphor, narrative, syntax, and linguistic invention at work in the literature they read and study. The undergraduate translation workshop functions as a nexus at which the concerns of writing, language, and literature meet and complement one another, and the fact that the workshop is usually divided evenly between these three constituencies only helps them to recognize their shared concerns through translation.

The multilingual workshop also demands that students revise and rethink their own language and thus what is expressed through it. To illustrate that process, I use the first three weeks to explore various exercises in English. Not only does this period give students time to work on the first translation from their source language, but it also levels the playing field for considering various critical problems and solutions as well as for developing a language of critique that will better inform the discussion of their work in the weeks ahead. One exercise involves six different versions of the passage from *The Iliad* (Book XVII) that describes Achilles' horses weeping at the death of Patroclus (the versions are by George Chapman, Alexander Pope, William Cullen Bryant, Richmond Lattimore, Robert Fagles, and A. T. Murray's prose version in the Loeb Classical Library). Students are asked to examine these versions and to come up with one of their own. They must then explain why they rendered the passage in couplets, blank verse, free verse, or even prose and consider the particular effects of word choice, line length, and syntax. Given that most students know little about meter, enjambment, or rhyme, this exercise also creates an opportunity to conduct short lessons on each formal feature while discussing the versions of the Homer passage, both professional and student.

Meanwhile the students are also at work on their first translations, the texts for which they choose themselves. I set no expectation of length, genre, or form, for I believe it important that students choose works they feel a connection to, as well as to consider the role they play in bringing those writers into English, especially if they are the first to do so. As for the length, I tell them less is more when starting out in translation, and that it is fine to begin with the first two or three pages of a story, or a single poem. They quickly appreciate how many problems occur in translating any given page, and even if they translate a work that has been translated before, they must justify their own approach in the process writing that accompanies the initial draft. Inevitably, several of the students end up choosing a text that is beyond their current skills, whether as readers of another language or even as writers in English, the latter especially being true for any native speakers of another language who happen to be taking the workshop. Thus, the first translation can sometimes end up as important for the lessons of its failures and shortcomings as it is for its hands-on engagement with the process itself, for such difficulties allow the student to gain a greater awareness of the level at which he or she is ready to work. Indeed, many students begin with something as demanding as Baudelaire but later choose something more manageable, sometimes moving from adult fiction to children's stories, yet still addressing important questions of tone and nuance.

During these first weeks I also assign excerpts from key theoretical discussions that appear in Rainer Schulte and John Biguenet's anthology, *Theories of Translation* (1992). The essays by Friedrich Schleiermacher and Wilhelm von Humboldt discuss the degree to which a translation should remain loyal to the linguistic character of the source text while serving the needs of readers in the target language. Another essay from the anthology that I find especially useful is Octavio Paz's "Translation: Literature and Letters," for it emphasizes that "translation and creation are twin processes" and that any piece of writing is only a version of the "ur-text" behind the eventual finished piece that is still trying to invoke the sources of its own inspiration (Schulte and Biguenet 1992: 160). I also assign several essays from Schulte and Biguenet's other anthology, *The Craft of Translation* (1989). These include Gregory Rabassa's "No Two Snowflakes Are Alike," which stresses that "translation is an approach, not an equivalency" (Schulte and Biguenet 1989: 11), and Margaret Sayers Peden's "Building a Translation," which reveals the many possibilities involved in several different renderings of a sonnet by Sor Juana. William Weaver's "The Process of Translation" is useful for giving the students an idea of the sense of detail and flexibility demanded of any translator, while Donald Frame's "Pleasures and Problems of Translation" and Christopher Middleton's essay on translating a Günter Eich poem take them through a meticulous approach to style.

In combining the practical specifics of rendering the passage from Homer with ideas and examples about craft and style, my hope is to move the students away from their initial notions of translation as a matter of finding the right word and toward thinking about how the source text can be rendered in several different ways. Since the workshop is open to students working from any language, one way I have found to explore the complexity of the source text is to examine more closely some original compositions in English. We look at the first page of Henry James's *The Portrait of a Lady*, Eudora Welty's "Why I Live at the P.O.," Virginia Woolf's *To the Lighthouse*, and Ernest Hemingway's "Big Two-hearted River: Part I." The aim of the classroom discussion is to consider what difficulties might arise in translating the passages into any language, including the language they are translating from, while also raising issues of narrative point of view, exposition, or the demands and opportunities of free indirect discourse.

For instance, we discuss what might be involved in translating James's notion of "the ceremony known as afternoon tea" at the start of *The Portrait of a Lady*, or the hilarious potential for malapropism in rendering the need for Welty's unnamed narrator "to try to stretch two chickens over five people," or the way syntax weds class and consciousness when Woolf describes James Ramsey as belonging, "even at the age of six, to that great clan which cannot keep this feeling separate from that, but must let future prospects, with their joys and sorrows, cloud what is actually at hand," or, finally, the echoes of war that haunt Hemingway's Nick Adams in the sonic bombardment heard as he sits "on the bundle of canvas and bedding the baggage man had pitched out the door of the baggage car." How is it even possible to capture *any* of this in translation? Yet these vastly different renderings of syntax, diction, sentence length, narrative distance, voice, tone, and so forth help point to the very same matters of nuance that the students need to understand and perform in their own translations. In the process, they learn that translating prose can be just as hard as translating poetry. I share with them my view that prose is actually more difficult to translate than poetry: we are quick to make compromises and rely on invention in translating a poem, whereas prose somehow gives rise to the expectation that we must get it exactly right, no matter how various and multiple the choices reveal themselves to be when it comes to dialogue, syntax, and diction.

As we work through the English-to-English exercises and the craft essays, students are completing drafts of their first two translations. Only in the fourth week do we begin the sessions in which their work is critiqued. They need that amount of time not only to produce their initial translations but also to appreciate the complexity of the process itself. For the most part, the first translation also tends to be the most wooden and doggedly loyal to the source text, revealing lock-step awkwardness and stilted phrasing. It is best that they receive some response from me on such issues before bringing the translation to the table for general critique. Students are also asked to seek out, respond to, and critique in writing six different published translations over the course of the semester. This assignment, which combines an anthology with a journal, helps them to build critical skills in examining specific choices translators have made, skills that enable them to assess their colleagues' translations during critiques.

In reading their colleagues' work, students are asked to think about what seems to work consistently well, what seems to stick out or be problematic, and whether anything seems particularly confusing or unclear. These questions are of course quite general, but I find it most productive to begin with them and work towards more specific concerns as the sessions unfold. For example, a translation of a short story may prove particularly fluid and natural in its expository and descriptive passages, but the dialogue may seem wooden. More likely than not, a number of students will pick up on just that, or at least will have a response at the ready when I ask what people think of the dialogue. Yet only in looking at specific lines and offering alternative possibilities do we start to get at the real consistencies or inconsistencies of the translation and whether or not it seems a reliable, engaging, and informed rendering of the text, or even what it means to arrive at that.

Students also write a page of critical response to each of their colleagues' translations, and they are encouraged to make notations and list questions on the manuscripts that they return to the translator after the critique has ended. At the start of the critique the translator is asked if there is anything specific he or she would like the class to focus on or discuss, or anything about the translation he or she would like to tell us. During the critiques, however, the translator is not allowed to talk unless we pose a specific question. This policy avoids back-and-forth debates about intent or differences of opinion, or justifications of choices made. Only at the end do we turn to the translator and ask if he or she has any questions. Depending on the student, some amount of defensiveness or even stubbornness can arise, especially in terms of saying "but that's what it says in the original." Then my job becomes reminding the class that the source text can be handled in many different ways. I also try to formulate an issue concerning how to handle dialogue, diction, cultural references, and so forth, which anyone will confront from time to time, and to pose that as a question for everyone to take away and think about in relation to their own translations.

This last element of finding some sort of commonality is an important aspect of any multilingual workshop. Because I have had students translating from languages as diverse as Arabic, Chinese, French, German, Hebrew, Italian, Japanese, Latin, Persian, Romanian, Russian, and Spanish, obviously no one in the class, myself included, can comment on the precise denotative, or often the connotative, meaning of the source text. How then is it even possible to teach the course or even grade the students' work? The answer lies in looking at the consistency, awareness, and inventiveness of the approach that they bring to the problems of performing the text in English. While this criterion does leave open the possibility that both the student and the class may miss or misunderstand the denotative meaning of a particular word or phrase, that is not crucial on the undergraduate level. More important is how the student renders the meaning or nuance that he or she understands to be there and, through the translation, arrives at an interpretation that is consistent in its register, diction, and style as well as convincing in its metaphorical logic and narrative sense as analogues for attributes of the source text that are employed for literary effect. In fact, what often happens when a passage seems particularly confusing is that the student is asked to return to the source text and ends up finding a mistake or more fully understanding the possibilities of the text's meaning.

This process points to the importance of revision. Midway through the semester, after completing three weeks of critique sessions, I again shift back to exercises and essays, this time to encourage students to think about the wide array of choices open to them in revision. Edmund Keeley's "Collaboration, Revision, and Other Less Forgiveable Sins in Translation" and John Felstiner's "Translation and Tradition in Paul Celan," both included in *The Craft of Translation*, are useful in illustrating how translators debate various choices and over time shift their views of the source texts they are translating. William Weaver's "In Other Words: A Translator's Notebook" (1995), comprised of excerpts from a journal he kept while translating Umberto Eco's novel *The Island of the Day Before*, is even more useful and generally a student favorite. It gives them a day-by-day, nuts-and-bolts view inside a master's workshop, such as when Weaver says halfway through his draft of the novel, "I keep thinking of my comparison of translator and sculptor. Now I have in front of me the mass of wet clay. Little by little, I am molding it. The material is all there, but I have to bring it to life" (Weaver 1995: 17).

Along with these essays I also hand out six different translations of Rilke's poem "Archaic Torso of Apollo," encouraging them to imagine them as six different versions by the same translator taken from different stages of the revision process. The idea is not so much to show them *what* to revise, but *how*, or at least the many opportunities available to them in doing so, along with the fact that their approach to the translation can change dramatically over the course of revising it. Finally, I give them John Frederick Nims's translations of two of Sappho's poems, 16 and 94, instructing them to complete the poem by filling in the lacunae and to feel free to alter Nims's version by doing so. When we discuss these versions in class, what we highlight is how the students imagine their way into what seem to be Sappho's aims, just as they need to imagine their way into the potential of their own translations in order to change them through the re-performance that is revision.

Near the end of the semester I further emphasize the importance of revision by turning the tables in the third set of critique sessions. Rather than ask the student translators to remain quiet during the critique, they are asked to do a presentation on a revision that has gone through several drafts. Specifically, I ask them to tell the class how they have changed their approach to the source text over time, what they have come to appreciate about its complexities, and what kinds of solutions worked or did not work along the way. The rest of the class then participates with its usual array of questions and comments, but the main emphasis is placed on the extent to which the translator has developed a sufficient and consistent command of what he or she is doing in the translation and how the translation might still evolve if given more time. In short, my hope is that each student will find a clear and detailed way to justify the approach of his or her translation in much the same way that they have seen Weaver or Peden or Felstiner do in the craft essays they have read.

Revision and what it accomplishes also raise the question of assessment and grading student translations. As with creative writing, there exists no clear standard or template, yet I do feel that distinctions can be drawn. I never give the drafts of translations a grade. Instead at midterm and at the end I ask students to submit a portfolio of their work thus far. The midterm portfolio includes two translations, one of them revised, while the final portfolio contains four translations, at least two of them revised. I also ask for an extended reflection of four to six pages that discusses how each translation has progressed, how a translator's approach has been informed by the theoretical and craft essays, as well as by the critiques, and what he or she has learned about the process of translation in general. The final grade takes into consideration this material, as well as the insight, creativity, and flexibility that students have brought to their translations, the thoroughness with which they have discussed published translations in their anthology journal, and the degree to which they have contributed insightful comments and questions to class critiques. I also try to figure in the degree to which they have grown in their practice by developing the ability to identify and discuss in detail the challenges and rewards of their work.

The effort to get students to take a step back from the language they wield and to recognize the wide array of possibilities open to them is what I see as the core experience of the undergraduate multilingual translation workshop and the essential lesson it has to offer. In fact, students will often say that after working with translation revising their own writing is much easier, and they come to see their own poems and stories as further versions that are continually evolving. Add to this increased awareness the array of voices, styles, formal strategies, and levels of diction that any translator must develop to translate different kinds of texts, and the result is that students leave a translation workshop more versatile writers and more exacting readers of literature.

I have often felt that I can teach more about literature and writing in a translation workshop than I can in a standard creative writing workshop or in a class on an author or genre since students end up much more directly involved with the shaping of language itself through translation. Translation is an art, and the essence of its art is the performance of a text from one language within another. The multilingual translation workshop allows undergraduates to explore and appreciate the means of such performance in and of itself, as well as to understand how lessons in the transformation of language apply not only to the translator but also the writer or the critical reader interested in the way the words make meaning and how such meaning is recast and remade in another tongue.

11 Teaching Theater Translation

David Johnston

The course described here, titled "Translating for the Stage," is an elective in the master's program in translation offered in the School of Modern Languages at Queen's University in Belfast. The students are both native and non-native speakers of English, commanding a variety of languages. A high level of competence in the source language and native ability in the target language are essential entry criteria. Two compulsory core courses function as prerequisites, so that "Translating for the Stage" assumes a degree of familiarity with basic issues of translation theory and practice, including the world of the professional translator. Particularly relevant among these issues are a *skopos* or purpose-oriented approach to translation, principally the awareness that the end-user's response is of primary importance in judging the efficacy of a translated text (Vermeer 1989); the way in which translation exposes the radical instability of the source text; the ethical engagements of translation; and the translator as both collaborative agent (who, in this case, will work with other theater-makers in assembling the final *mise en scène*) and professional practitioner (who, in all likelihood, will have dealings with publishers, marketing departments, executive producers, and literary agents).

The course is structured around a series of interconnected activities. Central among them are twenty-four class contact hours (one two-hour session per week over a twelve-week semester), three two-hour workshops, a series of weekly seminars given by visiting speakers, both theorists and practitioners (students enter their critical reflections on the speakers' visits in a weekly log submitted as part of their overall evaluation), a series of one-to-one meetings with the instructor in order to identify translation projects and to discuss particular issues arising therefrom, and at least two group visits to theaters so that students begin to familiarize themselves with the medium. They discuss their response to productions they have seen in fora that are organized outside class meetings. They are encouraged to attend as many productions as possible and to file 500-word reviews with the instructor for critical feedback. Class time is generally allocated 25 percent to theory and 75 percent to practice-based activities.

The rationale for the course lies in the increasing demand, in both professional and amateur as well as university theater, for retranslated classics and newly translated contemporary plays. The focus falls squarely on translation as a constituent activity within theater practice, with a clear emphasis on stagecraft and the dramatic actions that together constitute the performability of the play. At the outset students are asked to read two edited volumes, my *Stages of Translation* (1996) and Baines, Marinetti, and Perteghella's *Staging and Performing Translation* (2011), so as to ensure that they develop an understanding of the parameters within which the stage translator works. These readings expose students to the different translation practices suggested by the convenient shorthand of stage or page.

Performability, however, is not presented as an uncontested term. Indeed, a fundamental determination of the program as a whole is to teach the conflicts, to acknowledge the frequently conflicting strands of thought that both constitute the field and move it forward. The course begins, accordingly, with a discussion of what the perceived performability of the play text may be. The discussion is supported by readings drawn from both sides of the debate: Susan Bassnett's early work (1991), which argues strongly that shaping the translated text towards performance lies within the director's domain, vs. Patrice Pavis's seminal *Theatre at the Crossroads of Culture* (1992), which argues that translation practice is a crucial component of intercultural theater in performance.

The acknowledgment of debate does not mean that the course avoids taking its own position. We formulate a working definition of the stage translator's task—to ensure the performability of the target text—which is then elucidated throughout. The overall task itself is presented to the students as a series of phases. These phases are not intended to be seen as consecutive but rather as a series of concentric activities that together form a taxonomy of translator process linked at all times to theater practice. The taxonomy consists of the following checklist: background research; text work; writing for the actor; writing for the audience; working with other theater professionals.

Background research into the source text and author is not intended to support any notion of authentic reading and re-creation. The aim is rather to focus on the cultural work of the source text, how it engages with its time and place, and through that to acquire the sort of knowledge that the translator may need when setting scene and addressing actors early in rehearsal. By the same token, close reading of the source is carried out not to understand better the autotelic original but to deepen the translators' sense of characterization, dialogue (they have already studied speech-act theory in their core courses), setting, and the actions and devices that vivify the text and make it memorable in performance. The reading process is conceptualized in terms of a double perspective—text-inwards and text-outwards—that is similar to that of the actor who reads a script so as to understand character dynamics and their relationship with setting while at the same time contemplating how that understanding might be performed before a spectator.

The theater event is, of course, inseparable from audience experience. Students come to the course equipped with an enhanced awareness of fitness for purpose as a key element in assessing the efficacy of any particular translation. The course emphasizes translation for the stage rather than the page—in other words, translation that is carried out with the requirements of *mise en scène* as the lynch-pin of the process. That said, in a theater world in which hunger for new texts is constantly offset by the realities of funding difficulties, young translators may be asked to provide what are known as literal or plain translations of plays so that their performability may be assessed by the producing theater. Students are pro-vided with high-quality examples of such translations, thickened with explanatory notes and alternative renderings of any particularly problematic language (figu-rative, allusive, elliptical, and so forth). They also read Helen Rappaport's 2007 account of her work as a translator from Russian who provided literal versions for playwrights such as Tom Stoppard and Frank McGuinness. Because our main assumption, however, is that translators will work towards performance, that part of the reading process that is other-directed rather than text-focused is carried out with a dramaturgical awareness, a sense of what might work on stage.

The phases of background research and text reading are introduced and devel-oped through discussion of both classical and contemporary plays. In class, stu-dents offer analyses of what they see as the translation issues, difficulties, and opportunities presented by scenes from writers as diverse as Sophocles and Shake-speare, Pirandello and Brecht, Brian Friel, Juan Mayorga, and Alan Ayckbourn. Since the student analyses take into account their various target languages, one further explanatory—and perhaps justificatory—note needs to be inserted here, namely that, in the ecology of world theater, plays are not infrequently translated into other languages through what is effectively the staging post of English. As with the theatrical use of literal translations, the course tends to take a pragmatic stance on this issue, although students are also given the opportunity to debate the ethics of such practices and to decide for themselves what their own position might be. At this point in the course, however, the analysis of such play texts is academic in that it is solely intended to form the basis of classroom discussion.

Students are therefore encouraged to infuse their writing process with the sort of dramaturgical awareness that characterizes the work of other theater practition-ers. Important texts in this regard, assigned as preparatory reading for the course as a whole, are Eric Bentley's *The Life of the Drama* (1964), Shannon Jackson's *Professing Performance* (2004), and Peter Brook's *The Shifting Point* (1994). Students discuss all three books in a session titled "The Translator as Drama-turg." We identify stage translation as being directed towards two end-users, the actor and the spectator. To address writing for the actor, the class considers the notion of speakability, using Eva Espasa (2000) as a springboard. We explore a set of writing devices, such as rhythm and the verbal mirroring of speaker kine-sics (gestures) and kinetics (implied movement), along with the ways in which speech may be reflective of the speaker's motivation. Students learn how to fil-ter source-language dialogue through their own template of naturally occurring speech in order to ensure that both actor and audience understand what is happen-ing onstage. Small-group work based on pivotal scenes from Sheridan, Shaw, and Caryl Churchill allows students to test their growing awareness of the illocution-ary and perlocutionary dimensions of dialogue and to re-cast those dimensions in their own language or in English paraphrase.

There is a danger of oversimplification here, of course. Stage language is not simply naturally-occurring speech but language that is shaped and organized by the style of the play itself. The performability of the play depends no less on the quality of its impact in performance than on any measurement of intelligibility. Following Stephen Spender's famous reference to a "grammar of images" in Lorca's work (cited in Binding 1985: 51), students are asked to analyze excerpts from a range of classical and contemporary writers in order to identify both the structural grammar of the piece—that is, the interweaving and echoing of themes and expression that bring coherence to the text—and the isolated, unconnected image or metaphor that ensures the impact, or memorability, of any one particular exchange (Johnston's "Securing the Performability of the Text" [2004] is read in this particular context). The students return, once again in small groups, to the same excerpts from Sheridan, Shaw, and Churchill to identify what the course now calls the "long-term" and the "one-off" devices employed within these excerpts. They then select, in consultation with the instructor, a scene from a play of their choice and translate it into their own target language for discussion and feedback in class.

But what of the audience's expectations? Students draw on their own experience as spectators to develop a clear understanding of the expectations generated by different dramatic genres. Once again Bentley's study is useful in its discussion of the different types of audience complicity prompted by forms such as tragedy, comedy, and melodrama. Performance, of course, happens within the here and now of any given audience, and class discussion begins to broach both the ethics and the practicalities of relocating texts. Students are asked to read Upton's *Moving Target* (2000), particularly the introduction and any chapter that captures their attention, and to complete an assignment that requires them to consider how they would transpose the action of Friel's *Translations* to another context. By now fully aware that the translator must intervene substantially in the target text to secure its performability, students proceed to consider the ethics of ensuring target-culture relevance. They enter this particular course having already studied Lawrence Venuti's *The Translator's Invisibility* (1995) so that they are familiar with the ethical implications of domesticating and foreignizing effects in translation. The class discusses scenes from relocated translations such as Martin Crimp's version of *The Misanthrope*, set in modern-day Britain, and the Charabanc Theatre Company's *The House of Bernarda Alba*, relocated to Ireland's County Cavan in the 1930s. We recognize that both of these versions are clearly responding to the imperatives of commercial theater. But again the course takes a position, one that is more fully reflected in the understanding of translation that is set out in George Steiner's hermeneutic motion (1975a).

Steiner's concept of "restitution," however, as the fourth and final step of the hermeneutic motion, is problematic (1975: 160). What exactly is the translator able to restore in the translation so as to prevent it from usurping the place of the original? The class is introduced to the politics of recognition through Nancy Fraser (2000) and asked to consider in what ways multiple versions of plays by Chekhov reflect different senses of cultural ownership in representing the author to the English-speaking public. We then take up the question of how the translation of a play text might eschew domesticating strategies while simultaneously avoiding the pitfalls of mere exoticization. To address this question, Spanish playwrights—Lope de Vega, Calderón, and Lorca—are used as case studies. Both the language of the translations and the production decisions that accompanied them (very often involving the use of incidental music as a metadiscourse of place) are seen as engaging in a cultural politics of representation. Class members debate how the texts under examination might challenge hegemonic appropriation, always bearing in mind that theater, whether or not commercial, requires a directness of communication and connection that other art forms may achieve in a more leisurely manner.

The position emerging from this discussion is that translated plays present an opportunity to encourage audiences to look outwards from their own cultural matrix, imagining alternative ways of understanding of their own position in time and space. A multilingual course of this nature must also recognize that different power relations between languages come into play here, so students are constantly asked to assess whether the solutions found by a translator working into English would be equally effective in their own theatrical environment. This question of shifting linguistic, cultural, and institutional conditions is in fact applied to theoretical concepts and practical strategies throughout the course, connecting the discussions to the work that the students carried out with polysystem theory in the prerequisite courses (Even-Zohar 1978). They are rapidly attuned to the idea that stage translators work not only between texts but also between theatrical systems with distinct contexts of production and reception and between audiences with different horizons of expectations.

The emphasis on practice leads students to raise concerns about textual authenticity that are frequently articulated as "But is it okay to do that?" In partial response to what remains a pervasive and lingering doubt, two well-known directors are invited to a special workshop to discuss the pragmatics of theater-making. Students prepare for these talks with readings that emphasize an understanding of translation as a performative act whose inherent ephemerality requires constant repetition. Readings from Karin Barber (2003) and Richard Taruskin (1995) present a compelling challenge to the notion of authentic performance practice. Barber distinguishes between translation as text and as performance, suggesting that the former conception treats translation as an activity located within pre-set parameters while the latter locates it within a realm where only the contingencies of context determine meaning. Taruskin emphasizes that the aesthetic practices of the past are irredeemably lost to us, so re-interpretation is an inevitable component of any artistic practice.

Class discussion then returns, almost of its own accord, to a reconsideration of Steiner's restitution, the notion that the translator's intervention in the source text requires some sort of restorative justice. How something of the foreign may be restored within the production of a translated play becomes the subject of another supplementary workshop. Restorative solutions are discussed at the levels of production (music, design, costume, and so forth), paratext (program, poster, title, and so forth), and text. In the case of text, two generic solutions are identified and applied in the workshop: the deployment of specifically foreign elements in order to signal that a process of verbal transmutation is underway between source and target languages and the creation of disturbances within the target language so as to decenter the spectator, to uproot him or her from the sheltering matrix of the host language and culture. Students thus come to realize that theater translation may go beyond any residual sense of domesticating or foreignizing as disconnected strategies and move towards an articulation of the writing process that, like the reading process they have previously employed, is characterized by doubleness. The workshop concludes that the translator for performance engages with the cultural work of the source text, writing it forward into the experience of a spectator who is located in the here and now of performance while simultaneously writing backward, preserving elements of strangeness in the world of the source text. The writing forward can be illustrated by an updating of the referential dimension of the source, such as the construction of links between *The Miser* and the recent economic recession, while the writing backward can be illustrated by retaining a certain cultural or historical specificity, such as the recreation of an elevated style or the sonnet form in Lope's *The Dog in the Manger*. In this workshop, students develop their sense of the paradox of translation: it is a practice that presents the other to the self while at the same time preventing the self from appropriating the life and culture of the other.

Understanding theater translation as a practice that engineers movement between the here and there, the now and then, is one of the significant teaching objectives of the course. But, once again, students very often voice another concern, this time relating to the nature of spectatorship. The sense of movement, together with the ways in which the shifting existence of the play in time and space become a material feature of text and production alike, serves to destabilise the text, running counter to the students' sense or pursuit of consistency and cohesion, of what seems to hold together. We address these misgivings in a session that is devoted to the dynamics of spectatorship. Giles Fauconnier and Mark Turner's work (2002) on cognitive blending introduces students to the reality rather than the myth of spectator experience, namely that individual spectators blend in and out of performance, rather than completely suspend disbelief. In other words, the spectator moves between the world of the play and the realm of private experience—at times for positive reasons, such as the awareness of qualities of performance or production, at others for more negative reasons, such as boredom or as a consequence of interference from sources extraneous to the production. A kinetic translation method, we conclude, one that invites spectators to engage with the various temporal and spatial planes that are simultaneously inhabited by the translated play, reflects the shifting nature of spectator experience itself. Time and space become the tools of the translator's imagination.

Students are now in a position to undertake the performance-oriented translation of a short play or scene in the range of 1,500 words. They choose this play or extract in a meeting with the instructor. Additionally, they begin to develop a production brief that specifies such factors as the performance medium (e.g. live on stage or radio broadcast), a relocation in time or place, and a dialect or register (e.g. Lorca in Hiberno-English). This brief serves as the basis of a translation diary that contextualizes the work in progress that students present in class for peer feedback. In the last class meeting, at the same time as they are working on their translations and reflective diaries, the focus turns to considering the collaborative work of the translator within the production process.

Students are not exempt from the widespread assumption that collaboration is, in the best of situations, merely an efficient way to allocate tasks or, in the worst of them, inimical to true artistic vision. The concept of the "overtone," referring to a phantom note that emerges octaves above the rest as the result of perfect harmony, is used as a metaphor for the aura generated by the overriding artistic vision of any production, to which the translator remains a prime, but not the sole, contributor. Readings in the work of Jill Dolan (2005) and Pavis help to prise translators away from what is at times an overweening reluctance to engage and negotiate with other theater practitioners. These readings discuss theater as a necessarily collaborative medium in which the sum of the parts will, hopefully, be greater than parts taken in isolation. A central objective of the course is to enable students to work at a professional level within the theater, and, like the other graduates from the program, they become fully aware of the generic and transferable skills that they acquire working in this specialized environment.

Both Queen's University and the city of Belfast have a strong theatrical tradition. Students from the university's drama courses are invited to meet the translation students in order to discuss their work and to organize rehearsed readings in the Brian Friel Studio. These readings do not form part of the assessment process, principally because there is no guarantee that all student translations can be presented in this way. But every student in the course does benefit from these readings, both because they constitute theatrical events and because they offer opportunities for feedback from audiences and peers. Local professional actors also join us to share their approaches to a particular text chosen by the class (frequently Lorca), so that students begin to appreciate both the task and the methodologies of the actor. At this final workshop, we discuss the ethics of rehearsal room practice, namely rewrites, negotiated changes, lines of communication, translator-director relationship, and so forth.

Student work is assessed on the basis of a pack of material submitted at the end of the course. This material consists of the 1,500-word translation of a short play or excerpt begun earlier in the semester, a pitch to an imagined director proposing a performance of the translation (1,000 words), and a prefatory essay (3,000 words) that reflects on the translator's process by considering the traditions of playwriting and performance in the source culture as well as those in the Anglophone situation for which the translation is prepared. Students are expected, in other words, to account for their interpretations in terms of these two contexts, developing a concept of equivalence and a sense of theatrical efficacy grounded on research and realized in verbal choices. This account inevitably informs the pitch they devise to appeal to a director.

Ultimately, the course does not pretend to teach translators all they need to know in order to present themselves as seasoned stage translators. It does, however, offer those who take it the opportunity to experience in as much detail as possible the real-world demands of the professional theater environment. Within that context, the ethos that it presents to students is one of continuous professional development, seeking to instill in them the realization that the contingencies of time, space, and individual human agency provide the shifting contexts in which translations for the stage are written. And if that is so, then there is something to learn from each and every new engagement.

12 Teaching Audiovisual Translation

Markus Nornes

Teaching Between the Industry and Research

Audiovisual translation studies has fairly well exploded over the last two decades. The first courses were offered at the University of Lille in the 1980s (Gottlieb 1992: 161), and today departments, programs, and schools around the world specialize in teaching audiovisual translation (AVT), both within and without the academy. Despite these developments, strikingly little discussion has been given to pedagogy. Although one anthology allots a section to the topic, arguably few of its articles really address teaching (Bartrina 2009; Taylor 2009). The fact is that much of the scholarship on media translation amounts to the explication and defense of AVT's peculiar rules to the exclusion of any kind of theory—which is perhaps the reason why the relationship between translation research and AVT remains uneasy.

This situation is particularly regrettable since translation studies enjoys such a marvelous dialogue between theory and practice. Scholars and teachers of most forms of translation, however, do not have the distraction of a complex technical apparatus. The spinning gears and cycling chips of cameras and projectors impose novel space-time limits on the act of AVT. It is in response to the mechanics of capture and presentation—interfaced with the cognitive limits of human perception—that elaborate sets of rules for subtitling have been created to govern how many spaces are allotted to a line depending on the format (16mm, 35mm, 70mm, 3:4 video, 16:9 video, etc.), how many lines are allowed on the frame, where titles start and end in relation to both utterances and edits, how many letters (spaces) are available depending on the temporal length of the subtitle, their color, placement, their font, and more. The rules of dubbing are less severe—and have mainly to do with the issue of voice-lip synchronization—but they can be equally elaborate.

If ever an area of pedagogy cried out for critical theory, this is it. The problem is not simply that AVT is rule-bound: the industry aggressively enforces certain practices, so *regulation* is the regrettable reality for translators the world over. Yet teaching AVT involves far more than instilling the relatively straightforward rules. The question is rather how to submit received wisdom to constant interrogation while training students to translate creatively within industry-enforced stricture—i.e., to accomplish effective translations without getting fired, where "effective" means taking into account the theoretical issues raised by both translation and film.

This chapter describes an undergraduate course that introduces students to the field of AVT, although its basic design could be reformulated in a more sophisticated way for the graduate level. Offered in a large liberal arts college within a major research university in the United States, it attracts students from many different disciplines, including area studies, comparative literature, English, and film and television production. They bring a working knowledge of diverse languages, ranging from French, German, Spanish, and Russian to Cantonese, Japanese, Mandarin, Korean, and even Latin (a pre-med student who translated a scene from Derek Jarman's *Sebastiane* [1976]). None of them arrives in my classroom planning on becoming a translator, although some complete the course intent on exploring that possibility. All of them leave with a new relationship to foreign film.

Technology and Theory

Mastering the complex rules of subtitling and dubbing is necessary, both to find work and to know how to navigate the rules cannily in order to produce as effective a translation as possible. The problem is that AVT is remarkably technical. In the old days, translators were somewhat sheltered from this dimension by professional technicians. In the digital age, however, they must use powerful software packages that demand tens of hours just to attain a basic level of competence. This fact of current working conditions can overpower the learning process, leaving students and teachers little time or energy for addressing more fundamental translation issues such as equivalence and norms, aesthetics and ideology. A translation pedagogy must prevent technical intricacy from interfering with theoretically informed practice.

Corinne Imhauser, who teaches at the Institut Supérieur de Traducteurs et Interprétes in Brussels, offers a useful way to deal with this problem. She argues that introducing students to rules and software on Day One is a mistake that leads to slavish devotion to guidelines and untold hours wasted on the mastery of complex software packages (Imhauser 2009). Her strategy is shrewd: she starts off students with easy-to-use, nonprofessional software that allows for adequate time to discuss the fundamentals of subtitling. Her students begin subtitling, for example, with a simple word processor. Using page breaks, they assign one subtitle to a page and then position the page window just below the window of a media player such as QuickTime. They then manually run the subtitles using an arrow button while the film plays. This approach simultaneously prepares students for jobs at events like film festivals and theatrical performances, where subtitles are often projected manually from software like Microsoft PowerPoint. More importantly, introducing the software and technique can be done in a single sitting, so that the class can devote considerable attention to issues of space, time, elision, and paralinguistics (tone of voice, volume, screen movement, and the like).

My own approach to teaching AVT is similar to Imhauser's. For subtitling, I use freeware hacked by anime fans rather than the more complex professional packages. Students can master the basics of this software in a single class period. For dubbing, my initial exercises merely involve turning down the volume on the classroom video projector for live dubbing. I go further, however, by reserving the first third of the course for basic theories of translation and an introduction to the history of AVT, where we search for lessons for the present from past practices from around the world. This approach provides beginning AVT students with a basic knowledge of the technical issues while equipping them with a set of analytical tools to make them aware of the aesthetic and ideological assumptions on which conventional AVT practices are built.

History/Theory

The course is divided into three units: history/theory, a subtitling practicum, and a dubbing practicum. The first introduces AVT and lays the historical and theoretical groundwork upon which students can become sophisticated translators. The last two parts strive to bring theory to bear on practice through small projects that involve hands-on subtitling and dubbing.

The history/theory unit begins with a discussion of basic concepts in translation theory, using essays by Jerome and Dryden as an initial spring board. Jerome's distinction between sense-for-sense and word-for-word translation and Dryden's distinction between metaphrase, paraphrase, and imitation offer different ways of understanding the relations between concepts of equivalence and verbal strategies. We consider not only the impossibility of establishing a one-to-one correspondence between source and translated texts but also how kinds of correspondence may vary according to the genre of the source text and the function that the translation is intended to perform. These points enable us to see the sorts of pressures that the industrial rules of AVT put on the translator, further complicating equivalence.

We clear the air of prejudices over AVT modes by staging a dubbing versus subtitling debate. Students read articles by film critics like Bosley Crowther who initially wrote about the merits of subtitling but later championed the use of dubbing at the height of the 1950s art cinema (see Nornes 2007: 12–15). The classroom debate itself is triggered by a screening of *Crouching Tiger, Hidden Dragon* (2000), where I shift seamlessly *mid-film* from a 35mm subtitled print to the dubbed Blu-ray disc. *Crouching Tiger, Hidden Dragon* enjoyed a very impressive dubbing that was orchestrated by director Ang Lee and screenwriter James Schamus with English performances by the original actors. Dialogically playing such high-quality dubbing off the standard subtitles, as well as 35mm film against home-video, sets students off balance and constitutes their first baby steps toward scrutinizing their own assumptions and preferences in AVT.

Class then explores a variety of translation and interpretation options through a particularly pleasurable film. Inspired by Michael Cronin's close textual analysis of the representation of translation in the *Stars Wars* trilogies (Cronin 2009: chap. 5), I screen the first film in the series, *Star Wars* (1977), and hold class discussions on how translation is implicated in issues of power and ethics. We develop these issues further with readings in translation theory and commentary. Building on the basic concepts introduced through thinkers like Jerome, I use

Schleiermacher's lecture, "On the Different Methods of Translating," to provoke students to think about the implications of transporting the reader to the linguistic and cultural world of the foreign author or vice-versa. We then explore the elaborations of theorists like Antoine Berman, who locates an ethical imperative in Schleiermacher's idea and argues for translation strategies that show respect for the foreign text and culture. This conceptual trajectory, with the help of Goethe's notion of translation "epochs" linked to specific strategies, is integrated into a history of AVT through my book, *Cinema Babel* (Nornes 2007: 177–9). I draw a distinction between two kinds of AVT: one is called "corrupt," which violently appropriates the source text, forcing it to conform to cultural norms and industrial constraints, but conceals the appropriation and its ideological implications; the other is called "abusive," which experiments with linguistic features to reveal the violence of translation, to critique ideologies at work in corrupt practices, and to direct the viewer to the source text, turning the film into an experience rather than concealment of translation (Nornes 2007: 155–8, 176–87).

Concurrently, students complete three assignments that edge them toward a theoretically informed practice and prepare them for the practicums. The first assignment is titled "What is a 'Successful' Translation?" Students are given a one-page Norwegian comic strip called *Pondus*, chosen because it is unlikely that they will know the language. They use Google Translate or other dictionaries and translation tools to render the text bubbles into English. I use a comic because it is a simple analogue to cinema, with frozen images and no sound. Ignorance of the source language inspires students to read the dialogue carefully against the images, whereby they are forced to recognize a relationship that is key to the specificities of AVT. In class, they break into groups and collaborate on what they judge to be the best translation—as good as they can manage, not knowing Norwegian or the comic itself. In a final discussion with the class a whole, we tease out how the various groups defined a successful translation, especially in light of the theoretical readings.

The *Pondus* strip I use mixes the familiar and the unknown. The characters are clearly discussing Donald Duck and Pluto. The punchline, however, remains obscure, especially without knowledge of the homophobia for which the comic strip is notorious. When this attitude is revealed during a class discussion regarding translation and value, a range of ethical choices comes immediately into view for students—in addition to many other key issues for AVT, such as the relationship between word and image, spatial restrictions, and the like.

The final two exercises of the history/theory unit center on questions that appear simple at first glance but quickly become complex and vexing. The first is titled "What *is* the Source Text?" It is an analytical essay based on two movie clips along with corresponding excerpts from the shooting screenplay (which is easily available through stores in Hollywood such as Larry Edmunds Bookshop: http://larryedmunds.com/). The aim is to challenge the idea—held not only by many students but also by too many AVT scholars—that the spoken dialogue in the source text reflects the presumed intentionality of the characters. Gottlieb (1996: 284) shares this idea, which is why he advocates the teaching of subtitling without scripts. He considers scripts "translatory crutches" that distract students from the purity of the speech act. Christopher Taylor likewise explains that he teaches "from the premise that film scripts are 'written to be spoken as if not written,'" and that "subtitles are, in a sense, 'written to be read as if not written'" (Taylor 2009: 218, 226). These remarks point to a narrow notion of screenwriting, what is usually called the classical continuity style that fosters the realist illusion. There exist countless scripts that are, in Roland Barthes's terms, writerly texts, compelling the reader to construct meaning in a self-conscious way, even when the text is designed for performance before the camera (Barthes 1975: 4). When students are required to use scripts—particularly those that may be slightly different from the onscreen performance—they come to see film dialogue as a written object with layers of mediated authorship, they gain a heightened awareness of the dynamic between writing and performance, and they begin to think of their practice as akin to literary translation and not simply the transfer of naturally spoken utterances.

For this exercise, I use a mess hall scene from Robert Altman's *M*A*S*H* (1970) and the balcony scene from Woody Allen's *Annie Hall* (1977), where English subtitles reveal the inner thoughts of Alvie and Annie as they chat. The former features a typically Altmanesque overlapping of voices, and the latter uses synched visual and aural channels that compete for attention. Both clips lend themselves to theoretical contemplation regarding the production and location of meaning. The assignment is to analyze these paired texts—including the shooting scripts as well as the finished films—so as to describe the challenges they present to the translator, to identify what the source text could possibly be for each, and to imagine possible strategies for both subtitling and dubbing. Most importantly, students must justify their decisions on theoretical grounds using the concepts they have been learning in class.

The third exercise poses the question, "What *is* the Target?" Note that it does not ask about the "target *language*." Students are asked to think about audience and the context of reception. They watch a film clip while reading the script and think about how it would be most effectively translated. I use the famous balcony scene from the 1996 version of *Romeo and Juliet*, featuring Leonardo DiCaprio and Claire Danes. This film is perfect because Shakespeare is always handy for test cases in translation: every student knows the text and has typically studied it at some point in their schooling. Thus many are capable of quite sophisticated analyses. In class, we break into groups, and students collaboratively undertake a translation from *English to English*—from Early Modern English into some other form of the language. They typically choose the language of African Americans, high school students, Southerners, Canadians, five-year-olds, or hard-boiled characters in film noir, among other possibilities. Students in each group bring laptops to class and create a shared Google Doc; as they translate, one student serves as secretary while the others follow their progress live on the document. Upon completion, the class unifies, and each group selects two members to perform their new translation and introduce the problematics they worked through.

This exercise builds on "What *is* the Source Text?" while encouraging students to recognize the complexity of language in comparison to the arid simplicity of conventional subtitling language. The latter assumes a mass, even semi-literate audience no matter what the film may be, so that a subtitled film by Jean-Luc Godard deploys the same English as a Japanese anime. Because most translators of Shakespeare feel a strong sense of debt to the Bard and his distinct language, transforming the original into new forms of English provokes them to consider how all subtitling involves this dynamic. At the same time, the exercise frees students to work in the idiosyncratic language of a specific audience. Their task out in the real world will usually involve the use of a massified target language while hinting at source-text peculiarities for the actual, intended audience of the film.

Practicums

At this point, the course enters its second unit, a subtitling practicum. Each student chooses a five-minute clip that must pose various translation problems. The instructor has a chance to reject proposed scenes that are too straightforward. The unit begins with a short, five-page essay in which students analyze a scene from a film of their choosing. The assignment is framed by a quotation from Antony Shugaar (2014):

> I compare it [translation] to walking down the highway, if ordinary reading is driving at 60 m.p.h. And it seems, sometimes, when you're translating, measuring, and re-creating everything you read in another language, as if you can actually leave the highway and walk off into the landscape. Walk around the trees and buildings and see what's on the other side, how they're constructed.

The analytical essay is the students' chance to walk off that translation highway and leisurely poke around a text. Before they choose a film to analyze, I prepare them with in-class discussions of some challenging scenes from American film and television, such as the chess scene from Season 1 of *The Wire* (2002) with its thick African-American slang, a scene from Elmore Leonard's *Get Shorty* (1995) with its idiosyncratic syntax, and the mind-boggling seminar on astrophysics from Frederick Wiseman's *At Berkeley* (2013).

While students work on their analyses, they are introduced to the subtitling process and its software. They produce two sets of subtitles for the same scene, one rule-bound and conventional and the other experimental—or "corrupt" and "abusive" as theorized in the first unit of the course. Because students are responsible for their respective projects from beginning to end, a tight schedule based on typical professional workflow must be built into the syllabus.

First, students submit a proposal, and after vetting by instructor, they create a movie clip from a DVD using the freeware HandBrake and trimming it with QuickTime. They transcribe all dialogue and produce a full translation, annotating it to explain challenges and propose translation strategies. They begin "spotting" the transcript, using slashes to identify blocks of text that will be converted to individual subtitles. They use the freeware Aegisub to finish spotting by precisely setting the in and out points (or times) for each subtitle. This process results in a spreadsheet they can use to make their two sets of subtitles. Students are required to add a column to each spreadsheet for annotations detailing their translation decisions. At this point, they screen their draft subtitles in class for feedback from their colleagues. Finally, they edit and fine-tune their subtitles and submit the final version to the instructor along with an essay (approximately eight to ten pages) that presents a theoretical reflection on their work—justifying their choices and arguing for either an "abusive" or "corrupt" approach.

The dubbing practicum rounds out the third and last unit of the course, following a structure that is similar to that of the subtitling unit and likewise involving a complex workflow in the syllabus. Dubbing is a more elaborate and collaborative process, so students must work in groups. We begin by choosing five-minute scenes for translation. The groups each elect a producer, who sorts the students into roles: transcriber, translator(s), sound recordist, editor, and voice actors. A clip is created with HandBrake and QuickTime. The freeware Audacity has a "karaoke filter" that allows students to strip dialogue, leaving only sound effects and music. They produce a full, annotated translation and then create an annotated recording script for performance and lip-synch. We rehearse the dubbing in class in order to receive peer feedback for rewriting. At this point, they make a recording of their performances, which is ideally done in a studio so that the soundtrack can be instantly mixed and added to the image track. It could also be accomplished with a digital sound recorder or computer and added with editing software as rudimentary as iMovie. A low-tech version could simply turn down the original sound of a DVD and play a separate recording of the dubbing (this version sacrifices synch but hardly interferes with the learning process). Once finished, the dubbings are screened in class for discussion and peer feedback. Students each writes an essay in which they reflect on the project in theoretical terms (eight to ten pages), along with a separate self-evaluation of their contribution to the teamwork (two pages).

Assessment and Learning Outcomes

At the end of the course, students submit a portfolio of all their work. Because of their multilingual backgrounds, the evaluation rarely involves a vetting process that aims to isolate linguistic errors. Instead I expect conscientious attention to aspects beyond denotative meaning—everything from register to the interaction between speech and the image track—so that the evaluation is based primarily on their annotations and the theoretical reflections. They have plenty to write about because they must produce both abusive and corrupt versions of their clips; the assignment prompt requires that they decide which one is best and support that stance with a theoretically informed argument. Ultimately, I am assessing their ability to take a stance and to argue it. They can champion conventional subtitling, but they must defend it.

I wrap up the course by introducing students to the industry of AVT. After a semester of unfettered exploration of the translation landscape, buildings, and forests off the highway—enjoying a leisurely pace and the freedom to poke around and take chances—this discussion is a regrettably sobering climax to the course.

Students learn about the downsides of the digitization of film translation and the globalization of the industry, such as the electronically delivered genesis files that route all languages through subtitles in standard English. They discover that industrial standards are almost always imposed from without, generally not in favor of the translator or the source text. How to work creatively within the system will be their lifelong challenge. Students feel as if they are being forced to pile into their vehicles and translate down that highway at 60 mph, if not faster.

I teach the *art* of AVT. Too often, audiovisual translation studies focuses on the mechanical semantics of communication, whereas I emphasize the constructedness of moving image media—that it is, in the first instance, a *written* text that begins with a script. If film translation is indeed an art, it would be akin to Nelson Goodman's "allographic" art: that which starts with a scored object, like a symphony or a play, and is incomplete until it is performed (Goodman 1968: 113–15). The job of those performers/translators is to take the original scored text and work within the parameters of the prior object and its rule-bound, materially limited context and apparatus so as to bring it to brilliant completion. The film world is so thoroughly globalized that no film feels complete until it has crossed linguistic frontiers and a translation has been *performed*. Only a pedagogy rejecting a narrow vision of training and inspiring within students a historically informed, theoretically canny practice will achieve an outcome at the level of an art form.

13 Translating a Canonical Author

C. P. Cavafy

Karen Van Dyck

Afterlife

Focusing on a canonical author is an immensely productive way to teach students how to translate by showing them how to base their translation practice on research. The works of Homer, Dante, Proust, Rilke, or Césaire raise the question of reception in relation to many different critical approaches and illustrate many different strategies of translation and adaptation. The very issue of intertextuality that questioned author-centered courses after Roland Barthes's proclamation of the author's death (1977) reinstates them when the emphasis falls on translation. Confronted with a host of retranslations and multimedia adaptations, all bound in myriad relations to the receiving culture, students cannot rely on the intentional fallacy to control the possibility of endless interpretation. Translation, Walter Benjamin (1923a) reminds us, involves the afterlife of the work, not the author's life. Teaching canonical works with attention to the history of their survival enables students to move away from fixed notions of authorship and invention. Translation becomes a hermeneutic practice worthy of study in its own right, where learning how to interpret is indistinguishable from learning how to translate into different media.

These points form the basic rationale of my course on C. P. Cavafy (1863–1933), a poet of the Greek diaspora who lived in Alexandria and profoundly influenced many prose writers, poets, and artists, from E. M. Forster and Marguerite Yourcenar to James Merrill and Duane Michals. Presupposing no knowledge of Greek, the course is taken primarily by upper-level undergraduates in Modern Greek Studies, Comparative Literature, and Gender Studies. Students read widely in English translations of his poetry, but they are also immersed in works inspired by it. The course is organized both chronologically and thematically, according to the issues that have informed his reception. We begin by considering general questions about translation and world literature, devote a series of meetings to Cavafy's thematic preoccupations, and end with case studies based in Britain, Egypt, and America. Cavafy becomes the experimental ground for different practices: translations that inscribe interpretations through styles and discourses; commentary that engages social-historical issues such as diaspora, sexuality, and the postcolonial; and adaptations that reflect the constraints of particular media and the artistic concerns of the adaptors. Translation is thus construed with latitude to encompass various forms of cultural production, interlingual as well as intersemiotic.

Readings

At the first class I distribute a set of materials relating to Cavafy's poem "Ithaka": a printed version of the Greek text, a manuscript version in Cavafy's hand, a printed version with his corrections, and ten different translations, mostly English, but also French and other languages the students may know. Students take turns reading aloud the first three lines. The discussion usually begins with their questions about why certain words and phrases are repeated in the English translations while others are not. Why, they ask, is "Ithaka" spelled with a "k" sometimes and at other times with a "c"? Why does one translator use "pray" and another "hope?" Students wonder whether some words are more translatable than others, but they gradually see that the difference in different translations is rather a sign that translations are interpretations. Variation can point to a crux in the source text, a certain ambiguity or undecidability, but it can also illuminate the role that a translation plays in its own context, its intervention into the receiving culture. Are certain translations more modernist or more classicizing, more feminist or more gay, more English or more American? And this question in turn opens up a larger discussion about how reading translations can contribute to the study of world literature. Even before we review the syllabus, students have begun to grapple with the difficulty of establishing any one text as original or authoritative. They never fail to ask, Which Greek text did the translators translate? Translation is the door that opens this Pandora's box.

We then situate Cavafy scholarship in relation to work in comparative literature and translation studies by addressing three central questions: What is an original? What is world literature? What is translation? These introductory sessions set in motion the contrapuntal relation of primary to secondary sources that continues throughout the course. Students read English versions of Cavafy's poems, essays that examine his work, and theoretical texts. The task is to explore how these forms of writing present different modes of interpretation and supplement or comment on each other, questioning the boundary between primary and secondary. From the start students think about how they are going to intervene in a body of critical literature with their own translations. Later in the semester, as a result, when they have to submit a proposal for their final translation project, the readings and class discussions have equipped them with a catalogue of ways of thinking critically about existing scholarship and translations.

To introduce the question of what is an original, we read Cavafy's poem "In the Month of Hathor" alongside introductions and afterwords by various editors and translators (Keeley and Sherrard 2009: 387–91; Peter Mackridge's introduction in Sachperoglou 2007: xi–xxxix; Yourcenar 1980). The poem describes the difficulty of deciphering an epitaph and, more broadly, the other, whether a lover, a culture, or a historical period. Full of brackets and blanks that create a white space down the center of the page where time has eroded the gravestone, the Greek typography is handled in drastically different ways by different translators, who in effect suggest different originals to the Anglophone reader. Daniel Mendelsohn foregrounds it—"Amidst the erosion I see 'Hi[m] . . . Alexandrian'" (2012: 70)—while Edmund Keeley and Philip Sherrard ignore it. Content rather than the form delivers the message of illegibility in their translation. We then consider Cavafy's idiosyncratic distribution of his poetry as hand-sewn pamphlets containing different poems for different readers (Jusdanis 1987: 58–63), whereby students see that even in the age of mechanical reproduction originals are contested matters. Finally, we observe how the history of Greek epigraphy and textual editing impacts the original by reading David Damrosch (2003: 147–69) on the uncertain transcription of a poem in Egyptian hieroglyphics.

To develop the question of what is world literature, I use Cavafy's prose poem "The Ships" (2010). In this meditation on poetry as translation from the imagination to the page, the passage between place and language is fraught with the challenges of the sea—what is thrown overboard, what is confiscated by customs officials, and what survives the journey. As literature is worlded, it is subjected to historical vicissitudes that intensify the already precarious nature of its existence within national boundaries. We interrogate E. M. Forster's introduction of Cavafy to Anglophone cultures as the Anglicized cosmopolitan (Forster 1983). This interrogation is then deepened with essays by Gayatri Spivak (1983; 2003) that help to frame Cavafy's work and its translation in the terms of comparative literature and postcolonial theory.

For the final introductory question—What is translation?—we read Cavafy's poem "For Ammonis Who Died at 29, in 610," in which a poet is asked to perform an act of translation by pouring his Egyptian feeling into a foreign tongue. We relate it to W. H. Auden's essay on Cavafy in which he insists that "a tone of voice, a personal speech" is "immediately recognizable" in every translation (Dalven 1961: viii). How can a translation possibly communicate the source text in an untroubled manner? We question this fundamentally romantic conceit by pairing Auden with Lawrence Venuti's historicist manifesto, "How to Read a Translation" (Venuti 2013: 109–15). Translation studies, we learn, can show how to read a translation as a transformation, relatively autonomous from the source text. It reveals not only how a belletristic approach to translation is often fixated on the source author but also how the discourse of world literature erases the source text in favor of the forms and practices in which it is circulated.

The course now takes up Cavafy's thematic preoccupations by tracking his development through different periods, from his early, more formalist poems to his prose writing (prose poems, book reviews, journals) to his mature collections and his unpublished and unfinished poems. I pair poems from each period with critical and theoretical essays that reflect a main concern in Cavafy scholarship: poetic craft, biography, eros, the archive, geography, and history. On biography, for example, we examine Cavafy's claim in his poem "Hidden Things" that "from my most unnoticed actions,/my most veiled writing—/from these alone will I be understood" (Keeley and Sherrard 2009: 361). We read his English-language journal of his first trip to Greece against Robert Liddell's biography, mindful of what Kapsalis calls "autobiographical inventions" and what Foucault theorizes as the "author-function" (Cavafy 1982; Foucault 1977; Kapsalis 1983; Liddell 1974). To read psychoanalytically or with a Marxist, feminist, or deconstructive perspective creates different authors. If translation is a form of reading, we ask, can we think of it in terms of translator-functions?

When discussing the importance of geography we look at poems where Cavafy establishes his affinity for a Hellenistic Alexandria in decline. We contrast the claustrophobia of "The City"—"You will always end up in this city./ Don't hope for things elsewhere:/ there is no ship for you, there is no road" (Keeley and Sherrard 2009: 51)—with the upbeat openness of "Ithaka." Notions of translation as an extra-national zone (Apter 2006: 3–22) and as a diasporic practice (Edwards 2003: 1–15) help to complicate Keeley's assumption of Alexandria as a mythic place where the exile returns home to stay, an interpretation that acts as a geographical counterpart to his domesticating translation strategy (Keeley 1996).

On the archive we read about Cavafy's library, collections, and photographs (Haas 1995; Savidis 1964; 1983). To interrogate the collector's obsessive compulsion and connect it to the work of the editor and translator, we read Derrida (1998a) on "archive fever." The pathos of memory and desire in the name of an uncertain posterity, main themes in Cavafy's mature poetry but also problems for collecting and translating, is then critiqued through an examination of the materiality of the poem. We analyze how the fetishism of the archive is replaced by the creative act of refashioning in Cavafy's "Caesarion" when the boy from the history book—after ellipses and a stanza break—suddenly appears in the poet's room. The poem as a caesarean birth on the page undermines nostalgia. Students read my translations of Yannis Ritsos's poems about the contents of Cavafy's study, applying to translation what Ritsos learns about words as objects and their placement on the page.

To study the theme of eros, we read Margaret Alexiou's 1985 essay on the "dangerous drugs" in Cavafy's poetry while considering various queer approaches (Papanikolaou 2005; Sedgwick 2010). Keith Harvey (1998) helps us to think through the cultural and historical specificities of queering Cavafy, especially the Americanness of camp discourse in translation. Yet not every American translator takes this route. Rae Dalven's laconic translations are certainly attributable to a modernist poetics, but might they also harbor vestiges of Victorian prudishness? Why does she choose "covert" (Dalven 1961: 97) instead of "veiled" (Keeley and Sherrard 2009: 361) in her translation of "Hidden Things," "house of depravity" (143) rather than "of ill fame" (Mavrogordato 1951: 164) in "Two Young Men, 23 to 24," "excited ourselves" (94) rather than "aroused" (Keeley and Sherrard 2009: 183; Theoharis 2001: 104) in "To Remain?" But it is Mendelsohn's repeated choice of "boy" to replace "young man" or "ephebe" that establishes a palpable connection to post-Stonewall gay culture, moving us in a very different direction.

In the final part of the course, in anticipation of the students' own presentations, we consider cases of how Cavafy's poetry is reworked in various kinds of media in specific countries. The aim is to trace the similarities and differences among the interlingual translations and the intersemiotic adaptations in different cultural contexts. We map out the history of the strategies deployed by the translators we have so far been discussing, from Mavrogordato and Dalven to Keeley and Sherrard to Theoharis and Mendelsohn, including the poet James Merrill's distinguished versions (Merrill 2001). Students read commentary on the translations (Emmerich 2011; Friar 1978; Ricks 1993), and, taking their cue from these readings as well as our previous discussions, they come to class prepared to analyze the translators' verbal choices. Some students take an extra step to connect a translation to a critical work that cites it, drawing out how translator and critic share or hold competing agendas. Students learn to do the work that commentators for the most part avoid: the actual nitty-gritty reading of a translation as an interpretation.

The adaptations move the course into new areas of research. We examine how Lawrence Durrell integrates translations into his Alexandria-based novel *Justine* (1957), how Auden's poem "Atlantis" adapts Cavafy's "Ithaka," and how homoerotic visual interpretations are constructed in David Hockney's etchings (1967) and in Constantine Giannaris's biopic, *Trojans* (1990). How do different media, we ask, enable different kinds of critiques? The cultural appropriations are probed by pairing specialized articles with theoretical essays. Hala Halim (2013: 56–225) questions the colonial blinders of Cavafy's British legacy, while Vicente Rafael (2009) helps us to conceptualize how differently Cavafy is received in America, the new empire, and how translations navigate the repressive force of American monolingualism. Are adaptations, we ask, less sure than translations of their relation to the source text and therefore more attentive to thematic connections? Why do the poets Joseph Brodsky and Mark Doty title their homages to Cavafy "Near Alexandria" (1992) and *My Alexandria* (1993) respectively? Are American adaptations more insecure about their relation to the source culture than those produced in Britain or in Egypt?

Assignments

Students are assigned activities that help them not only to develop an incisive understanding of the readings in poetry, theory, and criticism but to marshal those readings in devising their own translations. They write weekly responses to various prompts formulated by the instructor, analyze a poem or group of poems that takes up critical preoccupations presented in the readings, and produce a final project that involves translating Cavafy's work into a medium of their own choice, whether linguistic or critical, theatrical or visual.

The prompts are based on the readings, asking students to reflect more deeply on a topic or to complete a pertinent exercise. Which bilingual edition of Cavafy's poetry, they might be asked, is the best to use for the purposes of this course, taking into account the editors' introductions? Other prompts have them comparing the representations of sexuality or the linguistic registers in two or more translations of the same poem, linking their findings to the translators' agendas or historical moments. Students who can work with the Greek texts—and are inclined toward linguistic experiments—might be invited to write a homophonic translation of a poem, reproducing the sound of Greek in English to demonstrate what they learned from Cavafy's intralingual homophonic rhymes. In another exercise, they examine how the homo-iconic counterspace between lovers in Duane Michals' photographs (1978) mirrors the typography of the poems he adapts. Students post their responses before the next class so they can comment on each other's work.

The analytical assignment is designed to compensate for the students' uneven linguistic background by enabling them all to consider the relations between the source texts and the translations. Students without Greek are asked to team up with a Greek speaker whom they use as an informant in order to write their own formal analysis of one of Cavafy's early poems. The collaboration influences the outcome for both Greek and non-Greek speakers, but students are asked to write up their own analyses. Paying particular attention to points of unstable identity and grammatical transgression addressed by Jakobson and Colaclides (1966), Nehamas (1983), and Robinson (1988), students formulate a line-by-line treatment. They read the notes on their chosen poems by Keeley and Sherrard (2009) and by Economou and Deligiorgis (2013), since both discuss the formal features of the source texts. In the end, students learn how to argue an analysis of a translation on the basis of textual evidence and scholarly research.

The final project creates an occasion for students to synthesize the knowledge and skills they have acquired by working with Cavafy's poems and various theoretical and critical materials. They must take a particular interpretation, whether derived from a published critical work or formulated by themselves, and create a translation or adaptation that inscribes it in the source text. Students analyze one or more poems of their own choosing, devise a strategy of translation or adaptation, and then produce their project. They think about how their handling of formal and thematic features might be shaped by various considerations, ranging from Cavafy's idiosyncratic publishing practices to the predominance of irony and multilingualism in his poems to gay translation theories to current debates in comparative literature. They submit an abstract and then give an oral presentation of their project and their goals. Their final submissions include their translation or adaptation of Cavafy's poetry as well as a critical analysis of how their project adopts, challenges, supplements, or ignores dominant preoccupations in Cavafy scholarship. These submissions are evaluated in terms of how effectively they realize and illuminate the hermeneutic project the students set for themselves.

In recent iterations of the course, students developed methods that were innovative as well as conventional. A student examined poems of linguistic excess that treated themes like arrogance and intoxication and translated them into English through a poetics of vanity. Another translated poems into the Klingon language from the television program *Star Trek*, while yet another adapted them—in Japanese—to the classical Japanese dance-drama known as *Kabuki*. The many cues for set design, lighting, and scene blocking in Cavafy's poems inspired a student to create maquettes for theatrical performance. Another took the punctuation and the visual presentation of the poem on the page as the interpretive framework for his translation (Smith 2008). A student without Greek analyzed six different translations of "Ithaka," using tracing paper to create a palimpsestic translation of her own that indicated where the versions coincided and diverged. Arguing against Auden's insistence that Cavafy's "tone of voice" is recognizable in English, the student found that what was most distinctive lay in those moments when the translators dissented rather than agreed.

Canonical authors provide fertile ground in translation courses for a very basic reason: many translations are available to compare. Multiple retranslations enable the reconstruction of a long and rich history of critical reception and translation practice. They tell us about changing literary taste, academic canons, and cultural institutions in the receiving situation even as they highlight the different traditions, interpretations, and evaluations that endow the source text with significance in its originary culture. Because translations, as Jakobson (1959) indicated, can be intralingual, interlingual, and intersemiotic, we can see how they interpret source texts by deploying different strategies (homophonic or semantic, domesticating or foreignizing, modernist or queer) in different media (pictorial, photographic, audiovisual, and musical). They help us to realize, in a particularly compelling way, that the death of the author is the life of the reader, the translator, the adaptor . . . and the work.

14 Translating a Literary Tradition

Modern Arabic Literature

Michelle Hartman

Translating a Tradition: The Contexts of Arabic Literature

No one familiar with Arabic literature considers it a "minor" literary tradition. Indeed the categorization of Arab authors by mainstream English-language publishers as "emerging" or recently discovered "new" voices is profoundly puzzling to anyone familiar with the depth and breadth of literary traditions in Arabic. Nonetheless, to teach Arabic literature in North America and the United Kingdom, all the more so to teach its translation into English, is to work on the margins of both mainstream literary and translation studies. Today all literatures might be considered peripheral in relation to English and to hold a lower place in the global hierarchy of languages and literatures. It is all the more important therefore to highlight the particularities of the relationships between languages and literary traditions when we teach translation. Arabic literature occupies a particularly fraught place in this hierarchy today. It is often considered to be esoteric, "controversial," difficult or simply untranslatable; Arab women writers are frequently invoked or used mainly to offer a peek "behind a veil" or show "us" how people really live "over there" (Hartman 2012).

This chapter describes and reflects upon the teaching of a course on the theory and practice of Arabic–English literary translation. The course's dual focus on theory and practice was developed with a firm commitment to foregrounding the politics of Arabic–English translation. These reflections highlight how the course prepared students to translate this particular literary tradition and to think about their own translation projects in relation to larger contexts. The unequal power relationship between Arabic and English languages and literatures was emphasized throughout the course. My experience teaching the translation of the Arabic literary tradition can be instructive in teaching other literary traditions—many of the strategies and techniques can be adapted or replicated in other contexts. The insights offered here suggest that we can work with students in such courses to develop grounded definitions of translation through teaching a literary tradition so as to bring together theory and history, politics and practice.

Shaping Content and Pedagogy: The Importance of Institutional Locations

This course was taught as a graduate seminar in fall 2010 at the Institute of Islamic Studies at McGill University. It enrolled a combination of graduate students and advanced undergraduates, all of whom had studied Arabic for at least three years and most of whom specialized in Arabic literature, Middle Eastern history or Middle Eastern studies. The fact that this course was offered in an institute that administers a long-standing program in Arabic language and literature as well as a large program in Middle Eastern studies meant that the course could assume a sufficiently advanced level of Arabic for students to undertake a range of translation projects. Most of the students did not have an extensive training in literature, linguistics, or translation studies, although some did.

The graduate level of the seminar allowed for the assignment of a fairly heavy reading load and substantial writing projects (undergraduates had to apply to enroll). Moreover, because of the program in which it was offered, a certain degree of familiarity with the field could be assumed. Only one professor was offering courses in Arabic literature, however, and at the time few other courses in the university were offered in literatures outside of white, Euro-North American traditions. A literary theoretical background that would include the study of how writers and literatures are marginalized within hegemonic Anglo-North American discourses could not be assumed. Course content had to be adjusted accordingly, so students were offered general information and background on Arabic literary traditions as well as basic introductions to postcolonial theoretical approaches and ways in which to understand unequal power dynamics between literary fields. Although few students had previous exposure to practical or theoretical translation studies, the university is situated in an officially French-speaking province in an officially bilingual country, and it uses English as its language of instruction. This means that all students on a daily basis deal with issues of translation, whether or not they have thought about it formally.

Setting Course Goals: Student Preparation

Like most courses that I have taught dealing with Arabic literature, this course was designed knowing the vastly different preparations of the students. The course demanded the ability to read and translate Arabic, but since I was aware of a considerable cohort of undergraduate students with advanced proficiency in Arabic, I sought to accommodate those who wished to develop their skills further. Students were required to have a "good reading knowledge of Arabic," which I set at the equivalent of three years of study. Most enrolled students did have that background. One student had only two years of formal study and struggled with some assignments; three other students were native speakers of Arabic. Not all students were native speakers of English, and I adjusted assignments so that students who wished to do so could translate into French rather than English. One student had strong French and Spanish (in addition to English), and she worked with translations in those two languages. Students with stronger theoretical preparation found that they more easily grasped many of the issues we confronted in the readings. Fluently bilingual (Arabic-English) students found they had more time to concentrate on integrating their theoretical and practical knowledge in assignments. About midway through the semester, I learned that students had set up their own study groups outside of class. These students organized to support each other and compensate for their different levels of preparation, which I thought was an excellent communal learning strategy.

The goals I set for the course took into account that not all the students would be equally fluent readers and writers of both languages. One way in which I addressed this mixed preparation was to closely integrate theoretical and practical discussions through interactive workshops. This allowed those with weaker linguistic skills to focus more on theoretical concerns while improving their Arabic. It was important to me that students be able to explore a full range of issues, no matter their preparation and background. I did not wish the course simply to place a higher value on more advanced linguistic preparation but on how students could work through practical and theoretical issues together.

Developing the Syllabus: Required Readings

In designing the syllabus not only did I strive to seek a balance between stressing theoretical and practical approaches to translation but also among a range of theoretical perspectives. I tried to keep the focus of the course broad, encompassing a range of issues crucial for translating Arabic literary works within a tradition, not as atomized individual works. My goal was to provide an expansive view of the Arabic literary traditions, to give a sense of the works available in English translation, to highlight the problems with existing translations, to tease out the major issues in translating Arabic into English, and then to raise questions about how we as readers, students, translators, scholars and teachers can improve Arabic–English literary translation.

Some of the required readings addressed the diversity of Arabic literary traditions, such as Fedwa Malti-Douglas (1994) on gender and criticism in Arabic literary studies and Amal Amireh's critique (2000) of the reception of Nawal El Saadawi in English. Other readings explored issues of cultural politics in translation studies including Gayatri Spivak's "The Politics of Translation" (1983), Sherry Simon's "The Language of Cultural Difference" (1992), and Maria Tymoczko's "Post-colonial Writing and Literary Translation" (1999). As a main text divided up throughout the semester, I assigned Lawrence Venuti's *The Translator's Invisibility* (1995) in order to give an introduction to the situation of literary translation into English. We also drew out techniques and strategies of translation into English from it, as well as definitions of "domestication," "foreignization," and "resistant translation." This work is important because many articles that address directly the cultural and political problems posed by translating Arabic literature into English refer to and build on Venuti's work directly.

The classic pair of articles by Edward Said (1990) and Hosam Aboul-Ela (2001), which propose Arabic literature as an "embargoed literature," opened the course to set up an understanding of the politicized environment in which translated Arabic texts are received and circulate. We also read Peter Clark's long article (2000) about the history of Arabic-English translation and his reflections on how he has changed his approach. This piece provided a good overview of the range of works translated into English and some of the history of the field. In later classes on pre-Islamic poetry and the Qur'an, we read Issa Boullata's call for resistant translation and André Lefevere's critique of translating pre-Islamic poetry (Boullata 2003; Lefevere 1992: 73–86). In sections that focused on translating women's writing, we read Marilyn Booth's twin articles (2008 and 2010) about the challenges she faced when her translation of *The Girls of Riyadh* was altered by the author and publisher. This was paired with my own piece comparing the flattening transla-tions of Arab women literary figures and their works (2012).

These readings were spread throughout the course and paired with readings of English translations of Arabic literary texts along with the Arabic sources. Stu-dents who were fluent enough in Arabic to read all of both texts were encouraged to do so. Some students read Arabic and English versions of all of the works, including the novels. All students read the English and Arabic versions of short Qur'anic suras (Sells 1999), at least one pre-Islamic poem (Sells 1989), and trans-lations of Yusuf Idris's 1971 short story "House of Flesh" (1971; "Bayt min lahm") by Denys Johnson-Davies and C. Lindley Cross as well as an essay by one of the translators (Cross 2009). We worked together on one collection of poetry, avail-able in a facing page bilingual edition, Mahmoud Darwish's *The Butterfly's Bur-den* (2007). The longer and more sustained analyses of published translations of fiction included four novels, Alexandra Chreiteh's *Always Coca-Cola* (*Da'iman Coca-Cola*), Iman Humaydan's *Wild Mulberries* (*Tut Barri*), Sonallah Ibrahim's *Stealth* (*Al-Lusus*), and Hanan al-Shaykh's *The Story of Zahra* (*Hikayat Zahra*).

This selection of texts may seem eclectic, but it reflects a number of principles as well as the practical matter of connecting readings with my own expertise. In order to underline the breadth of the Arabic literary tradition, I began with several weeks dedicated to pre-Islamic poetry and the Qur'an. This is not to suggest that all courses must start with ancient works but rather to foreground some of the par-ticular and peculiar translation issues that arise in relation to Arabic literature—ancient and modern, religious and secular. Translator Michael Sells has produced some of the most interesting and thoughtful critical work in theorizing Arabic translation, and I also wanted students to work with some of his experimenta-tions with poetry and the Qur'an. It is unusual for students to share any common bases for thinking about Arabic–English translation. An exception are words and phrases connected to religion. The question of how to translate the word "Allah" is exemplary: do you leave it transliterated and emphasize difference or translate it as "God" to underline links to other religions?

This turned out to be a very useful place to start. Students greatly appreciated Sells' fresh ways of expressing classic religious phrases, many of which they had encountered in previous translations of the Qur'an. "In the name of God the Com-passionate, the Caring" is one example. Also successful was the week devoted to Fady Joudah's translation of Mahmoud Darwish's *The Butterfly's Burden*. It struck me as important to emphasize poetry and not focus merely on fiction, my area of interest. This section proved to be too rushed, however, since one poetic text in one week was too little to delve into the particular issues facing poetry in translation. My choice of novels was dictated partly by the opportunity to invite the translator of Sonallah Ibrahim's *Stealth* to class. Students prepared a detailed analysis of his translation and interviewed him in a productive session. The three other novels are all very different in terms of language, genre, and themes, but all were written by Lebanese women, and I translated two of them. The focus on these works enabled me to share my perspectives and self-critiques as a translator as the students were producing and critiquing their own translations. While I feel that they did benefit from my modeling of self-critique, it proved very difficult to encourage them to critique my work. Only the graduate students, whom I knew very well and who were very comfortable with me, engaged in a—very polite—questioning of some of my translation choices.

The pairing of these texts with theoretical readings in order to explore issues and debates in translation studies worked very well. This approach provided frameworks through which students could focus their analyses and critiques of translations. Class time was devoted partly to a discussion of readings, partly to the critique and discussion of translations. Some classes were devoted to workshops, practical sessions in which translation strategies and verbal choices were discussed and debated. In these sessions, we read sections of published translations that students had analyzed at home and discussed them in small groups and as a class.

As the class progressed and students had more theoretical terminology and concepts with which to work, their analyses grew in sophistication. They would question if translators used foreignizing or domesticating strategies, for example, and were encouraged to define concretely what these strategies were. This included a discussion of overall structure, packaging and marketing, and major changes in the texts—including censorship of passages, changes to titles, chapters, reordering of the book, and so on—as well as word choices. Partly because of the focus of critical articles on Arabic literature, partly because of the particular political position of Arabic literature in English-speaking contexts in the twenty-first century, students were very interested in whether different texts could be defined as "resistant translations" or not (cf. Venuti 1995: 12, 18–19, 32). I encouraged students to think about how and why different kinds of texts might engage with this label. Another concept that proved to be very useful was drawn out of Spivak's article, and we devoted considerable discussion to investigating translations for "traces of intimacy," as she defines them (Spivak 1983: 313, 316, 319). Some of our most productive conversations were generated by students in relation to thinking through these terms of analysis defined in readings but connected to actual examples from translated texts.

The best class discussion, in my opinion, was a debate about glossaries. Students generated this conversation out of what had become to them the increasingly familiar concept of bringing "the text to the reader" or "the reader to the text" drawn from Friedrich Schleiermacher's lecture on the different methods of translating. The case study was my translation of Iman Humaydan's *Wild Mulberries*, which included translator's notes as a sort of compromise glossary. Students took divergent opinions and argued them forcefully. Some said that such techniques increase the readership of Arabic literature in English, a worthy goal.

Others powerfully argued that novels should be left as novels and not explained to English-language readers, who can take on the task of understanding Arabic words, Googling those they don't know.

Developing the Syllabus: Assignments

The assignments emphasized practical elements of translation with an eye to integrating theoretical discourses. They were also made somewhat flexible to account for the mixed preparation of students in the course. The major assignment, consisting of three papers, was cumulative. The first two were constructed as short projects, while the third, a research paper, required components that were typical of graduate seminars in our institute. For the first project students were asked to analyze a published (or unpublished) translation of any work of Arabic literature in a 4,000-word essay. They were encouraged to choose a text that matched their interests and linguistic ability in terms of complexity, length, genre, and so on. They were to use the terms of analysis discussed in class and developed through theoretical readings to produce this analysis. They developed their own criteria for analysis and were required to lay it out clearly in their paper. The second project was an essay of the same length that analyzed the students' own translation of a work of Arabic literature, which had to be submitted together with the essay. They could use the same piece of writing they analyzed in the first project and translate it themselves or change to a different source text. I wanted to give students an opportunity to change their text and focus if they were not satisfied with their initial choice. They could choose something previously untranslated or work on a text with a published translation. They handed in both the translation and the analysis in which they detailed their proposed theory of translation, why and how they chose it, how they implemented it, and whether they felt it was successful.

These two projects proved extremely productive. The majority of students took them very seriously and produced excellent, thoughtful work. I therefore encouraged students to use the final research paper to expand on the second project—combining it with the first when relevant—and produce a long paper that would include references to theoretical approaches to translation, situating their text in the context of the Arabic literary tradition and so on. Because this was not required from the beginning of the class, students who wished to write a final research paper focused in another direction were also allowed to do so. About half of the students chose to expand their second paper (and at times together with their first paper). Several who did not wish to include their translation work expanded only the first paper. The remaining several students produced papers structured differently.

The projects definitely exposed disparities in the linguistic preparation of students. Though they were designed with this in mind, students with weaker linguistic skills felt that the translating was extremely time consuming and that their ability to reflect on their practice was hindered because of time constraints working with language. Although they were encouraged to choose pieces to translate that were shorter or longer depending on their abilities, this did not always mean that they did so. To improve the assignments for this course, I would further specify that the final assignment should necessarily build on the previous ones and I would spend more time workshopping the translations the students produced together during class time. Perhaps formalizing what students did on their own—forming study groups where they could support each other—would also be an effective way to help improve the completion of the assignments. The translation project itself could be longer if more of their work was dedicated to it.

The different kinds of assignments are evaluated using different criteria. Critiques of translations, whether focused on the students' own work or that of others, are expected to employ successful argumentation that draws on theoretical concepts from readings, research, and class discussions. Not only must the critical terms be defined clearly (i.e., domestication, foreignization, resistant translation, and so on), but the relevance of these terms to the translation must be established through a textual analysis that weighs the relative merits of different translation choices. In assessing translations, creativity and innovation are two important evaluative criteria. If students attempt creative solutions to difficult translation problems, such as humor, idiomatic expressions, and tense agreement between Arabic and English, they earn points, especially when they can make a case in their critical reflections.

Towards a Definition of Translation: Theory, Practice, and Politics

The overall goal of this course is to advance a theory of translation to be implemented in practice, where both the theoretical concepts and practical strategies are rooted in a deep understanding of the cultural and political contexts of a particular literary tradition—here Arabic literature. The course is designed to enable students to develop this theory on their own, both individually—in their written work—and also collectively—in the classroom space, where the group's insights are brought to bear on individual translation work. By producing close readings of literary texts in translation together with the original texts, developing their own translations of these same texts (and others), and critiquing both in class time dedicated to workshops, students are encouraged to develop their theoretical positions through practice. By assigning theoretical, critical, and literary historical readings in every class, their practice is always connected to larger concepts. The inextricable links between theory and practice were not only articulated in the abstract but also continually demonstrated to the students. The definition of translation developed by this course was therefore rooted in these links and also an engagement with the political, cultural, and social position of Arabic literature in English translation.

By focusing the course on translating a tradition—and defining it as such—the position of Arabic literature vis-à-vis English becomes more transparent. Like all other literary traditions today, Arabic literature finds itself in a minoritized position as it travels into English. Unlike most other traditions, the position of Arabic literature is one that is simultaneously desired and reviled. It has been contending with gross stereotypes, dramatic misunderstandings and egregious mistranslations since it was first translated, long before September 11, 2001. The course's focus on Arabic as a literary tradition therefore de-emphasizes individual moments of translation as existing divorced from other realities. It prods students to grapple with the notion that translation is not just about finding "the right answer" or the perfect equivalence between words or phrases. A historically and politically situated approach like this one emphasizes that some translations might be "better" at a given time, in a given context, and others at another. The larger historical and political frameworks provided helps to explain this. The course therefore also emphasizes the complexities of the rhetoricity and language of the source text in conjunction with the complexities of reception contexts. Exploring all of these connections, particularly those between theory, practice, and politics, suggests possibilities for teaching the English-language translation of a marginalized literary tradition like Arabic.

Part III

Studying Translation Theory, History, and Practice

15 Translation Theory in a Translator Training Program

Anne Malena and Lynn Penrod

This chapter describes an introductory course in an undergraduate program offering a Certificate in Translation Studies. Designed to complement the various language-specific courses where students actually learn how to translate (between English and several languages, Asian as well as European), this course familiarizes them with the process of translation as well as the basic theoretical issues associated with it. The integration of theory and practice is its primary focus. The foundation for the approach taken here is the notion of equivalence, which is studied at different levels, from lexical to pragmatic, and in relation to various text types, including advertisements, prose fiction, children's literature, poetry, memoirs, and journalism.

Two basic texts are required for this course: Mona Baker's *In Other Words* (2011), which relies on systemic-functional linguistics and pragmatics, and Douglas Robinson's *Becoming a Translator* (2012), which surveys translation theories as well as the translation profession, constructing an image of the translation process as simultaneously deliberate and intuitive. Other materials are supplied to students through online links and selected video clips. Although our institutional site is a Canadian university, the course is taught in English. Students must have achieved an intermediate-level competency in at least one other language in order to enroll. The range of other languages varies from year to year for students taking the course as an elective, but certificate students, for whom the course is required, are all enrolled in language-specific translation courses as well.

We start with an introduction to perspectives on translation, a historical overview of translation both as an academic field and as a profession, effectively providing students with an appropriate context for the course. Salient trends are presented and illustrative in-class exercises are assigned. Starting with brief mentions of Cicero and Jerome to explain the long-standing debate about literal versus free translation and moving on to a discussion of the map of the field drawn by James Holmes (Toury 1995: 4), we challenge students to reflect on the link between translation theory and practice. Since most of them still have little knowledge of the skills required to become translators, we ask that they consider the person at the center of the activity of translation—the translator. This focus helps them to identify themselves as future translators and to grasp the idea that theory emerges from practice and that, in spite of the division of labor suggested by

Holmes between "pure" and "applied" translation studies, translators need to be aware of the "pure descriptive" side of things, mindful of what (text type), where (culture), when (period and timeline), why (function), and for whom (client and targeted audience) they translate.

To anchor these points in practice, we set two relatively simple exercises. The first is the intralingual translation of a short British text into North American English, which usually generates extensive discussion of regional dialects of English, British, Canadian, and American. The second exercise is the analysis of one sequence from the comic strip *One Big Happy* where the main character, Ruthie, asks her friend Fatima about what she was saying to her mother, since Ruthie had not understood the conversation. When Fatima answers that she had been speaking Farsi, Ruthie responds: "No, I *don't* see! I understand how you could *look* far but not *speak* far!" (emphasis in the original). This exercise forces students to reconsider the meanings of words. As they grapple with explaining the joke, they realize that they may be lacking adequate conceptual terms to make it clear. Once they learn that Ruthie's error is based on her wrong interpretation of morphemes, they understand the need for translators to develop sophisticated linguistic skills.

These exercises prepare students for Baker's discussion of equivalence "at" and "beyond" the word level, in which she introduces several linguistic categories: dialect, collocation, morphemes, and lexical meaning (Baker 2011: chaps. 2 and 3). Baker identifies four types of meaning that are deployed throughout the course: (1) propositional, or meaning found in a dictionary; (2) expressive, which cannot be judged as true or false and reflects the speaker's attitude; (3) presupposed, which "arises from co-occurrence restrictions," either selectional (i.e., a dog cannot be studious), or collocational (i.e., teeth are "brushed" in English but "washed" in Polish); and (4) evoked, which arises from dialect (geographical, temporal, social) and register (field, tenor, mode) (Baker 2011: 11–15). Students now have a few tools to analyze issues of nonequivalence.

At this stage, we aim to develop their skills in semiotic analysis by using a rich corpus of advertisements. We ask that they first analyze a given ad by referring explicitly to Baker's categories and terminology; we then ask that they imagine having to translate the ad into another language and explain where and why they detect instances of nonequivalence and how they might deal with them. Typically ads for beauty products include images of mostly white and beautiful young women with poetic captions, a goldmine for the kind of analysis that we require. Car ads, particularly those produced by Volkswagen, are also excellent material for budding semioticians (see http://www.greatvwads.com for vintage ads). Images of vehicles are linked to witty captions, such as an upside-down Beetle and the question, "Will we ever kill the bug?" along with a 142-word text. Neither native nor non-native speakers of English may have ever had occasion to consider the polysemy of the word "bug" or the metaphorical possibilities of the verb "to kill." Students are asked to identify examples of the different types of meaning, to discuss examples of terms that are register-specific (the field is advertising, the tenor semi-formal, and the mode the ad itself) or dialect-specific (North American, twentieth-century, middle class), and then to analyze at least two common problems of nonequivalence.

Baker lists problems of nonequivalence and strategies to deal with them, accompanied by numerous examples from different languages (Baker 2011: 15–44). Most advertisements are steeped in culture, and students quickly recognize this fact as the main problem they must face. They will have to choose different terms for dialect-specific examples, depending on the target culture for which they imagine themselves translating the Volkswagen ad. If the target language is French, the target culture may be Québécois or French, but it can just as easily be African, Caribbean, or Asian. The point is not to come up with a correct translation but to present a cogent argument for why "bug" is better rendered as "coccinelle" than "insecte," "petite bête," "bestiole" (familiar), or even "bibite" (Québécois and familiar), all of which may be listed as equivalents of "insect" and first entries for "bug" in an online dictionary.

This type of activity works best in small groups composed of students working in the same language and later reporting to the entire class. Whether we assign translation exercises (some from Baker, others from Robinson, and still others from books in the Routledge *Thinking Translation* series) or scenarios designed for students to apply newly learned theoretical concepts, this method ensures a learner-centered constructivist approach (Kiraly 2000; Vygotsky 1978). We particularly favor the idea of reverse scaffolding: removing the teacher's safety net piece by piece as students' learning moves through the novice, intermediary, and expert stages. For example, when introducing new concepts, we may first assign brief practical exercises to give students the opportunity to discover translation-related issues on their own. To introduce Baker's chapter on collocations, idioms, and fixed expressions, we start by asking students to think of an idiom in English in order to translate it. Interestingly, they often have no idea of what constitutes an idiom, and group discussion aims at a definition with our and Baker's help. In this case, forming multilingual groups also works well, so that when students come to translate the idiom, they share information about equivalents or lack thereof in several languages. Students typically delight in finding out that we have an English frog in our throat but a French *chat* (cat) in our *gorge* (throat), or that the moon is feminine in French but masculine in German. Discussions often become very animated, and students in each group enjoy sharing these cultural vagaries. In this way, over the course of the term, students deepen their understanding of both source and target languages while gaining confidence in their ability to translate.

At this point, we introduce students to concepts about translation studies from a slightly different perspective. Robinson's introduction to theory and practice develops an approach that combines intuitive discovery with reasoned analysis, treating such topics as the kinds of cultural knowledge translators should have, useful theoretical discourses for understanding translation practices, and various practical matters of concern to translators such as contracting for projects and meeting deadlines.

One of the very interesting facets of Robinson's work is to allow students to discover what their own particular style of translating might be. Students learn the differences between internal and external learning and explore various ways in which the translator must be a learner as well as the ways in which this kind of learning occurs. Again group work is important here, and students often report on evaluation forms that Robinson's exercises have been easily extrapolated into their other courses. Translators' learning styles are dependent upon various kinds of intelligence: musical, spatial, bodily-kinesthetic, personal/emotional, logical/ mathematical, and linguistic. Students are quick to sense their own dominant styles, and they discover that working with someone else, whether as a partner or in a larger group, is helpful when translation problems occur (Robinson 2012: 56). They also appreciate exploring the importance of the physical and social environment in which they do their work. An effective exercise drawn from Robinson is to have students choose a fairly simple process (using an ATM, boiling an egg, parking a car), divide into groups, come up with different ways of presenting or teaching it in another language, and then translate it into that language. What kinds of problems does the translator encounter? How do different learning styles and different environments affect the translation process or the final product?

Potential answers to these questions can be explored by discussing a few practical aspects of the profession and the dual nature of the translator as both a professional and a constant learner. Borrowing from Karl Weick and Charles Sanders Peirce, Robinson conceptualizes the translator as "a *professional* for whom complex mental processes have become second nature" and "a *learner* who must constantly face and solve new problems in conscious analytical ways" (Robinson 2012: 94). This view reinforces the cyclical characteristic of translation practice and encourages students to start developing their own strategies. In Robinson's view, the cycle consists in three stages: translate; edit; sublimate. Robinson's model is very effective since he uses language that students can easily relate to and understand: (1) translate: "act; jump into the text feet first; translate intuitively"; (2) edit: "let yourself feel the tension between intuitive certainty and cognitive doubt"; (3) sublimate: "internalize what you've learned through this give-and-take process for later use; make it second nature; make it part of your intuitive repertoire" (Robinson 2012: 102–3). To link practice to theory, we ask students to translate a short paragraph individually and to keep track of those three stages as they work. As they report back to the class, it becomes evident that multiple iterations of the cycle are required for them to feel that their working pattern is becoming second nature.

Now that students have a better understanding of the translator as perpetual learner, we turn to the translator as professional. The emphasis is placed on concepts of external or internal knowledge, the social networks translators operate within, and the habits of translators. An exercise adapted from Robinson consists in asking students to form groups of three—a translator, an agent, and a client— and to create a scenario in which the client contacts the agent about a job, the agent communicates with the translator, and then the agent reports back to the client. An added twist to this exercise works wonders in stimulating students' imaginations as well as helping them forget their inhibitions: they have the choice of playing these roles either with professional politeness or rudely, with expected results. The skits they then present in class demonstrate how well they have absorbed the concepts presented by Robinson.

For the sake of keeping with the integration of theory and practice, as the alternation between Robinson and Baker demonstrates, we then return to Baker and introduce grammatical equivalence (chap. 4). By now students have become accustomed to discussing the differences between languages, and they quickly grasp the importance of developing a common language to do so. For students who may not have truly confronted grammatical issues in their formal education until they begin learning a second (or third) language, the study of grammar provides the necessary building blocks for students to produce translations respectful of categories of person, number, gender, tense, aspect, and voice. They discover that these categories carry meaning and that translating without regard for grammatical variance runs the risk of producing nonsense. To illustrate this point, we use an international translation blooper (http://www.jnweb.com/funny/ translation.html): "It is forbidden to enter a woman even a foreigner if dressed as a man" (found in a Bangkok temple). Groups of students working to explain the syntactical problems in this sentence have also launched into lively discussions about Thai culture and more specifically gender and religious issues. They question whether the source-text phrase means that women are never allowed to enter the temple or whether it means that all women wishing to enter are required to wear female garb. This ambiguity will most likely be impossible to maintain in the target text. The example provides an occasion to point out that grammar is necessary to express lived experience.

Before introducing the topic of textual equivalence in Baker's subsequent chapters, we turn to Michael Apted's film *Nell* (1994) for an exploration of translation beyond the written text. The film, based on Mark Handley's play *Idioglossia* (1992), portrays the true story of a young woman who was raised in isolation in the mountainous backwoods of North Carolina and appears to have developed her own personal language. Her situation offers students of translation the opportunity to consider issues of equivalence when dealing with an unknown language in an unfamiliar setting: the two doctors observing Nell are like anthropologists attempting to make sense of a language and culture reduced to a set of signs that they need to organize so as to produce meaning. As students watch selected clips, they do the same, picking up clues from Nell's speech but also from her behavior and surroundings. These clues include her fear of strangers and of daylight and the Bible where her mother left a note about her identity.

Before solutions are offered in the film, we show an early scene with English subtitles. The language Nell speaks is actually a deformation of English, which is explained by the fact that she has been raised with no human contact except her twin sister, who died at a very young age, and her mother, who had a speech impediment caused by a stroke that paralyzed the left side of her face. The sole book in the remote family cabin was a Bible, so Nell's language consists of elements of idioglossia, Bible verses, and mispronounced English vocabulary. Some students usually make these inferences fairly quickly. We then show the same scene with Spanish subtitles and, freezing the screen, we all work together to see what the translators have done. For example, Nell's lines, "Ga'inja / Fo'tye Maw waw wi'a law / [. . .] / An Maw a leess'a Nell, Maw say . . ./ 'Af'ah done go, ga'inja come,'" are rendered into standard English as "Guardian angel / Before Ma went with the lord / [. . .] / and Ma taught Nell, Ma said . . ./ 'After I'm gone, a guardian angel will come.'" The Spanish version, however, is the following: "ange'gua /

Pa tiem Mau ana co Dio / [. . .] / Ma lisa Nell. Ma dis: / 'Desés hiso adó, ange'gua llega.'" In both cases, the translators have represented Nell's speech by adhering to the proper, albeit simplified, syntax and favoring familiar and truncated forms, although the Spanish version is closer to the soundtrack. Through this activity students learn about the difficulties in transcribing oral speech, interpreting an obscure idiolect, and evaluating its translation into Spanish. The case also illustrates Roman Jakobson's categories of intralingual, interlingual, and intersemiotic translation, which we briefly introduce early in the course (1959: 127).

We now take up the text as the unit of translation by considering the concepts of theme (topic) and rheme (comment on the topic) as well as pragmatic equivalence, including cohesion (connections between actual words and expressions in a text) and coherence (conceptual relations) (Baker 2011: chaps. 5–7). Baker bases her explanation of thematic analysis on the Hallidayan linguistic model for "illuminating certain areas of discourse organization," although she is careful to point out that it does not work for all languages (Baker 2011: 139). Thanks to her many examples, students quickly recognize the importance of selecting thematic elements from any text. In our own language-specific teaching practice, for example, we have often found that students do not always fully understand the French source text we have assigned for translation. The tools offered by Baker are therefore quite helpful in convincing them that they first need to analyze the information structure of the text, thereby understanding the thematic links that punctuate it, before they attempt to translate. In addition, once they have understood the main syntactical elements of the clause—subject, predicate, object, complement, and adjunct—they are ready to confront cohesion issues.

Once notions of cohesion have been assimilated, we move to the more difficult concept of lexical chains by explaining that, according to the Hallidayan model, there are "two main categories of lexical cohesion: reiteration and collocation" (Baker 2011: 211). Reiteration may proceed with the repetition of an earlier item, or using a synonym, a superordinate, or a general word. For example, the boy is swimming, where "boy" might be replaced with "lad," "child," or "athlete." Collocation, already familiar to students, includes opposites (e.g. boy/girl), an association of words from the same ordered series (e.g. Tuesday/Thursday), and metonymic associations from an unordered series (e.g. car/brake; mouth/chin; red/green) (Baker 2011). Students are then asked to work on Baker's example of lexical cohesion, an excerpt from the text titled *A Hero from Zero*, by first asking themselves what type of text it is, what the theme is, and what words are likely candidates for lexical cohesion. For this exercise, students are expected to select examples of the categories and explain both how these items are connected and how they form lexical chains. Slides of a color-coded and annotated version of the text can then be posted and discussed during the lecture. We follow this in-class exercise with a take-home assignment, an analysis of the entry on Martin Luther in the *Encyclopedia Britannica*, which also serves as preparation for the discussion of coherence.

Before students read Baker's chapter on pragmatic equivalence, we find it helpful to introduce them to Jakobson's model of communication in order to provide a few more tools of semiotic analysis and to assist in their interpretation of the conceptual relations of coherence (Jakobson 1960). Indeed, students need to figure out how a source text makes sense before attempting its translation. Learning the elements of communication and their related functions—context (referential), message (poetic), addresser (expressive), addressee (conative), contact (phatic), code (metalingual)—ties in with pragmatic equivalence and points to the translator as reader. This communicative model is particularly helpful in enabling a more sophisticated analysis of advertisements. When students become adept at interpreting the source text, they understand the need to scrutinize their target text with the same care. They practice these skills through more in-class exercises involving the analysis of advertisements and the translation of captions, which are then peer evaluated.

Baker's presentation of Paul Grice's cooperative principle and implicature (Baker 2011: 234–9) follows. Students enjoy learning how to read what is not said as we proceed with simple examples of the type, "I failed the exam. I have other career plans." Group discussions help them to grasp what implicature entails, to detect irony, and to think of ways to maintain it in translation. We talk at length about conventional rules that implied meaning does not always respect as well as about conversational maxims (quantity, quality, relevance, manner) that are so often flouted. We conclude with translation strategies that students can deploy when encountering these issues of coherence. We do point out, however, that according to Baker the co-operative principle is universal while implied meaning and maxims may be culturally bound.

Throughout the course students have the option of making use of the volumes in the Routledge *Thinking Translation* series (see, for example, Haywood, Thompson, and Hervey 2009). These books, listed in the syllabus as recommended texts, are useful to students in their language-specific translation courses as well. The French, German, Italian, and Spanish texts follow the same model, while the Chinese, Japanese, and Russian texts develop their own. Except for the Russian, they all contain a very useful table of "Schema of Textual Matrices" or "Filters," which we post on the course website and discuss in class. This schema provides a list of "questions to ask about the text" concerning genre, significant cultural markers, formal and semantic features, and instances of linguistic variation, and each of the categories refers to specific chapters that deals with them. In class, we have students work on exercises drawn from the books across languages— exercises in "gist translation," "translation loss," and "dialect, sociolect, and code-switching"—and report back to the whole group. We guide the discussion by relating the issues emerging from this activity as much as possible to Robinson and Baker. Even when working on exercises with slightly different objectives, students from all groups can profit from the general discussion.

We have found this course to be popular: the enrollment often exceeds sixty students, many of whom are not seeking the certificate and so just take the course as an elective. It provides a strong impetus to language students to continue their study of translation while sensitizing them to the critical importance of translation studies across disciplinary boundaries.

16 Translation Theory in a Comparative Literature Department

Jane O. Newman

Teaching Translation in/as Comparative Literature

Debates about translation track well with the historical evolution of comparative literature, especially in the United States, as the early reports of the American Comparative Literature Association (ACLA) make clear (Bernheimer 1995: 21–48). Emily Apter in fact declares questions of translatability to be at the "theoretical fulcrum" of the discipline (Apter 2013: 3–4). It thus made sense that in 2002, in coordination with the opening of the International Center for Writing and Translation at the University of California at Irvine (UCI), the doctoral program in the Department of Comparative Literature launched its emphasis in Translation Studies and Literary Translation. Nationwide, the field of comparative literature was undergoing a major shift in a genuinely global direction at the time (Saussy 2006a). The intersection of translation studies with both traditional critical theory *and* postcolonial theory and globalization studies, on the one hand, and the fact that translation theory and practice always already pay close attention to the traditional staples of comparative literary study, such as close reading and literary history, on the other, made the founding of a translation emphasis within a doctoral program in comparative literature a timely event.

While UCI's emphasis is housed in what is now the Department of Comparative Literature, it is open to students from all departments in the humanities division. Students take five courses: one seminar in "Theories of Translation"; two "Translation Workshops," which focus on the methodologies and practice of translation; one independent study, in which the student produces an extensive translation of a single work or group of related works, into English or another language in which our faculty have expertise (the project is required to relate in some way to the student's specific field of interest and thus functions as a preliminary step in the conceptualization of the dissertation); and one course in the student's major-focus language. A portion of the doctoral qualifying examination addresses the theory and practice of translation, and the student's dissertation consists of either an independent translation project or a thesis on theories of translation.

The seminar in "Theories of Translation" described below is offered annually. For the theoretical readings, students post a substantial commentary on an online message board before each session. They also submit a series of translating exercises that include preparing a standard trot of a text along with a more polished translation and then retranslating this translation into both a current standard dialect of English and a "minoritizing" dialect (Venuti 1998: 11). These exercises, which are presented to the seminar twice during the quarter, culminate in a final project: a fifteen-to-twenty-page translation accompanied by an introductory essay that discusses the student's practice in relation to at least five theoretical texts. For example, Ivory Coast novelist Ahmadou Kourouma's *Allah n'est pas obligé* (2000; *Allah is not Obliged*), a narrative about tribal wars in West Africa against the background of decolonization, led the student to draw on postcolonial theory and address the question of the "thickness" of translation (Appiah 1993) in order to consider what kind of English might best render Kourouma's creolized forms of French. The student opted for a form of hip-hop-identified Black English as a way of capturing the oppositional point of view of the youthful protagonist, a child soldier. Because the translation projects require excellent control of two languages, successful completion of the final project fulfills one of two language requirements for the comparative literature PhD.

The Seminar

The governing thesis of this course is that translation is central to comparative literature, a field that has long displayed a proclivity for crossing borders of all sorts. Indeed, there could be no "comparative" literature without mapping the spaces between languages and cultures, nationalities and traditions, and diverse media and discursive forms. Studying translation *theory* in particular allows a specific set of questions to emerge about the states(s) of Theory in the United States academy as those questions have come to occupy the discipline, including the conundrum of what "Theory" actually is, given that many of the assigned readings, traditionally designated as "theoretical," are based on arguments from specific examples of translation (e.g. Chow 1995; Deleuze and Guattari 1986; Derrida 1998b; Spivak 2005; Venuti 1998). Participants in the seminar often hail from a broad range of departments (classics, comparative literature, East Asian languages and literatures, English, French, and Spanish), and this diversity is a real asset since it requires the translation of different disciplinary assumptions into common terms. Often the students either are or seek to become published translators. These experiences and goals make for a productive awareness of the boundedness of a specifically academic set of questions about translation, on the one hand, and a sensitivity to the impact of the pressures of the nonacademic publishing industry on translation, on the other.

The course begins with two weeks of introductory readings. The first week (Peden 1989; Reiss 1981; Venuti 1998) introduces students to the basic vocabulary of translation theory and examines the recent history and evolution of the debates. Key issues here include the relation between source and target language and text, the aptness of various kinds of translation theory to a variety of "text types" (Reiss), and the generalizability of discussions of translation from written to oral works. This series of readings allows students to understand the factors that shape both the historiography and geography of the field. "Violence" in translating, for example, emerges as differentially valued over time, from Peden's endorsement of creatively "destructive" (134) forms of translation in 1989 to Venuti's concern ten years later about the inevitable "institutional exploitation of foreign texts and cultures" (4). (By 2006, the violence of translation had come to be associated with ever more literal "war zones" [Apter 2006: xi]). These diverging assessments of the intervention that translation occasions in the source text, empowering versus disempowering, allow the students to observe the embeddedness of the respective generations of translation theory in the sociopolitically inflected academic discourses and worldly realities of their times. Likewise, the several ways in which the relationship between the authority of the source-text author and the authority of the translator is described in this series of texts reflect the different degrees of sensitivity to power relations in the creation of agency and voice that emerged in academic thinking beginning in the late 1980s. Usually associated with gender and ethnic identity construction, the association of these categories also with the work of translation signals the integration of translation theory into these same late twentieth- and early twenty-first-century debates as they have become central to comparative study.

In the second week, we take the question of the often contextually influenced dynamics of the more recent history of translation theory and apply it to a longer time frame, juxtaposing what has come to be considered a tradition of ancient "Western" "foundational" texts from Cicero, Augustine, Luther, and Dryden to equally as "foundational" but more modern postmodern and postcolonial texts, including Schleiermacher, Nietzsche, Benjamin, Jakobson, and Derrida (Robinson 1997a; Schulte and Biguenet 1992; Venuti 2012b). Along with these two sets of texts, we read two essays by Burke (2007) and Spivak (2005) to pose the question of how various conventions of geography and time, on the one hand, and directional logics, on the other, can shape (and limit) the way that the history of translation theory is told. Reading Burke's examination of translations from the "modern" vernaculars into Latin in the early modern period against Spivak's critique of the (post) modern hegemonies of always already "translating into English" makes it possible to understand the sometimes unexamined philosophies of history implicit in many recent claims, where it has become axiomatic that translating ought to move from homogenizing and standardized forms of ancient (or even modern) languages such as Latin or English into the celebration of a heterogeneous plurality of often hybridized modern (and postmodern) ones. Such assumptions overlook the heterogeneity and creolized forms of Latin (and English) that were more often the norm than the exception in earlier periods, making it difficult to recognize that there may have been times when it was forward-looking, even revolutionary, to reverse the process by translating diverse languages into a more universal tongue. Thus Burke (2007: 70) discusses the case of Protestant Reformers in Italy translating potentially subversive texts from their vernaculars into Latin for wider distribution.

The Burke-Spivak juxtaposition is a useful frame within which to assess this week's other readings, which include selections from the canon of foundational texts of translation theory that has emerged and been made available in anthologized form. Similar chronologies and directional logics often inform the ways in which anthologies are put together, when they always already move from "old fashioned" Western and "ancient" to more recent "progressive" ones that "provincialize Europe" (Chakrabarty 2000). In the process, crucial areas of translation theory derived from older European traditions, such as the focus on the relation between sacred and human languages, are too easily left behind. Recalling the religious vocabularies of immanent or transcendent meaning and the attractions of linguistic sameness or notionally universal tongues that so interested some pre- and early modern authors of translation theory is useful in today's no-longer-so-monolithically secular globalized world. These very same earlier terms can also help to explain the sometimes vatic claims made by the postmodern icons of translation theory, such as Benjamin's "pure language" (1923b: 78) or Spivak's "experience of contained alterity in an unknown language" (2005: 314). Recognizing the linguistic theologies implicit even in these most postmodern of theoretical texts is in turn relevant as Theory writ large takes a postsecular turn (de Vries and Sullivan 2006).

The directional logics and secularist principles that condition (and can limit) the ways translation theory is presented transfer well into the context of the readings for the third week, when we turn to the story of the place of translation in comparative literature by examining the "Three Reports" to the ACLA (Bernheimer 1995: 21–48) in conversation with Chow's "position paper" (1995) and more recent essays on the role of translation in the discipline by Corngold (2005: 139–45) and Saussy (2006b). These readings allow students to think about the temporality and rhetorical force of statements made by major professional organizations like the ACLA. Just how accurately do such gestures of disciplinary self-narration measure the status actually accorded to translation studies in departments and programs on the ground? Are they possibly already belated by the time they appear as normative accounts that inevitably go on to acquire immense potency? The selectivity of the history of comparative literature and of the place of translation theory and practice in the discipline created by the collective publication of the ACLA documents in the Bernheimer volume is striking when approached in this way. By tracking the evolution of the discipline in the United States from its "classical" "Eurocentric" age (1950s–1960s) to its "multicultural" iteration (1970s–1980s) to its international-"globalized" forms (1990s–2000s) in progressivist fashion, these accounts can predispose us to think in too narrow and often essentializing ways about the languages of comparative literature. For example, the pan-African decolonization movements of the 1960s and their reverse impact on the colonial languages of French and Portuguese (as well as English) in the metropole are not mentioned in the earlier reports by either Levin (1965) or Greene (1975) (these reports are included in Bernheimer 1995: 21–38). Likewise, Bernheimer (1995) pays no attention to the political earthquake that shook Europe in 1989, and this omission should cause theorists to wonder which of the "Eurocentric" languages whose dominance they were critiquing they had actually been talking about the whole time.

Discussing the essays by Chow, Corngold, and Saussy in this context is useful, for they too tamper with standard claims made about the history of comparative literature and its relation to the permanent plurality and hybridity of languages and traditions by reaching back to earlier eras of comparative literature outside of the United States and by showing how allegedly "Euro"-derived categories, such as the secular nation-state, created the specter of a single, homogenized language in non-European locations as well (Chow 1995: 109). These essays thus allow students to question positions commonly attributed to so-called traditional Comp Lit in additional ways, including the notion that the languages imagined in such statements as "the knowledge of foreign languages remains fundamental to our raison d'être" (Bernheimer 1995: 43) are only privileged European ones or that reading a newly expanded set of "global" texts—either "in the original" or in translation—can do the lion's share of the heavy lifting in the work of transnational or even subnational representation. The second topic is particularly important as the number of languages and literary-cultural traditions demanding a seat at the comparatist table ironically both expands exponentially and shrinks in the wake of the discipline having come to share more of its space not only with world literature but also with cultural and media studies. In both cases, so many of the assigned core texts have been translated into English that familiarity with them does not necessarily require the language competencies formerly associated with the field.

It is in connection with questions about how narratives of the discipline had been shaped by the assumption of language as an (un)easy vehicle of identity and representation that we then turn to two areas central to discussions in comparative literature as they are deployed in the service of critical translation studies, namely postcolonial studies and theories of sexuality and gender. In the first case, we read Deleuze and Guattari in the company of Corngold's critique (2004) of their claims about Kafka's work representing a "minor literature" ("Kafka") alongside Gentzler's (2008) and Venuti's (2005) more recent theorizations of "translation nationalism." Here "Translation nationalisms [. . .] assert a homogeneous language, culture, or identity where none is shared by the diverse population that constitutes the nation" (Venuti 2005: 189); it then becomes the task of subnational languages to "interrupt" such narratives of nation in productive ways (Gentzler 2008: 33, 35). Here, in spite of their shared critique of the production of a homogeneous "national voice," both Gentzler and Venuti assume that language is strongly representational; in both cases, a political identity—either hegemonic or resistant—can be brought into being via translation. Corngold's usefully cautionary commentary on the work that "minor languages" in particular are asked to do when performing this kind of "representational" work resonates with what Apter elsewhere critiques as "ethnic nominalism" (2008: 581). Theoretical reflections on translation as a tool either of "official" discourses and the hegemonic "suppression" of difference (Venuti 2005: 199) or of contestatory subnational self-voicing reflect positions articulated in the kinds of postcolonial theory commonly privileged in comparative literature as a discipline.

The next week on "Translation and the Difference of Gender" reveals similar patterns of an evolving set of claims from the mid-1980s (Chamberlain 1988) through the 1990s (Simon 1996) to the early-to-mid 2000s (von Flotow 2007), with the marked shift from the treatment of translation within the context of "the women's movement" to the rise of translation within academic feminism and gender and sexuality studies (von Flotow 2007: 92–3). Throughout these essays, there is an audible refrain that a feminist approach to and/or gender analytic of translation poses questions that "clearly" differ from the "traditional," "long-dominant," and "longstanding and sterile" ones (Simon 1996: 7, 27, 36) that "for many years" made simplistic, sexist assumptions (von Flotow 2007: 98). The students are asked to locate these alternative approaches within the readings and thus to assess the robustness of the progressivist rhetoric that governs such claims. While Simon, for example, describes von Flotow's "three practices of feminist translation: supplementing, prefacing and footnoting, and 'hijacking'" (Simon 1996: 14), she quickly goes on to admit that some of the initiatives she discusses are "not exclusive to feminist theory" (Simon 1996: 28). And yet, gender *is* one of the prevalent tropes for translation theory in ways that several of these theorists note via reference to the famous adage *les belles infidèles*, on the one hand, and the allusion to gendered relations of power and prestige, on the other. Thinking the future of the relation of gender to translation theory is often one of the most vexed of the issues discussed in the course. Von Flotow suggests that there has been an "androcentric slide into gender as a trope in postmodern translation theory" (2007: 95) such that actual women themselves have been effaced. Placing in the spotlight of transnational feminist studies the issues of the languages that the world's women use in their day-to-day lives and of global women's literacy and schooling remains the real desideratum.

The final weeks continue to track the ways that translation theory and comparative literature share paradigmatic questions, often in conjunction with larger institutional, political, and social events, especially with regard to the conjuncture of language, representation, and cultural identity. We juxtapose the discourses of psychoanalysis central to discussions of translation by Chow 2008, Derrida 1998b, and Ricoeur 2006—and in discussions of psychoanalysis that use the vocabulary of translation, such as Laplanche (1992)—with discussions about cultural translation and the translation of culture (Appiah 1993, Bassnett 2007) that move the discussion into the realm of an other-than-interlingual transposition or exchange. In both cases, the common question of "origin" as a multivalent term used to refer to the construction of self, language, culture, and nation looms large, suggesting that the structures of multilayeredness and the temporality of memory governing both individual and collective self-voicing intersect with one another and with translation theory in fundamental ways. For example, Derrida's essay on monolingualism discusses French as a colonial language and the violence of a metropole-centric linguistic colonialism in general (1998b: 23–7). Yet he also dwells on the specificity of his particular case as being able to write about Maghreb Judaism only in a "pure French" (46–74) that is a "monolanguage" (67) to which he has a "neurotic attachment" (56). Chow's deployment of the vocabulary of a subject-oriented psychoanalysis in understanding the role of culture in translation is somewhat more figurative; she calls upon Freud, Butler, and Cheng to argue that the "melancholy turn" in translation—which mirrors the "melancholic subject's essentially unfinished relationship with the lost/dead loved object"—"makes it possible to hold onto the notion of a certain original condition (language, literacy, culture) while advancing the plaint that this original condition has been compromised, injured, incapacitated, interrupted or stolen—in a word, lost" (Chow 2008: 571–2). Here the achievements of what Appiah (following Clifford Geertz) calls "thick translation" rest on the claim that language is always already fundamentally involved in the "conventions" of the culture that produced the "object-text" (Appiah 1993: 339). Constructing a relation to that culture through language nevertheless often relies on mechanisms of occlusion, displacement, delay, and recovery with which we are familiar from the individual case study. Theories of collective cultural identity and of individual subject positions and their mutual discontents that are often of interest to students of comparative literature are thus set in conversation with one another in profitable ways.

Translation as the Object of Comparative Literature

This course in translation theory makes clear that interlinear, interlingual translation is as much a "translational model" of the theories (and histories) central to the study of comparative literature (and of the humanities writ large) as vice versa. That is, both translation theory and comparative literature seek to retain a "kernel of 'the foreign'" as a way of reaching beyond the forms of homogenizing literary and cultural theories and methods that are often found in cartographies and chronologies of knowledge based on a "unipolar logic" (Apter 2008: 583–4) and housed in methodological silos. Derrida writes of the "double postulation" that defines language in relation to translation:

> —We only ever speak one language . . .
> (yes, but)
> —We never speak only one language . . .

This is "not only the very law of what is called translation. It would also be the law itself as translation" (Derrida 1998b: 10). This "postulation" might also usefully describe comparative literature as a field. At any given time and place, it only ever speaks one language. But over time and in different locations, it never speaks only one language. The "law of translation" is thus also the law of comparative literature.

17 Interdisciplinary Humanities

An Introduction Through Translation

Sean Cotter

The multilingual and multicultural experiences of my students at the University of Texas at Dallas fall somewhere along a spectrum, between those completely at home in the dominant culture—English-speaking, Anglo, conservative—and those of different ethnicities, some immigrants or their children, some with limited written or spoken English. A minority of my students identifies with the first pole. While the campus participates in the norms of English hegemony, it is in fact one of the most diverse student bodies in the country: just 36 percent of roughly 21,000 students identify as Anglo, 23 percent are international, and 39 percent list themselves as Hispanic, Asian-American, Native American, African-American, or multiracial. Of course, ethnic identity is far from the only diverse factor. Some students returning from military service in Iraq or Afghanistan identify as Anglo and conservative but do not feel at home in our dominant culture. Most of the students, therefore, group toward the second pole, at a variance to normative culture.

This fact has consequences for disciplinary teaching in the humanities, the area that, more than any other, emphasizes language. Traditional classes in creative writing, English literature, and American history give an advantage to students who were raised and schooled in English-language culture, but they penalize those who come from outside. As a teacher of translation, I attempt to turn my students' outsider experiences into advantages for academic study. This transformation depends on a dialectical relationship between the students and the field. The students must become better readers and writers of humanistic texts. And rather than presenting an idealized, monolingual humanities, I want to decenter English as the language of instruction through the material I teach. Translation is the linguistic and cultural practice that uniquely sets this dialectic going.

Hence I have made it the basis of "Reading and Writing Texts," a course that most undergraduate humanities majors must take as an introduction to interdisciplinary study. The course is highly structured, moving from a seven-line poem to a monograph, from highly directed research to independent application of theoretical material, and from modules on creative writing to literary analysis and historical study. It includes material that assumes the hegemonic status of English and uncovers the dependence of monolingual culture on the work of translators and the erasure of other languages. At the same time, it reframes canonical texts and disrupts monolingual culture, creating support and space for outsider experiences. Translation is defined as both individual and social: it occurs in a gap between languages where a translator makes interpretive choices, using language systems implicated in complex networks of social power.

I move the students into the practice translation as quickly as possible. The longer they remain outside, the more calcified their prescriptive, conservative ideas of translation become (for instance, "translators should stay close to the original," or "translation is impossible," or "translators lie"). We begin with two short mock-translation exercises in which I provide poems in word-for-word trots and the students work these trots into English poems. I use two Romanian poems in the first assignment, since rarely do any students know the language, and poems by Goethe, Baudelaire, and Mistral in the second, when students with knowledge of the source languages have practice asking relevant questions.

We spend one day in a workshop format, discussing the students' translations in groups. The workshop structure challenges Romantic, solipsistic ideas of inspired creativity. Inspiration is ultimately individualistic, and by that definition a workshop has nothing to contribute to the bettering of a creation. Language cannot be individual, however: it is social. Translation is a type of collaboration with another author for the social purpose of moving a work from one group of language speakers to another. To make this point concrete, I ask the students to accept at least one change from the workshop, handwritten on their submissions, and I grade the altered version. This assertion of the social broadens our examination of translation, building a bridge to issues considered later in the term, namely the power relationships that structure cultural contexts and the historical determinants that affect the translator's interpretive choices.

Since the students work on the same texts, the workshop is also an introduction to one of the semester's central motifs: multiple translations. I ask the students to explain their translation choices to each other, connecting their choices across the poem and aiming for a consistent interpretive stance. This exercise becomes a concrete demonstration of variation in interpretation. As students acquire the skills to read variations as motivated rather than as mistakes, they gain experience in exploring nuances of meaning. These exercises accompany a set of translated poems, each in at least two versions, both of which are intelligent, creative renderings of the source text that disagree on central interpretive questions.

Analyzing multiple translations of the same poem serves several purposes. The shifting texts provoke students to develop strong attachments to specific verbal choices in the translations. This investment in words is a central value in literary study, an end in itself. I avoid, at first, comparing the source text and translation to the source text, since students' attachment to the author's special status will inevitably lead them to favor the original composition, and the translation will always seem secondary. Multiple translations demonstrate the mobility of meaning in reception. Rather than a version of literary study in which students passively acquire knowledge of canonical texts, reading multiple translations moves them toward active participation in textual production.

The concrete details in Anna Akhmatova's portrait of a marriage, "He Loved," make the poem an effective example. We read Judith Hemschemeyer's version (1998):

> He loved three things in life:
> Evensong, white peacocks
> And old maps of America.
> He hated it when children cried
> He hated tea with raspberry jam
> And women's hysterics.
> . . . And I was his wife.

We also read an earlier version by D. M. Thomas (1985):

> He loved three things alone:
> White peacocks, evensong,
> Old maps of America.
> He hated children crying,
> And raspberry jam with his tea,
> And womanish hysteria.
> . . . And he had married me.

Students are usually quick to note that the translations offer different interpretations of the speaker's relationship with the "he." In particular, Thomas's rhyme, "tea"/"me," suggests that the speaker is on the list of things hated, while Hemschemeyer's "life"/"wife" associates the speaker with things loved. Students are generally able to imagine that different people can picture a love affair differently, and a tolerance for ambiguity in social relationships opens them to ambiguity of interpretation in literature. Multiple translations offer effective entry into more sophisticated literary questions as well. In the case of Charles Baudelaire's "The Broken Bell," translators disagree on whether the final image of a soldier dying beneath a mound of corpses should be read as wistful or shocking (see Schulte 1994: 147, 149, 153). Paul Celan's "Deathfugue" may indict German mythology or the German language itself (see Felstiner 2001; Hamburger 1989).

While the shorter poetic texts make introducing the exercise more manageable, it is also productive to read longer, prose texts in more than one version. We read translations of Franz Kafka's *The Metamorphosis* by A. L. Lloyd and by Willa and Edwin Muir (the earliest English versions). I ask the students to follow an interpretation throughout these long, complicated texts. The Muirs and Lloyd read Gregor in opposite ways. The Muirs strive to dehumanize Gregor completely, simplifying moments of ambiguity between insect and human. The Lloyd version, to a fault, maintains Gregor's partial humanity. This distinction shows in the choices made for an early sentence in the German text. When the chief clerk arrives at the Samsa home and insinuates that Gregor's tardiness has jeopardized his job, Gregor, on the other side of the door, exculpates himself in a rambling speech. The clerk does not understand the language and declares to Frau Samsa, "Das war eine Tierstimme" (Kafka 1967: 68). The word "Tier," meaning both insect and animal, contains a diversity of meaning that no one English word can accommodate. The Muirs rephrase the sentence as a negative: "That was no human voice" (Muir 1952: 32). Their choice creates a parallel between the clerk's exclusion of Gregor from humanity and the translators' exclusion of "Tier" from English. Gregor is "no human," and "Tier" is "no language." Lloyd chooses a half-way point. "That was an animal's voice" (Lloyd 1946: 26) is positive, in the sense that it suggests an equivalent does exist, and something about Gregor is at least partially recognizable to language. "Animal" signifies part of the range of the German word, and it is willing to translate something it cannot recognize completely. The clerk is in a parallel position, once again. While still disturbed, he does not find himself outside language and does not, therefore, maintain an ambiguity in the verbal depiction of Gregor.

This distinction makes an important difference in another scene, when Grete recoils in horror at seeing Gregor looking out the bedroom window, "well placed to look like a bogey" (Muir 1952: 53) or "in such a position as to inspire terror" (Lloyd 1946: 52). What is this position? The Muirs have Gregor "braced against the chair," which suggests the back of the chair toward the window, and the insect legs spread against the arms. Here, Grete is frightened by the utterly alien insect. Lloyd has Gregor "propped on the seat," that is, on a chair that faces the window, sitting like a human, perhaps with one (or even two) legs crossed. Grete is frightened by the ambiguous combination of human and insect.

The larger pay-off comes when the students are able to predict how the translations will differ. We examine the Muirs' description of Gregor's dead body as the charwoman encounters it, a long paragraph that ends with her exclamation, "Just look at this, it's dead! It's just lying here, dead and done for!" (Muir 1952: 84). I ask the students to deduce, given Lloyd's other choices, how his version will maintain a sense of Gregor's humanity. Every class has been able to predict (among other changes) that the last line will change its pronoun. Indeed, Lloyd preserves a human aspect even in Gregor's lifeless body: "Come and look! He's stone dead! He's lying there, absolutely dead as a doornail!" (Lloyd 1946: 92). The fact that Lloyd does not follow Kafka's pronoun—the explicitly neuter "liegt es, ganz und gar krepiert" (Kafka 1967: 109)—demonstrates the overwhelming force of his commitment to his reading of Gregor.

The course extends the implications of the students' reading of multiple translations to reading multiple critical interpretations. The end assignment for this section is an essay contrasting two academic articles, chosen from a list of six that I provide. We read two book chapters as a full class: Deleuze and Guattari's "What Is Minor Literature?" (1986: 16–27) and David Damrosch's "Kafka Comes Home" (2003: 187–205). I ask students to write an abstract for the Damrosch chapter. Once they have my comments, I assign each student one of four essays on Kafka's *The Metamorphosis* (Bouson 2008; Sokel 1995; Straus 1989; Zilcosky 2011), and again they write abstracts. The class then repeats the workshop structure we followed for their translations, arriving at a similar point: scholarship, like creativity, is social. The students discuss their abstracts in groups, and again I ask them to make one, handwritten change. Only after I grade and return these abstracts do they move into an information-gap exercise. I place the students in groups in which each has read a different article, and I ask them to explain their articles to each other and establish grounds for comparison among four pairs. The other students help determine which articles would be useful to study for the assignment. Because the students' work leads directly to their comparative essay, they have an investment in their fellows' presentations.

Using a similar teaching method in these sections of the course allows translation to function in an interdisciplinary way. It is not only an object of study but also a teaching methodology, not only a topic of discussion but also an experience for the students. The commonly understood benefits of group work appear in this setting of exceptional diversity: the groups interrupt students' usual social activity and create meaningful engagements with those of different backgrounds, conversation styles, and viewpoints. The exercise with the academic articles usually precipitates conflicts. Students may find it difficult to trust the version of the article presented because of motives traceable to class difference, accented English, or other markers of otherness. I circulate during the exercise and help students to decompress afterwards, whether in office hours or over email. The students (and the instructor) practice translation in this way too.

These experiences of translation, as well as the fundamental connections between translation, interpretation, and social context, form the basis for the subsequent sections of the course. The readings in Kafka criticism, multiple perspectives on a shared central object, are followed by readings in cultural encounters, variations on ideas of power. We start again from Deleuze and Guattari's arguments for the political significance of language and their reading of orthographical changes and anti-metaphorical imagery in Kafka's writing. Mary Louis Pratt's 1991 article, "Arts of the Contact Zone," shifts emphasis from language to genre, explaining the acts of resistance encoded in Guaman Poma's auto-ethnographic letter to the King of Spain. Damrosch's chapter on post-Encounter Aztec poetry (2003: 78–109) explores ways in which a less powerful language may, through its creative and poetic possibilities, seduce the more powerful party. Excerpts from Gloria Anzaldúa's *Borderlands / La frontera* (2001) discuss the connection of language and individual identity, locating the strategic value of a restrictive adjective such as "border artist." An excerpt from Richard Rodriguez (1981) accepts the hegemonic role of language but argues in favor of adopting English in order to participate in public discourse.

We finish this set of readings with two works concerning immigration: Eva Hoffman's memoir, *Lost in Translation* (1989), and Euripides' play *Medea*. Hoffman's text examines what selves she is able to inhabit when she changes social contexts. We watch her youthful ability at the piano become "Talent" in Poland, something that simultaneously belongs to both her and her culture. She struggles to maintain this identity in Vancouver, Canada, where no corresponding piano culture exists. Hoffman's seductive and fascinating introspection allows students to inhabit her transformation into a literary career. The students are also invited to experience a cross-cultural discontinuity in the trap-play, *Medea*. Euripides first offers a choice between two cultural sympathies: a version of Greekness heavily parodied through the character of Jason and Medea's Colchian culture, made noble by the pathos of her immigrant sacrifices. Once the play establishes sympathy for Medea on these relativistic grounds, Euripides posits a second choice, this time between relativism itself and a universalist aversion to the murder of children. Yet the appearance of Medea's supernatural dragon-wagon questions the transcendental basis of this aversion. By the end of the play, the audience has experienced an emigration from its attachment to its cultural identity to a type of placelessness: a hopeless embrace of a groundless universal. Many of my students (or their parents) have experience with immigration, and these texts help bridge textual translation questions to a larger scale, to those cultural crossings that create the need for translation.

This broader perspective leads the class to consider translation in history. My experience has been that of the majors I teach, the historical studies students hold most doggedly to ideas of self-evident truth. In the only reading we do explicitly about a discipline, we spend one class meeting on Paul Valéry's short essay, "Historical Fact" (1962), which argues that the work of history lies in the present, not the past, because its focus is on argument and interpretation. The connection of historical to literary study does not reside solely on the primacy of interpretation in both fields. If the theme of the course is to remain productive in this last section, the plasticity of translation must also obtain here. We read Lydia Liu (1999) and André Lefevere et al. (1995), who argue for the historicity of equivalence. We focus on an insightful and manageable monograph: Peter Thuesen's study of Bible translation in Protestantism, *In Discordance with the Scriptures* (1999). Students generally find his material compelling, whether they come from conservative Christian backgrounds or have lived in a culture like Dallas which is saturated with conservative Christian discourse.

Thuesen makes the argument that the current proliferation of English-language Bible translations can be explained by an irony built into Protestantism's theological structure at the Reformation. The Protestant position that one may have access to God through scripture, without the mediating role of a Church, requires the translation of scripture into the relevant vernacular. Yet the inherent difference between source text and translation leads, over six hundred years, to a crisis of interpretation around the 1946 Revised Standard Version translation. Thuesen documents the divergence between Protestant theology and translation ideology, focusing on the nineteenth and twentieth centuries, which results in textual changes—the prophecy that the messiah would be born of "a young girl" rather than "a virgin"—on academic grounds. This difficult challenge to the idea of self-authenticating scripture causes nationwide protests, even book burnings. The tension of translation ironically triggers the creation of "superchurches," national organizations that authorize various translations, intervening between the believer and scripture as the pre-Reformation church had done.

Rather than concluding this section with a disciplinary exercise (for example, one that involves reading a primary document for historical information), I ask for an essay interpreting, in light of an author from the syllabus, a multilingual or multicultural event that the student has experienced. I insist that the paper focus on the most minute details possible, so that it analyzes rather than recounts a story. A student who had come to Dallas to flee Hurricane Katrina analyzed the cultural content of a moment at dinner when her sister-in-law pushed away her salad and declared, "Honestly, if I didn't have to eat, I wouldn't." Pratt helped the student to identify the imbalance of power that allowed the sister-in-law to deny her body and prevented the student from asserting the central importance of food, which her home culture of New Orleans took for granted.

While the assignment assesses the student's ability to analyze an event, its scope is broader. It presses the point that everyone has had a multilingual or multicultural experience, which is to say that translation is a part of everyone's world. Despite a broad definition (I suggest that "multicultural" could include moving from high school to college, or that "multilingual" could describe writing translations for the course), perhaps 5 percent of students have claimed that they have not had an experience worthy of analysis. The assignment allows most students to bring personal experiences to bear on academic work, experiences that impede their work in other settings but that here prove to be advantages. Through their analysis, these experiences become parseable in academic terms and connected to the experiences of others. Used in this way, cultural theory turns personal struggle into a source of insight, and, after all, insight into translation, reading, and writing has been the goal of the course throughout the semester.

Term ends with the juxtaposition of a history, Michael Cronin's *Translating Ireland* (1996), and a play, Brian Friel's *Translations* (1981), which stages translation in early nineteenth-century Irish/English interaction. Students discuss the ways each discipline's genres of thought shape the presentation of translation in each text. The history readings help students spot the great variety of translations, literal and metaphorical, presented in the play. The final project of the term requires the students to rewrite one of their earlier assignments.

If I have focused here on what students bring to the class, then I may end with what they take away. Some students bring travel experience to the class, while others travel afterwards, with new ways of interpreting their encounters. One exceptional student, the daughter of American missionaries in Mexico, accepted a position in Army Intelligence upon graduation and served in Afghanistan. A few years later, in an email, she described a surprising social role for the course material:

> I study reports, history, intelligence injects, and quite literally sometimes, translations. My knowing the delicate differences between what one tribe might mean when they use the word "rockets" vs. the way another tribe uses it—though the translator may have used the same English word for both translations—actually influences what military actions the unit might then take or not take in that area.

In no other course of mine have I seen such a direct connection between course material and the abatement of violence in the world. Even in the midst of an exercise in American hegemony, translation can make a small but significant change. The interdisciplinary nature of translation can transform the humanities by creating the grounds for social connections, avoiding Romantic, individualistic ideas, and practicing collaboration. By the same token, the interdisciplinary study of translation can transform students into more nuanced readers, better able to interpret multiple versions of a truth. These great benefits await a more thorough interaction of the humanities with translation.

18 Teaching Literature in Translation

Karen Emmerich

Institutional Contexts

Comparative literature could not exist without translation, which allows students and advanced scholars alike to access texts written in languages they do not know. Yet while texts in translation are widely cited, discussed, and taught—not just in departments and programs of comparative literature but in departments of national literatures as well—the *way* they are taught often cultivates a mistrust of, or at best obscures or ignores, the mediating work of translation. Like countless such departments and programs across the country, the Department of Comparative Literature at the University of Oregon teaches texts that were first written in a far broader range of languages than either our students or our professors can read. Yet unlike many such departments, ours takes seriously the idea that the responsible teaching of translated literature involves a recognition of the fact and consequences of translation as an interpretive activity, as well as a contextualization of one's own reading practices and pedagogical choices. We think it particularly important that our graduate students develop a nuanced understanding not only of the complex processes involved in the production and circulation of literature in translation but also of the various theoretical approaches that have been brought to bear on these processes. The aim is to enable them to foster a similarly nuanced approach to translated texts among their own students, both at our university and in their future teaching careers. If translation can be seen as both an opportunity and a problem, we treat the teaching of translated texts as one way of making a pedagogical opportunity *of* the problem.

To this end, all doctoral candidates in our department are required to satisfactorily complete a course titled "Translation Pedagogy" before they can serve as instructors in courses of their own design (most students complete it in their first term). "Translation Pedagogy" is an introduction to key texts in the field of translation studies; it interrogates notions of equivalence and explores the ethics and politics of translation as well as the role of translation(s) in the academy and the global literary marketplace. It also seeks to supplement the methodology of close reading that currently holds sway in literature departments with other forms of analysis that account more adequately for the fact and implications of translation, such as distant reading, historicization, translation comparison, and the placement of translation in a spectrum of other forms of rewriting or textual mediation.

The course is taught as a weekly seminar in conjunction with a series of pedagogy workshops (run by another faculty member) that focus on such practical issues as designing a syllabus, leading classroom discussions, planning in-class and take-home activities, and grading.

Taking these workshops in the same term as the seminar encourages doctoral candidates to view the theoretical readings we discuss during our weekly meetings as immediately and practically relevant to their own teaching. Many of the activities conducted during the pedagogy workshops feed directly into the final project for the seminar, the designing of a syllabus for an undergraduate course in world literature. These two functions were originally combined into a single course, but since our university operates on the quarter system, we decided to divide them to enable a fuller engagement with the theoretical readings on which the seminar focuses and to offer doctoral candidates more practical support as they begin teaching sections of large undergraduate lecture courses. At universities that operate on the semester system, these two components could fruitfully be incorporated into a single course.

Readings and Activities

The first week of the seminar places the issue of translation pedagogy in the context of larger debates concerning the role of translation in the teaching of comparative and world literature. Assigned texts include Gayatri Chakravorty Spivak's "Translating into English" (2005), Emily Apter's "A New Comparative Literature" (2006: 243–51), Sandra Bermann's "Teaching in—and About—Translation" (2010), Lawrence Venuti's "The Pedagogy of Literature" (1998: 88–106), and excerpts from André Lefevere's *Translation, Rewriting and the Manipulation of Literary Fame* (1992). Emphasis is placed on the theoretical basis for the range of approaches that scholars have articulated for teaching translated literature, from Spivak's call for supplemental contextualizing and a push toward the source text to Venuti's insistence that reading translations entails a double reading, one that is attentive to the network of "domestic values inscribed in the foreign text during the translating process" (1998: 89). Since this course emphasizes graduate students' own future role as educators responsible for designing syllabi, Venuti's chapter is particularly useful because it privileges as teaching texts translations with a "rich remainder" (i.e., a rich network of embedded values from the receiving culture) (1998: 103). Lefevere's work is also crucial in treating translation not as an exceptional threat to the study of literature from other languages but as one form of interpretive mediation among others—including editing, anthologization, literary criticism, and so on—many of which are also brought to bear on source texts.

During this first week, the doctoral candidates stage a series of debates over the perceived value and danger of reading in translation. I divide them into two groups: one plays the role of undergraduate students who are highly resistant to reading translated literature; the other responds as a professor might to the students' concerns or objections. I then have the groups switch sides: the professorial group is now highly resistant to *teaching* in translation; the student group brainstorms possible responses, discussing how their professors' beliefs and approaches will affect their current and subsequent encounters with translated texts in and out of the classroom. This role-playing session makes doctoral candidates aware of the potential effect of their own attitudes toward translation and attunes them—throughout the term and beyond—to the diverse ways in which translation is discussed by individuals at every level of the university, from their own undergraduate students to the most senior professors with whom they work.

The rest of the course is divided into two sections, each of which is further broken down into rubrics that are addressed in individual class meetings. The first section takes up the question of "What is (a) Translation?" by offering an overview of some important texts and trends in translation studies, while the second section, titled "How to Read a Translation," brainstorms means of circumventing the suspicion of translation that pervades both popular and academic discourse.

Our meeting on "Translating 'Translation'" uses texts by Bella Brodzki (2011), Lori Chamberlain (1988), Michael Emmerich (2013), Lydia Liu (1995), and Maria Tymoczko (2010) to think through the entrenched understandings of translation that manifest themselves in the ways we talk about it. Chamberlain's "Gender and the Metaphorics of Translation" is particularly useful in helping students to think about the "important consequences in the areas of publishing, royalties, curriculum, and academic tenure" (1988: 306) that can arise from the metaphors we often encounter in translation commentary. Translation is an abstract, intellectual enterprise, and the language we use to describe it often runs to metaphor. But what does it mean—and what effects can it have—to think of translation as loss, damage, destruction, or distortion, as rape or pillage, as abuse, as a *belle infidèle*, or even in more positive terms as bridging and cultural ambassadorship? This discussion sensitizes students to rhetoric surrounding translation, encouraging them to be mindful of this issue when approaching the other texts on the syllabus; they also become remarkably aware of the assumptions about translation embedded in their own statements about it. Playing off of Emmerich's notion that "[t]ranslation must be viewed as a node within which all the ideas of translation in all the languages there ever have been or could ever be might potentially congregate, intersect, mingle" (2013: 47), I ask class members to share words connoting "translation" in the languages they know and to discuss points of overlap and divergence. How linguistically and culturally specific, we ask, might the field of translation studies itself be?

The next three weeks treat canonical texts in this field. In "Tasks of Translation 1: Translation as Interpretation?" we look at work by Roman Jakobson (1959), Eugene Nida (1964), and George Steiner (1975a) to consider the hermeneutic function of translation and to think through the various notions of equivalence that Nida puts forward. In "Tasks of Translation 2: Languages, Nations, Literary Traditions," we consider Itamar Even-Zohar's polysystem theory (1978), Yopie Prins's examination (2005) of how the hexameter entered nineteenth-century English poetry through translations of Homer, and Charles Bernstein's comments (2011) on homophonic translation, but we also put them in productive dialogue with Walter Benjamin's "The Task of the Translator" (read in both Harry Zohn's and Steven Rendall's translations). All of these texts treat translation as a means of expanding the literary possibilities of the translating language, and they do so in ways that help us challenge the traditional categories of equivalence discussed in the previous week.

We now take up "Foreignizing Translation vs. Radical Domestication," not only explaining these approaches but returning to Benjamin to consider how "The Task of the Translator" has contributed to a late twentieth-century valorization of "foreignizing" strategies. This thread is traced back to Friedrich Schleiermacher's seminal text "On the Different Methods of Translating" (in Susan Bernofsky's translation) and forward to Antoine Berman's "Translation and the Trials of the Foreign" (in Lawrence Venuti's translation). Important to this week's readings is Douglas Robinson's argument (1997a) that many of the goals of foreignizing translation—including making the interpretive work of translation visible to the reader—are more adequately achieved by a translation strategy he calls "radical domestication": for instance, a slangy English translation of Luther's treatise on translating the Bible into German rather than Latin.

These weeks also involve activities meant to model certain techniques that graduate students may later use in their own classrooms. One is translation comparison, in which several different translations of a single source text—the opening lines of the *Iliad* or a poem by C. P. Cavafy or a passage from a short story by Kenzaburo Oe—are examined side-by-side. Among the Homeric translations, I always include George Chapman's seventeenth-century version in iambic pentameter, at least one prose translation, and David Melnick's *Men in Aida* (1983), a homophonic translation that follows the sound rather than the sense of the Greek text, as well as several twentieth-century translations whose differences from one another are less extreme. Looking at these translations together not only makes students aware of the historical, mutable nature of literary forms and literary taste but also helps them to understand the hermeneutic nature of translation as they see various interpretations of what a text means and even *how* it means taking shape in the translations. We discuss the various goals one might have for including a particular translation on a syllabus, as well as the costs and benefits of assigning multiple translations or only one.

The course then passes into its second section, "How to Read a Translation." In a meeting titled "Translation at the Margins," we read Marcia Nita Doron and Marilyn Gaddis Rose's "The Economics and Politics of Translation"—written in 1981 but sadly not dated today—as well as selections from Venuti's *The Translator's Invisibility* (1995) and *The Scandals of Translation* (1998). We look at sample translator contracts and materials from sources such as PEN American Center and Three Percent in order to think through the marginalization of translation not just in the academy but also in the popular sphere. In preparation for an assignment to write reviews of recently published translations, students are asked to look at a host of online resources regarding translated literature, including the forum "On Reviewing Translations" posted on the online magazine *Words Without Borders*. Each student finds two reviews to share with the class: a positive example of what they consider a responsible review that accounts for the fact and complexity of the work of translation and a negative example that fails to provide any such account. Since students are encouraged to look at reviews in languages other than English in completing this assignment, they develop an awareness of the disproportionately scant representation of translated literature in the United States as compared to other countries.

The next week, "Stylistic Analogues: Translation as Comparative Literature" borrows its key term from Lawrence Venuti and uses his bilingual edition of Antonia Pozzi's poems and letters to consider the task of translation as an inherently comparative project. One of Venuti's stated aims in the translation is to "suppl[y] what [Pozzi] lacked in Italian: a tradition of modernist women poets" (Pozzi 2002: xxii), in part by translating the poems so as to highlight a likeness between Pozzi and Anglophone poets such as H.D., Amy Lowell, Mina Loy, and Lorine Niedecker. Students are often resistant to Venuti's approach, seeing it as too "creative," "invasive," or "interpretive," but they acknowledge that his translation and their own response are productive for discussing what translation is as well as various demands for and understandings of equivalence. During this meeting, we also discuss the role of the translator's note or introduction in contextualizing both a work of literature and the translator's approach.

The week titled "Objects of Translation: Unstable Texts" recalls our earlier reading of Lefevere on editing as a form of rewriting in order to consider the instability of source texts. We read recent work by textual scholars such as David Greetham (1998) and Peter Shillingsburg (1996) and take *Gilgamesh* as our case study. We look at two very different translations of the epic: Andrew George's rather scholarly version (1999), which presents a highly fragmentary composite text that is reconstructed from numerous tablet sources and includes brackets, ellipses, and italics to mark missing and interpolated passages, and Stephen Mitchell's popular version (2004), which fills in those gaps and treats the epic primarily as a narrative focusing largely on plot and character. Class discussion explores the kinds of conversations that each edition encourages or discourages, and in the process we assess their value in meeting the various pedagogical goals one might have in assigning the work. I myself routinely teach both these translations in the same undergraduate lecture course, where I split the students into two groups and have them argue the pros and cons of each translation. In the graduate course I similarly divide the doctoral candidates into two groups and have them once more play the role of undergraduates while trying to anticipate what students might appreciate or find frustrating about the two translations, particularly if they are taught consecutively.

The final week of readings for the course, titled "Translation and World Literature: Close Reading, Distant Reading," returns to the debate staged in the opening week concerning the role of translation in the teaching of comparative or world literature. The texts for this meeting are David Damrosch's "World Enough and Time" (2003: 281–303), which treats world literature as "writing that gains in translation" (281) and proposes collaboration as a primary mode of comparative literary studies, and Franco Moretti's "Conjectures on World Literature" (2000), which argues the need for "distant reading" as a supplement or antidote to the supremacy of the model of close reading that, Moretti believes, can do nothing but reinforce the canons implicit in the "profoundly unequal" system of world literature (56). Given the emphasis throughout the term not only on the close analysis and contextualization of source texts and translations alike but also on networks of literary production, reproduction, mediation, and dissemination, the course ultimately makes an argument for the value of both Damrosch's and Moretti's approaches over and against the "distaste for translation" (Damrosch and Spivak 2011: 460) that so commonly characterizes the teaching of translated texts.

Assignments

Students submit informal responses, one or two pages in length, to the texts assigned for each week. This assignment facilitates classroom discussion as well as critical engagement with the readings. Students also keep a journal for the duration of the term, in which they record translation-related experiences in the graduate seminars they are taking, in the undergraduate lecture courses they attend as instructors, and in their own undergraduate sections. Keeping this journal heightens their awareness of how their professors talk about translations while encouraging them to behave differently as instructors *and* as graduate students. They learn to engage their undergraduates, their peers, and their professors in more frequent conversations about translation and in a more nuanced fashion than they otherwise might have done.

Midway through the term, when we begin to think about the discourse surrounding translation in the nonacademic world, I ask the students to turn in brief reviews of two translations, one from a language they read and one from a language they do not. This assignment forces them to confront their own biases and assumptions about translation head-on, particularly as they face the challenge of talking about a translation without recourse to the source text. They must thus take the translation at face value, reading it both for its representation of the source text and for its own structures of meaning. This experience may temper their tendency, in comparing a translation to a source text, to focus on what they take to be word-level mistakes. For each translation, they must decide how much information the reader of their review requires about the author, the historical and literary context, the language, and so on. Hence the assignment also helps them to decide how much contextualization might be needed for undergraduate students in their courses.

"Translation Pedagogy" culminates with the final assignment: the construction of a proposed syllabus for a course in world literature, accompanied by a brief essay explaining the specific decisions that have gone into the crafting of this syllabus. Beginning in their third year of study, most graduate students in our department teach lower-division undergraduate courses in comparative literature that also fulfill general education requirements. They are asked to design a course suitable for this purpose and to prepare at least two classroom exercises or take-home assignments that put translation at the center of the discussion of literary texts; we spend our final seminar workshopping drafts of these syllabi, exercises, and assignments. The final projects reflect a nuanced understanding of translation and envision a wide range of methods for conveying that understanding to undergraduates. These methods include not only basic tasks like noting translators' names on the syllabus and choosing texts on the basis of the merits and interest of the translations as well as the source texts they translate but also more challenging techniques like analyzing multiple translations of a single text and assigning secondary materials that contextualize both the source text and the translation. On occasion, graduate students have designed entire courses around issues of translation and adaptation, incorporating various second-order practices such as dramatic performance and film adaptation as well as interlingual translation. A course on fairytales, for instance, looks at the circulation of particular narratives in multiple editions and translations as well as in the adaptations of children's books and films. In a handful of cases so far, our graduate students have gone on to teach the courses they designed for this project.

Potential Outcomes

"Translation Pedagogy" ideally serves a double purpose: to sensitize graduate students in comparative literature to the issues of reading in translation, which will inform their future scholarly work with translations of literary, critical, and theoretical texts, and to cultivate pedagogical methods that treat translated literature more responsibly than it is often treated today. Judging from numerous class discussions, our graduate students become aware of the limitations of their own professors' knowledge and treatment of issues of translation. Targeting a population of graduate students with such a course thus has the potential to encourage a broader departmental shift in the way translations are taught in undergraduate and graduate classes alike. Professors might also choose to retool their own syllabi or to refocus class discussions (even if only occasionally) on the fact and consequences of reading texts in translation. Similar courses can easily be instituted in departments and programs of comparative literature at other institutions. Alternatively, intensive, short-term versions of the course could be offered as opportunities for professional development to bring scholars of comparative literature at all levels up to speed on the many ways that translation affects their discipline.

19 Translation and World Literature

The One Thousand and One Nights

Sevinç Türkkan

This chapter describes an undergraduate course that focuses on translations, adaptations, and rewritings of *The One Thousand and One Nights*. The course treats translations as translations so as to problematize notions of authenticity and originality while highlighting the role of translators as interpreters. The study of adaptations and rewritings enlarges students' understanding of the translators' role in constructing a text out of which other texts and media proliferate to form what we call "world literature." Students become aware that translation is essential to how we perceive the rest of the world as they develop skills in reading translations without sacrificing close reading to "distant reading" (Moretti 2000: 56). The course not only involves a cultural translation from a supposed medieval Arab literary tradition to what Pascale Casanova has called the "world republic of letters," but it also teaches students to read translations as artifacts of mediation between various cultural logics: Arabic-European, Eastern-Western, and Islamic-secular. As such, the course serves as an introduction to the ethics and politics of translation, representation, and world literature.

Student Body, Objectives, and Pedagogies

Listed as an upper-division offering in an English department, the course includes mostly English majors, in both literature and creative writing, but also some students who declare a minor in English with majors in such other fields as journalism, political science, international studies, and women's studies. Students have advanced preparation in close reading and academic writing, strong skills in reading texts in context, and some exposure to literary theory and criticism, including such concepts as intertextuality and postmodern rewriting. Even though most of them are monolingual, some belong to second- and third-generation immigrant families, and so they have been exposed to some linguistic variety. But they do not bring to the course any familiarity with postcolonial studies, translation theory, or the debates surrounding the concept of world literature.

Hence I aim to introduce students to the multiple and divergent translations of the *Nights* and trace the development of European consciousness about the Arab world based on these translations. I want students to develop skills in reading each translation within its particular cultural and historical context and in relation to the translators' interpretive strategies. Adaptations and rewritings allow me to discuss issues of intertextuality, literary self-reference, and the self-reflexive nature of the *Nights*. Ultimately, we formulate a definition of world literature that recognizes the politics of translation in canon formation and the translators' role in literary influence and cross-cultural studies.

Given the students' background and preparation, I set aside time for workshops in which small groups concentrate on specific aspects of the translations and discuss their findings. These workshops give me an opportunity to refocus class discussions in the frame provided by the theoretical readings. I also encourage students to set up their own study groups to address assignments and to develop communal learning strategies. They create discussion boards online, post questions and responses to the readings, write reports on their progress, and share their group projects through Google Documents. Discussion boards are especially useful in monitoring students' questions and in addressing them directly during class meetings. Interactive sessions allow students with weaker theoretical preparation to articulate their concerns and to benefit from their peers' perspectives.

Readings, Assignments, and Classroom Activities

The course begins with an overview of recent debates on world literature and a discussion of the place of translation in these debates. I assign Damrosch's introduction to *What Is World Literature?* (2003: 1–36), Casanova's "Literature as a World" (2005) and Moretti's "Conjectures on World Literature." I juxtapose these texts with Grossman's *Why Translation Matters* (2010) to give students an eminent translator's view on the value of translation and the degree of close reading, creative effort, and hard work necessary to produce effective and responsible translations. Before we venture into an in-depth study of selected tales from the *Nights* and their multiple translations, I provide students with a background for the Arabic text. Students read Littman's "Alf Laylah wa-laylah" (1960), Horovitz's "The Origins of the Arabian Nights" (1927), and selections from Gerhardt's *The Art of Story-Telling* (1963). These materials enable us to reflect on several forms of translation inherent in the very composition of the *Nights*, namely how it makes use of its Arabic, Chinese, Greek, Indian, Persian, and Turkish origins, how the text derives from oral story-telling, and how the frame story carries the potential to generate more stories.

We then begin our study of the translations. I organize the readings so that we consider foundational statements in translation theory in conjunction with English versions of the *Nights*. To address the problems posed by linguistic theories of translation, Nida's concept of "dynamic equivalence" (1964), which was formulated to support Bible translation as a form of Christian proselytizing, is paired with Burton's version (1885), which appropriates the *Nights* so as to challenge the moral conventions of Victorian society. Venuti's chapter on "Heterogeneity" in *The Scandals of Translation* (1998: 8–30) is paired with Lane's translation (1839–41), allowing us to trace the Anglophone "remainder" in Lane's verbal choices, to highlight the translator's role in forming cultural identities, and to be more aware of our own cultural situation and historical moment as readers of translations. We discuss Lewis's concept of "abusive fidelity" (1985), which focuses on the signifying process of the source text, in relation to Haddawy's translation (1990), which aims to reproduce the aesthetic effects of the Arabic. Powys Mathers' translation (1923) of Jean-Charles Mardrus's "literal and complete" French version is paired with Borges's "The Translators of *The One Thousand and One Nights*" (1935), which includes an illuminating commentary on Mardrus, noting that "he adds Art Nouveau passages, fine obscenities, brief comical interludes, circumstantial details, symmetries, vast quantities of visual Orientalism" (Borges 1935: 102).

As students begin to realize how the translators' varying interpretations inscribe French and English values in the Arabic text, we spend a class session on Schleiermacher's "On the Different Methods of Translating" and Nabokov's "Problems of Translation" (1955). Both readings privilege translations that adhere closely to the source text, and although their reasons seem different, they share a certain nationalistic or chauvinistic tendency: Schleiermacher aims to develop the German language and literature against French cultural domination; Nabokov has a deep investment in Pushkin's Russian, even if he argues that it is inflected by French influences. This discussion is developed further in a workshop in which we select a passage from Haddawy's translation and compare it with its corresponding passage in other translations. Students debate the effects of translation strategies: "literal" vs. "free," "foreignizing" vs. "domesticating," "assimilating" vs. "exoticizing." They weigh the translators' use of paratextual materials like introductions and annotations against the addition of explanatory insertions in the text to clarify names and culturally specific items like foods and customs. Among the questions we ask is the following: How should readers understand translations that erase the mention of nightly lovemaking when Shahrazad falls silent and Dunyazad asks for a "more amazing tale"?

I request, in other words, that students carefully identify literary techniques and formal elements employed by translators and support their interpretations by establishing relations to a specific cultural context. This task can be facilitated by introducing other, related materials produced by the translators, such as Lane's ethnographic study, *An Account of the Manners and Customs of the Modern Egyptians* (1836), and Powys Mathers's poetry anthology *The Garden of Bright Waters* (1920). To understand the context of Lane's translation, for instance, students study his notes along with his ethnography, which was published a couple of years before the translation. They consider the language and style of these materials, contemplate the reasons for the differences and similarities among them, and think about the purpose and target audience behind each. This work leads students to become aware of how the context shapes the translation, how the translation occupies a place in the translator's overall output, and how text and context join to elicit readers' responses. We then evaluate the translation within the framework provided by Venuti's concepts of domesticating and foreignizing translation. Students consider Lane's translating method in light of the effect it produced. Does his purging of "certain passages which, in the original work, are of an objectionable nature" really serve his purpose of accurately representing the "Arab manners and customs" (*The Thousand and One Nights*, I: xvii)? Or was he simply making his translation agreeable to Victorian sensibilities? We finally discuss the ethics of rendering into English a collection of folk tales as if they were an ethnographic account of the people who produced them.

We go further, however, to recreate the broader context in which each translation was published and circulated. Class discussions of book covers, title pages, illustrations, and typographical elements generate an awareness of how editors, publishers, and printers influence the reception of translations. To these features of book production, we add periodical reviews to show how each translation was received at the time of publication, what literary conventions guided or constrained its reception, and what critical discourse was employed in reviews. My goal here is to have students reflect on what happens to the message of the translated text when it is interpreted within or against the linguistic and literary constraints of another tradition by a translating subject and a host of gatekeepers in the publishing industry and the receiving culture at large.

Paratextual materials help students to adopt the translators' perspectives, yet in the process they risk accepting the beliefs and prejudices that underlie the Orientalism informing the translations. To encourage students to recognize, critique, and resist Orientalist assumptions, I have them examine the world that the translators create and the pictures that they paint of their tasks as translators. I then ask students to compare these constructions and self-presentations with the translations. I point out how these images are not fixed but ever shifting and contradictory as they construct cultural others based on assumptions of difference. I push my students to see beyond the linguistic and communicative purposes of translation by recognizing that translation is a cultural practice with ethical and political implications. To introduce students to the concept of Orientalism and the role of translators in this project, I pair Said's introduction and relevant sections on Lane in *Orientalism* (1978) with sections from Irwin's *For Lust of Knowing* (2006). These readings introduce a new dimension to the earlier discussions of Lane as a translator. Students debate the issue of Orientalism with specific examples from primary and secondary sources as they counter Irwin's dismissive criticism of Said's work as "malignant charlatanry" (Irwin 2006: 4).

A discussion devoted to Jakobson's concept of intersemiotic translation (1959) initiates the unit on adaptations between different sign systems, mostly literature, on the one hand, and drama, film, music, and visual art, on the other. The concept of fidelity (or lack thereof) to the narrative, thematic, and stylistic features of the *Nights* is the lens through which I approach the adaptations. As we listen to Rimsky-Korsakov's *Scheherazade*, a musical spin on the tales, we try to identify the power of the violin and harp to represent the voices of Shahrayar and Shahrazad. I choose al-Shaykh's adaptation (2011) of the stories for Tim Supple's theatrical production to show students how the exigencies of performance impact the narrative form of the *Nights*. We discuss not only how the writer maneuvers theatrical constraints but also how the physical requirements of the theater resist the reconciliation and rejoicing with which the source text ends.

To establish a context for our discussion of film adaptations, I assign readings on the frequently adapted stories, Molan's "Sinbad the Sailor" (1987) and Cooperson's "The Monstrous Births of Aladdin" (2006). These readings help students to reevaluate their common understanding of popular representations of Sinbad and Aladdin as simple adventure heroes. They rather learn to read the tales structurally, identifying the morals that underlie them and the ways in which these stories overtly comment on the frame tale.

I use Pasolini's film adaptation *Il fiore delle mille e una note* (1974) precisely because students are least likely to be familiar with it. It presents a radical alternative to popular adaptations, which empty the *Nights* of any moral consideration, end up in neat resolutions, and reinforce orientalist stereotypes. In such versions, protagonists are dancing girls; romance, power, and wealth are the motivating principles; and marital union triumphs at the end. In contrast, Pasolini's adaptation of the stories "Aziz and Aziza" and "The Porter and the Tree Ladies" explores love and marital desire as contradictory and pervasive. We contrast Pasolini's protagonists, the passive Nur al Din and the overly active Zumurrud, with their conventional counterparts in popular representations. We also compare Pasolini's anti-hero Zumurrud with Shahrazad of the *Nights*, noting the resemblance in their abilities to challenge patriarchy and expose its oppressive regimes. Central to our discussions is how Pasolini abstains from moral judgment and gives us the shortest circuit between the subject and the object of desire.

I set up the discussion of adaptations in visual art by pointing out that, in the medieval Arab world, miniatures and illuminations were the only means of pictorial representation, while the tradition of odalisque painting in Europe was entirely fantastical and based on Orientalist assumptions. We juxtapose examples from the Renaissance portraiture with plates from Owen Jones's *The Grammar of Ornament* (1856), which represents styles of drawing for educational purposes, Assyrian and Chinese, Egyptian and Moorish, Persian and Turkish. With the help of *The Grammar*, students identify how illustrators of the *Nights* combined Eastern and Western elements of style and mise en scene. Thus in Adolphe Lalauze and Albert Letchford's illustrations for Burton's translation we trace the Spanish and Moorish motifs, locate the inclusion of Japanese objects and Italian landscapes, and discuss the influence of the French painter Gérôme on Letchford. In considering the illustrations by Léon Carré, Kees van Dongen, and Furasawa Iwami for French and Japanese translations, we observe how confusion about the origins of the *Nights* is reflected in the mixture of arabesque and Renaissance styles with their Japanese and Chinese counterparts. By the end of this unit, students question approaches that judge adaptations by the yardstick of fidelity, adopting a more flexible and complex understanding of them as works in their own right.

In the last unit, we consider subversive appropriations of the *Nights* by writers and their translators. The novelists include John Barth, Naguib Mahfouz, Orhan Pamuk, Salman Rushdie, and Alia Yunis. We focus on the multiple levels of signification in each rewriting but also illuminate the role of the translator in recreating these levels. Class discussions center on identifying structures, characters, themes, and techniques from the *Nights*. I point out how translators recognize intertextuality and possess the linguistic and critical competence to formulate its significance and to recreate it in their translations. I ask students to ponder not only the point at which a text loses its original identity and signifies anew as it crosses national, historical, and literary boundaries, but also the cultural status that the *Nights* occupies as a narrative sourcebook.

Especially rewarding is the discussion on Pamuk's *The Black Book* and its two English translations by Maureen Freely (in 2006) and Güneli Gün (in 2002). We analyze how Pamuk rewrites the form of interlacing stories from the *Nights* to narrate his protagonist's quest for identity. In order to criticize despotic governments, Pamuk superimposes the caliph Harun el-Rashid's nocturnal adventures in disguise onto the social and political milieu of the modern Turkish Republic. I initiate the discussion of intertextuality in translation by encouraging students to think about how sound might translate (or not) into English. Since the alliterative Turkish title, "Kara Kitap," translates as either "The Black Book" or "The Dark Book," we consider what different significations each English version might have and how they might be supported (or not) by the narrative. Should a translation retain the alliteration of the Turkish title, aim for an aesthetic recreation, or create an allusion to other texts through a free rendering or replacement?

We also discuss the protagonists' names, their meanings, and their allusions to Eastern literary traditions. We debate whether the names should be rendered as they are, transliterated into the alphabet of the target language or supplemented by annotations and explanations. What happens, I ask students, when the name "Celal," a Turkish reference to the Persian poet Mevlana Celaleddin Rumi, is transliterated as "Jelal" in Gün's translation? Gün's "Jelal" can suggest the Biblical figure of Jesus, but it also echoes Rumi's classical Persian name, "Jalal." Thus the translation might be seen as restoring the Sufi overtones in the source text or substituting them with a Christian point of view. Here I point to the translator's effort to fix a meaning in the Turkish only to proliferate the interpretive possibilities in the translation. Freely, meanwhile, retains the name "Celal," thereby indicating the openness of the Turkish language to the Sufi poet. After recognizing the problems posed by intertextuality in translation, students assess the trade-off between source-text loss and target-text gain with the help of Walter Benjamin's concept of translation as an "afterlife" (1923b). This exercise further problematizes theories of equivalence as well as the assumption that translation is a transparent act of communication. Translation, we conclude, is a practice that deconstructs the source text first by decontextualizing it, emptying it of source-language significations, and then by recontextualizing it for a new audience in the translating language and culture.

Writing Assignments

In addition to midterm and final examinations that test students on material covered in class, I ask them to write two short essays and a final research paper that takes class discussions in related but different directions. Each of the short essays corresponds to the two core units of the course. For the first, I ask students to choose a passage we have not examined from one of the translations and to compare it with a corresponding passage from another version, posing questions about the aesthetics, ethics, and politics of translation. Students are asked to define precisely what they mean by "translation" and carefully lay out their theoretical assumptions. Isolating similarities and differences between the two passages, they must formulate each translator's interpretive strategies by analyzing vocabulary, syntax, literary tropes, and style and by situating the strategies in the cultural and historical context in which the translator worked. The second essay, similarly, focuses on one of the adaptations, exploring the relationship between a story from the *Nights* and its intersemiotic transposition. Once again, students are asked to present a theoretically informed definition of adaptation and then to articulate and contextualize the interpretation that a drama, film, or work of visual art inscribes in the source text.

Although they are initially concerned about the open-ended nature of the assignments, I find that students execute them with rigor and creativity. For the first essay, they develop productive applications for the translation theory we study throughout the course, focusing on the translators' verbal choices as well as factors in the packaging and marketing of the translations while taking up issues of canon formation, nation-building, and colonialism. Some students engage with contemporary cultural and political debates in the United States. Others test the abstraction of theoretical concepts by examining them against current practices in publishing and reading translations. For the second essay, most students choose to write on film or painting, primarily because these media are most accessible. One student explored the effects of an absent Shahrazad and a frame story in the film adaptation, suggesting that this absence allowed Pasolini to concentrate exclusively on the love-stories in the *Nights*. Another student traced the transformation of the female body from a sexual object to a story-telling subject in paintings and illustrations. Yet another student, who actually saw Supple's dramatization of al-Shaykh's *Nights* at the Luminato Festival in Toronto, analyzed its representation of sensuality and the erotics and politics of gender struggle.

I construct the assignment for the final research paper by returning to the debates on world literature with which we began the course. This longer assignment asks students to draw on theoretical concepts in both translation and world literature to frame the discussion of the translations, adaptations, and rewritings with the goal of modifying and reformulating the concept of world literature itself. I want students to consider how we can perform readings of translations alongside rewritings and adaptations with sensitivity to the reader's and translator's subjectivity in a nontransparent act of communication. Students engage with problems of "fidelity" and "accuracy," the place of translation in understanding linguistic others, and the translator's role as interpreter and creative writer, all in the context of the ethics and politics of translation and the global inequalities that affect literatures in English translation.

20 World-Wide Translation

Language, Culture, Technology

Ignacio Infante

The undergraduate course described in this chapter examines theoretical and practical approaches to translation from an interdisciplinary perspective. It constitutes an introductory survey of the field of translation studies for students majoring in literary and cultural studies as well as for those with academic interests outside of foreign languages and literatures. While the course is housed in a comparative literature program (cross-listed with international and area studies and used for credit in the applied linguistics minor), it has also attracted students majoring in anthropology, English, foreign languages, psychology, and pre-medicine, as well as those in business, engineering, and the fine arts. As this wide-ranging constituency demonstrates, the structure and scope of the course offer a productive model for studying translation that includes but extends beyond literary criticism and linguistic approaches to translation.

Aims and Methods

The course considers the central position that translation occupies in the world today, involving professionals who work in diverse fields and deploying new technologies and digital media. One of the main pedagogical objectives is to provide students with an opportunity to experience creatively the relative foreignness of cultures and to take an active role in the process of both linguistic transmission and transcultural exchange. While most students who enroll have a command of a foreign language, the interdisciplinary approach does not require fluency.

Roughly the first half of the course focuses on translation theory, while the second half studies how translation is actually used in different professional contexts. Students are first exposed to key theoretical texts that examine how translation has been traditionally studied from the perspectives of linguistics, literary criticism, and film studies. These readings allow students to gain familiarity with the central concepts of translation studies, including notions of equivalence, the relation between literary translation and world literature, semiotic approaches to translation, forms of subtitling, and film adaptation considered as an act of translation. The aim is to provide a basic critical terminology to analyze translations and translation-oriented cultural works for students majoring not only in the humanities but also in other fields where translation does not enter the curriculum in a direct or sustained way.

The second half of the course emphasizes the role of translation in various professions such as anthropology, business, health care, and law. It is also here that students are given the option of working in the real world through community-based teaching and learning (CBTL). The addition of this component was inspired by the experiences of a student who took an earlier version of the course and later worked as a volunteer in a health clinic. The student, who unexpectedly had to interpret for a Spanish-speaking patient, found the course material extremely helpful in order both to understand her role as an interpreter and to provide a more efficient and skilled translation into English. After learning of the student's experiences, I realized the potential benefit that implementing CBTL could have for students as well as for various local communities who may need their assistance. This component allows students to connect the critical study of translation explored during the first eight weeks of classes with the particular service they carry out with a community partner. Students who elect the CBTL option currently collaborate with a nonprofit organization, the World Pediatric Project in St. Louis.

Readings and Activities

The course is structured around four main sections that closely relate to the different aspects of translation we examine throughout the semester: language and literature; culture; the world; and technology. After each section has been completed, a full class session is dedicated to student presentations and class discussion. The presentations examine key ideas, relate them to particular cases of the students' own choosing, and create various activities that stimulate intellectual exchange and active classroom participation. Students also submit a short response paper that discusses specific aspects of translation addressed in the readings. A midterm exam tests their knowledge of the main concepts examined during the first two sections.

We begin by exploring translation as a mechanism of transmission between different languages through the analysis of literary translation from a historical perspective. Goethe's taxonomy of translation strategies in the *West-Easterly Divan* (1819) is extremely useful in discussing how literary translation is employed to construct the nation during European Romanticism as well as how transnational relations give rise to his influential concept of "world literature" (*Weltliteratur*). Jorge Luis Borges (1935) situates particular translations of *The One Thousand and One Nights* in their historical moments, highlighting the intimate connection between translation and the creative act of literary invention. These readings are complemented by a workshop where students are divided into groups and assigned the task of comparing the same passage from the various translations that Borges discusses. Through the comparison, students learn how differences in rhetorical style and thematic emphases in a literary translation can be historically determined, greatly altering the reception of the same source text in different cultural contexts.

We then consider how translation has been understood from the perspective of modern linguistics. Roman Jakobson (1959) and Eugene Nida (1964) provide two different linguistics-oriented approaches. Both theorists emphasize the importance of translation as a process of interpersonal communication and the transmission of meaning. While Jakobson offers a semiotic model for understanding translation beyond literature (based on the categories "intralingual," "interlingual," and "intersemiotic"), Nida addresses the question of equivalence through his distinction between "formal" and "dynamic" correspondence. We contrast these approaches with selected passages from Walter Benjamin's "The Translator's Task" (1923b), which advances a theory of translation that is opposed to the communication of information.

Finally, we examine how translation is related to film adaptation and to the more recent phenomenon of fansubbing, the amateur subtitling made by fans of movies and television shows and shared online (our readings are Francesco Casetti [2007] and Luis Pérez González [2006]). While the adaptation of a text into an audiovisual medium and the phenomenon of fansubbing constitute quite different translational processes, they both demonstrate how the creative act of translation is connected to film and television. Thus not only is this exploration of audiovisual translation related closely to the literary practices examined in previous classes, but it opens a new line of inquiry. We discuss such materials as movie adaptations of *Romeo and Juliet* and fansubbed TV shows with which students are generally much more familiar than the work of such writers as Goethe, Benjamin, and Jakobson.

The first section of the course generates presentations that match the variety of the required materials, theoretical, literary, and audiovisual. Students have applied notions of equivalence in analyzing different translations of a novel by Gabriel García Márquez. They have compared movie adaptations of the Cinderella fairy tale that articulate different "communicative situations," in Casetti's terminology, in order to discuss the process of film adaptation in different cultural contexts (Casetti 2007: 83–5). And they have produced, shared, and discussed their own fansubbing efforts with their favorite contemporary American sitcoms, such as *Modern Family* and *The Big Bang Theory*.

The next section examines how various cultures have historically depended on translation in their encounters with each other, whether during colonial and postcolonial periods or during our current era of globalization. We start by reading Robert McCrum's *Globish* (2010), a popular history of the English language that traces its evolution into the radically simplified version referred to as "Globish" with the expansion of the British Empire, the political preeminence of the United States in the twentieth century, and the development of global capitalism and new media today. As an illustration, we view Danny Boyle's Oscar-winning movie *Slumdog Millionaire* (2009), whose screenplay intentionally deploys a globalized version of the English language. Our examination of McCrum's *Globish* serves to highlight several points, namely that the English language is the direct result of various processes of cultural translation, that cultural translation is intrinsically connected to specific socioeconomic and political processes that support nation-formation, and that colonial ventures have shaped major world languages such as English, Spanish, and Chinese.

To develop these points further, we read a series of texts that cut across different practices and disciplines. Talal Asad (1986) and James Clifford (1997) study the problems of translation in anthropology, particularly as they address Western ethnographic practices in relation to non-Western cultures. Vicente Rafael (1988), working in history, examines the politics of conversion, translation, and violence during the colonial expansion of the Spanish empire in the Philippines. From the standpoint of literary and cultural studies, Alfred Arteaga (1994) and Gayatri Chakravorty Spivak (1983)investigate the ethical problems posed by the translation, publication, and circulation of literatures that originate in marginalized and minority cultures.

The presentations that follow this section tend to show students closely scrutinizing contemporary cultural trends in the United States and abroad. They have questioned the problematic politics of photojournalism in representing non-Western cultures as well as the (mis)representations of American high school culture in contemporary French music videos. They have treated the circulation of "Chinglish" in contemporary China by relying on McCrum's analysis of Globish. They have thought about the questions of authenticity and originality raised by the hybrid cultural objects that have emerged in various Asian immigrant communities in American cities.

The course then tackles the relation between translation and a number of practical, real-world issues. This section generally elicits strong responses from students, particularly since it involves divisive social debates and traumatic contemporary events. To what extent, we ask, are issues and experiences like sexual orientation, human rights, war crimes, torture, and illness translatable across different cultures and societies? The readings are drawn from such fields as gender theory, legal scholarship, literary criticism, medical history, and sociolinguistics. We start with Michael Cronin's work (2003) on minority languages within the larger context of globalization so as to consider the material conditions that determine interlingual translation in our world today. We then read Lori Chamberlain (1988) and Keith Harvey (1998) to learn how translation has been gendered feminine in theory and commentary as well as how the translation of homosexual and nonheteronormative identities across cultures creates problems that are simultaneously stylistic, social, and political.

We then focus on issues of interlingual and cultural translation as they emerge in medical contexts both in the United States and abroad. Brad Davidson (2000) provides a detailed examination of medical interpretation in American hospitals, including the sociolinguistic role played by interpreters in interviewing, diagnosing, and treating immigrant patients who lack fluency in English. Julie Livingston (2006) helps to develop this inquiry by considering whether the Western concept of disability can be translatable to a non-Western language and culture. Her case study involves Setswana, a language spoken in Botswana. By examining these two cases, students are able to see how pragmatic, epistemological, and ethical problems are closely connected to medical translation within specific institutional frameworks in the United States and globally.

The next set of readings takes up the issue of translation in wartime. Both Emily Apter (2006: 129–38) and Zrinka Stahuljak (2010) focus on the Balkan conflict in the former Yugoslavia, although from very different perspectives. Apter discusses the concept of Balkanization in relation to the global dominance of English over minority languages, while Stahuljak examines the role played by Croatian interpreters who not only witnessed the conflict but also sought to establish a position of neutrality when interpreting the testimony of other witnesses. With the help of Craig Scott, we then consider the problem of torture, where the differing status of human rights violations in national legal systems and international law creates tension that in fact constitute a "problem of translation" (2001: 45). Scott offers an opportunity to bring translation studies to bear on the manifold legal ramifications of human rights from a transnational perspective.

The presentations after this section do not shy away from controversial topics. Students have analyzed the representation of homosexual identities in the English translation of Cuban writer Reinaldo Arenas's autobiography, *Before Night Falls* (1993). They have treated the McGill Pain Questionnaire as a form of medical translation, elucidating the various cultural determinants at work in its codification of pain. And they have considered the legal and human rights issues raised by the case of the transwoman PFC. Chelsea (née Bradley) Manning, asking whether the United States Army's solitary confinement and refusal to allow her to undergo hormonal therapy constitute a form of torture after her imprisonment for espionage.

In the fourth and final section of the course, we focus on how contemporary technological advances and the digital revolution have radically changed the practice of translation as well as its socioeconomic conditions. We start with Apter's assertion that "everything is translatable" (2006: 226) in an era characterized by DNA mapping, the digitally driven form of language referred to as Netlish, machine translation, and various forms of software art. Because students today have a close familiarity with digital technology, they can establish a series of connections between the act of translation, various digital processes, and software applications. Cronin also helps us to develop this line of inquiry by arguing that contemporary translators occupy a "third culture" constituted by their location in a "supranational" space while experiencing a "fluid temporality" shaped by the institutional and economic forces of globalization (2003: 108, 105). For Karin Littau, the development of hypertext, anticipated by poststructuralist concepts of textuality, both realizes and redirects the various efforts to make the translator visible in translation studies by presenting "a multiplicity of variant translations" and by foregrounding "the seriality of translation" (1997: 445).

We conclude this final section of the course with a translation digital lab in which we explore different forms of machine translation and carry out a series of interlingual experiments with Google Translate as well as with various translation applications for tablet and smartphone. Even though students regularly use Google Translate for basic translation needs and composition in foreign languages, they are not necessarily familiar with the probability-based models of Natural Language Processing (NLP) at the core of Google's translation technology. By critically thinking about the different translation outcomes provided by Google Translate when using specific constraints (such as translating between two or more foreign languages or inserting text with words that cannot be processed by the models of NLP), students are able to see that it does not represent a universally applicable translation technology. Instead it constitutes a model that is linguistically determined by the grammatical structures of the English language and culturally determined by Anglophone culture.

Students develop particularly engaging presentations after the final section of the course. They have explored how the outcomes of different systems of machine translation compare with the probability-based model developed by Google Translate. They have also analyzed how digital photographic applications articulate customized translations of actual experiences that can be instantaneously shared online to create different social networks in various cultural contexts. Finally, they have devised their own digital applications able to process and translate different product choices into various customer profiles within a newly created online marketplace for different communities in the city of St. Louis.

Final Projects and Community Service

Students are required to develop a final project that includes both a practical engagement with translation and a critical analysis of their engagement that makes use of the required readings. The practical component is a translation—construed with latitude—of a text, film, webpage, event, or object into any medium (the media that students usually choose are linguistic, audiovisual, electronic, or digital). If a student elects to produce a retranslation of something previously translated, he or she must justify the new version on the basis of an assessment of the first version. The critical component of the project is an essay in which students discuss the relevance of their translation strategies to their source materials. This essay generally includes a description of the main challenges posed by the source materials, the theoretical approach adopted, and a critical analysis of the student's own translation or critique of an existing translation.

The final projects have included a wide range of materials and approaches. Students have translated previously untranslated texts, poetry, prose fiction, and drama. They have produced a series of translations into English of the same poem by Borges, applying different theories of translation and adaptation. They have subtitled an entire Catalan movie into English. They have created an intersemiotic translation of a short story by Kate Chopin, turning it into a work of visual art. They have treated Western photojournalism of non-Western cultures as a form of cultural translation, critically examining the ethical problems raised by such visual representations. While some of these projects originally emerged as part of a presentation, others were unrelated to previous work carried out in class.

Students who participate in the track for community-based teaching and learning do not submit a final project. Instead they perform service with a community organization in one of three areas: immigration, health, education. Depending on their language skills as well as the needs of our community partners, students are likely to engage in interlingual translation and interpretation and to assist recent immigrants in their integration into American culture. Students deploy in the most practical way the theoretical and critical concepts about translation that they learned from the readings and class discussions while making a significant contribution to the improvement of community life. They identify and work to revise detrimental stereotypes as they encounter a range of linguistic and cultural differences. As part of their community service for the World Pediatric Project, students help the families of children receiving medical treatment in various hospitals in the St. Louis metropolitan area. These families originate from different countries in Central and South America, they are unfamiliar with American culture, and they do not usually speak fluent English. Hence students organize various events and activities for children and their families, including American birthday parties and trips to various cultural sites in St. Louis, while helping them with basic shopping and translation needs.

The CBTL track requires ten hours of community service and the completion of a final presentation to the rest of the class. In small groups, students share their experiences by describing the different cultural and linguistic needs of the families they work with, the various events and activities they organize, and the ways in which their service is connected to issues of cultural and interlingual translation. Students individually submit a short written report in which they connect specific aspects of the content of the course with their particular community experience. At a time when colleges and universities stress the importance of study abroad for undergraduates, the CBTL track allows our students to obtain a greater understanding of a multicultural world through local communities.

Ultimately, World-Wide Translation is a course that allows students simultaneously to become globally aware and locally committed. The course provides a general introduction to the field of translation studies while emphasizing its real-world applicability in different professional contexts, academic fields, and theoretical frameworks. By emphasizing the literary, linguistic, cultural, and technological aspects of translation, the course offers an interdisciplinary approach that allows students to explore translation from various critical perspectives and in various social practices. While being solidly grounded in the field of comparative literature as its institutional home, World-Wide Translation offers a model for opening the humanities and bringing the vital skills they provide to a wider undergraduate population of students majoring in other areas of study.

21   (Post)Colonial Translation

Shaden M. Tageldin

If comparatists are riven by heteroglossia, teaching (largely) in translation while working (largely) in original languages, postcolonial critics more often are trapped in monoglossia, casually gesturing to multiple languages (dominated as well as dominating) while engaging only one: the imperial tongue. I teach translation to bring comparative literary method and postcolonial theory to bear on one another—and to unsettle both. Through the prism of translation, I maintain, teachers of comparative literature can at once reprise the paradigms and surprise the limits that postcolonialism imposes on dominant understandings of world literary relations today.

My graduate seminar on "(Post)Colonial Translation," offered in the Department of Cultural Studies and Comparative Literature at the University of Minnesota, provides a case in point. Shuttling between critical translation theory, literary history, and imaginative literature, the seminar interrogates the role of translation—interlingual, ontological, epistemological, cultural—in imperialism and (post)coloniality. Readings span Africa, the Americas, the Arabic-speaking world, Asia, and Europe. We explore how modern Western empires have used translation to assert power; how native intellectuals have pursued translation to resist it or to propel their cultures toward some real or imagined equivalence with the imperial West; why many modern cultural developments in the global South took translational forms, ranging from the Indian "renaissance" and the Arab *nahda* to the Chinese May Fourth movement and pan-African *négritude*. Finally, through post-1945 poetry and novels that rewrite empire *as* and *through* translation, we see how imperial English or French has translated Arabic, Bangla, Creole, Korean, or Urdu and wonder, as writers remake the former to approximate the latter, if English and French are (or are not) equally translated. Such translational fictions enable my students to grasp the riddles of language that translation presents despite the fact that we hold no or few languages in common.

In sum, the course untangles the asymmetrical dynamics of translation under (post)colonial conditions, showing how these engender both the universals that underpin empire and the particulars that issue from and against them. By apprehending the geopolitically unequal ground on which languages met in modernity, students not only see why imperial languages came to dominate today's world but also recognize that the modern literatures of recently colonized "non-Western" spaces do not magically appear postindependence. As a site of struggle and seduction, translation reasserts the linguistic and cultural presence of what comes before, persists within, and survives empire—of all that comparative literature and postcolonial studies still mark absent—and compels us to rethink both on polycentric, not Eurocentric, terms.

The course unfolds in three units: "(In)commensurabilities: The Particular, the Universal, the Sovereign"; "Between Theology and History: Seductions, Conversions, Subversions"; and "Rezonings: Colony/Nation/Diaspora, Old/New Media, Globality/Vernacularism." Each student posts 500-word reflections on assigned readings to our course website; presents readings in class; and writes a twenty-page final research paper based on a prospectus submitted one month prior. Hailing from diverse disciplines, my students write papers that bring critical translation theory to bear on a range of topics: from translations of vernacular and literary Telugu in British India and the struggles therein for intimacy with the colonized to willful mistranslation in the 1889 Treaty of Wichale and Italo-Ethiopian interimperial politics; from intersemiotic translations of medieval poetry in contemporary Icelandic music, opposing Iceland to Danish and United States imperialisms, to those of text and image in a photo-essay on Shanghai by a Chinese-born writer and a United States-born photographer, opposing historicity to imperial nostalgia; from the translation of "race" in Brazil in the shadows of globalization and the Universal Declaration on the Question of Race (1950) to that of *banh mi* into "Vietnamese po'boy," in post-Katrina New Orleans, as a barometer of Vietnamese American inclusion/exclusion in United States politics; from the translational politics of Ottoman and Turkish modernity in the novels of Ahmed Midhat and Orhan Pamuk to the commerce between translation and death in Walter Benjamin's essays on translation and on storytelling. From the ensemble of assignments, refrains emerge: complicity/opposition, agency/situation, particularity/universalism. These cut across the architecture of the syllabus and redraw (post)colonial translation along new "fault" lines.

Between Complicity and Opposition

In extra-European texts, students sometimes seek an anticolonial or a postcolonial posture more (or less) oppositional than it really was or is. Translation redefines their views of domination and resistance, veering as it does between complicity and opposition. Witness our seminar discussion of *négritude*. When we read Aimé Césaire's *Notebook of a Return to the Native Land*, students assert that Césaire's translation of European scientific racism into a liberationist poetics is not especially revolutionary, since he never breaks free of the limits imposed on Blackness by French colonial rhetoric and epistemology. Why swallow and regurgitate, they ask, the poisonous idea that Blackness is to emotion what Whiteness is to reason?

Read with Brent Hayes Edwards's argument that translation in interwar Black internationalism dislocated the idea of Blackness (Edwards 2003: 13–15), Césaire can be seen as seizing and recuperating from white understanding even the most abject image: the pejorative "nègre" ("nigger") as opposed to the whitewashed "noir" ("black") or "homme de couleur" ("man of color"). To say "nègre" in a new key is to translate the term into an altered and potentially radical state of mind and being. Césaire rejects a claim for Black humanity premised on the very ideas of reason, civilization, history, and sovereignty that underpinned the French colonial *mission civilisatrice*. I point out that Eshleman and Smith's choice of "nigger" for *nègre* imitates Césaire's conscious recuperation of colonial logic, but their version of his assertion "il est place pour tous au rendez-vous de la con-quête" (Césaire 1983: 57–8) as "there is room for everyone at the convocation of conquest" (Césaire 2001: 44) defangs it: "convocation" stages the reinvention of humanity as a harmonious coming-together rather than the appointed time ("ren-dezvous") of conquest, concealing the fact that anticolonialism often called on the colonized to occupy the position of the colonizer in order to upset the colonial order of things.

We then shift to the Moroccan theorist Abdelfattah Kilito, using translation to explore the similar issue of whether he upholds the binaristic logic of Orientalism. How do we understand, I ask, Kilito's declaration in *Thou Shalt Not Speak My Language* that, had the ninth-century intellectual Matta ibn Yunus rightly trans-lated into Arabic Aristotle's concepts of tragedy and comedy, instead of "mis-rendering" them as panegyric and satire, Arabic letters would have undergone a renaissance akin to Europe's (Kilito 2008: 95–8)? Students question whether Kilito anachronistically ascribes an Arab/European binary to the Middle Ages, refusing a literary history that might view the "Arabic" and "European" streams in confluence with one another so as to buttress a demand that Arab culture catch up to the West. In response I notice the hint of irony, the fact that Kilito might be not so much stating his own position on Arab literary history as restating the problematic position of Arab intellectuals who style the so-called nineteenth- and early-twentieth-century renaissance of Arab letters on European models, intent on subjecting Arabic literature to European temporalities. That restatement, I sug-gest, is a sly dose of savage critique; the very preposterousness of the counterfac-tual upends its imagined potentialities (if only Arabs had translated Greek texts correctly, how Western they would be!). Kilito's Janus-faced text plunges students into the bewildering linguistic, epistemic, temporal, and political thicket that is translation.

Between Agency and Situation

Next we take up the problem of agency in translation, starting with Gayatri Chakravorty Spivak's "The Politics of Translation." This anti-imperialist theory of translation argues for the "surrender" of the First World translator to the rheto-ricity of the original Third World text (Spivak 1983: 315). Flush with the lin-guistic, historical, and political nuances that insert gaps in its language, Spivak suggests, this text cannot but insert a space between itself and its translator, a space that refuses easy assimilation of its aesthetics and politics to those of its translator. Students unfailingly test the limits of Spivak's theory in debate. *Should* anyone, some ask, forget his or her linguistic, social, and political position as she or he translates? To do so, they argue, is to forget history. Others agree with Spivak. Is it not important to remember who translates whom? Maybe a translator who hails from a dominant world power *needs* to surrender authority to a text from a dominated language.

We consider other, opposing theories of translation by intellectuals writing in Bangla, Chinese, and Arabic (Tageldin 2012: 265–7). These intellectuals argue that languages in translation pay with their own words for everything they get (Rabindranath Tagore), or cook their own flesh in the fire of others (Lu Xun), or lose words in gaining others (Kilito, channeling the nineteenth-century Syro-Lebanese polymath Ahmad Faris al-Shidyaq). Such theories of translation, issuing from various points in the global South, reinject resistance into the elasticity of "surrender." Situation, we conclude, is all-important.

The discussion continues with Naoki Sakai's illuminating *Translation and Subjectivity*. Sakai takes the constructions of modern Japan and a unitary Japanese language in the face of the imperial West as paradigms for a critical reconsideration of translation theory. For him, every language—even when it seems at its most self-same, issuing from or addressing so-called native speakers—is inherently in-translation, as foreign in the mouths of its addressers as it is to the ears of its addressees. All language, then, is not "homolingual" but "heterolingual address," in which "the act of inception or reception occurs as the act of translation" (Sakai 1997: 2–10). What most interests us in Sakai is his refusal to affirm only one subject position for the translator; instead he posits an ever-disrupted series of multiple positions in relation to the source text (Sakai 1997: 13). In the end, Sakai tells us, the translator is a bystander between the source and the target languages, inside both and thus inside neither at the moment of translational enunciation. But perhaps the position of bystander is too passive, too non-agential. The question that students ask of Spivak also haunts our reading of Sakai: is translation always only dictated by the source text?

Here too reading a literary text in tandem with theory helps us to rethink the translator's agency. We pair Sakai with Theresa Hak Kyung Cha's generically hybrid *Dictée*. From the first page, this text confronts us with a scene of translation that is also a scene of dictation. We wend our way through the broken lines of French and English on a page that seems torn from the notebook of Cha's deeply autobiographical narrator, although that page is typed, not scrawled, and thus not quite a facsimile of the likely medium in which a student of Cha's generation would have undertaken a classroom assignment. What does it mean if the opening scene of writing is also a scene of dictation? Is the text we see, presumably typewritten from a saved or remembered script, another layer of dictation, by fingers to keys, then to the printhead that strikes the page?

Cha calls into question the agency of the writer who is told from the start, "Aller à la ligne" (1982: 1). She savvily plays on the blurred boundary, in French, between the infinitive, the most fundamental form of the verb, and the imperative, the tense of command. "Aller à la ligne" means at once "To go to the line," a sentence that strikes a meditative tone, and "Go to the line," a sentence that brooks no refusal. To speak, then, is not just to command, as we might imagine, but also to be commanded. Turning now to the opening line of the English translation at the bottom of the same page, students noted that it does not match the French. "Open paragraph," the English intones (1982).

With a flick of her rhetorical wrist, Cha both ratifies and upends Lu Xun, whose 1930 essay " 'Hard Translation' and 'The Class Character of Literature'" calls for a practice of what we might think of as literal translation, one that does not smooth over the gaps between words. For the most literal rendering of "Aller à la ligne" actually bears more of the playful nuance of the source. It evokes both the "line" of the page—the rule the writer must follow as she pens her dictation—and the "line" of the map: the border, one of many, to which the writer must go if she is to write herself into the political cartography of twentieth-century Korea, Japan, China, and the United States (including Hawaii). By contrast, the more interpretive rendering, "Open paragraph," we agree, transmits only what Walter Benjamin (1923b: 75) calls the "inessential," reducing the French to its informational core, signaling that the writer is taking dictation and following an invisible teacher's orders. The English gains richness in intertextual juxtaposition with the French, but alone it says little. Lu Xun might say that it makes the foreign more easily digestible to the local reader, semantically and politically.

We come to see that Cha offers a resolution to the conundrum of the translator's agency. The translator surrenders, on some level, to a voice that is not her own but that calls to her in tones that can be detached neither from its own location nor from her own. Cha suggests that in making the passage from French to English, her narrator had to submit—each time she assumed a speaking position—not only to the rules of idiom but also to the dictates of situation. We cannot wrest language from context, which is also to say that we cannot think language outside society, outside politics. It dictates us even as we speak it. The translator is agent and acted upon.

Between Particularity and Universalism

Idiom brings us to our final foci: the native versus the hybrid, the vernacular versus the transnational, the untranslatable versus the translatable, and the particular versus the universal. Viewing (post)colonialism through the looking-glass of translation theory, our class discussions uncover how claims to particularity (radical untranslatability) and dreams of universalism (radical translatability) interlock in politics as in language. To explore this conundrum of all translation, my students and I engage Benjamin, Roman Jakobson, Lu Xun, and the nineteenth-century Egyptian intellectual Rifaʻa Rafiʻ al-Tahtawi. Our transcontinental repertoire unseats the imperial assumption that only the West writes foundational translation theory, and always first.

We notice that both al-Tahtawi and Lu Xun understand all language as translatable, although they reach that conclusion from divergent premises. In al-Tahtawi's account of 1834, a shared substrate—a Chomskyan deep grammar—unites all languages and makes them exchangeable in translation, however marked their surface incommensurabilities (Tahtawi 2004: 184–5; see also Tageldin 2011: chap. 3). In Lu Xun, by contrast, translatability inheres in the hard matter of language—precisely the surfaces al-Tahtawi deems too stubborn to translate. Lu Xun tells us, in effect, that any language is translatable if we try *not* to overcome its resistance to our "own"—if we resort to whatever circumlocutions necessary to render the nuance and force of a "foreign" language within the limits (and possibilities) of our "own."

Turning to Benjamin and Jakobson, students remark Benjamin's doublespeak, itself a riddle of particularity and universalism. At times, Benjamin echoes al-Tahtawi; he premises "pure language" on an "a priori," "suprahistorical kinship" of languages, "related to each other in what they want to say" (Benjamin 1923b: 77, 78). At others, he chimes with Lu Xun, arguing that what voyages to the zone of translation "where languages are reconciled and fulfilled," that is "pure language," is the untranslatable (Benjamin 1923b: 79). Indeed, for Benjamin, only by moving word-for-word—rendering, in fragments of fragments, the untranslatable—can a translation reconcile itself to the original. What then of Jakobson? Weaving between online posts and in-class readings, we find that Jakobson's "On Linguistic Aspects of Translation" strikes familiar chords. Even if one does not know what "cheese" is and cannot offer an equivalent in one's own language, Jakobson says (1959: 126–7), one can understand it if it is explained and therefore translate it—a point al-Tahtawi also makes (with different examples). Suspicious, like Lu Xun, of the "dogma of untranslatability" (which, Lu Xun opines, diverts subversive ideas from our native language by declaring those ideas ineluctably "foreign"), Jakobson writes, "All cognitive experience [. . .] is conveyable in any existing language. Whenever there is deficiency, terminology may be qualified and amplified by [. . .] circumlocutions" (Jakobson 1959: 128). Still, students observe, translatability for Jakobson inheres only in ordinary language, in "information"; as for al-Tahtawi (2004: 182), and for precisely the same reasons, it founders in poetry, where sound weds sense in paronomasia. "[P]oetry," Jakobson concludes, "by definition is untranslatable" (1959: 131).

With these theories, we compare others by Emily Apter, Tagore, Kilito, Subramanian Shankar, and Ngũgĩ wa Thiong'o (2009) that invoke untranslatability as a bulwark against imperialisms, cultural and epistemic. We notice that such anti-imperial resistance at times unfolds in standard (ostensibly universal) languages, at others in vernacular (ostensibly particular) languages. A whiff of Apter's "Untranslatable," aligned with the sacred, clings to both (Tageldin 2014). We note that Tagore's insistence, in his "Presidential Address" of 1923, that the language learner (a translator?) must pay with his or her own language for everything he or she gets from another—like Kilito's intimation (via al-Shidyaq) that bilingualism is a subtraction from a "first" language—suggests a fundamental untranslatability at the heart of all language that cannot be mystified by the introduction of a Marxian third term enabling the exchange of unlikes (Tagore 2001). No currency mediating exchange-value will do—only barter. The foreignness of the imported word never vanishes for Tagore as it does for Shankar, who envisions social translation as a process that over time domesticates foreignness, makes it translatable.

As students observe in online posts, Shankar's *Flesh and Fish Blood* highlights the inextricability of translation as praxis from translation as trope. Arguing that the actual practice of translation teaches us that translation is never simply an

act of violence (at worst) or a problem (at best) but also always a creative compromise and thus a hopeful opportunity, Shankar contests Tejaswini Niranjana's
contention that colonial translation is always a structure of "containment," a violent effort to fix the meaning of the languages, texts, and ontologies of the colonized, and that postcolonial translation—what she dubs "disruption"—is always
its (equally violent) opposite (Niranjana 1992: chap. 6). Shankar's provocative
insights, we agree, include his observation that untranslatability, like translatability,
is historically and materially contingent. Through what he calls "social translation"—
a practice of "gradual, collective, anonymous, and oral translation"—what seems
untranslatable in one time and place might become eminently so in another
(Shankar 2012: 111). Still, if such is the way of social translation—to gradually wear away the particularities of the local until it dissolves in the global
dominant—should we eye it with equanimity, or celebrate it as promise, or recognize it as the violence it often is? (Post)colonial translation compels us to address
this question, crucial even now to our understanding of world literature in the
shadow of politics.

Indeed, Shankar himself—even as he premises the translatability of all language on the historical and material situatedness of the vernacular, as opposed
to the ahistorical and inviolable sacredness enshrined in classical or standard
language—hints that the vernacular is the most untranslatable language there is.
Plucking a point from online discussion for in-class debate, my students ponder
this contradiction: how to insist on a "local" inassimilable to the hybrid or the
transnational—a local that resists translation—while also insisting that nothing is
too "local" to translate, if the historical-material conditions for its interpretation
elsewhere are ripe, and right? We conclude that Shankar casts indigeneity—the
stuff of daily life that defines "native" experience (Benjamin's *Brot*)—as particular yet unknowable, but the vernacular as particular yet knowable: a site at which
the local negotiates external forces, including the universal, on its own terms.

Finally, in Kilito and Ngũgĩ, we confront the *noli me tangere* that makes
"untranslatable" language so tantalizing *to* touch. Scrutinizing Kilito's encounter
with an American student fluent in Moroccan dialect, we are struck by the fact
that—however sharply her fluency dispossesses him of his "native" language—it
is not vernacular but standard Arabic that is the most intimate (hence untranslatable) language for Kilito. It is the *standard* language he hopes the American
woman does not speak, whose untranslatability he defends from her imperial
"invasion." By contrast, Ngũgĩ's *Something Torn and New* understands *vernaculars* as untranslatables—lose an African language, Ngũgĩ argues, and one loses
a cultural memory—even as it calls for translational traffic among African vernaculars and between those languages and the world's, bypassing the mediation
of essentially colonial European languages. Yet what do we make of the role of
European colonialism in "translating" many oral African vernaculars into writing (usually Roman scripts) and along new epistemic lines? Here my students
find especially relevant Lydia Liu's theory of the super-sign, "a hetero-cultural
signifying chain that crisscrosses the semantic fields of two or more languages
simultaneously" (2004: 13). In an imperial conjuncture of "native" and "foreign"

signifiers of the sort that Liu's *Clash of Empires* describes, extra-lingual power dynamics often torque the native toward the foreign. Might the foreign wear, at times, a disarmingly indigenous, vernacular face? Might the native—to flip Liu's script—at times masquerade as more foreign than it really is? These questions, which assume particular urgency in (post)colonial translation theory, are also universal. They speak to what my students understand, and rightly, as the *political* task of the translator.

22 Mirrored Texts

Bilingual Authorship and Translation

Jan Walsh Hokenson

This course in self-translation explores the history of bilingual literary writings since the Middle Ages, with emphasis on modernists in Europe and the Americas. Accordingly, it also tracks the rise and fall of literary nationalisms, the role of sociopolitical dislocations in the legacy of bilingualism, and the changing concepts of translation and originality in literary history and critical theory. Following readings in history and theory, class discussions focus on the self-translated texts of such writers as Julien Green, Samuel Beckett, Stefan George, Giuseppe Ungaretti, Vladimir Nabokov, and Rosario Ferré, plus two self-translators' own memoirs of the process, one by Ferré (1995), the other a bilingual book by Green (1987). Bilingual authorship is a fertile subset of translation studies that offers students the opportunity to do some exciting, close comparative translation analysis while investigating the basic but often unstated assumptions of translation theory.

As in most translation studies courses, students are required to have advanced skills in at least two languages, including English. "Mirrored Texts" is usually an advanced graduate seminar, but it can easily be tailored to students at different levels. Optimally, students hold bachelor's degrees in either comparative literature or in the literature and culture—or linguistics—of one specific language. Rather like many of the self-translators studied in the course, these days several of the students themselves often come from different language heritages and can help instruct the others about the cultural politics of bilinguality and the realities of trying to preserve one's native language while struggling to move into another. The students' own languages, however acquired, can become an opportunity for testing out the theoretical ideas that the class as a group is developing. Also, as the course advances, the seminar structure invites students to act as interpreters or ambassadors for the literary traditions of the languages with which they are working.

Conceptually, the course is structured to develop answers to certain questions arising from gaps or blanks in literary and translation history. Although students usually do not believe me until mid-semester, I always tell them that the course is a collaborative effort in which all of us weekly share our labors, thoughts, discoveries, problems, and questions, so that we can as a group come to some real conclusions about this weird and onerous practice of authors' self-translating: Why do they do it? For money, for control, for expanding audiences? Why are their two versions so different? Why has translation theory neglected these bilingual writers? Does their work reveal common features from which we might develop a theory of self-translation? Why has writers' bilinguality been elided by historians of canon formation and national literatures, as in translation theory? Is the chief obstacle to their inclusion the fact that the so-called original text somehow exists in two languages? To which national canon or tradition does the bilingual text belong? To neither? Or to both? Does the bilingual text break out of what we habitually think of as a national canon or tradition into something transnational? How do we know?

"How do we know?" becomes an important refrain in such an endeavor, as everyone's training and skills are brought to bear on new materials and conjectures. In order to get this course off the ground, students have to rethink the basic model of translation theory, source > target language by a second-hand translator, and that means reconceiving the nature and role of the translator *tel quel*. Students already familiar with the history and theory of translation welcome this aim as a kind of bold, breathtaking challenge. It is clear to them that translation theory continues to conceive of translators as belonging to one culture only, usually the target-language culture, for which they interpret the foreign. Students not versed in translation theory, those coming straight into the course from literary studies in a specific language, are often more helpful to their classmates in explaining how canon-formation was politically shaped to be monolingual (erasing Chaucer's French, for instance) and how the concepts "author" and "translator" came to be seen as mutually exclusive (whereas with Wyatt's Petrarch they were not).

Thus the course is designed as a collaborative effort to scrutinize the historical contexts of selected texts by self-translators while steadily querying the relations of ancient and modern notions of authorship and biculturality. Supplemented by other books and shorter readings, the panoptic textbook for the course is Hokenson and Munson, *The Bilingual Text* (2007, hereafter abbreviated as TBT). For teaching, it is helpful that this book is divided into three sections covering broad historical periods and that each section entails an overview of changing concepts of language and translation in that period followed by analyses of specific bilingual texts. Given that self-translation is still usually neglected in the (monolingual) histories of major literatures, it is useful to have everyone read the introduction ("Aims and Terms") and the conceptual sections of that study in the first three weeks of the course: "Vulgar Tongues: Medieval and Renaissance Conditions (1100–1600)," "The Widening Compass of the Vernaculars: Early Modern Conditions (1600–1800)," and "Facing Language: Romantic, Modern, and Contemporary Conditions (1800–2000)." On that foundation, buttressed by supplementary readings, the group swiftly acquires a common conceptual base and lexicon.

Initially, to facilitate the roundtable format, the various parts of each conceptual section can be assigned to individual students to present orally to the group, producing discussions that at first often center on the historically unstable notions of "nation" and "author." Hence discussions in the first week focus on the critical legacy of the "version" in philological tradition and in the second week on the bilingual writer through history (because literary historians have so effectively buried the realities of other languages' presence in their canon). Meanwhile students are scouring literary and translation histories looking for an appealing bilingual author whom they might study all semester. Each student selects one self-translator as an object of independent study and presents a brief weekly report that relates the writer to issues scheduled for that week. The final project includes a working annotated bibliography at mid-semester, an oral presentation of the project to the seminar, and a final critical essay on the bilingual author's self-translated texts.

One of the challenges in teaching "Mirrored Texts" is students' preconceptions—perfectly understandable in the long legacy of German Romantic translation theory—about the unitary self as a kind of one-dimensional consciousness that is happiest and most original in the maternal language. Even though most students have a good intellectual grasp of bilingualism, and probably rightly flatter themselves that they are indeed pretty bilingual themselves, the idea of original artistic creation by a second self in another language is daunting. So the third week focuses on the self in self-translation, because even today many students have internalized the notion that it is only in the maternal language that one can be authentic, original, or even creative. We tackle the issue of subjectivity immediately in several ways. To recover some historical perspectives on this issue, following the TBT reading, we examine some eighteenth-century notions of different languages as simply tools appropriate to certain definite purposes, analogous to different registers or stylistic levels within any one language (why switching languages was for so long likened to changing clothes, with languages as "outward dress" to suit the occasion or the audience). We explore notions of bilingual subjectivity in concrete, contemporary terms with such translation theorists as Douglas Robinson on "the fragmentation and 'scattering' . . . of traditional subjectivity across wide psycho-social networks" (2001: 147).

I also invite an applied linguist to visit the class to review contemporary linguists' views of bilinguality in the individual and to take a lot of questions. Students readily agree with the main point that bilinguals can never be perfectly so, because languages can never be identical in meaning and the speaker has had different experiences in each. That point becomes crucial later in the course, but for the moment students are fascinated with reports on the brain of the bilingual (briefly, in monolinguals the left hemisphere is dominant, bilinguals tend to be more symmetrical in lateralization, and some sites are specific to each language but there are also clear areas of overlap). Such information renders bilinguality a material as well as a cultural or linguistic issue, like something we all carry around in our own heads. In particular students lacking any linguistics background need this briefing on diglossia as functional specialization of languages and on code-switching among bilinguals. One striking example that both echoes early modern thinkers in contemporary terms and dramatizes the cultural freight of languages, not to mention language choice, impresses students: a Kenyan woman goes to her brother's bakery to get free bread and asks for it in their dialect, but he retreats from her into Swahili, the official language of cold commerce.

By the fourth week, focusing on translation theory and the bilingual text, the class as a group confronts, in a preliminary way, the more specific difficulties of theorizing bilinguality in mirrored or parallel literary texts. Everyone reads the epilogue in TBT, charting trends in critical work to 2007, as well as the introduction to Anthony Cordingley's 2013 collection of essays on self-translation, and students have each been provided a copy of a venerable theoretical article or chapter from various theorists and critics who deeply disagree with one another (such as Beaujour 1989; Fitch 1998; Oustinoff 2001). Once students perceive that there are fundamentally different ways to conceptualize the bilingual text, then they can better strike out on their own, approach their selected bilingual author with multiple perspectives, and ultimately tailor their final essays with an eye toward possible publication. Indeed, several fine articles have eventuated from this course over the years.

By this point, another challenge is to hold the course together. With students working on texts in five or six different languages, coming from such different traditions and contexts, and working on bilinguals as distinct as German-British in the 1810s, Chilean-French in the 1950s, and Puerto Rican-American in the 2010s, the group risks splintering into various, faintly nationalistic notions of cultural difference. In order to open up that relationship, Anthony Pym's *Method in Translation History* is always a great success. In this context, students quickly discern how Pym's book entailed a radical proposal to redesign the model of translation as movement or transfer from one monoculture to another by (1) viewing translators as human bodies, that is, not split in two by national borders but living and traveling in two languages at once, comprising intersections and overlaps of cultures, such that each translator is "a minimal interculture" (Pym 1998: 181); (2) revisioning translation itself as *not* the translator's transfer of the text into his or her (target) culture but as overlap or interculture, serving neither monoculture but combining both as intercultural document; and (3) declining to define "culture" except or until "interculture" is defined, which is to define culture negatively, solely by the points of "resistance" in the translative process from the intercultural overlap (i.e., only the untranslatable is monocultural) (Pym 1998: 191). A particularly useful corollary is Pym's assertion that the "entire discourse on fidelity" arises from the institutionalization of translation designed to eclipse all traces of interculturality (Pym 1998: 186). It is crystal clear to students that self-translators, of all historical periods, lived and breathed those precepts every day. Thence another week's focus on the translator as interculture.

Adopting wholesale Pym's objective of a translation history based on interculturality, students track this concept through their bilingual writers' cultural contexts, as well as the two texts, just as the group is beginning to do together for the other writers in discussion. Once students start tracing the bits and pieces of linguistic hybridity in their writer's life and times, the authorial situations seem to leap into life for them in exciting ways. Also, because historical background is much easier for them to adduce than intercultural material or effects in the bilingual texts themselves, the week after Pym is devoted to the bilingual reader, using various readings from linguistics and referring to Marilyn Gaddis Rose's concept of reading literary texts and their translations stereoscopically. That week, on liminal spaces between languages, brings the concept of interculture into the students' applied, literary critical modes of reading.

After refining the concept of the translator, this next step, the question of reading or how to read a text in two language versions, is just as crucial. Students are so heavily grounded in translation analysis as dictionary work that it is difficult for them to take that next 180-degree turn and see so-called errors as authorial, artistic creations. That's where Rose's concept is useful (one could use many different metaphors, but it's fitting here that stereo- replace monoscope). Rose suggests that stereoscopic reading of all texts and their (standard) translations uncovers "the interliminal richness" generated by harmonies and disjunctions between the versions, and it directs our attention to "the affective, semantic space between" languages and texts (Rose 1997: 54). For self-translated texts, this interliminal space between versions is just where students need to start working if they are to grasp the mechanics—cultural and linguistic—of the actual practice of self-translation. For example, when Beckett translates *Happy Days* as *O les beaux jours*, Winnie's scraps from Shakespeare ("Ensign crimson" followed by "Pale flag," from *Romeo and Juliet*) become fragments from Ronsard ("bouchette blémie," from "Quand au temple nous serons"). Lexically the translation is indefensible. But as Knowlson (1978) pointed out long ago, Winnie's classics are used functionally rather than referentially.

Building on this cardinal difference between reader-oriented functionality and dictionary-oriented referentiality, it is useful at this point to introduce the problem of defining translation itself and to review medieval to postmodern takes on the matter. "Version and Originality" govern another week's discussions. Some students will be tempted to reify the "inter" zone between versions, the intercultural and interliminal, as an actual ontological space that has reality and substance in a Benjaminian way or following Beaujour or Fitch. To prevent the topic from evaporating in vagueness, a pragmatic definition of translation that can bridge wide lexical gaps is needed for keeping the seminar's focus on the literary *practice* of self-translation, that is, the authorial production of two versions as commensurate literary works. No single definition suffices. The most helpful I have found for this task is Andrei Fedorov's concept of the ideal translation as achieving "functional and stylistic correspondence" (quoted in Oseki-Dèpré 1999: 95). Examples, using a short bilingual text or two, help to anchor the lively discussion of what this means.

The instructors' choice of examples depends on whichever of the students' languages they hold most in common (usually Romance languages and German in my experience). One of the best texts for this purpose is Étienne Dolet's bilingual encomium for his son (see the analysis in TBT 7–8). He wrote Latin and French versions of his *Genethliacum* (1539), celebrating the birth of his son. Dolet's French text is gentle and orthodox, his Latin incisive and heretical. His *Natura* is a pagan wonder, imperious and awesome, whereas *La Nature* is a material fount of God. In Latin the writer wishes for his son the republican Roman value of security, in French the *romanz* virtue of constancy. How can we call this a translation? When students apply the concept of the translator as interculture, things become clearer. It is in Latin that the sheer power and wisdom of nature overwhelms the new father, who can invoke for his son the still living descendence of Roman values, while in the world of Christian vernacular French the more nurturing mother figure of nature, while equally powerful, sheds her imperial aspect to serve as a feminine protectrice for the child. Dolet as self-translator negotiates two futures for his son under the aegis of both residual and recently dominant cultural heritages.

The texts coexist as parallel versions of their occasion, and it is only through stereoscopic reading of the two languages that we can apprehend—in full—the paternal ideas, thoughts, and emotions, as well as the intercultural conditions in which the texts arise. The striking similarities and overlaps in the two texts, as in the interechoing strains of paternal wonder, pride, and no little fear for his son, should weigh as heavily as differences in any critical interpretation. Many students quickly discern how the divergences between security and constancy or imperious nature and motherly nature are partly those of the languages and their literary traditions (what Dolet termed "rhetorical harmonies") as the writer interpreted them. But in teaching, it must be stressed that the divergences are inextricable from the common core of Dolet's encomium, its irreducibly dual nature as text. Only in the play between both *distinguo* and *similitas* can the bilingual text reach full expression, in this case a bilingual Renaissance father's joy, as fully realized only in the interliminal space (or the stereoscopic process) of reading bilingually.

A variety of examples will serve to anchor in such ways the various conceptual tools being developed in this course in a provisional way, such as (in this case) bilingual author as interculture, textual bilinguality as interliminality, self-translation as functional and stylistic correspondence, in versions aimed at different reading audiences and their (monolingual) literary traditions. Renaissance Latin-vernacular samples are particularly effective insofar as Latin is foundational to many of the students' languages and the two texts exhibit the kinds of tension between languages undergoing cultural change, especially shifts in ruling authorities, that will preponderate in many of the postcolonial bilingual authors whom students will want to study. Also, to introduce historically distant material, such as medieval and Renaissance texts, helps them appreciate the long rich history of self-translators.

Spanish examples, usually fairly accessible to such a class since most students have some acquaintance with Latino culture, might include the Latin-vernacular case of the Mexican nun Sor Juana de la Cruz, the Spanglish case of comic code-switching by Ana Lydia Vega of Puerto Rico, the bilingual version *Yo-Yo-Boing!* (with English and Spanish texts *en face*) by Giannina Braschi, or the self-translations by Claude Esteban, Maria Luisa Bombal, Esmeralda Santiago, Roberto G. Fernández. To broaden both the reservoir of examples as well as the course's literary horizon, one can call upon the self-translating Nobel laureates: Frédéric Mistral, Rabindranath Tagore, Karl Adolph Gjellerup, Luigi Pirandello, Samuel Beckett, Isaac Bashevis Singer, Czesław Miłosz, Joseph Brodsky.

It is at this point that the class focus shifts from bilinguality or languages to authorship, that is, keeping literary creation prominent in the conceptual landscape of this course, insofar as most students' critical focus will increasingly become more literary than linguistic. And it is helpful at this point, in discussing whatever array of concrete examples, to review also some basic translation terminology and have the class agree as a group to adopt some definitions in common: specifically terms devised to span the gap between what Lawrence Venuti (1995) terms foreignizing and domesticating translations, others versions and adaptations, Oustinoff (2001) naturalizing and decentering translations and—for self-translators—recreative translations. Some such analytic tools and labels will be needed for written analyses.

Also by this time, a week or so before midpoint in the semester, I start thinning out assigned readings so students can focus on their authors and group discussions can focus on the texts by the five or six major bilingual authors assigned. The class usually needs to review the major theories and critical concepts of bilingual texts, in particular Beaujour's notion that "a polylinguistic matrix is basic to their life and art," "a kind of constantly shifting balance or flexible synthesis" (1989: 27, 53); Fitch's theory (following Walter Benjamin) that the two texts are "variants of something that has no tangible textual existence" (1998: 135); Oustinoff's idea (following Fitch) that the theoretical problem is *where* the text exists, each version being the imperfect incarnation of an ideal work (2001: 248); and Cordingley's sense that even as cultures are becoming increasingly hybrid, so self-translators' "stereolinguistic optics" keeps them highly conscious of "the internal bilingual and bicultural space out of which their creativity emerges" (2013: 3).

Indeed, for the last plank in this conceptual scaffolding of the course, I assign Anthony Cordingley's anthology of essays, both because the essayists update many of the field's major theorists and because such more recent work moves away from Benjaminian ideals into the pragmatic territory of actual texts in concrete cultural, bicultural, and culturally hybrid contexts. If one had to select only a few essays for the course, I would use those on self-translation as a play of mirrors (Julio-César Santoyo, "On Mirrors, Dynamics and Self-Translations" [Cordingley 2013: 27–38]), on its history (Jan Hokenson, "History and the Self-Translator" [Cordingley 2013: 39–60]), and on its sociology (Rainer Grutman, "A Sociological Glance at Self-Translation and Self-Translators" [Cordingley 2013: 63–80]). These essays exemplify contemporary scholarship on the typologies of self-translators as a group across periods and languages.

Over the first six to seven weeks, then, the course moves rather gradually through historical, literary, and theoretical material (with lots of brief literary examples throughout) into six weeks of close readings of a half-dozen bilingual authors. Thus about midway it shifts gears, applying all the knowledge and skills acquired so far to the intensely focused matter of a single writer's bilingual production—always being compared and contrasted with the students' own selected authors (whose life and work have become rather well known to the seminar as a group), then another major bilingual author, and so on, week by week. To keep things compassable and the focus clear, I prefer to limit the authors to bilinguals born before 1945, so that the corpus of critical sources is substantial. Across whatever array of texts one chooses, they should be case studies that widen the horizon of the course while helping students discern different self-translation strategies and aims. Constantly reining in delightful distractions, one must take care not to let dictionary differences outweigh artistic similarities.

Once students perceive how difficult it is to describe literary self-translation with many of the standard terms of criticism and theory, they can approach "mirrored texts" as rich laboratories for working out the uniqueness of their own chosen bilingual author. Among the most productive outcomes of the course is the fact that concepts of "text," "self," "translator," and "version" undergo substantial redefinition.

23 Folklore in Translation

Lee Haring

Objectives

This chapter describes a course that explores the relations between translation studies and the study of folklore (henceforward called folkloristics). The focus is the translation and adaptation of verbal folklore materials. The course can be offered on either the undergraduate or graduate levels, and although not every student commands proficiency in a foreign language, those who do can employ it in various activities.

Several objectives guide the instruction. The first is to locate parallels between practices and principles in the two fields. The instrumental model of translation has its counterpart in treatments of folklore as anonymous and freely available for rewriting, detached from the cultural and political contexts in which proverbs are spoken, songs are sung, and tales are told (Bauman 2012). Because folkloric transmission involves performance, it betokens reinterpretation, as does translation. To study this essentially hermeneutic process, students compare texts and contexts, translations and adaptations, as well as a variety of performances. (In the exposition that follows, required readings are given in parenthetical citations.)

A second objective is to uncover ethical issues. Native American narratives in English illustrate the effect of dominance and subordination on the representation of a people. Thus students take into consideration the cultural and political hierarchies in which translation and adaptation can position folklore and how the impact of those hierarchies might be mitigated or preempted.

A third objective is to examine the concept of genre in the two fields. The course studies three oral genres, proverb, folktale, and epic, although other genres are added by pointing students to online performances on YouTube, Vimeo, and Ustream. Fundamental topics are the form and content of a communication, its intended audience, the tone or manner in which it takes place, the channels and codes of communication, and the norms for performance and interpretation.

Readings and Activities

The two fields are introduced through questions asked of the initial readings (Oring 1986: 1–44). What is meant by *folk* and *lore*? Why has no one definition of folklore been accepted? How have these two conceptions changed through history? How does nationalism influence the conception of folklore? How does folklore differ from literature (Jakobson and Bogatyrev 1931)? Introducing folkloristics is easy because students are already familiar with songs, jokes, rhymes, and folk beliefs. Discussion is facilitated by dividing the class into groups who will work together throughout the course. Groups first exchange instances in which something they recognize as folklore has been moved from one language to another or from one medium to another. Here students who command a second language are the best resource for the class. The groups then decide how the instances or items should be classified by applying the instructor's lectures on genre (Bascom 1965; Oring 1986: 91–174).

Moving to translation studies, students quickly see that "The Frog King," "Rapunzel," "Snow White," and other tales they know from childhood were told long ago in many languages, then translated and retranslated into other languages, and finally adapted in various media (Bacchilega 1997). Questions drive us deeper into the readings in translation studies. Why is translation not merely substituting a word in the translating language for a word in the source language? What is the problem with the concept of *equivalence*, and how do different authorities try to solve it? What parallels exist between different translations and the variant forms of a folktale? What is meant by untranslatability? Can you derive how-to rules from the readings? Semiotic transformation, it turns out, immediately draws in cultural and social context (Bassnett 1980: 21–44; Bohannan 1966; Jakobson 1959; Nida 1964).

To interrogate the instrumental model, an experiment in intralingual translation addresses metaphor in proverbs. Students find five metaphorical proverbs (Strauss 1984) and reword them literally, thus eliminating the metaphor. German, for example, has the saying, *gibt man ihm einen Finger, nimmt er die ganze Hand* (give him a finger, he takes the whole hand). To make this activity even more revealing, if not maddening, the translating language is limited to the 850 words in C. K. Ogden's Basic English vocabulary (http://ogden.basic-english.org/words. html). In Basic the metaphor disappears: "Some people demand too much." Staying in English while experiencing the translator's agonies, students begin to sense that no translation can be transparent (de Caro 1986). Hence they are now ready to confront Walter Benjamin's impossible demand for transparency and pursue further reading about translation and the sociology of culture (Bassnett 1980: 79–131; Bourdieu 1992).

Next comes a fieldwork exercise in transcription, prefaced by some guidelines (Finnegan 1992: 72–90; Wilson 1986) and an exemplary field account (Herskovits and Herskovits 1958). Folklore fieldwork creates a source text by recording literally, often electronically. Literary translation does not, but it often rests on previous textual editing. To try out the folklorist role, students transcribe the words of a performance from a website. The instructor's approval or recommendation is necessary, because so many obvious sources—songs by Woody Guthrie, children's rhymes—have already been transcribed and published. Online performances by African-American artists such as Elizabeth Cotten or Horace Sprott promise better results, as do interviews with jazzman Jelly Roll Morton or folk music collector Alan Lomax (http://www.youtube.com/watch?v=MPt0IlmHJhs). Verifying the accuracy of one's transcription raises questions. How should the sound of oral literature be translated or represented? Should repetition be concealed or written verbatim in translations?

Since folkloristics probes the movement of cultural products as intently as translation studies, readings on folktale variation come next (Uther 2008). Students read a selection of Grimm tales (Grimm and Grimm 1884; 1992; Magoun and Krappe 1960), noting how many translations are outdated, rewritten, or unreliable (Margaret Hunt's Victorian version is useful). Group discussion discovers *motifs*: actor motifs for persons or characters, including animals, object motifs for things, and incident motifs for plot elements moving the story forward. Student groups try to agree on how to describe the resemblances, relying (or not) on the principal indexing tool (Thompson 1955–1958).

Students submit an essay that addresses the question of how borrowed material is reinterpreted, through translation, to fit pre-existing cultural emphases. They are asked to discuss variant forms of the same folktale, although by imagining that versions in different languages are translations of a lost source text (they aren't, of course). Starting from a Grimm tale on the syllabus, students find and compare two variant forms of the plot from outside Europe (D. L. Ashliman's website, "Folklore and Mythology," is a helpful resource: http://www.pitt.edu/~dash/folk texts.html).

A pair of texts, one European, one African, can serve to illustrate different emphases. In "Fitcher's Bird" (Grimm no. 46), three sisters, one after the other, fall into the power of a sorcerer, who kills the first two. The youngest sister—active, ingenious, courageous—escapes, revives the other two, pretends to marry the sorcerer, and finally tricks him into being killed. In the Indian Ocean tales, this plot portrays a desirable young woman who actively disobeys convention. She turns away all eligible suitors in favor of an animal or a supernatural creature whose disguise as a handsome rich man makes him irresistible. After they marry and she finds out his true nonhuman identity, the marriage is broken (Haring 2007: 147–67). The tale symbolizes any young woman's capacity for desire as well as the superior power of ancient custom. Either she is rescued and goes back submissively to her parents, or she loses her life for her disobedience. The two tales are distantly related historically, as the versions studied by students will be, but there is no original, no archetypal source for it. The only pan-human pattern in the variant forms is the reshaping of actors, objects, and incidents. Never arbitrary, the substitution of one character or object for another is to be explained through information external to the text. That need motivates the hermeneutic model.

The essays written for this assignment are exchanged for peer review, a process seen as a two-way kind of translation. The critic first states the author's main idea in a sentence and then describes how that idea is supported in the essay. Next the critic explains what is done well in the essay and says specifically what could be done better. In reply, the author addresses the accuracy of the translation, decides whether the positive evaluation is acceptable, and considers the suggestions for improvement. Revision of one's essay, after peer review, sharpens critical thinking and self-awareness.

It also raises the next pair of topics: how readers impose their own notions on folklore and how translators modify the effects of their source texts. Students examine the dynamics whereby those who translate and publish folktales shape materials from other languages. As translators' choices are constrained and possibly censured by cultural and social norms (Toury 1978), so the history of folkloristics can seem to some students to be censuring the Grimm brothers for their editorial practices (Briggs 1993; Tatar 1987; Zipes 1988).

Because genres differ, they are mistranslatable (Ben-Amos 1976; Shuman and Hasan-Rokem 2012). Epic, for example, is familiar through being misapplied to films. At one time, epic was denied to Africa (Finnegan 1970: 108–10; Johnson, Hale, and Belcher 1997). Defining concepts prepare students to decide what an epic is (http://journal.oraltradition.org/issues/18i and 18ii). They then read my online translation of *Ibonia* from Madagascar (http://www.openbookpublishers. com/product/109/). Students test the translator's claim that this long, elaborate folktale has epic status. Members of each student group can also collaborate on sketching an imitation epic. Their description enables comparison with those of the other groups, thus refining the definition further.

From anonymous, exotic folktale to a nonexistent source text is a short step. No student wants to believe that the most popular poet in English after Shakespeare was James Macpherson, especially after reading his work (Macpherson 1760). His self-named translations don't look like poems they have seen before. If he is an extreme case of translator's invisibility, Ossian, his putative source, is even less visible. Reading Macpherson is an opportunity to discover what the eighteenth century thought folklore should look like and to consider an instance of pseudotranslation (Rambelli 2009). Is Macpherson's work folklore? How does a reader know a text is poetry in some other language, or in any language? What constitutes poetry, whether oral or written? These questions guide our discussion. Handbooks of literature show the Euro-American conception of poetry (Abrams and Harpham 2012; Kennedy 2009; Mikics 2010), but in this course the most frequently heard byword is, "It's more complicated than that."

To debate fundamental issues for folkloristics and translation studies, the English translations of Native American narratives are examined. Henry Rowe Schoolcraft's rewritings of Native narratives mark a moment in the history of translation (Bauman 1993). To focus discussion on the ethics of difference, students read two translations, seventy years apart, of the Kathlamet "Myth of the Sun" (Boas 1901; Hymes 1975). In this heartbreaking story, Charles Cultee narrates "the destruction of a people through the selfishness of a chief whose fascination for a bright object clouds his sense of responsibility to his people" (Toelken 1996: 253). Dell Hymes's more recent translation and commentary show the extent to which a translator may obscure the content and pattern of a transcribed performance. The prominence he gives to an individual narrator like Charles Cultee informs the debate about authorship (Hymes 2003: 121–299). Student groups read one story aloud and comment on the narrator's style. Although Hymes's forte is the patient scrutiny of verbal detail (Hymes 2003: 36–80), his microscopic observations lead to hypotheses about poetry that extend far beyond individual Native American narrators (Hymes 2003: 95–118). Group discussion arrives first at clear statements of these hypotheses then turns to his propositions about complexity and variation in patterns. What are the obstacles, we ask, to finding poetry in the oral literature of a dominated people?

The Chinook languages Hymes translates are in a subordinate language; ethnographies and translations tend to be written in dominant languages. Students who speak such subordinate languages can help their monolingual classmates perceive the process of translating. No longer a neutral act, translation turns out to be enmeshed in global power inequalities. The hierarchical relations that underlie modes of translation are discussed in readings that open the question of intellectual property (Sturge 1997; Toelken 1998). Three groups of students debate the restrictions in class, one group speaking for Native Americans, another for the dominant culture, while a third plays critic. The class as a whole reviews the findings, assessing the effectiveness of the debate.

The property issue also applies to translation between media. In the next assignment, students choose a film portraying Native people and discuss a story told by a character in the film. Basic questions are raised about performance. What are the features of the story? Who tells it? Is the teller translating in any sense? Do audience reactions influence the narrator's performance? How does translation into film affect the representation? Among the recommended films are Arthur Penn's *Little Big Man* (1970), Ryszard Bugajski's *Clearcut* (1991), Chris Eyre's *Smoke Signals* (1998), Zacharias Kunuk's *Atanarjuat: The Fast Runner* (2001), Courtney Hunt's *Frozen River* (2008), and Sterling Harjo's *Barking Water* (2009).

This section of the course points students toward an ethical engagement. Human beings continually mix lexicons, quote, sample, shift genres and attitudes, and rearrange the components of the messages they receive. Every point in these processes presents ethical challenges to translators and collectors of folklore alike, beginning with the choice of texts to translate and of performers to study and including the question of who owns the result. Only in scale are the ethical issues that bear on student projects different from those raised by the interactions between cultures. Discussion of the geopolitical scale opens with the vigorous controversies provoked by UNESCO's 2003 Convention for the Safeguarding of the Intangible Cultural Heritage (http://www.unesco.org/culture/ich/index.php?lg=en&pg=00006). Socially situated performances attract the interest of folklorists and translators, whereas UNESCO's abstract language effaces their specificity. Similarly, nations signing the Convention are directed to inventory the traditions and expressions of their peoples (i.e., collect folklore) with no regard for the diversity of economies or ways of life. Traditions protect themselves and are translatable without help from the World Intellectual Property Organization (Vaidyanathan 2001; Venuti 1998: 47–66). Where should the translator or folklorist stand? Readings about the ethical problems expose their geopolitical implications, enabling students to debate them (Bendix, Eggert, and Peselmann 2012).

The last section not only engages in cultural criticism but seeks to deepen thinking about the cultural agency of translators and folklorists. If Walt Disney's *Snow White and the Seven Dwarfs* (1937) is not the source, then reducing the complexity of folktales for an audience of children constitutes only one choice among different signifying practices. If a world language like English is inevitably an instrument of domination (Venuti 1998: 158–89), are creole languages and literatures instruments of counterhegemony (Baron and Cara 2011)? Such questions ask students to imagine the range of possibilities in translating and representing other cultures, compelling them to project utopian solutions to the inequalities we have confronted throughout the course.

The Final Project

The course ends with the submission of a final project for which students choose between two main alternatives. One capitalizes on any fluency they may possess in a language other than English. These students can elect to produce an English translation of a folktale, myth, legend, or collection of proverbs or riddles. If the source material has already been translated, then the previous translation must be criticized and evaluated. A folkloristic essay states the rules (Bascom 1964). Next the student presents her or his own translation and explains the differences, giving an account of translation problems against the background of issues studied in the course.

The other alternative is a collection of folklore from a speaker of another language. Recording an item and its context gives a practical introduction to the hermeneutic approach. Students are directed to take down fixed-phrase folklore exactly as the informant speaks it in the source language, whatever it may be. If the source language is not English, the informant will have to write it out for the student. Then comes transliteration of the item in English characters; again the informant may help. Next, in a literal translation, the student shows what each word in the source material means. Now comes free translation, for which the student uses idiomatic English, producing what is in effect a retranslation (Venuti 2013: 174). Finally the student records meaning in context. The informant is asked to describe an actual or hypothetical situation where the item might be used and to explain the meaning that it might carry in that situation. The student includes his or her own interpretation, clearly separated from the informant's explanation.

Advanced students with special interests are offered other options. Freud's theory of dream interpretation, for instance, presents analytic concepts (condensation, displacement, repression) that are readily applicable to folktale and other folklore forms (Dundes 1987; Dundes and Falassi 1975; Freud 1952). The concepts also apply to the translator's work, even if his or her invisibility conceals the workings of the unconscious (Venuti 1995; 2013: chap. 2). The directions for translating the language of dreams arose in a setting of unequal power, Freud's consulting room; translators and folklorists often work in dominant languages, regardless of the cultural status of the source materials. A student could explore these unequal power relations between languages or between the fields of folklore and literature, insofar as oral forms have been seen as subservient to writing. Yet another option would be to consider these relations in terms of gender, a category that has been used to illuminate both fields (Chamberlain 1988; Haring 1999).

Earlier versions of this course attracted students from classics, philosophy, and comparative literature; a later iteration added students of economics and political science, one of whom went straight into law school. Since both translation studies and folkloristics examine the movement of cultural products among diverse groups and peoples, the course points toward career paths in translating, anthropological fieldwork, literary history and criticism, public presentation, and intergroup relations.

24 Translation in the Human Sciences

Joshua Price

Aim and Methods

This chapter describes a course that explores the centrality of translation to knowledge production across the humanities and social sciences. It is designed for graduate students and advanced undergraduates who have declared concentrations in those disciplines. Assigned readings are drawn from anthropology, history, linguistics, literary theory, philosophy, legal and political theory, and sociology, along with translation studies. Taken together, the readings present an overview of the issues at stake in translating such material, issues that are at once theoretical and practical, linguistic and historical.

The initial class meetings set up a conceptual framework and establish a shared referent for the term "human sciences." We first sketch the rise and differentiation of the disciplines in the West (Simeoni 2007; Wallerstein 1996: 1–69). Then we consider the international, multilingual history of this differentiation through the entry on *Geisteswissenschaften* in the *Dictionary of Untranslatables* (Cassin 2004: 368–72), distinguishing this term from *sciences humaines* and relating them to terms more widely used in the North American academy, such as the "humanities" and the "social sciences." Starting with the translation history of "human sciences" also serves to introduce the methodology of the course, which is organized around the genealogy of key concepts as they migrate across languages and disciplines. We review briefly the distinction between *verstehen*, the interpretive understanding characteristic of the human sciences, and *erklären*, often associated with explanation in the natural sciences. This distinction anticipates our discussion of translation as a hermeneutic practice, in which the meaning of a text is not fixed but rather emerges as it is subject to an interpretive process—in this case, as it is translated (Venuti 2010: 74).

The course next examines the rhetorical and institutional mechanisms through which academic writing in the human sciences is disseminated (Hermans 2002; Kuhn 1962: 23–34, 43–51, 111–34; Lefevere 1982: 205). These discussions elaborate a sociologically rich sense of how a work is transformed for a new audience through translation, the process that Lefevere calls "refraction" (1982: 204). We consider how the translation of academic texts is organized, institutionalized, and regulated differently from the translation of literary texts. Academic journals and university presses play important regulatory functions by determining which texts are worth publishing and therefore translating. Normative expectations that establish authority are constructed, inculcated, and maintained through formal procedures such as the granting of degrees, tenure, fellowships, and awards, as well as double blind peer review and funding for research and publication. Conferences and professional associations simultaneously foster and contain intellectual movements and disciplinary shifts. The aim of this discussion is to indicate the actors, structures, and procedures that figure in the production, circulation, and reception of translations.

Academic writing in the human sciences is also a question of technical mastery, what Lefevere might call a "poetics" (1982: 205). Each discipline, subdiscipline, and the competing movements within them have their own linguistic and intellectual conditions of possibility, including tropes, styles, canons of texts, and presuppositions. Paradigms, in Kuhn's sense, dictate certain theoretical assumptions, rules of evidence, and forms of argumentation while excluding others as out-of-bounds or nonsensical. At any one time, different research trends and methodologies vie for prominence or disciplinary hegemony. The constitutive aspects of a text are both internal—its poetics—and external—its institutional site—and these aspects are mutually determining.

In view of the multiple factors that both enable and constrain academic discourse, we consider how language in the human sciences is used in two distinct but related ways (Durston 2007: 4). A language is, on the one hand, a means of communication and, on the other, a repository of lexical and syntactical items, styles and genres, discourses and ideologies, usually affiliated with a particular social group. The translation of academic writing must take into account both functions. We sample several scholarly journals in different disciplines, identify the characteristic features of the writing, and distinguish it from other genres and text types such as poetry, an instruction manual, and a transcript of everyday speech. Framing the discussion of translated texts in this way does not presuppose that the source text contains an essential meaning, but it does risk reifying disciplinary norms and therefore treating translation conservatively instead of dynamically, as reflecting and influencing academic discourses. Indeed, translations often break, broaden, or problematize norms, expectations, and presuppositions. This point is most effectively made through the case studies that drive the rest of the class discussions.

Keywords

The course is based on the premise that conceptual terms pose particular challenges to translation in the human sciences, revealing the historical and epistemological foundations of the disciplines (Price 2008). Organizing class meetings around a concept or phrase anchors the discussion, serving as an entry point or introduction to a disciplinary tradition or problematic that may be unfamiliar to students with diverse backgrounds. For this reason, I invite students to bring in samples of how a keyword we are scheduled to discuss has been translated into other languages. Comparing translations, not only to the source text but to each other, can illuminate aspects of translation as an interpretive act as well as sharpen students' own interpretive skills (Rose 1997).

Our first case study involves the different ways in which the French term *l'imaginaire* has been translated into English across such disciplines as history, philosophy, political theory, and psychology. We consider the historian Alain Corbin's use of the term as well as Arthur Goldhammer's decision to avoid a close rendering like "the imaginary" and rather choose "the imagination" and similar forms (Corbin 1990; 1992). At the same time, we create a larger context for understanding this case by reading criticism of Goldhammer's translation. For Philippe Carrard, it exemplifies the English-language publisher's effort to "normalize" Corbin's highly theoretical prose for a general audience in the United States (Carrard 1993: 81). For Lawrence Venuti, Goldhammer's choice is symptomatic of an empiricist approach both to history and to translation, whereby Corbin is assimilated to the dominant form of historiography in the British and American academy (Venuti 2010). The class discussion is considerably deepened by Claudia Strauss's detailed account (2006) of the concept of "the imaginary" as it appears in various thinkers and scholars, including Benedict Anderson, Cornelius Castoriadis, and Jacques Lacan. She fails, however, to register the fact that the term has been translated, commenting on the French authors as if they were writing in English. The case offers remarkable insights into the differences between French and Anglo-American academic institutions, the use of translation to maintain a status quo in scholarship and in publishing, and the marginality of translation in Anglophone cultures.

We return to *verstehen*, partly because our initial spadework has identified it as a keyword and partly because it is central to Max Weber's sociology. We read excerpts from Talcott Parsons' translation of *The Theory of Social and Economic Organization* (1947), where in an extended footnote he justifies his use of "understanding" to render the German word. We observe how this footnote, arguably the most important in American sociology, prepared the way for entirely new approaches to the study of culture and society. We are aided by Keith Tribe's incisive critique (2007) of Parsons' translation, which shows how the American sociologist revised Weber to fit his own theory of social action. Students are asked to consider whether Tribe presupposes a true or invariable meaning of Weber's German text as the basis of his critique. We turn briefly to Clifford Geertz's essay, "Thick Description" (1973), where the formulation of an interpretive, idiographic method of social inquiry illustrates the influence of Parsons' translation in such other disciplines as anthropology. Geertz described the connection succinctly: "Believing, with Max Weber, that man is an animal suspended in webs of significance he himself has spun, I take culture to be those webs, and the analysis of it to be therefore not an experimental science in search of law but an interpretative one in search of meaning" (Geertz 1973: 5).

We next consider the French term *surtravail*. Wallerstein argues that because it is a technical term in French Marxist discourse, generally rendered into English as "surplus labor," the translator needs to know whether such terms carry nuances in the French Marxist tradition that they lack in English (Wallerstein 1981: 89–90). We thus situate our discussion of *surtravail* in the framework of Wallerstein's translation guidelines, which recommend that a translator in the social sciences possess the equivalent of a scholarly specialization in the discipline in which he or she is translating. This recommendation raises the issue of whether translators should aid in standardizing discipline-specific terms through repeated use and, more generally, whether such standardization is feasible or desirable (Price 2008). Students compare Wallerstein's argument for standardized translation with Dipesh Chakrabarty's claim (2000) that a term like "work" is subject to cultural variations that cause problems for classical Marxist theory. If Chakrabarty's argument for the cultural differences of "work" is convincing, we ask, is Wallerstein's faith in a standardized terminology misplaced?

We continue this discussion by considering the term "travail" in Venuti's translation of Jacques Derrida's essay, "What Is a 'Relevant' Translation?" (1999). Chosen to translate Derrida's use of the French word "travail" (usually rendered into English as "work"), "travail" functions in the English version as an unstable point of polysemy: it retains the French, variously signifies "hard work," "painful effort," or "difficult experience," and is archaic in relation to the current standard dialect of English, most often poetical in effect. Although the English "travail" thus indexes a different, non-Marxist provenance, it would nonetheless seem to bear out Wallerstein's call for disciplinary expertise: it reflects Venuti's familiarity with the French philosopher's distinctive mixture of philosophical speculation with literary effects insofar as "travail" is used in the translation to recreate patterns of alliteration and wordplay in the source text. Yet since the choice is a poetical archaism that recurs with greater frequency in the English version than in the French source, it constitutes an example of what Philip Lewis calls "abusive fidelity" (1985), deviating from current standard English, challenging the abstract, homogeneous language in which Anglophone philosophy is usually written, and therefore questioning Wallerstein's effort to cast the translator as supportive of an academic status quo. These points become more apparent as we take into account Venuti's introduction to his translation (2001) and the essay he subsequently wrote about the "disciplinary resistance" of his strategies (2013: 57–80).

We address the untranslatability of conceptual terms by considering Diana Taylor's argument that "performance" is not only an object of academic study and a discipline but a way of knowing "transmitted through a nonarchival system of knowledge" (2003: xvii). Hence, she argues, the term "performance" is untranslatable into Spanish, although this very feature can be productive when it is employed throughout the Americas. Taylor's claim occasions our effort to make explicit the conditions that allow an author to judge some terms as translatable but others as not. We articulate various perspectives on the question—philosophical (Is everything translatable or is nothing translatable? Can any discipline-specific term be translated?), linguistic (What counts as an adequate or acceptable translation?), and methodological (What criteria and materials are used to arrive at a decision as to untranslatability?). Class discussion aims to refine students' sense of translation as refraction, as we see performance studies (or *estudios de performance*) institutionalized throughout the hemisphere.

We then approach untranslatability in legal theory by considering different applications of the term "tribe." Whether a particular group is recognized as a tribe in the eyes of the United States government is highly consequential for land claims and access to various resources. The incommensurability between jurisprudence and native concepts of group membership serves as the starting point for a discussion of the intralingual translation of legal terms (Torres and Milun 1990). Do the Mashpee, we ask, have legal standing to sue the Commonwealth of Massachusetts? American jurisprudence relies on legal precedent and fixed rules of evidence, tying the past to the present in a linear way. The Mashpee have a fluid definition of membership: they take in runaway slaves, Hessian mercenaries, and other indigenous people. In fact, anyone who has lived among them becomes Mashpee. This criterion invalidated their claim to continuity and tribal integrity as defined by United States courts. Torres and Milun, writing as critical race theorists, take up the challenge of gaining understanding across the boundaries of two cultures, enacting what Raimon Panikkar (1988) might term a diatopical hermeneutics. The aim of the class discussion is to understand how the legal and institutional question rests on the translation of a contested word. We continue our interdisciplinary approach by reading the anthropologist James Clifford's essay (1988) on the Mashpee trial, in which the link between language and identity is foregrounded.

Anthropology poses an interesting—some would say, an insidious—case of translation in the human sciences. Although anthropologists commonly think of themselves as translators, they are often oddly silent and unreflective on the most crucial aspects of their translating; some even go so far as to render dialogue in the target-audience's language and then to analyze the translation as if it were the source text. As a result, their work sometimes reveals glaring fallacies and errors, both linguistic and epistemological. We explore these problems with the help of Kate Sturge's examination (1997) of translation strategies in ethnography. For an exemplary case, we turn to Tullio Maranhão's account of a common form of category confusion in anthropological translation: he exposes "the habit of using taxonomies of cosmopolitan beliefs and practices—economics, religion, politics, and so on—to understand Amerindian beliefs and practices" (Maranhão 2002: 66–7). Students assess the methodological dilemmas created by legal and anthropological perspectives on Native American cultures. Does a diatopical hermeneutics deliver insight into two culturally divergent points of view? Or do legal scholars and anthropologists just present their own contradictions by assuming a bird's eye view while providing little sense of how they acquired this privileged position?

We end by studying the two controversial English translations of Simone de Beauvoir's *Le Deuxième Sexe*, the versions of Howard Parshley (1952) and of Constance Borde and Sheila Malovany-Chevallier (2009), both titled *The Second Sex*. Although Parshley's translation was essential for the second wave of North American feminism, transforming the lives of millions of women (and men), it omits roughly 15 percent of the French text. Emily Apter (2013: 158–67) and Margaret Simons (1998) show how he eliminates or significantly masks her use of Marxist and phenomenological vocabulary while eliding references to

Kierkegaard and Hegel, Heidegger and Sartre, Virginia Woolf and Gaston Bachelard, among other European authors.

We consider the translators' prefaces and compare excerpts from the two translations, focusing on the famous assertion in which Beauvoir seems to articulate a notion of gender as constructed rather than innate: "On ne naît pas femme: on le devient." Parshley's version inserts an indefinite article—"One is not born, but rather becomes a woman" (Beauvoir 1952: 281)—whereas Borde and Malovany-Chevallier remove it: "One is not born, but rather becomes, woman" (Beauvoir 2009: 283). In a critique published in the *London Review of Books*, Toril Moi wrote that this removal constitutes

> an elementary grammatical mistake: French does not use the indefinite article after *être* ('to be') and *devenir* ('to become'), but no such rule exists in English. (*Comment devenir traducteur?* must be translated as 'How to become a translator?') This error makes Beauvoir sound as if she were committed to a theory of women's difference.
>
> (Moi 2010: 5)

Other readers defended the translation on precisely these terms. Moi's review generated a fascinating cache of letters from editors and translators, feminist scholars and publishers that we consider as so many refractions of the question of scholarly translation through a variety of discursive lenses.

Using conceptual terms as a means of organizing the course allows for the possibility of wide variation in different iterations. Cassin's "dictionary of untranslatables" is a bountiful source of such terms, each inserted in "a cartography" of "philosophical differences" (2004: xx). Yet this work technically falls in one discipline: philosophy. The history of the humanities and the social sciences in fact displays an embarrassment of riches for building a translation-oriented course, what with the genealogies of terms like "bricolage," "Dasein," "ego," "hegemony," and "jouissance." Different terms will point up different themes, of course, but they will all yield insights into the nature of translation as an interpretive act, mediated by language and influenced by the various institutional sites, cultural formations, and historical moments in which it is performed.

Assignments

I require two kinds of writing assignments for the course. The first involves the weekly submission of what I call motivated questions about the readings, touching on any translated-related issues that the material might raise for the students. The question may put texts in conversation with one another, point out contradictions or flaws in them, or evoke previous class discussions. In addition, students write one or two pages explaining what precisely motivates the question, justifying its relevance or importance, rehearsing pertinent elements of the readings, and, if necessary, contextualizing their argument by linking it to our ongoing debates. The motivated questions help students to prepare for class, driving them deeper into the readings, and at the same time enable the instructor to gauge the level of their understanding and engagement. If the questions are submitted with sufficient lead time, I try to select particularly productive examples to incorporate into my lesson plan.

The second assignment is a final project. For most students, this project is a research paper that takes as a springboard a theme or question from the course, whether a conceptual term, a disciplinary issue or the history of the English translations of a particular text in the human sciences. With the instructor's approval, students may take the option of translating a text and accompanying their translation with a critical introduction that describes their strategies, notably the interpretation they inscribe in the source text and the relation between that interpretation and the discourses in the discipline in which the text was produced. This option gives them the opportunity to address the practical implications of the theoretical issues we considered throughout the semester. If they choose to translate a text that has been previously translated, their introduction must include a rationale for the retranslation that is based on a critical analysis of the previous translator's work.

The projects that students have submitted can be imaginative and quite original. A major in linguistics and Near Eastern studies translated a historical text by a contemporary critic of Zionism who, some have charged, is anti-Semitic. The student's introduction wrestled with this charge in an effort to think through the intellectual and ethical questions it posed for her work as translator, paying special attention to the verbal choices she had to make. Another student studied English translations that render the French term *mondialisation* as "globalization," noting how each word sketches a different referential field and inquiring into whether the varying contexts created by the source text and the translation introduce any change in meaning. Other students developed equally challenging projects that involved the difficulties associated with translating a seemingly familiar discourse into English, such as Latin American literary theory or Arabic commentary on homosexuality. Students who translate find it immensely rewarding, but they confess that a translation probably requires more work than writing a free-standing paper: not only must their translation function as a viable interpretation of the source text, but they must conduct sufficient research to provide a cogent justification for their translation strategies.

Part IV

Resources

25 A Survey of Translation Pedagogies

Sonia Colina and Lawrence Venuti

Translation studies has become a field in its own right in the last few decades, as demonstrated by the number of presses, journals, conferences, and organizations dedicated to scholarly work on translation. As the field has become increasingly established, the question of how to teach the practice of translation has been given a diverse range of answers. This chapter presents a critical survey of prevalent translation pedagogies by situating the teaching of translation within the broader context of translation studies and related disciplines.

Pedagogies make assumptions about teachers, students, and the learning process that ultimately rest on specific epistemologies. The teaching of translation has witnessed a shift from a positivist to a constructivist epistemology, from teacher-oriented to student-oriented approaches, from the veneration of the source and target texts to a veritable discovery of the translator and the translation process. This evolution can be tracked in current academic practices, although it occurred as consciously articulated responses to developments in such other fields as psychology, sociology, and educational theory.

At the same time, translation pedagogies have undergone a certain unevenness of development in the wake of the burgeoning research in translation. While varieties of linguistics as well as translation theories geared to pragmatic and technical text types have had a noticeable impact on teaching, developments in literary and cultural studies have been slow to reach the classroom except through a changing list of translation-oriented readings in surveys of translation theory. The translation pedagogy in creative writing courses and programs has perhaps been the most resistant to change, remaining deeply invested in a limited version of the workshop model.

From Read-and-Translate to the Learner

Among existing approaches to translation teaching, some are anecdotal and asystematic, reflecting an intuitive inclination to teach as the teacher was taught. In the absence of an articulated methodology, these approaches assume the positivist epistemology in which reality is autonomous from the knowing subject and not constructed for knowledge, which is therefore regarded as objective and can be transmitted as such. The expert in possession of this knowledge is the teacher whose job is to pass it down to students, while students are passive receptors and imitators of the teacher. Implicit is the belief that the transmission of knowledge from teacher to class occurs through lecturing and correction of student work. Consequently, interaction takes place only between the teacher and one student at a time, or between the teacher and the class as a whole, and it is limited to questions and answers. Interaction among students is minimal or nonexistent.

This transmissionist view of learning carries important implications for the education and training of translators. Positivist epistemology claims that knowledge can be transferred from teacher to student, but the manner in which the transfer takes place is not a matter of interest. The assumption that the transfer happens more or less automatically implies as well that teaching need not be improved or even that teacher training is not needed (Kiraly 2003: 8). If teachers are expert translators who possess the relevant expert knowledge, they should be able to teach it to their students without specialized preparation other than the experiences with foreign languages and translation that establish their expertise.

In the translation classroom, the transmissionist view is reflected in an emphasis on the source and target texts rather than on the students, their learning, or the translation process. Texts are often translated in a vacuum without any reference to the producer or to the cultural, social, and political context of the source text. No mention is made of the purpose or any other contextual information regarding the translation. Only one correct translation can exist, normally the one produced by the teacher, and the teacher aims to get students to come as close as possible to that master translation, marking their deviations from it. Teaching focuses not on decision-making and procedural skills but rather on identifiable content such as terminology lists and specialized data in fields like science, medicine, and law.

The transmissionist pedagogy in translator training is a read-and-translate method, also known as "chalk-and-talk." Donald Kiraly describes it in some detail:

> When I was first introduced to translator education, at the School of Applied Linguistics and Cultural Studies (FTSK) of the University of Mainz in Germersheim in 1983, translation was taught universally in a conventional "chalk-and-talk" manner, with a teacher sitting in front of each translation practice class, requesting verbal contributions by individual students who would read off their respective translations of parts of a larger text (chosen by the teacher, most often from a newspaper). The teacher would ask if other students had comments to make and would then provide his or her own commentary on the proposed solutions. This would go on for the duration of class after class, from the first through the final semester of the eight-semester *Diplom* (MA level degree) program of studies. [. . .] To my knowledge, observing ongoing classes was the only education or training in translator education available to me or any other new instructor at the time.
>
> (Kiraly 2015: 10)

Today, in the United States, the read-and-translate method is typically deployed in the "rapid reading" courses where graduate students prepare for the translation exams that satisfy foreign-language requirements. Although these exams are supposed to assess reading proficiency, comprehending a foreign-language passage is rather different from translating it effectively. In rapid reading courses, however, as in the proficiency exams, translation is not distinguished from reading comprehension. Cecilia Brickman's *A Short Course in Reading French*, a textbook designed for such courses, "is intended for English speakers who want to learn to translate written French into English" (2012: xvii). Brickman's chapters outline French grammatical principles, including sections that describe strategies like "Translation of the Present Tense/*Présent de l'indicatif*" and "Various Ways in Which to Translate Reflexive Verbs" (2012: 16, 45). Most chapters contain translation exercises involving brief extracts, and a final section provides extended passages drawn from literature and philosophy. In keeping with the read-and-translate method, minimal information is provided about the source text, and the translating is detached from any context that might enable the translator to decide how to frame an interpretation. In the classroom, the teacher inevitably assumes the role of corrector who transmits lexical and syntactical knowledge as well as translation strategies while criticizing student work, often line by line, word by word.

Developments in educational research, notably the work of Jean Lave and Étienne Wenger (1991), shifted the focus of translation teaching from read-and-translate to the learner and the learning process, including contextualized or situated learning. The pedagogical context is precisely what Dorothy Kelly addresses in her handbook on training the translator trainer. She presents a general description of "an actual curricular or syllabus design process, as it deals with outcomes of the training process" (Kelly 2005: 4). She offers an example of an outcome: "Students will be able to work cooperatively with the different professionals who intervene in translation activity (fellow translators, revisers, documentary researchers, terminologists, layout specialists, editors), identifying the potential difficulties involved in each situation, designing strategies for dealing with them" (Kelly 2005: 39).

Kelly acknowledges that teaching outcomes vary according to diverse factors, including social needs and industry requirements, professional standards and institutional policy, disciplinary trends and student backgrounds. She is most concerned in linking course content and activities to intended outcomes in accordance with trainee and teacher profiles, taking into account such factors as educational level and styles of learning and teaching. Student and course assessment are the next steps in this process, allowing teachers to evaluate outcomes and to improve or adjust the curriculum and course design.

While Kelly's proposals have been criticized as too general and even obvious in some cases (A. Darwish 2007), particularly to experienced teachers, they have been influential in translation teaching insofar as they raise awareness about how various contextual factors influence pedagogical decisions. Her treatment reflects a situation in which teachers have been assigned to teach translation for various reasons, whether because their expertise lies in foreign-language instruction, because they entered the teaching profession on the basis of their experience as professional translators and interpreters, or because they were educated in a positivist environment that did not consider the need for teacher training. The relatively recent proliferation of translator training programs has meant that these factors still affect the field.

The Impact of Educational Theory

As Kiraly (2000; 2003) points out, much of the responsibility for the shift to the learner and the learning process can be assigned to the advent of a constructivist epistemology. Social constructivism views knowledge not as an objective datum in the mind that can be transferred but rather as a product actively created by the learner in interaction with others and with the environment. As a result, the teacher's role is that of a facilitator who guides the learners in their process of knowledge construction. In constructivist teaching, students are active participants in the lesson, classroom interaction is mostly between students, and learning is collaborative and project-based. As Kiraly explains,

> expertise and professionalism emerge through praxis and conversation, not as the result of transmissionist interaction with the teacher, but through hypothesis developing and testing, through discussion and debate, and as a result of concerted effort exerted with a team of present and future members of the community in question.
>
> (Kiraly 2003: 17)

Kiraly proposes that the translation classroom center on an authentic project for an actual client. Students participate in a community of practice, working with other students, with experts (professional translators, foreign-language informants), and with pertinent resources (theoretical concepts, dictionaries) to identify translation problems and solutions. The class thus learns to interact like professionals in a team collaborating on a project. The teacher sets up and oversees the process, guiding students and introducing them to experts and resources. The goal is not to find the correct translation but to develop expert behavior, that is, the ability to make effective decisions and to interact appropriately with the community. Self-reflection becomes an important element of the process.

Kiraly's constructivist proposals have been criticized for lacking sufficient structure and placing too much responsibility on the learner (Schäffner 2004: 158–9). He does not, however, advocate a passive teacher who abdicates responsibility to the students. On the contrary, the teacher is a crucial factor in the facilitation and implementation of the learning process. While in a transmissionist pedagogy specific issues—whether linguistic or procedural, cultural or professional—are separately identified and addressed in some type of predetermined list or syllabus, in Kiraly's constructivism they are addressed as they arise within the context of work on the project. This sort of teaching may look less structured, but it actually proceeds inductively within a flexible structure formed by a specific project.

Nonetheless, a constructivist pedagogy can be most productive if it implements sequenced activities that enable a cumulative development of skills with increasing complexity. Maria González-Davies, who has also been inspired by social constructivism, has sought to satisfy this need by developing a task-based approach that relies on collaborative and small-group work in the classroom. She describes the "principles" of this approach as follows:

> the aim of the teaching and learning process is to encourage intersubjective communication in a positive atmosphere mainly through team work, to acquire linguistic, encyclopedic, transfer and professional competence and to learn about translation.
>
> (González-Davies 2004: 13–14)

González-Davies presents a myriad of "procedures" that fit various teaching goals and can be adapted to different levels of student competence (González-Davies 2004: 2). She distinguishes between three kinds of procedures: activities, or brief concrete exercises that help to practice specific points; tasks, or a chain of activities with the same global aim and a final product, which may involve the translation of various text types but can also focus on writing, research or editing; and projects, or multicompetence assignments in which students engage in professional activities and tasks and work together toward a product that is an authentic translation for an actual client.

A project, for example, might require students to produce a translation for a hotel door hanger to be distributed to hotels in a foreign country. Typical texts for such signs include "Do Not Disturb" and "Please Make Up This Room." The client offers ready-made hangers through the internet in the foreign country, but he would like to add a translation since many guests and staff are speakers of the foreign language. To carry out the project, students perform several activities and tasks. Guided by the instructor, the class begins by brainstorming about the text type, analyzing the characteristic language, content, and function of door hangers. They might then divide into small groups to locate parallel texts in nearby hotels, examples of door hangers in the target language, and to compose several texts of their own, experimenting with stylistic variations suited to different kinds of hotels, whether a traditional luxury establishment or a conventional chain franchise or a stylish boutique accommodation. Students learn to use language fitted to varying social contexts, as they will have to do with the translation projects they subsequently undertake. Each group exchanges their text with the other groups, and the class as a whole evaluates the results. This task chain, or sequence of activities, is followed by another that takes up the door hanger project: the same groups each analyze and translate the source text, whereafter they revise their translations according to the parallel texts, and the class assesses the translations, discussing the rationale for different choices and working out the most effective version to deliver to the client. The activities and tasks build upon each other, ultimately leading students to think of translation as a special writing activity.

González-Davies's approach can be considered an advance over Kiraly's in providing an instructional framework that is less apparently serendipitous and more rationally structured. Her wide array of activities, tasks, and projects is engaging and productive. Yet because her approach depends so heavily on research in education and psychology, the aims of procedures too often remain at a fairly low level—in the case of those procedures that develop linguistic skills, at the level of word and phrase—without encompassing larger units like genre, style, rhetoric, or ideology. These units are equally important in translation and could be introduced through broader research in such areas as discourse analysis (Colina 2006: 148).

González-Davies's task-based pedagogy can be most effectively implemented by teachers who have gained some experience in course design as well as classroom teaching. The development of activities, tasks, and projects requires the construction of a syllabus where each assignment builds upon earlier ones, taking into account the students' profiles, the foreign-language knowledge and translation skills they bring to the course. Additionally, teachers should be careful to integrate discrete activities and tasks into the comprehensive translation process, lest students, especially those who are less skilled, fail to grasp the entire process, not realizing that the function of a text can in fact determine decision making at every level.

Interdisciplinary Research and Translation Teaching

Translation pedagogies have been underpinned by various kinds of research, whether theoretical or empirical, whether specific to translation or drawn from other disciplines. These interdisciplinary syntheses have resulted in useful approaches to teaching, but they have also displayed the fragmentation that besets the field of translation studies, where research trends and methodologies reflect disciplinary divisions that may be so highly specialized as to produce incommensurable concepts of translation. Hence research-based pedagogies have led to widely divergent emphases in the classroom, forming translators equipped with different kinds of knowledge and different skills.

Sonia Colina has proposed a pedagogy of "communicative translation" that rests both on a specific theoretical approach to translation, functionalism, and on a "data-based empirical description of translator competence" (2003: 30). Following Christiane Nord's development of the functionalist discourse known as "Skopostheorie," Colina argues that the translation process should be guided by the function or purpose that the translation is intended to serve in the receiving situation. To emphasize function is to establish a set of relations among various factors, including a specific use of language, whether "informative," "expressive," or "operative," a specific genre or text type, and what Colina calls "pragmatic" or "situational features," such as an identifiable group of receptors, a time and place of reception, and the motive for producing the translation (2003: 16–20). She justifies her adoption of functionalism with empirical data from studies of novice translators that include error analysis and think-aloud protocols, a research method from cognitive psychology in which subjects verbalize their actions while performing them. The data show, among other findings, that novices stress the formal or grammatical structure of language to the detriment of its communicative function, and they fail to consider situational features while translating.

Colina's proposals for an introductory course aim precisely to fill these gaps in students' knowledge and skills so as to develop their communicative translational competence. She devises activities that focus on various factors—textual, generic, and situational—as well as their impact on specific translation strategies. A typical activity involves the analysis of these factors of the source text, which is further developed by discussing a translation "brief," or the client's instructions to the translator, which provide additional details about how the translated text is to function (2003: 19–22). Students analyze the genre of the source text, noting its linguistic and rhetorical features and locating parallel texts in the translating language, and they give special attention to the changes that these features may need to undergo in order to perform the required function in the receiving situation. Students also carry out activities in connection with a real project. In translating a Spanish recipe for a general Anglophone readership, for instance, students become aware not only of how information is organized and presented in the genre but which linguistic and cultural aspects of the Spanish text (e.g. the metric system, cooking processes, local ingredients, and structural differences between languages) must be reworked so that the recipe is both intelligible and serviceable in an English-language context.

Colina's pedagogy is susceptible to criticisms that can be leveled against any functionalist theory of translation (Peverati 2008). The function or purpose of a text may not be so simply isolated; the text may be characterized by a hybridity or complexity that prevents its potential effects in the source culture from being easily formulated, predicted, and recreated. Functionalism may be most effective in teaching students how to translate pragmatic and technical texts, the genres that Colina in fact considers: "technical manuals, business correspondence, instruction brochures, and advertising" (Colina 2003: 10). Humanistic texts like historical narratives and philosophical treatises, in contrast, might be motivated by authorial intentions to make a certain kind of scholarly contribution, but they can cause disciplinary or institutional effects, possibly unanticipated, that require other kinds of theoretical discourses to understand and figure into the translation process, such as sociological or political concepts. Functionalism, in other words, risks oversimplification in its effort to locate clear purposes and intentions. Empirical data, moreover, can be useful in locating problems that a student is likely to encounter in working with fairly straightforward text types, but studies can be compromised by the researcher's assumption of a particular translation theory. The studies cited by Colina, relying on text types that lend themselves to a functionalist account, can overlook or exclude data that may also be pertinent but that become intelligible only on the basis of different theoretical assumptions, such as those that foreground social and political issues.

Other research-based pedagogies have sought to open up translator training to precisely such issues, encompassing but going beyond the text. Joanna Drugan and Chris Megone argue for the need to instruct students in ethics, made urgent by a geopolitical economy subject to massive recessions. This need is not fulfilled by "codes of professional conduct" for translators, which "focus instead only on matters of technical competence" (Drugan and Megone 2011: 187). Although Drugan and Megone see such instruction as involving an interdisciplinary collaboration between a philosopher and a translator trainer, they are careful to indicate that "the point of studying ethics for translators is not that they become philosophers but that they develop good judgement" (Drugan and Megone 2011: 189). The aim is to develop "ethical reasoning skills" (Drugan and Megone 2011: 191), a learning outcome that they describe as follows:

> training will be to enable translation students to *identify* the ethical issues as they arise in particular circumstances, to *analyze* how these issues should shape their actions, and thus to choose an action which constitutes an *effective response* in the situation faced.
>
> (Drugan and Megone 2011: 188)

To achieve this aim, Drugan and Megone propose a pedagogy that integrates the teaching of ethics into the translation curriculum through the use of case studies. In a course "where practical translation exercises are discussed" (Drugan and Megone 2011: 191), students can be asked to consider ethical dilemmas deriving from actual situations and to outline possible responses. In one of Drugan and Megone's examples, a client has presented inaccurate or erroneous material and demands consistency across their translations, confronting the translator with the question, "What ethical considerations should be borne in mind when making—or justifying—specific translation choices?" (Drugan and Megone 2011: 203). Possible responses include whether to assign priority to meaning or style, whether to alter content or emphasis, and whether to apply standardized translation strategies. The discussion might be facilitated through the introduction of ethically oriented translation theories, such as the work of Antoine Berman, who has criticized "deforming tendencies" like "clarification" (Berman 1985: 244–52), or that of Andrew Chesterman, who has insisted that clarity is "a genuine ethical principle" (Chesterman 1997: 150). For Drugan and Megone, the ethical issues raised by this particular case involve "matters of justice and entitlement or property ownership" that bear on the translator's expertise or competence (2011: 204). In applying translation strategies, should the translator serve the client who owns the translation, at least in economic and legal terms, or the audience who must use it, unaware of inaccuracies and errors? Or should the translator control the text for which he or she is responsible, even if copyright law or a contract preempts signing that text?

Although Drugan and Megone's proposals can certainly enhance training by increasing the translator's critical self-awareness, implementing them poses certain problems, both theoretical and pedagogical. They are certainly right in arguing that ethical reasoning skills should not be treated as independent of skills in translation practice, particularly since practical and ethical decisions are often intertwined. But ethical reflection can lead to conflicts with a translation theory like functionalism, with the idea that the production of a functional or purposeful translation should guide the translator's decision-making. The function of a translation might be judged unethical (consider documents for oppressive governments or exploitative businesses), forcing the question of whether the translator should accept the commission in the first place. Similarly, the history of philosophy, even the history of translation theory and commentary, contain multiple and conflicting concepts of ethics that can easily foil Drugan and Megone's aim of teaching student translators good judgment. Following the "cooperative principle" formulated by ordinary language philosopher Paul Grice, Chesterman's translation ethics assumes that "clarity will survive as an ethical linguistic value long after the postmodern textual anarchists are dead and buried" (1997: 150). Yet Berman's thinking might be considered postmodern because he follows the existential phenomenologist Martin Heidegger in distinguishing between an ethical "manifestation" of the "utter foreignness" of the source text and an unethical "clarification" that enacts a reductive "movement from polysemy to monosemy" (1985: 240, 245). What constitutes good judgment in translation, in other words, can depend on the ethical theory that the translator uses to evaluate a project—and that a teacher introduces in the classroom. Drugan and Megone, after all, base their pedagogy on ethics in ancient Greek philosophy, the thinking of Plato and Aristotle. Ethical concepts drawn from quite different, even antithetical philosophers—Nietzsche, for example, or the contemporary French philosopher Alain Badiou—would result in the identification of different issues, in the analysis of different actions, and in a different determination of what constitutes an effective response.

Literary Translation and the Workshop

The workshop format became prevalent in teaching translation in the early 1960s, primarily in the master's programs in creative writing that began to be instituted at universities in the United States. The genres were strictly literary, poetry and prose fiction, and notwithstanding the rare program that permitted a book-length translation as a master's thesis, translation was subordinated to original composition, treated as an ancillary practice that is useful in developing writerly skills and resources but that does not take priority over writing a poem or story. Nonetheless, the institutional site of the teaching ensured that translation would be seen as creating a literary work in its own right, relatively autonomous from the source text, possessing its own aesthetic features.

In a typical workshop, this literary or aesthetic recognition becomes the goal of the teaching and learning. Students present their translations of poetry or fiction, explain their rationale for selecting the source texts, and comment on specific problems posed by translating the texts into English. Then the class submits the translations to a critique under the teacher's guidance. Because workshops are usually multilingual and neither the instructor nor every student commands every source language, the critique emphasizes the literary effects of the translation at the expense of its equivalence to the source text. The class discussion can certainly function as collaborative learning, with students pooling their skills and resources to help their peers improve their translations as literary works. Yet if the teacher is a noted translator of poetry or fiction, especially one who is also a noted poet or fiction writer, students are more than likely to defer to the teacher's judgments, and the pedagogy quickly devolves into a literary variety of traditional transmissionist teaching: instead of error correction, the teacher performs what might be called stylistic editing, bringing the translation in line with the literary or aesthetic values that are embodied in the teacher's own translating or writing. The teacher's authority as translator and author will incline students to treat these values implicitly as true or right.

Missing from this workshop pedagogy is any assignment of readings in translation theory and commentary. Some teachers have in fact voiced their opposition to the use of theoretical texts in the translation workshop, characterizing theory as unnecessary to the production of translations; when readings about translation are assigned, they tend to be practically oriented, written by professional translators and focused on the task of how to recreate the formal features of the source text (Venuti 2013: 240–3). As a result, students do not see that translation strategies always rest on theoretical assumptions about literature and translation, so that any attempt to draw a hard-and-fast distinction between theory and practice is deeply questionable. The exclusion of theoretical texts deprives students of the conceptual resources they need to think critically about their own work as well as the teacher's comments. Without developing a critical self-consciousness, students are unlikely to learn to translate independently of the teacher's guidance.

Only recently has the teaching of literary translation received the sort of scrutiny that has been given to the teaching of nonliterary translation for more than a decade. Kelly Washbourne aims to introduce a constructivist pedagogy into the workshop by reimagining it "as a site for collaborative, process-oriented learning" (2013: 49). Instead of devoting the workshop solely to a teacher-moderated class discussion of products, namely the literary translations written by individual students, Washbourne urges instructors to develop a broad range of alternative activities that bring translation processes to the fore and engage students in small groups. These "creative-reflective variations" include "readarounds," in which students read and discuss multiple student versions of the same source text; "insourcing," in which one group of students produces source texts while another group translates them, whereafter the roles are switched; and "open elections," in which students' translations along with their justifications for their strategies are posted on a common platform for assessment by their peers (2013: 56). Following constructivist pedagogues like Kiraly and González-Davies, Washbourne seeks to turn the literary translation classroom into "a community of practice," although this move involves restoring the workshop to its historical function as a setting "where participants are committed to artisan-community-level quality of production, as opposed to the standardization of a factory" (2013: 49, 54).

Washbourne's recommendations are strong on method, but they stop short of considering whether literary translators should learn a particular body of knowledge to develop their skills—or even to perform the sort of activities that he recommends. Thus he suggests that students might be asked to "develop evaluation criteria for a translation of the text you have translated or for a text with multiple target texts" (2013: 59). Yet such criteria are not self-evident. Students need to be introduced to theoretical concepts and analytical tools in order to describe, explain, and evaluate translations. Where will students find these materials if they are not provided by the instructor in the form of readings submitted to rigorous discussion and debate? Washbourne wants to foster an interdisciplinary pedagogy by drawing on related fields such as literature and creative writing to formulate learning goals for literary translators. The goals he describes remain schematic, however, devoid of the content to which they are linked in literary studies. He cites as one such learning goal "the awareness of the traditions in which one is working" (2013: 51), but students will not achieve this awareness unless they explore the traditions of theory, criticism, and practice that constitute literary and translation history and learn how to bring these traditions to bear in their translation projects. Washbourne does not specify any traditions whatsoever, let alone ways of teaching them in the workshop.

Future Directions

The scholarship on translation pedagogy has been dominated by functionalist theories and by methods that are constructivist, empirically based, and linguistics-oriented. The research that has transformed translation studies since the 1980s, approaches that have brought it closer to developments in literary and cultural studies by pursuing sociological and political orientations, has yet to make a significant contribution to teaching the practice of translation. This area may well see development in the future, but at this point we might notice the efforts that have been made and consider where they might lead.

The crucial question is how to mediate between research that is largely theoretical speculation, on the one hand, poststructuralist in its basic assumptions and postcolonial or feminist in its ideological standpoint, and the teaching of translation practice, on the other hand, when that practice can involve pragmatic and technical as well as humanistic texts. Carol Maier has taught workshops in which she employed a widely used activity, the analysis of multiple versions of the same source texts, in order to "prompt and sustain discussion about ways in which gender might, and has, figured in the work of various translators" (2003: 159). The texts were Spanish, poems by the seventeenth-century Mexican nun Sor Juana Inés de la Cruz; the translations were English, produced by such accomplished hands as Willis Barnstone, Margaret Sayers Peden, and the team of Electa Arenal and Amanda Powell. Maier asked participants to prepare material beforehand, not only the source texts and translations but also essays in translation theory informed by poststructuralism and feminism and an English-language short story that raises issues of gender, authorship, and translation. The workshops were attended by faculty and students, both undergraduate and graduate, although in such different locations as Spain, the United Kingdom, and the United States.

The workshops were remarkable for the absence of any sustained discussion of theoretical concepts as tools to analyze the translators' practices, the specific verbal choices they made in the translations. The Spanish setting was a translator training program where various theoretical discourses are taught, but when Maier asked the faculty participants "for their thoughts about the amount of background material an instructor might best present to students before asking them to work on the translations," they did not propose methods of showing students how theory is linked to practice; instead, Maier observes, "the general consensus was that I had given them too much information" (2003: 162). In the other settings, a British graduate program in literary translation and an American liberal arts college, the participants readily addressed the issue of gender, although only in terms of translation practice, as it "arose spontaneously from a comparison of the multiple versions" (2003: 165).

Maier concludes by formulating "flexible pedagogical strategies" that involve the suggestion that the teacher "initially provide minimal background information, or none" (2003: 166). But this strategy seems counterproductive, if not self-defeating. If students cannot put theoretical concepts to instructive uses in analyzing translations, shouldn't they be taught how to read theory carefully and how to explore its practical implications? Translation issues that seem to be raised "spontaneously," like gender, actually reflect previous work in the area or at the very least a cultural situation, such as those in the United Kingdom and the United States, where there exists an acute awareness of those issues. If the teaching includes the unsystematic introduction of concepts, can students learn how to apply them systematically? Maier wants to train translators "to work knowingly with respect both to the trust they invariably place in a text and the limits placed by any and all approaches to translation" (2003: 66). But the ideological critique motivated by discourses like feminism constitutes a hermeneutics of suspicion, as Paul Ricoeur (1970) called it, not trust, and the limits that theoretical concepts impose on translation analysis and practice are not simply constraining but enabling. These concepts need not preempt a pedagogy that fosters what Maier values, "an individual, contextual interpretation" rather than "an ultimate universal deciphering" (Maier 2003: 160).

This goal is shared by Rosemary Arrojo, who authored one of the theoretical essays that Maier assigned in her workshops. Arrojo sets out from "a perspective generally associated with postmodern, poststructuralist, or even postcolonial notions of language and the subject which have as a common ground a disbelief in the possibility of any neutral, purely objective meaning" (Arrojo 2005: 239). From this perspective, the functionalist, empirically based, linguistics-oriented scholarship that dominates translation pedagogy—she cites the work of Basil Hatim and Ian Mason, Mona Baker, and Paul Kussmaul—is riddled with "essentialism" (Arrojo 2005: 225–6) in their failure to treat meaning in language and equivalence in translation as a variable interpretation contingent upon specific cultural and social situations. Arrojo argues that "if translation is an interpretive task that cannot be in any sense neutral or above ideological and historical constraints, it seems logical that translation students should be taught the responsibilities involved in being active interpreters and writers of translated texts" (Arrojo 2005: 231).

To this end, she presents a classroom activity that she used with Brazilian students. They were asked to write a Brazilian Portuguese translation of a piece of English prose, "a short, rather informal text which is supposed to be a note left by an American guest to his Brazilian host" (Arrojo 2005: 239). After completing the translation, the students were shown William Carlos Williams's 1934 poem, "This Is Just To Say," which is the text they translated, although it was printed as prose. They are now tasked with translating the English poem into a Brazilian Portuguese poem. What they learn, Arrojo explains, is that "whether a text is literary or not, whether it is a poem or not, does not really depend on something which is intrinsically found in its language or in its structures but, rather, on the conventional interpretive strategies which readers activate in order to (literally) make sense of it" (Arrojo 2005: 240). The activity forces students to become aware of those strategies and to take into account how the translator's interpretation constructs a context and a function that provisionally fix the meaning of the source text.

Still, one wonders how students come to learn those interpretive strategies, described here as "conventional." Arrojo acknowledges that, for the activity to be effective, the students must be members of a cultural community "which is familiar with the prevalent conventions generally guiding the reading of poetry" (Arrojo 2005: 240). Students of literary translation, then, must command several distinct bodies of knowledge: they need to be proficient not only in both source and translating languages but also in interpreting the poems written in them in order to arrive at an awareness of their interpretive strategies—unless of course they are first taught the poststructuralist theory that underpins Arrojo's activity. She also cites a specific interpretation of Williams's poem, Jonathan Culler's reading, suggesting that "if a translator decides to elaborate on this reading" (Arrojo 2005: 241), certain words (namely "plums") will pose problems that receive different solutions according to changes in Brazilian culture. The question again arises of how much information the teacher should provide to students in order for them to perform and learn from the activity. Arrojo does not indicate whether she introduced Culler's reading into the classroom, but it seems necessary to her argument. Given the pertinent materials, students can learn not just that translation is an interpretive act but that their interpretations are informed by various conditions that at once constrain and enable those interpretations, conditions that are linguistic and poetic and that derive from literary traditions and theoretical discourses as well as from the source and translating cultures.

Clearly, the more sophisticated we expect translators to become, the more knowledge and skills we must teach them. Constructivist pedagogies have introduced an emphasis on collaborative work at the expense of teacher intervention, but students need to master diverse bodies of knowledge to develop a self-critical awareness about their translating as well as greater resourcefulness as translators. Whether the institutional site of the teaching is a translator training program or a department of languages and literatures, students can be required to practice translation in workshop-like courses while they study languages and cultures, translation theory, and the fields and disciplines in which they plan to specialize. But to avoid the naïve dichotomy between theory and practice, the indissoluble link between them should be demonstrated and underscored through activities in every course, whether collaborative or individual or a combination of both.

26 A Review of Textbooks in Translation Studies

Sarah Maitland

The exponential growth of translation studies over the past two decades has led to a parallel growth in textbooks designed specifically for the field. They range from anthologies of translation theory and commentary to primers or introductory expositions of influential theories and research trends to reference works that include encyclopedias, handbooks, and companions to manuals offering instruction in translation practice. This chapter provides a necessarily selective review of textbooks for use in translation-oriented courses at both the undergraduate and graduate levels. The emphasis falls squarely on those books with broad applicability, but some attention is also given to others that can prove effective in specific pedagogical contexts. The review is divided into four sections, each devoted to a particular type of textbook: readers, primers, reference works, and manuals. The goal throughout is to examine how these texts construct a relationship between theory and practice and what kinds of research and translating they enable.

Readers

Anthologies that gather theoretical statements and other kinds of commentary tend to be organized chronologically, aiming to cover a broad historical range. But even within these parameters significant differences emerge among the available books. Rainer Schulte and John Biguenet's *Theories of Translation* (1992) may well have been the first entrant in the field: it moves from antiquity to the twentieth century, covering Roman translation through an essay by Hugo Friedrich and including such major theorists as Friedrich Schleiermacher, Walter Benjamin, and Jacques Derrida. Of the twenty-one essays and excerpts, eight were written by canonical poets that include John Dryden, Dante Gabriel Rossetti, Octavio Paz, and Yves Bonnefoy, some of whom comment on their own translation practice. This fact may explain why the anthology is often adopted in the translation workshops offered in creative writing programs. The readings themselves receive no accompanying apparatus that would allow the book to serve as an introduction to the field of translation studies and thereby make it more useful in research-oriented courses. In fact, the editors preface the volume by reducing thinking about translation to the production of translated text: "Translation thinking is always concerned with the reconstruction of processes" (Schulte and Biguenet 1992: 9).

Douglas Robinson's *Western Translation Theory* (1997b, 2nd ed. 2002) overlaps with Schulte and Biguenet's volume to some extent but actually presents a very different selection of materials. Intended primarily for courses on the history of translation theory, it moves from antiquity to the nineteenth century and brings together 124 texts by ninety authors, nine of whom are women. Fourteen authors, including Burgundio of Pisa, King Duarte, Etienne Dolet, Jacques Peletier du Mans, Nicolas Perrot d'Ablancourt, and Mikael Agricola, appear for the first time in English translation. Each entry includes a biographical headnote and copious footnotes, but these commentaries are heavy on biographical detail and do not give a sense of what influences have been brought to bear on the ideas expounded, to what debates they respond or how they connect with or depart from the historical development of translation theory. Robinson himself translated a number of the German texts, but he does not state why he produced fresh translations rather than rely on existing versions or what theories guided his strategies. His translations of two letters by Luther appear to assign priority to maximum readability: they have a decidedly informal feel, with conversational contractions and a few anachronistic clichés. The breadth of Robinson's selections, especially in the medieval and early modern periods, allow for detailed work in specific periods, but a lack of critical engagement with the theories themselves, together with a few important omissions (Jacques Amyot is absent, for instance), make this anthology a selective point of departure.

Lawrence Venuti's *The Translation Studies Reader* (2000, 3rd ed. 2012b) addresses the need for an extensive overview of the key approaches to understanding the field. In the third edition, thirty-one authors are presented in seven chronological sections, the first of which contains "foundational statements" dated before 1900. Subsequent sections are divided into decades of the twentieth and twenty-first centuries. The selection emphasizes authors whose work has been influential, whether translators or poets, philosophers or literary theorists, linguists or scholars of translation. Juxtaposing readings from different periods and disciplines brings them into critical conversation, inviting reflection on the limits of our knowledge and assumptions about translation. The organization encourages the exploration of such issues as equivalence, translation strategies, cultural norms and movements, ethics and ideology, world literature, and translation in linguistically divided cultures.

Venuti prefaces each section with an extensive essay that describes both the period in which the chapters are placed and the intellectual and scholarly trends in which they emerged. The prefaces clarify the theoretical bases of the readings, enabling instructors and students alike to navigate the rich proliferation of research methodologies and translation practices that have characterized the field. The latest edition, however, includes fewer linguistics-oriented pieces and omits James Holmes's seminal essay, "The Name and Nature of Translation Studies" (1972), considered by some as the founding statement for the field but critiqued by Venuti as resting on empiricist assumptions that reflect a questionable scientific model.

A move away from linguistics-orientated approaches is also evident in Mona Baker's *Critical Readings in Translation Studies* (2010). This anthology presents twenty-five texts organized thematically and drawn from a range of disciplines, including anthropology, literature, and sociology. Basic issues are covered, such as translation strategies and the translator's voice and ideology, and considerable attention is given to the role of translation in cultural representation and canon formation, in minor cultures, in social and political institutions, and in new media. Among the distinctive features of this collection is its commitment to the theory and practice of interpreting in various situations, medical and military, especially with immigrants and refugees.

Like Venuti, Baker is assiduous in her commitment to enhanced pedagogy. Each reading is preceded by an introductory comment highlighting crucial passages and elucidating core concepts from a critical perspective. Follow-up questions for discussion are also provided. Yet since Baker does not clarify what makes the readings "critical," we must presume that this feature coincides with her largely politicized view of translation. Situations of inequality and conflict are foregrounded, and ideological critique and political commentary take precedence over linguistic practices. Over half of the readings were published after 2000, insuring that the presentation of the field is up-to-date but without giving the comprehensive overview to which the book aspires.

Primers

A number of textbooks take as their project the presentation of major theoretical movements in translation studies. Jeremy Munday's *Introducing Translation Studies* (2001, 4th ed. 2016) starts with a chronological tour of the development of the field and defines the debates before the twentieth century as issues of literal versus free translation, faithfulness, and the valorization of the foreign. The rest of the book is structured according to developments in translation research over the past thirty years, addressing functionalist and systemic theories, discourse and register analysis, cultural and ideological dimensions, the visibility, ethics, and sociology of translators, and translation technologies.

Each chapter contains pithy definitions of chief concepts alongside recommended texts for supplementary study. Yet much of the thinking is linguistics-oriented, with only three of the twelve chapters tackling theories that are cultural or philosophical and not grounded on varieties of linguistics. The materials, moreover, are not always presented in thoughtful juxtapositions. In treating "philosophical approaches to translation," Munday concentrates on George Steiner's hermeneutic motion, Ezra Pound's experimentalism, and Jacques Derrida's notion of "différance." Most of this chapter is devoted to Steiner, pre-empting a fuller discussion of more complicated notions like Walter Benjamin's "pure language" and Paul Ricoeur's "linguistic hospitality." In fact, Munday erroneously suggests that Ricoeur's rejection of a "perfect" translation entails a rejection of Benjamin's "pure language," and that Ricoeur had offered practical solutions where Benjamin was concerned only with "ideal, abstract" concepts (Munday 2016: 262). This limited survey offers only the briefest of engagements with philosophical accounts of translation.

Anthony Pym's *Exploring Translation Theories* (2009, 2nd ed. 2014) similarly seeks to present a comprehensive analysis of contemporary developments organized according to overarching concepts. Pym foregrounds equivalence as well and in two separate chapters looks to structural linguistics and relevance theory before turning to functionalism. He describes his work as explaining the "central paradigms" of translation theory (2014: 3), but he in effect oversimplifies what are actually diverse, contested, and mutually interrogating concepts by reducing them to a series of distinct and internally coherent points of departure. He asserts, for example, that every theory responds to the "fundamental conflict between uncertainty and equivalence" (2014). As a result, he misleadingly construes Venuti's concept of foreignizing translation as a form of "directional" equivalence secured through a particular discursive strategy (2014: 32), whereas Venuti formulates it as an ethical effect of translated text that can be produced through various means, not only different and even opposed discursive strategies but also the very choice of a source text—provided that the translation challenges dominant values in the receiving culture. The engagement with the concept of cultural translation is likewise limited. Pym considers only two approaches, using Talal Asad to discuss ethnographic representation and Homi Bhabha to discuss hybridized opposition to representation through the ambivalence of human migrancy (Pym 2014: chap. 8). Both Munday's and Pym's primers are useful introductions for certain theories but distorting of others.

The ten books in the series "Translation Theories Explored," initially published by St. Jerome but now available through Routledge, tend to be more reliable. The theories under exploration are linguistic, functionalist, systemic, feminist, deconstructive, postcolonial, and anthropological. Among the strongest volumes are Kathleen Davis's *Deconstruction and Translation* (2001), a lucid and precise account of Derrida's thinking about translation that also considers English versions of his texts, and Kate Sturge's *Representing Others* (2007), a wide-ranging examination of the place of translation in ethnography and museum collecting. These incisive treatments, when read along with the primary texts they discuss, can be helpfully illuminating to both undergraduate and graduate students.

Reference Works

A sure sign of the growth of translation studies during the 1990s was the appearance of glossaries that defined terms and concepts as the variety of research methodologies increased. Mark Shuttleworth and Moira Cowie's *Dictionary of Translation Studies* (1997) contains over 300 clear and accessible entries. Terms that refer to the linguistic dimensions of translation predominate, however, with relatively little attention to the impact of such other disciplines as literary and cultural studies, philosophy, and sociology. No entries discuss feminism, for example, or postcolonial theory. Giuseppe Palumbo's *Key Terms in Translation Studies* (2009) fills in these gaps with an up-to-date survey of over 170 terms that include "essentialism," "habitus," and "ideology" as well as "calque," "equivalence," and "relevance theory." Palumbo uses cross-references to related entries, not so much to extend definitions, like Shuttleworth and Cowie, as to give a sense of the debates in which the terms are enmeshed. He also includes a section on influential thinkers in the field, although it is admittedly rudimentary and omits some figures who are obviously worthy of inclusion.

Mona Baker and Gabriela Saldanha's *Routledge Encyclopedia of Translation Studies* (1st ed. 2002, 2nd ed. 2009) reflects the diversity of research trends and methodologies that currently characterize the field. It is divided into two parts, the first of which provides over seventy entries on terms and concepts while the second examines the translation histories of over thirty linguistic and cultural communities. In addition to linguistic material covered in the glossaries, the encyclopedia addresses such translation-related issues as asylum, censorship, gender and sexuality, ethics, and globalization as well as various forms of interpreting. The translation of particular genres, text types, and media is also explored, including advertising, comics, film and video, news, and scientific texts. Each entry functions as a critical review of the scholarship on a particular topic, clarifying points in current debates. Yet few contributions actually advance those debates, and some stop short of fulfilling the expectations created by their titles. The entry on "Poetry," for instance, although it comments on "the relationship between theory and practice" (Baker and Saldanha 2009: 196), does not discuss how different theories of translation or of poetry might lead to different treatments of formal features like meter and line breaks. Nor does it consider the concepts and strategies advanced by important poet-translators like Pound, who receives no mention.

Translation studies has also seen the publication of many companions and handbooks within the past decade. This genre of edited volume is intended to survey dominant research trends, but the actual books vary widely because of the interdisciplinary nature of the field. Piotr Kuhiwczak and Karin Littau's *A Companion to Translation Studies* (2007) presents nine chapters devoted to such areas as literary translation, linguistics, philosophy, history, gender, and politics. The coverage is patchy, however. The chapter on theater and opera, for example, traces the emergence of stage translation as a domain of study, explains a number of fundamental concepts, and concludes by discussing avenues for future investigation. Yet since the last work cited appeared in 1997, virtually a decade of influential research is omitted, a problem from which the book generally suffers.

Kuhiwczak and Littau's companion stresses cultural approaches to translation at the expense of linguistics, whereas Kirsten Malmkjær and Kevin Windle's *Oxford Handbook of Translation Studies* (2011) reverses this emphasis by defining the "central concepts in the study of translation" as primarily linguistics-oriented, a matter of stylistics, meaning, and universals. The thirty-two chapters in this handbook are organized in sections on history, genres and text types, interpreting, multimedia translation, technology, and pedagogy. Yet in the three-chapter section titled "The History of Translation Theory," attention is diverted away from covering current theoretical positions, and discussions remain very broad. Sandra Bermann and Catherine Porter's *A Companion to Translation Studies* (2014) is perhaps unique in gathering the diverse approaches that currently dominate the field: the forty-five chapters were contributed by scholars in comparative literature, foreign languages, and literary theory, as well as translation studies, including the work of several translators. The pieces do not show much cross-fertilization, however, since some deploy strictly empirical, linguistics-oriented methods while others are informed solely by philosophical speculation and still others limit their references mostly to literary history or to translation studies. Rachel Galvin's chapter, to take one exception, relies on a remarkably varied set of theoretical concepts to examine the asymmetrical and disjunctive exchange involved in North American and Latin American poetry translation during the twentieth century. She makes use of Schleiermacher and Antoine Berman, Munday and David Bellos, and Édouard Glissant as well as Gilles Deleuze and Félix Guattari, developing an argument that is at once theoretical, historical, and practical.

Manuals

The mushrooming of translator training programs around the world has created the need for textbooks that teach translation practice, and instructors have obliged with various kinds of pedagogies. Routledge's "Thinking Translation" series concentrates on translating into English from a number of languages, including Arabic, Chinese, French, German, Italian, Russian, and Spanish. Sandor Hervey, Ian Higgins, and Louise Haywood's book in this series, *Thinking Spanish Translation* (1st ed. 1995; Michael Thompson replaced Higgins for the second edition in 2009), is based on an actual twenty-week undergraduate course. Assuming that students already possess advanced proficiency in Spanish, it aims to develop their competence in weighing up specific linguistic and cultural challenges across a range of text types. Theoretical developments are treated as a means of devising possible solutions to practical problems, an approach that centers on analyzing source texts, identifying problematic items, and applying strategies. The opening chapters distinguish between different types of translation (intralingual and gist), consider the issue of translation loss, and present such strategies as cultural transposition and compensation. Subsequent chapters explore linguistic and textual features, translation in specialized domains (scientific, technical, legal, financial, and consumer-oriented), and the demands of stylistic editing and revision. In-class discussion is stimulated through practical exercises and concrete translation tasks that illustrate the topics introduced in each chapter. A variety of Spanish and Latin American sources are used, with extensive references to online material.

The bulk of this text is devoted to the development of what the editors call a "scheme of textual 'filters'" (Haywood, Thompson, and Hervey 2009: 6) to represent different stages in the translator's analysis of the source text. Each filter—"genre," "cultural," "formal," "semantic," and "varietal"—is used as a practical lens through which to introduce concepts from linguistics, ranging from dialect, register, idiom, and code-switching to lexis, cohesion, and coherence. The authors relate these linguistic and textual features to translation practices through broad practical themes such as literal and connotative meaning, exoticism, particularization, and generalization.

The material is presented over the course of eight chapters without reference to the theoretical concepts on which it is predicated. Although the authors acknowledge that they borrow freely from linguistics, the only specific references are to Roman Jakobson's distinctions between different types of translation and his classification of the nonreferential functions of language (Haywood et al. 2009: 11, 60, 91); Geoffrey Leech's six classifications of connotative meaning (Haywood et al. 2009: 171); Hans Vermeer's *Skopostheorie* as developed in Christiane Nord's functionalist approach (Haywood et al. 2009: 47–8); and Venuti on domestication and foreignization and their ideological significance (Haywood et al. 2009: 73). This decontextualized presentation makes it difficult to discern the conceptual frameworks that underpin the authors' analytical tools as well as their assumptions about translation. By devoting more space to the explanation of those tools and their application to source texts, the text gives the discussions a sense of efficiency, enabling students to move quickly to the practical implications of their chosen translation strategy.

Mona Baker's *In Other Words: A Coursebook on Translation* (1st ed. 1992, 2nd ed. 2011) is a how-to manual for students tackling translations in mostly nonliterary contexts. Based on what Baker describes as "modern linguistics," the text makes use of M.A.K. Halliday's model of discourse analysis, functional linguistics, and pragmatics. These concepts enable her to take a systemic approach to the structure of texts, giving attention to how word forms vary between languages and how translators facilitate meaningful communication through translation. Early chapters address the issue of equivalence and introduce basic tools for identifying and solving difficult problems of nonequivalence, such as when the target language lacks words that express the same meaning as the source text. More complicated problems of collocations, idioms, and fixed expressions are considered alongside word order, the flow of information, and the organization of texts. Later chapters examine how translation might deal with the network of internal features that link the various parts of a text as well as the relationship that a translation constructs with its audience.

Among the strengths of *In Other Words* is its commitment to preparing students for the myriad linguistic problems that they can expect to encounter with translation. Every chapter concretizes main points through examples drawn from real translations into English as well as into such other languages as Arabic, Brazilian Portuguese, Chinese, French, German, Greek, Russian, and Spanish (back-translations into English are provided). And every chapter ends with exercises that further illustrate and reinforce the concepts introduced in the exposition. The last chapter, which was added to the second edition, seeks to encourage critical thinking about ethical dilemmas facing translators and interpreters. It reviews different kinds of ethics, distinguishing broadly between "deontological" models associated with concepts of virtue and duty and "teleological" models concerned with the consequences of actions and usually exemplified by utilitarianism (Baker 2011: 277). For Baker, the translator performs a complex social role not only by producing texts but also by interacting with clients and other agents involved in the commissioning and reception of a translation. Yet the treatment of ethical concepts is cursory, and their application to specific dilemmas is not fully explained. Baker does not develop a clear position, although she does seem to be following Kant in advocating virtue ethics.

Douglas Robinson's *Becoming a Translator* (2012, 3rd ed. 2012) uniquely focuses on the figure of the translator and the need for self-awareness during the translation process. It aims to teach students how to translate faster and more accurately while building reflective skills. Translators, Robinson explains, need to process linguistic materials efficiently and effectively, but they also need to recognize problems when they arise, to identify a range of strategies, and to evaluate their practical implications. Robinson's manual "shuttles" between two cognitive extremes: the "natural" or intuitive ways that translators learn in the professional world and the conscious analytical problem-solving that translators learn in the classroom (2012: 2). This shuttle movement shapes the structure and content of the book, but it can be challenging, depending on the previous educational experiences that the reader brings to the text. "Teachers and students accustomed to traditional analytical pedagogies," Robinson recognizes, "will probably shy away at first from critical perspectives and hands-on exercises designed to develop subliminal skills" (2012: 3).

The opening chapters discuss the commissioning of a translation and the external and internal factors (such as timeliness, cost, and project management) that influence how translators approach their work. Robinson then introduces the theoretical framework for the shuttle movement that he uses to explain the translator's mental processes. He defines two sets of concepts and applies them to translation: from the philosopher Charles Sanders Peirce, Robinson derives the notions of "instinct," "experience," and "habit," on the one hand, and "abduction," "induction," and "deduction," on the other; from the social psychologist Karl Weick, he derives the notions of "enactment," "selection," and "retention" (Robinson 2012: 62–71). The result is a model, graphically displayed, to describe the translator's accumulation of experience, recognition of patterns, and subsequent incorporation of knowledge and skills into subliminal activity.

Perhaps the greatest merit of Robinson's manual is its treatment of theoretical concepts primarily as *enablers* of practice, proceeding directly from the needs and constraints that a translation project imposes upon the translator. Speech-act theory and pragmatics are used to define the function of the translation as a text that must fulfill a certain need for its users (Robinson 2012: 128–35). Translation in this light can be seen as a verbal act that causes translators to become aware of the performative effect of their decision-making. Pierre Bourdieu's concepts of "field," "capital," and "habitus" are used to discuss the translator as an agent in a sociocultural community who at the same time works under the overarching conditions of the translation market (Robinson 2012: 110, 144, 161–2). Milton Bennett's hierarchy of intercultural communication is expanded to include the role of translation and interpreting in fostering ethnocentrism, cross-cultural tolerance, and integration (Robinson 2012: 183–4). Robinson also makes use of Richard

Jacquemond's comparison of power differentials between dominant and less powerful cultures and Lori Chamberlain's feminist approach to metaphors used for
translation (Robinson 2012: 185–7). His final chapter considers the importance
of reflective competencies by considering the "alarm bells" (Robinson 2012: 200)
of translation quality, what the translator does when a problem arises, and the
analytical skills and sources of support that the translator employs in response.

Through numerous exercises, Robinson attempts to show that theory can illuminate rather than obstruct the translator's progress. Yet too much space is devoted
to theoretical exposition, and readers must wade through what are at times lengthy
digressions before entering into the practical discussion promised by the title of
the book. Robinson acknowledges, moreover, that since the book is not written
for a specific language combination, exercises are framed only in English, and
instructors will need to adapt them to student language pairs.

For students preparing to undertake research in translation studies, Gabriela
Saldanha and Sharon O'Brien's guide, *Research Methodologies in Translation Studies* (2014), is intended as something of a sequel to Jenny Williams and
Andrew Chesterman's *The Map: A Beginner's Guide to Doing Research in Translation Studies* (2002), which focused on enabling novice researchers to decide
between different theoretical models and research topics. Given the raft of methodological developments since publication of *The Map*, from keystroke logging
to Internet-mediated research, as well as greater attention to translation ethics
and sociological approaches, *Research Methodologies* presents approaches from
applied linguistics, social science, psychology, and cultural studies and describes
how to apply them within translation research contexts. The picture that emerges
is not one of a discrete translation studies research methodology but one of critical
synthesis, addressing translational concerns by adapting the diverse apparatuses
that are in operation in related disciplines.

Focusing on empirical methods, the book outlines a number of theoretical models that students may employ in their research. The chapter devoted to "Product-
orientated research" (Saldanha and O'Brien 2014: 50–108) discusses approaches
to researching the text that results from the translation process and the application of critical discourse analysis and corpus linguistics in the description and
qualitative evaluation of translations. The chapter on "Process-oriented research"
(Saldanha and O'Brien 2014: 109–49) considers methods that seek to understand
translator behavior, competence, and cognitive processes. This chapter covers a
range of practices, including self-observation, eye-tracking, contextual enquiry,
situational observation, and physiological measuring. A chapter titled "Participant-
oriented research" (Saldanha and O'Brien 2014: 150–204), meanwhile, is directed
towards the human agents involved in translation processes and draws on the use
of common sociological research methods such as questionnaires, interviews, and
focus groups. A chapter on "Context-oriented research" (Saldanha and O'Brien
2014: 205–33) highlights ethnographic models used to investigate social, political, and ideological factors affecting translators, the circumstances in which translations take place, and the ways in which they influence receiving cultures. Here

emphasis is placed on the case study method, which, according to the authors, has been misunderstood as a single unit of investigation or free-form option unconstrained by the demands of a particular investigatory approach. An introductory chapter raising issues of reliability, validity, and ethics and a final chapter on producing research reports sandwich these discussions.

Although aimed at both students and established researchers, *Research Methodologies* is essentially an extended survey of the most frequently applied empirical methodologies in translation research. As a result, it tends to prioritize prevailing debates in the literature over the voices of the authors themselves. It would have been useful, for example, to articulate case studies of existing translation research so as to offer practical demonstrations of the methodologies described in the four main chapters. The focus on empirical research, moreover, which reflects the authors' own expertise, necessarily gives rise to the erroneous impression that this approach is either the only area of translation research in operation or that it is the only one that requires greater methodological precision for its deployment.

The authors are careful to note that they do not believe in clear-cut distinctions between conceptual and empirical research or between descriptive and evaluative models. Yet they have in fact created an artificial distinction by separating the study of translation "products" from the sociopolitical contexts in which translations take shape. The authors further explain that, as with all disciplines concerned with cognitive processes, it is inappropriate to make inferences about translators' psychological processes because corpora of texts do not give access to underlying cognitive structures. Yet they miss an opportunity to signal one of the distinguishing features and fundamental benefits of translation research—namely, that because the production of a translation is at base a social practice, the study of translation must in turn avoid any isolation of specific features or processes to the exclusion of others.

By targeting two distinct audiences at once, students and established researchers, the authors must at times address one to the detriment of the other. Students will benefit from the authors' assiduous commitment to detail with every methodology presented and the attendant discussion of the respective benefits and challenges, but they will not find definitive answers on how to choose a research topic or how better to formulate research questions. By contrast, the substantial explanatory digressions aimed at instructing students about basic ontological and epistemological categories like realism, positivism, and constructivism, or about how to produce a case study or research report, will prove less relevant to established researchers.

The textbooks considered here show quite clearly that translation studies has become a recognizable and fairly coherent academic field but also that it is riven by methodological divisions that reflect the different areas and disciplines where translation research and practice are carried out in the academy. Translation by its very nature demands an interdisciplinary approach if we are to develop a comprehensive understanding of it, but the very complexity of that approach poses difficulties for the creation of equally comprehensive textbooks. To be sure, textbooks in any field tend to be decisively shaped by the research interests of their authors, inevitably excluding material that does not conform to those interests. Yet in translation studies the range of academic specializations that are most decisive in the making of textbooks can lead to disagreements about the readings, topics, and methods that should be brought into the classroom. As the field continues to advance, a consensus may emerge as to what students should know when they study and practice translation. For now, however, the textbooks that display the divisions may be useful in enabling us to interrogate precisely what translation studies is and to identify in what direction we may now wish to take it.

Bibliography

Abdel Haleem, M.A.S. (trans.) (2004) *The Qur'an*, Oxford: Oxford University Press.

Aboul-Ela, Hosam. (2001) "Challenging the Embargo: Arabic Literature in the US Market," *Middle East Report* 219 (Summer): 42–4.

Abrams, M. H., and Geoffrey Gault Harpham. (2012) *A Glossary of Literary Terms*, Boston, MA: Wadsworth Cengage Learning.

Adamson, Andrew, and Vicky Jenson (dirs.) (2001) *Shrek*, DreamWorks Distribution.

Alexiou, Margaret. (1985) "C. P. Cavafy's Dangerous Drugs: Poetry, Eros, and the Dissemination of Images," in Margaret Alexiou and Vassilis Lambropoulos (eds.) *The Text and Its Margins*, New York: Pella, pp. 157–96.

Allen, Esther, and Susan Bernofsky. (eds.) (2013) *In Translation: Translators on their Work and What it Means*, New York: Columbia University Press.

Amireh, Amal. (2000) "Framing Nawaal El Saadawi: Arab Feminism in a Transnational World," *Signs: Journal of Women in Culture and Society* 26/1: 215–49.

Anderson, Lorin, and David Krathwohl. (2001) *A Taxonomy for Learning, Teaching and Assessing: A Revision of Bloom's Taxonomy of Educational Objectives*, New York: Longman.

Anzaldúa, Gloria. (2001) "Chicana Artists: Exploring Nepantla, el lugar de la frontera," in Bob Coleman, Rebecca Brittenham, and Scott Campbell (eds.) *Making Sense*, New York: Houghton Mifflin, pp. 17–25.

Appiah, Kwame Anthony. (1993) "Thick Translation," in Venuti (2012b), pp. 331–43.

Apted, Michael. (dir.) (1994) *Nell*, Egg Pictures/PolyGram Filmed Entertainment.

Apter, Emily. (2006) *The Translation Zone: A New Comparative Literature*. Princeton, NJ: Princeton University Press.

———. (2008) "Untranslatables: A World System," *New Literary History* 39/3: 581–98.

———. (2009) "Translation—9/11: Terrorism, Immigration, Language Politics," in Esperanza Bielsa and Christopher Hughes (eds.) *Globalization, Political Violence and Translation*, New York: Palgrave Macmillan, pp. 195–206.

———. (2013) *Against World Literature: On the Politics of Untranslatability*, London and New York: Verso.

Arberry, A. J. (trans.) (1955) *The Koran Interpreted*, New York: Macmillan, 1967.

Arenas, Reinaldo. (1993) *Before Night Falls*, trans. Dolores Koch, New York: Viking.

Aristeas. (c. 130 BCE) "The Work of the Seventy-Two," trans. Moses Hadas, in Robinson (1997b), pp. 4–6.

Arnold, Matthew. (1861) "The Translator's Tribunal," in Robinson (1997b), pp. 250–4.

Arrojo, Rosemary. (1998) "The Revision of the Traditional Gap between Theory and Practice and the Empowerment of Translation in Postmodern Times," *The Translator* 4: 25–48.

————. (2005) "The Ethics of Translation in Contemporary Approaches to Translator Training," in Martha Tennent (ed.) *Training for the New Millennium: Pedagogies for Translation and Interpreting*, Amsterdam: Benjamins, pp. 225–45.

————. (2012) "Translators' Codes of Ethics," in Carol A. Chapelle (ed.) *Encyclopedia of Applied Linguistics*, 5 November.

Arteaga, Alfred. (1994) *An Other Tongue: Nation and Ethnicity in the Linguistic Borderlands*, Durham, NC: Duke University Press.

Asad, Talal. (1986) "The Concept of Cultural Translation in British Social Anthropology," in Baker (2010), pp. 9–27.

Association of Departments and Programs of Comparative Literature. (2006) "2005 Report on the Undergraduate Comparative Literature Curriculum," in *Profession 2006*, New York: MLA, pp. 177–97.

Auden, W. H. (1945) "Atlantis," in *The Collected Poetry of W. H. Auden*, New York: Random House, pp. 20–2.

Augustine. (427?) "The Use of Translations," trans. D. W. Robertson, Jr., in Robinson (1997b), pp. 31–4.

Bacchilega, Cristina. (1997) *Postmodern Fairy Tales: Gender and Narrative Strategies*. Philadelphia, PA: University of Pennsylvania Press.

Baer, Brian James, and Geoffrey S. Koby. (eds.) (2003) *Beyond the Ivory Tower: Rethinking Translation Pedagogy*, Amsterdam: John Benjamins.

Baines, Roger, Cristina Marinetti, and Manuela Perteghella. (eds.) (2011) *Staging and Performing Translation: Text and Theatre Practice*, Basingstoke and New York: Palgrave Macmillan.

Baker, Mona. (1996) "Corpus-Based Translation Studies: The Challenges that Lie Ahead," in Harold Somers (ed.) *Terminology, LSP and Translation: Studies in Language Engineering in Honour of Juan C. Sager*, Amsterdam: John Benjamins, pp. 175–86.

————. (2006) *Translation and Conflict: A Narrative Account*, London and New York: Routledge.

————. (ed.) (2010) *Critical Readings in Translation Studies*, London and New York: Routledge.

————. (2011) *In Other Words: A Coursebook on Translation*, 2nd ed., London and New York: Routledge.

———— and Gabriela Saldanha. (eds.) (2009) *Routledge Encyclopedia of Translation Studies*, 2nd ed., London and New York: Routledge.

Ballard, Michel. (1992) *De Ciceron à Benjamin*, Lille: Presses universitaires de Lille.

Bandia, Paul. (2005) "Esquisse d'une histoire de la traduction en Afrique," *Meta* 50/3: 957–71.

————. (2010) "Post-Colonial Literatures and Translations," in Gambier and van Doorslaer (2010), pp. 264–9.

Barber, Karin. (2003) "Text and Performance in Africa," *Bulletin of the School of Oriental and African Studies* 6/3: 324–33.

Barnstone, Willis. (1993) *The Poetics of Translation: History, Theory, Practice*, New Haven, CT: Yale University Press.

Baron, Robert, and Ana C. Cara. (eds.) (2011) *Creolization as Cultural Creativity*, Jackson, MS: University Press of Mississippi.

Barthes, Roland. (1975) *S/Z: An Essay*, trans. Richard Miller, New York: Hill and Wang.

————. (1977) "The Death of the Author," in *Image, Music, Text*, trans. Stephen Heath, New York: Hill and Wang, pp. 142–8.

Bartrina, Francesca. (2009) "Teaching Subtitling in a Virtual Environment," in Díaz Cintas and Anderman (2009), pp. 229–39.

Bascom, William. (1964) "Folklore Research in Africa," *Journal of American Folklore* 77: 12–31.

———. (1965) "The Forms of Folklore: Prose Narratives," *Journal of American Folklore* 78: 3–20.

Bassnett, Susan. (1980) *Translation Studies*, 3rd ed., London and New York: Routledge, 2002.

———. (1991) "Translating for the Theatre: The Case Against Performability," *TTR: Traduction, Terminologie, Rédaction* 4/1: 99–111.

———. (1993) *Comparative Literature: A Critical Introduction*, Oxford: Blackwell.

———. (2007) "Culture and Translation," in Kuhiwczak and Littau (2007), pp. 13–23.

——— and Harish Trivedi (eds.) (1999) *Post-Colonial Translation: Theory and Practice*, London and New York: Routledge.

Bauman, Richard. (1993) "The Nationalization and Internationalization of Folklore," *Western Folklore* 52: 247–69.

———. (2012) "Performance," in Bendix and Hasan-Rokem (2012), pp. 92–118.

Beaujour, Elisabeth Klosty. (1989) *Alien Tongues: Bilingual Russian Writers of the 'First' Emigration*, Ithaca, NY: Cornell University Press.

Beauvoir, Simone de. (1952) *The Second Sex*, trans. H. M. Parshley, New York: Knopf.

———. (2009) *The Second Sex*, trans. Constance Borde and Sheila Malovany-Chevallier, New York: Vintage.

Ben-Amos, Dan. (1976) "Analytical Categories and Ethnic Genres," in Dan Ben-Amos (ed.) *Folklore Genres*, Austin, TX: University of Texas Press, pp. 215–42.

Bendix, Regina F., Aditya Eggert, and Arnika Peselmann. (eds.) (2012) *Heritage Regimes and the State*, Göttingen: Universitätsverlag Göttingen.

Bendix, Regina F. and Galit Hasan-Rokem. (eds.) (2012) *A Companion to Folklore*, Oxford: Wiley-Blackwell.

Benjamin, Walter. (1923a) "The Task of the Translator," in Hannah Arendt (ed.), Harry Zohn (trans.), *Illuminations*, New York: Schocken, 1969, pp. 69–82.

———. (1923b) "The Translator's Task," trans. Steven Rendall, in Venuti (2012b), pp. 75–83.

Bentley, Eric. (1964) *The Life of the Drama*, New York: Atheneum.

Berman, Antoine. (1984) *L'Epreuve de l'étranger: culture et traduction dans l'Allemagne romantique*, Paris: Gallimard.

———. (1985) "Translation and the Trials of the Foreign," trans. Lawrence Venuti, in Venuti (2012b), pp. 240–53.

Bermann, Sandra. (2010) "Teaching in—and About—Translation," *Profession 2010*, New York: MLA, pp. 82–90.

Bermann, Sandra and Catherine Porter (eds.) (2014) *A Companion to Translation Studies*, Malden, MA: Wiley Blackwell.

Bermann, Sandra and Michael Wood (eds.) (2005) *Nation, Language and the Ethics of Translation*, Princeton, NJ: Princeton University Press.

Bernheimer, Charles (ed.) (1995) *Comparative Literature in the Age of Multiculturalism*. Baltimore: Johns Hopkins University Press.

Bernstein, Charles. (2011) "Breaking the Translation Curtain: the Homophonic Sublime," in *Attack of the Difficult Poems: Essays and Inventions*, Chicago: University of Chicago Press, pp. 199–202.

Binding, Paul. (1985) *Lorca: The Gay Imagination*, London: GMP.

Blum-Kulka, Shoshana. (1986) "Shifts of Cohesion and Coherence in Translation," in Venuti (2000), pp. 298–313.

Boas, Franz. (1901) *Kathlamet Texts*, Bulletin/Smithsonian Institution, Bureau of American Ethnology, Washington, DC: G. P. O.

Bohannan, Laura. (1966) "Shakespeare in the Bush," *Natural History* 75: 28–33.

Bonnefoy, Yves. (2004) *Shakespeare and the French Poet*, ed. John Naughton, Chicago: University of Chicago Press.

Booth, Marilyn. (2008) "Translator v. Author (2007): *Girls of Riyadh* Go to New York," *Translation Studies* 1/2: 197–211.

———. (2010) " 'The Muslim Woman' as Celebrity Author and the Politics of Translating Arabic: Girls of Riyadh Go on the Road," *Journal of Middle East Women's Studies* 6/3: 149–82.

Borges, Jorge Luis. (1935) "The Translators of *The One Thousand and One Nights*," trans. Esther Allen, in Venuti (2012b), pp. 92–106.

Boullata, Issa. (2003) "The Case for Resistant Translation from Arabic to English," *Translation Review* 65: 29–34.

Bourdieu, Pierre. (1992) *The Rules of Art: Genesis and Structure of the Literary Field*, trans. Susan Emanuel, Stanford, CA: Stanford University Press, 1996.

———. (2002) "Les conditions sociales de la circulation des idées," *Actes de la recherche en science sociales* 145: 3–8.

Bouson, J. Brooks. (2008) "Insect Transformation as a Narcissistic Metaphor in Kafka's *Metamorphosis*," in *Bloom's Modern Critical Interpretations: The Metamorphosis*, New York: Bloom's Literary Criticism, pp. 35–46.

Bowker, Lyn. (2000) "Towards a Methodology for Exploiting Specialized Target Language Corpora as Translation Resources," *International Journal of Corpus Linguistics* 5/1: 17–52.

———. (2002) *Computer-Aided Translation Technology: A Practical Introduction*, Ottawa: University of Ottawa Press.

———. (ed.) (2006) *Lexicography, Terminology and Translation: Text-based Studies in Honour of Ingrid Meyer*, Ottawa: University of Ottawa Press.

Boyle, Danny. (dir.) (2009) *Slumdog Millionaire*, Fox Searchlight Pictures.

Breton, André. (2006) *Poems of André Breton: A Bilingual Anthology*, trans. Jean-Pierre Cauvin and Mary Ann Caws, Boston, MA: Black Widow.

Brickman, Cecilia. (2012) *A Short Course in Reading French*, New York: Columbia University Press.

Briggs, Charles L. (1993) "Metadiscursive Practices and Scholarly Authority in Folkloristics," *Journal of American Folklore* 106/422 (Fall): 387–434.

Brisset, Annie. (2010) "Cultural Perspectives on Translation," *International Social Science Journal* 199: 69–80.

Brodsky, Joseph. (1992) *To Urania: Poems*, New York: Farrar, Straus and Giroux.

Brodzki, Bella. (2011) "Translating Gender/*Traduire le genre:* Is Transdiscursive Translation Possible?," in Luise von Flotow (ed.) *Translating Women*, Ottawa: University of Ottawa Press, pp. 263–82.

Brook, Peter. (1994) *The Shifting Point: Theatre, Film, Opera 1946–87*, New York: Theater Communications Group.

Bruni, Leonardo. (2008) *De interpretatione recta-De la traduction parfaite*, ed. and trans. Charles Le Blanc, Ottawa: University of Ottawa Press.

Burke, Peter. (2007) "Translations into Latin in Early Modern Europe," in Peter Burke and R. Po Chia Hsia (eds.) *Cultural Translation in Early Modern Europe*, Cambridge: Cambridge University Press, pp. 65–80.

Burton, Richard F. (ed. and trans.) (1885) *A Plain and Literal Translation of the Arabian Nights' Entertainments Now Entitled the Book of the Thousand Nights and a Night*. London: The Burton Club, 10 vols.

Buzelin, Hélène. (2005) "Unexpected Allies: How Latour's Network Theory Could Complement Bourdieusian Analyses in Translation Studies," *The Translator* 11/2: 193–218.

Carne-Ross, D. S. and Kenneth Haynes (eds.) (1996) *Horace in English*, New York: Penguin.

Carrard, Philippe. (1993) "Taming the New History: Alain Corbin and the Politics of Translation," *History of the Human Sciences* 6: 79–90.

Carrell, Patricia. (1987) "Content and Formal Schemata in ESL Reading," *TESOL Quarterly* 19: 461–81.

Casanova, Pascale. (2002) "Consecration and Accumulation of Literary Capital: Translation as Unequal Exchange," trans. Siobhan Brownlie, in Baker (2010), pp. 287–303.

———. (2005) "Literature as a World," *New Left Review* 31: 71–90.

Casetti, Francesco. (2007) "Adaptation and Mis-adaptations," in Robert Stam and Alessandra Raengo (eds.) *A Companion to Literature and Film*, Malden, MA: Blackwell, pp. 81–91.

Cassin, Barbara. (ed.) (2004) *Dictionary of Untranslatables: A Philosophical Lexicon*, trans. Steven Rendall, Christian Hubert, Jeffrey Mehlman, Nathaneal Stein, and Michael Syrotinski, ed. Emily Apter, Jacques Lezra, and Michael Wood, Princeton, NJ: Princeton University Press, 2014.

Catford, J. C. (1965) *A Linguistic Theory of Translation*, Oxford: Oxford University Press.

Cavafy, C. P. (1982) "Journal of the Poet's First Trip to Greece," in Filippou G. Fexi (ed.) *Peza*, Athens: Pantazi Fykiri, pp. 286–307.

———. (2010) "The Ships," in Peter Jeffreys, ed. and trans. *Selected Prose Works* Ann Arbor, MI: University of Michigan Press, pp. 84–5.

Césaire, Aimé. (1983) *Cahier d'un retour au pays natal*, Paris: Présence Africaine.

———. (2001) *Notebook of a Return to the Native Land*, ed. and trans. Clayton Eshleman and Annette Smith, Middletown, CT: Wesleyan University Press.

Cha, Theresa Hak Kyung. (1982) *Dictée*, Berkeley and Los Angeles: University of California Press, 2001.

Chakrabarty, Dipesh. (2000) *Provincializing Europe: Postcolonial Thought and Historical Difference*, Princeton, NJ: Princeton University Press.

Chamberlain, Lori. (1988) "Gender and the Metaphorics of Translation," in Venuti (2012b), pp. 254–68.

Chen, Alice. (2006) "Doctoring Across the Language Divide," *Health Affairs* 25/3: 808–13.

Chesterman, Andrew. (1997) "Ethics of Translation," in Mary Snell-Hornby, Zuzana Jettmarová, and Klaus Kaindl (eds.) *Translation as Intercultural Communication*, Amsterdam: John Benjamins, pp. 147–57.

———. (2001) "Proposal for a Hieronymic Oath," *The Translator* 7: 139–54.

Cheung, Martha. (2002) "Power and Ideology in Translation Research in Twentieth-Century China: An Analysis of Three Seminal Works," in Theo Hermans (ed.) *Crosscultural Transgressions: Research Models in Translation Studies II*, Manchester: St. Jerome, pp. 144–64.

Chow, Rey. (1995) "In the Name of Comparative Literature," in Bernheimer (1995), pp. 107–16.

———. (2008) "Translator, Traitor; Translator, Mourner (or, Dreaming of Intercultural Equivalence)." *New Literary History* 39/3: 565–80.

Chreiteh, Alexandra. (2009) *Da'iman Coca-Cola*, Beirut: Arab Scientific Publishers, 2009.

———. (2011) *Always Coca-Cola*, trans. Michelle Hartman, Northampton, MA: Interlink.

Cicero, Marcus Tullius. (55–44BCE) "Translating Greek Orations into Latin," "The Best Kind of Orator," "TransLating Greek Philosophy into Latin," trans. E. W. Sutton, H. M. Hubbell, and Harris Rackham, in Robinson (1997b), pp. 6–12.

Clark, A. C. (ed.) (1911) *Pro Archia Poeta Oratio: M. Tulli Ciceronis Orationes*, Oxford: Oxford University Press, vol. 6.

Clark, Peter. (2000) *Arabic Literature Unveiled: Challenges of Translation*, Durham, NC: Center for Middle East Studies, Middle East Paper 63.

Clifford, James. (1988) "Identity in Mashpee," in *The Predicament of Culture: Twentieth-Century Ethnography, Literature, and Art*, Cambridge, MA: Harvard University Press, pp. 277–346.

———. (1997) *Routes: Travel and Translation in the Late Twentieth Century*, Cambridge, MA: Harvard University Press.

Colina, Sonia. (2003) *Teaching Translation: From Research to the Classroom*, New York: McGraw Hill.

———. (2006) Review of González-Davies (2004), *Studies in Second Language Acquisition* 28: 147–9.

Conzemius, Anne, and Jan O'Neill. (2001) *Building Shared Responsibility for Student Learning*, Alexandria, VA: Association for Supervision and Curriculum Development.

Cook, Guy. (2003) *Applied Linguistics*, Oxford: Oxford University Press.

Cooperson, Michael. (2006) "The Monstrous Births of Aladdin," in Ulrich Marzolph (ed.) *The Arabian Nights Reader*, Detroit, MI: Wayne State University Press, pp. 265–82.

Copeland, Rita. (1991) *Rhetoric, Hermeneutics, and Translation in the Middle Ages: Academic Traditions and Vernacular Texts*, Cambridge: Cambridge University Press.

Corbin, Alain. (1990) *Le village des cannibales*, Paris: Aubier.

———. (1992) *The Village of Cannibals: Rage and Murder in France, 1870*, trans. Arthur Goldhammer, Cambridge, MA: Harvard University Press.

Cordingley, Anthony. (ed.) (2013) *Self-Translation: Brokering Originality in Hybrid Culture*, London: Bloomsbury.

Corngold, Stanley. (2004) "Kafka and the Dialect of Minor Literature," in Christopher Prendergast (ed.) *Debating World Literature*, London and New York: Verso, pp. 272–90.

———. (2005) "Comparative Literature: The Delay in Translation," in Bermann and Wood (2005), pp. 139–45.

Cronin, Michael. (1996) *Translating Ireland: Translation, Languages, Cultures*, Cork: Cork University Press.

———. (2003) *Translation and Globalization*, London and New York: Routledge.

———. (2009) *Translation Goes to the Movies*, London and New York: Routledge.

Cross, C. Lindley. (2009) "Perspectives Behind Translating *House of Flesh* by Yusuf Idris," http://home.uchicago.edu/~ksalib/papers/Idris-Perspectives.pdf (accessed 11 February 2014).

Cunningham, Michael. (2010) "Found in Translation," *New York Times*, 2 October, p. 10.

D'Ablancourt, Nicolas Perrot. (1640/1654) "Preface to Tacitus" and "Preface to Lucian: To Monsieur Conrart," trans. Lawrence Venuti, in Venuti (2012b), pp. 31–7.

———. (1654) "To Monsieur Conrart," trans. David G. Ross, in Robinson (1997b), pp. 157–9.

Dalven, Rae. (trans.) (1961) *The Complete Poems of Cavafy*, New York: Harcourt, Brace and World.

Damrosch, David. (2003) *What Is World Literature?* Princeton, NJ: Princeton University Press.

Damrosch, David and Gayatri Chakravorty Spivak. (2011) "Comparative Literature/World Literature: A Discussion with David Damrosch and Gayatri Spivak," *Comparative Literature Studies* 48/4: 455–85.

Darwish, Ali. (2007) "Review of Kelly (2005)," *JoSTrans: The Journal of Specialised Translation* 7 (January), http://www.jostrans.org/issue07/rev_kelly.php (accessed 4 January 2016).

Darwish, Mahmoud. (2007) *The Butterfly's Burden*, trans. Fady Joudah, Port Townsend, WA: Copper Canyon, 2007.

Davidson, Brad. (2000) "The Interpreter as Institutional Gatekeeper: The Social-Linguistic Role of Interpreters in Spanish-English Medical Discourse," in Baker (2010), pp. 154–73.

Davis, Dick. (2002) "All My Soul is There: Verse Translation and the Rhetoric of English Poetry," *Yale Review* 90/1: 66–83.

——. (2004) "On Not Translating Hafiz," *New England Review* 25/1–2: 310–18.

Davis, Kathleen. (2001) *Deconstruction and Translation*, Manchester: St. Jerome.

De Campos, Haroldo. (2007) "Translation as Creation and Criticism," trans. Diana Gibson and Haroldo de Campos, in Antonio Sergio Bessa and Odile Cisneros (eds.) *Novas: Selected Writings of Haroldo de Campos*, Evanston, IL: Northwestern University Press, pp. 312–26.

De Caro, F. A. (1986) "Riddles and Proverbs," in Oring (1986), pp. 175–97.

De Fonclare, Guillaume. (2014) *Inside My Own Skin*, trans. Yves Henri Cloarec, New York: Hanging Loose.

De Launay, Marc. (2006) *Qu'est-ce que traduire?* Paris: Vrin.

Deleuze, Gilles, and Félix Guattari. (1986) *Kafka. Toward a Minor Literature*, trans. Dana Polan, Minneapolis, MN: University of Minnesota Press.

Delisle, Jean, Hannelore Lee-Jahnke, and Monique C. Cormier. (eds.) (1999) *Terminologie de la Traduction: Translation Terminology, Terminología de la Traduccíon, Terminolo- gie der Übersetzung*, Amsterdam: John Benjamins.

Derrida, Jacques. (1978) *Writing and Difference*, trans. Alan Bass, Chicago: University of Chicago Press.

——. (1985) "Des Tours de Babel," trans. Joseph F. Graham, in Joseph F. Graham (ed.) *Difference in Translation*, Ithaca, NY: Cornell University Press, pp. 165–207.

——. (1998a) *Archive Fever: A Freudian Impression*, trans. Eric Prenowitz, Chicago: University of Chicago Press.

——. (1998b) *Monolingualism of the Other, or the Prosthesis of Origin*, trans. Patrick Mensah, Stanford, CA: Stanford University Press.

——. (1999) "What Is a 'Relevant' Translation?" trans. Lawrence Venuti, *Critical Inquiry* 27 (2001): 174–200.

De Vries, Hent, and Lawrence E. Sullivan. (eds.) (2006) *Political Theologies: Public Reli- gions in a Post-Secular World*, New York: Fordham University Press.

Días Cintas, Jorge and Gunilla Anderman. (eds.) (2009) *Audiovisual Translation: Lan- guage Transfer on Screen*, London: Palgrave Macmillan.

Dolan, Jill. (2005) *Utopia in Performance: Finding Hope at the Theater*, Ann Arbor, MI: University of Michigan Press.

Doron, Marcia Nita, and Marilyn Gaddis Rose. (1981) "The Economics and Politics of Translation," in Rose (1981), pp.160–7.

Dorst, Tankred, and Ursula Ehler. (2012) *This Beautiful Place*, trans. Anne Posten, New York: Hanging Loose.

Doty, Mark. (1993) *My Alexandria*, Urbana, IL: University of Illinois Press.

Drugan, Joanna, and Chris Megone. (2011) "Bringing Ethics into Translator Training: An Integrated, Inter-Disciplinary Approach," *The Interpreter and Translator Trainer* 5/1: 183–211.

Dryden, John. (1680) "From the Preface to *Ovid's Epistles*," in Venuti (2012b), pp. 38–42.

Duff, Alan. (1981) *The Third Language: Recurrent Problems of Translation into English*, Oxford: Pergamon.

Dundes, Alan. (1987) "The Psychoanalytic Study of Folklore," in *Parsing Through Customs: Essays by a Freudian Folklorist*, Madison, WI: University of Wisconsin Press, pp. 3–46.

Dundes, Alan and Alessandro Falassi. (1975) *La Terra in Piazza: An Interpretation of the Palio of Siena*, Berkeley and Los Angeles: University of California Press.

Dunne, Keiran J., and Elena S. Dunne. (eds.) (2011) *Translation and Localization Project Management: The Art of the Possible*, Amsterdam: John Benjamins.

Durston, Alan. (2007) *Pastoral Quechua: The History of Christian Translation in Colonial Peru, 1550–1650*, South Bend, IN: University of Notre Dame Press.

Eaglestone, Robert. (2005) "Levinas, Translation, and Ethics," in Bermann and Wood (2005), pp. 127–38.

Eco, Umberto. (1976a) "Peirce's Notion of Interpretant," *MLN* 91: 1457–72.

———. (1976b) *A Theory of Semiotics*, Bloomington: Indiana University Press.

———. (1979) *The Role of the Reader: Explorations in the Semiotics of Texts*, Bloomington, IN: Indiana University Press.

Economou, George, and Stavros Deligiorgis. (trans.) (2013) *Complete Plus: The Poems of C. P. Cavafy in English*, Bristol: Shearsman.

Edwards, Brent Hayes. (2003) *The Practice of Diaspora: Literature, Translation, and the Rise of Black Internationalism*, Cambridge, MA: Harvard University Press.

Einsohn, Amy. (2006) *The Copyeditor's Handbook*, Berkeley and Los Angeles: University of California Press.

Emery, Peter G. (2004) "Translation, Equivalence, and Fidelity: A Pragmatic Approach," *Babel* 50/2:143–67.

Emmerich, Karen. (2011) "The Afterlives of C. P. Cavafy's Unfinished Poems," *Translation Studies* 4/2: 197–212.

Emmerich, Michael. (2013) "Beyond Between: Translation, Ghosts, Metaphors," in Allen and Bernofsky (2013), pp. 44–57.

Espasa, Eva. (2000) "Performability in Translation: Speakability? Playability? Or Just Saleability," in Upton (2000), pp. 49–62.

Esselink, Bert. (2000) *A Practical Guide to Localization.* Amsterdam: John Benjamins.

Euripides. (1955) "The Medea," trans. Rex Warner, in David Grene and Richmond Lattimore (eds.) *Euripides One: Four Tragedies*, Chicago: University of Chicago Press, pp. 57–108.

Even-Zohar, Itamar. (1978) "The Position of Translated Literature within the Literary Polysystem," in Venuti (2012b), pp. 162–7.

Fairclough, Norman. (2005) *Critical Discourse Analysis: The Critical Study of Language*, London: Longman.

Fauconnier, Giles, and Mark Turner. (2002) *The Way We Think: Conceptual Blending and the Mind's Complexities*, New York: Basic Books.

Ferré, Rosario. (1995) "On Destiny, Language, and Translation; or, Ophelia Adrift in the C. & O. Canal," in Anuradha Dingwaney and Carol Maier (eds.) *Between Languages and Cultures: Translation and Cross-Cultural Texts*, Pittsburgh, PA: University of Pittsburgh Press, pp. 39–49.

Felstiner, John. (1980) *Translating Neruda: The Way to Macchu Picchu*, Stanford, CA: Stanford University Press.

———. (2001) "Deathfugue," in John Felstiner (ed. and trans.) *Selected Poems and Prose of Paul Celan*, New York: Norton, pp. 31–2.

Finnegan, Ruth. (1970) *Oral Literature in Africa*, Oxford: Clarendon.

———. (1992) *Oral Traditions and the Verbal Arts: A Guide to Research Practices*, London and New York: Routledge.

Fitch, Brian. (1998) *Beckett and Babel: An Investigation into the Status of the Bilingual Work*, Toronto: University of Toronto Press.

Forster, E. M. (1983) "The Poetry of C. P. Cavafy," in Denise Harvey (ed.) *The Mind and Art of C. P. Cavafy: Essays on His Life and Work*, Athens: Denise Harvey, pp. 13–18.

Foucault, Michel. (1977) "What Is an Author?" in Donald F. Bouchard (ed.) and Donald F. Bouchard and Sherry Simon (trans.), *Language, Counter-Memory, Practice: Selected Essays and Interviews*, Ithaca, NY: Cornell University Press, pp. 113–38.

Foz, Clara. (1998) *Le traducteur, l'Eglise et le Roi*, Ottawa and Arras: Les Presses de l'Université Ottawa et Artois Presses Université.

France, Peter. (ed.) (2000) *Oxford Guide to Literature in English Translation*, Oxford: Oxford University Press.

Fraser, Nancy. (2000) "Rethinking Recognition," *New Left Review* 3 (May–June): 107–20.

Freud, Sigmund. (1952) *On Dreams*, trans. James Strachey, New York: Norton, 1952.

Friar, Kimon. (1978) "Cavafis and His Translators into English," *Journal of the Hellenic Diaspora* 5/1: 17–40.

Friel, Brian. (1981) *Translations*, London: Faber and Faber.

Gambier, Yves, and Luc van Doorslaer (eds.) (2010) *Handbook of Translation Studies*, Amsterdam: John Benjamins, vol. 1.

Gasché, Rodolphe. (1986) *The Tain of the Mirror: Derrida and the Philosophy of Reflection*, Cambridge, MA: Harvard University Press.

Gascoigne, David. (1935) *A Short Survey of Surrealism*, London: Enitharmon, 2001.

Geballe, Elizabeth Frances. (2013) "Literary Disorders and Translation Treatment: Curing Chekhov's 'The Black Monk'," *Literature and Medicine* 31: 256–76.

Geertz, Clifford. (1973) "Thick Description: Toward an Interpretive Theory of Culture," in *The Interpretation of Cultures: Selected Essays*, New York: Basic Books, pp. 3–30.

Gentzler, Edwin. (2008) *Translation and Identity in the Americas: New Directions in Translation Theory*, London and New York: Routledge.

George, Andrew. (ed. and trans.) (1999) *The Epic of Gilgamesh: The Babylonian Epic Poem and Other Texts in Akkadian and Sumerian*, London: Allen Lane.

Gerhardt, Mia I. (1963) *The Art of Story-Telling: A Literary Study of the Thousand and One Nights*. Leiden: Brill.

Giannaris, Constantine (dir.) (1990) *Trojans*, Arts Council of Britain and Greek Film Center.

Gibbons, Reginald. (1985) "Poetic Form and the Translator," *Critical Inquiry* 11/4: 654–71.

Gil Bardají, Anna. (2009) "Procedures, Techniques, Strategies: Translation Process Operators," *Perspectives* 17/3: 161–73.

Goethe, Johann Wolfgang von. (1819) "Translations," trans. Sharon Sloan, in Schulte and Biguenet (1992), pp. 60–3.

González-Davies, Maria. (2004) *Multiple Voices in the Translation Classroom*, Amsterdam: John Benjamins.

González-Davies, Maria and Christopher Scott-Tennent. (2005) "A Problem-Solving and Student-Centred Approach to the Translation of Cultural References," *Meta* 50/1: 160–79.

Goodman, Nelson. (1968) *Languages of Art: An Approach to a Theory of Symbols*, Indianapolis, IN: Bobbs-Merrill.

Gottlieb, Henrik. (1992) "Subtitling—A New University Discipline," in Cay Dollerup and Anne Loddegaard (eds.) *Teaching Translation and Interpreting: Training, Talent and Experience*, Amsterdam: John Benjamins, pp. 161–70.

———. (1996) "Theory into Practice: Designing a Symbiotic Course in Subtitling," in Christine Heiss and Rosa Maria Bollettieri Bosinelli (eds.) *Traduzione Multimediale per il Cinema, la Televisione e la Scena*, Bologna: CLUEB, pp. 281–95.

Green, Julien. (1987) *Le langage et son double/Language and Its Double*, Paris: Seuil.

Greetham, David. (1998) "A Suspicion of Texts," in *Textual Transgressions: Essays toward the Construction of a Biobibliography*, New York: Garland.

Grimm, Jakob, and Wilhelm Grimm. (1884) *Grimm's Household Tales*, trans. Margaret Hunt, London: George Bell and Sons, 2 vols.

———. (1992) *The Complete Fairy Tales of the Brothers Grimm*, trans. Jack Zipes, New York: Bantam.

Grossman, Edith. (2010) *Why Translation Matters*, New Haven, CT: Yale University Press.

Haas, Diana. (1995) "Biographical, Autobiographical and Epistolary Material from the Archives of C. P. Cavafy: A Report on Recent Research," *Molivdo-kondilo-pelekitis* 5: 39–49.

Haddawy, Husain. (trans.) (1990) *The Arabian Nights*, New York: Norton.

Halim, Hala. (2013) *Alexandrian Cosmopolitanism: An Archive*, New York: Fordham University Press.

Hamburger, Michael. (1989) "Death Fugue," in Michael Hamburger (ed. and trans.) *Paul Celan: Poems*, New York: Persea, pp. 62–5.

Han, Zhaohong. (2004) *Fossilization in Adult Second Language Acquisition*, Clevedon: Multilingual Matters.

Hardenberg, Wendeline A. (2009) "Self-Translation: Identity, Exile, and Beyond," *Metamorphoses* 17/1 (Spring): 152–74.

Haring, Lee. (1999) "The Multilingual Subaltern: Creolization as Agency," *Estudos de Literatura Oral* 5: 109–19.

———. (2007) *Stars and Keys: Folktales and Creolization in the Indian Ocean*, Bloomington, IN: Indiana University Press.

Hartman, Michelle. (2012) "Gender, Genre and the (Missing) Gazelle: Arab Women Writers and the Politics of Translation." *Feminist Studies* 38/1: 17–49.

Harvey, Keith. (1998) "Translating Camp Talk: Gay Identities and Cultural Transfer," in Venuti (2012b), pp. 344–64.

Hassan, Waïl, and Susan Muaddi Durraj. (eds) (2012) *Approaches to the Teaching the Works of Naguib Mahofouz*, New York: MLA.

Hatim, Basil, and Ian Mason. (1990) *Discourse and the Translator*, London and New York: Routledge.

Hayward, Maysa Abou-Youssef. (2012) "Teaching Mahfouz: Style in Translation," in Waïl S. Hassan and Susan Muaddi Darraj (eds.) *Approaches to Teaching the Works of Naguib Mahfouz*, New York: MLA, pp. 130–41.

Haywood, Louise, Ian Higgins, and Sándor Hervey. (1995) *Thinking Spanish Translation: A Course in Translation Method. Spanish to English*, 1st ed., London and New York: Routledge.

Haywood, Louise, Michael Thompson, and Sándor Hervey. (2009) *Thinking Spanish Translation: A Course in Translation Method. Spanish to English*, 2nd ed., London and New York: Routledge.

Heaney, Seamus. (trans.) (2001) *Beowulf: A New Verse Translation*, New York: Norton.

Hemschemeyer, Judith (1998) "He Loved . . .," in Judith Hemschemeyer (ed. and trans.) *The Complete Poems of Anna Akhmatova*, Somerville, MA: Zephyr, vol. 1, p. 261.

Herder, Johann Gottfried. (1766–1767) "The Ideal Translator," in Robinson (1997b), pp. 207–8.

Hermans, Theo. (ed.) (1985) *The Manipulation of Literature: Studies in Literary Translation*, London: Croom Helm.

———. (1999) *Translation in Systems: Descriptive and Systemic Approaches Explained*, Manchester: St. Jerome.

————. (2002) "The Production and Reproduction of Translation: System Theory and Historical Context," in Saliha Paker (ed.) *Translations: (Re)shaping of Literature and Culture*, Istanbul: Bogaziçi University Press, pp. 175–94.

————. (2004) "Metaphor and Image in the Discourse on Translation: A Historical Survey," in Harald Kittel, Armin Paul Frank, Norbert Greiner, Theo Hermans, Werner Koller, José Lambert, and Fritz Paul (eds.) *Übersetzung, Translation, Traduction*, Berlin: De Gruyter, pp. 118–28.

Herskovits, Melville J., and Frances S. Herskovits. (1958) *Dahomean Narrative*, Evanston, IL: Northwestern University Press.

Hockney, David. (1967) *Fourteen Poems by C. P. Cavafy Chosen and Illustrated with Twelve Etchings by David Hockney*, trans. Nikos Stangos and Stephen Spender, London: Alecto.

Hoffman, Eva. (1989) *Lost in Translation: A Life in a New Language*, New York: Penguin.

Hofstadter, Douglas. (1997) "A Vile Non-verse," in *Le Ton beau de Marot: In Praise of the Music of Language*, New York: Basic Books.

Hokenson, Jan, and Marcella Munson. (2007) *The Bilingual Text: History and Theory of Literary Self-Translation*, Manchester: St. Jerome.

Holmes, James S. (1972) "The Name and Nature of Translation Studies," in *Translated! Papers on Literary Translation and Translation Studies*, 2nd ed., Amsterdam: Rodopi, 1988, pp. 67–80.

Horovitz, Josef. (1927) "The Origins of the *Arabian Nights*," *Islamic Culture* 1: 36–57.

Humaydan Younes, Iman. (2001) *Tut Barri*, Beirut: Masar.

————. (2008) *Wild Mulberries*, trans. Michelle Hartman, Northampton, MA: Interlink.

Hymes, Dell. (1975) "Folklore's Nature and the Sun's Myth," *Journal of American Folklore* 88/350: 346–69.

————. (2003) *Now I Know Only So Far: Essays in Ethnopoetics*, Lincoln, NE: University of Nebraska Press.

Ibrahim, Sonallah. (2007) *Al-Talasus*, Cairo: Dar al-mustaqbal al-'arabi.

————. (2010) *Stealth*, trans. Hosam Aboul-Ela, London: Aflame.

Idris, Yusuf. (1971) "Bayt min lahm," in *Bayr min lahm wa-qisas ukhrá*, Cairo: 'Alam al-Kutub.

————. (1978) "House of Flesh," in Denys Johnson-Davies (ed. and trans.) *Egyptian Short Stories*, London: Heinemann, pp. 1–7.

————. (2009) "House of Flesh," trans. C. Lindley Cross, http://home.uchicago.edu/~ksalib/translations/HouseOfFlesh.pdf. (accessed 11 February 2014).

Imhauser, Corinne. (2009) "The Pedagogy of Subtitling," in Gilbert C. F. Fong and Kenneth K. L. Au (eds.) *Dubbing and Subtitling in a World Context*, Hong Kong: The Chinese University Press, pp. 231–41.

Irwin, Robert. (2006) *For Lust of Knowing: The Orientalists and Their Enemies*, London: Allen Lane.

Jackson, Shannon. (2004) *Professing Performance: Theatre in the Academy from Philology to Performativity*, Cambridge: Cambridge University Press.

Jakobson, Roman. (1959) "On Linguistic Aspects of Translation," in Venuti (2012b), pp. 126–31.

————. (1960) "Closing Statements: Linguistics and Poetics," in Thomas A. Sebeok (ed.) *Style in Language*, Cambridge, MA: MIT Press, pp. 350–77.

Jakobson, Roman and Petr Bogatyrev. (1931) "On the Boundary Between Studies of Folklore and Literature," trans. Herbert Eagle, in Ladislav Matejka and Krystyna Pomorska (eds.) *Readings in Russian Poetics: Formalist and Structuralist Views*, Cambridge, MA: MIT Press, 1971, pp. 91–3.

Jakobson, Roman and Peter Colaclides. (1966) "Grammatical Imagery in Cavafy's Poem 'Thimisou, Soma . . .'," trans. Peter Jeffreys, *Linguistics* 4/20: 51–9.

Jerome. (395a CE) "The Best Kind of Translator: Letter to Pammachius," trans. Paul Carroll, in Robinson (1997b), pp. 23–30.

———. (395b CE) "Letter to Pammachius," trans. Kathleen Davis, in Venuti (2012b), pp. 21–30.

Johnson, John William, Thomas A. Hale, and Stephen Belcher. (eds.) (1997) *Oral Epics from Africa: Vibrant Voices from a Vast Continent*, Bloomington, IN: Indiana University Press.

Johnston, David. (ed.) (1996) *Stages of Translation. Essays and Interviews on Translating for the Stage*, Bath: Absolute.

———. (2004) "Securing the Performability of the Text," in Sabine Coelsch-Foisner and Holger Klein (eds.) *Drama Translation and Theatre Practice*, Berlin: Peter Lang, pp. 24–43.

Jones, Owen. (1856) *The Grammar of Ornament*, London: Day and Son.

Judaeus, Philo. (20 BCE ?) "The Creation of the Septuagint," trans. F. H. Colson, in Robinson (1997b), pp. 13–14.

Jusdanis, Gregory. (1987) *The Poetics of Cavafy: Textuality, Eroticism, History*, Princeton, NJ: Princeton University Press.

Kafka, Franz. (1967) *Erzählungen*, Frankfurt: S. Fischer.

Kapsalis, S. D. (1983) " 'Privileged Moments': Cavafy's Autobiographical Inventions." *Journal of the Hellenic Diaspora* 10/1–2: 67–88.

Kaster, Robert. (1988) *Guardians of Language: The Grammarian and Society in Late Antiquity*, Berkeley and Los Angeles: University of California Press.

Keeley, Edmund. (1996) *Cavafy's Alexandria*, Princeton, NJ: Princeton University Press.

——— and Philip Sherrard (trans.) (2009) *C. P. Cavafy: Collected Poems*, ed. George Savidis, Princeton, NJ: Princeton University Press.

Kelly, Dorothy. (2005) *A Handbook for Translator Trainers: A Guide to Reflective Practice*, Manchester: St. Jerome.

Kennedy, X. J. (2009) *Handbook of Literary Terms: Literature, Language, Theory*, New York: Pearson/Longman.

Kilito, Abdelfattah. (2008) *Thou Shalt Not Speak My Language*, trans. Waïl S. Hassan, Syracuse, NY: Syracuse University Press.

Kintsch, Walter. (1998) *Comprehension: A Paradigm for Cognition*, Cambridge: Cambridge University Press.

Kiraly, Donald C. (2000) *A Social Constructivist Approach to Translator Education*, Manchester: St. Jerome.

———. (2003) "From Instruction to Collaborative Construction," in Baer and Koby (2003), pp. 3–27.

———. (2005) "Project-Based Learning: A Case for Situated Translation." *Meta* 50/4: 1098–111.

———. (2015) "Occasioning Translator Competence: Moving Beyond Social Constructivism Towards a Postmodern Alternative to Instructionism," *Translation and Interpreting Studies* 10/1: 8–32.

Knowlson, James. (1978) "Afterword," in Samuel Beckett, *Happy Days/O les beaux jours: A Bilingual Edition*, ed. James Knowlson, London: Faber and Faber, pp. 84–128.

Kolb, David. A. (1984) *Experiential Learning Experience as a Source of Learning and Development*, Upper Saddle River, NJ: Prentice Hall.

Kourouma, Ahmadou. (2000) *Allah n'est pas oblige*, Paris: Seuil.

Kuhiwczak, Piotr, and Karin Littau (eds.) (2007) *A Companion to Translation Studies*, Clevedon: Multilingual Matters.

Kuhn, Thomas. (1962) *The Structure of Scientific Revolutions*, Chicago: University of Chicago Press, 2012.

Kundera, Milan. (1992) "Author's Note," in *The Joke*, trans. Milan Kundera, New York: Harper Collins, pp. 319–23.

Ladmiral, Jean-René. (1994) *Traduire: Théorèmes pour la traduction*, Paris: Gallimard.

Lane, Edward William. (1836) *An Account of the Manners and Customs of the Modern Egyptians*, London: Charles Knight.

———. (trans.) (1839–41) *The Thousand and One Nights, Commonly Called in England, The Arabian Nights' Entertainments*, London: Charles Knight, 3 vols.

Laplanche, Jean. (1992) "Psychoanalysis, Time and Translation," trans. Martin Stanton, in John Fletcher and Martin Stanton (eds.) *Jean Laplanche: Seduction, Translation, and the Drives: A Dossier*, London: Institute of Contemporary Arts, pp. 161–77.

Latour, Bruno. (1996) "Portrait de Gaston Lagaffe en philosophie des techniques," in *Petites leçons de sociologie des sciences*, Paris: La Découverte, pp. 15–24.

Lave, Jean, and Etienne Wenger. (1991) *Situated Learning: Legitimate Peripheral Participation*, Cambridge: Cambridge University Press.

Lee, James F., and Bill Van Patten. (2003) *Making Communicative Language Teaching Happen*, New York: McGraw Hill.

Lefevere, André. (1982) "Mother Courage's Cucumbers: Text, System and Refraction in a Theory of Literature," in Venuti (2012b), pp. 203–19.

———. (1992) *Translation, Rewriting and the Manipulation of Literary Fame*, London and New York: Routledge.

———. (1995) "Introduction: Comparative Literature and Translation," *Comparative Literature* 47: 1–10.

——— with Michel Ballard, Clara Foz, Anthony Pym, Lourdes Arenciba Rodriguez, Sherry Simon, D.J.M. Soulas de Russel, George Talbot, and Colette Touitou-Benitah (1995) "Translators and the Reins of Power," in Jean Delisle and Judith Woodsworth (eds.) *Translators through History*, Amsterdam: John Benjamins, pp. 131–55.

Levý, Jiří. (1967) "Translation as a Decision Process," in Venuti (2000), pp. 148–59.

Lewis, Philip E. (1985) "The Measure of Translation Effects," in Venuti (2012b), pp.220–39.

Liddell, Robert. (1974) *Cavafy: A Biography*, New York: Pocket.

Littau, Karin. (1997) "Translation in the Age of Postmodern Production: From Text to Intertext to Hypertext," in Baker (2010), pp. 435–48.

Littmann, Enno. (1960) "Alf laylah wa-Layla," *Encyclopedia of Islam*, 2nd ed., Leiden: Brill, vol. I, pp. 358–64.

Liu, Lydia. (1995) "Introduction: The Problem of Language in Cross-Cultural Studies," *Translingual Practice: Literature, National Culture, and Translated Modernity—China, 1900–1937*, Stanford, CA: Stanford University Press, pp. 1–42.

———. (1999) "Legislating the Universal: The Circulation of International Law in the Nineteenth Century," in Lydia Liu (ed.) *Tokens of Exchange: The Problem of Translation in Global Circulations*, Durham, NC: Duke University Press, pp. 127–64.

———. (2004) *The Clash of Empires: The Invention of China in Modern World Making*, Cambridge, MA: Harvard University Press.

Livingston, Julie. (2006) "Insights from an African History of Disability," *Radical Review of History* 94: 111–26.

Lloyd, A. L. (trans.) (1946) Franz Kafka, *The Metamorphosis*, New York: Vanguard.

Luhmann, Niklas. (2013) *Introduction to Systems Theory*, trans. Peter Gilgen, Cambridge: Polity.

Luther, Martin. (1530) "Circular Letter on Translation," trans. Douglas Robinson, in Robinson (1997b), pp. 84–9.

Lu Xun. (1930) " 'Hard Translation' and 'The Class Character of Literature'," in *Lu Xun: Selected Works*, trans. Yang Xianyi and Gladys Yang, 3rd ed., Beijing: Foreign Languages Press, 1980, vol. 3, pp.75–96.

Macpherson, James. (1760) *Fragments of Ancient Poetry, Collected in the Highlands of Scotland and Tr. from the Gaelic or Erse Langrage*, Edinburgh: G. Hamilton and J. Balfour.

Magoun, Francis B., Jr. and Alexander H. Krappe. (trans.) (1960) *The Grimms' German Folk Tales*, Urbana, IL: Southern Illinois University Press.

Mahfouz, Naguib. (1947) *Midaq Alley*, trans. Trevor Le Gassick, New York: Doubleday, 1975.

Maier, Carol S. (2003) "Gender, Pedagogy, and Literary Translation: Three Workshops and a Suggestion," in Baer and Koby (2003), pp. 157–72.

Malmkjær, Kirsten, and Kevin Windle. (eds.) (2011) *Oxford Handbook of Translation Studies*, Oxford: Oxford University Press.

Malti-Douglas, Fedwa. (1994) "Dangerous Crossings: Gender and Criticism in Arabic Literary Studies," in Margaret R. Higonnet (ed.) *Borderwork: Feminist Engagements with Comparative Literature*, Ithaca, NY: Cornell University Press, pp. 224–9.

Maranhão, Tullio. (2002) "The Politics of Translation and the Anthropological Nation of the Ethnography of South America," in Tullio Maranhão and Berhard Streck (eds.) *Translation and Ethnography*, Tucson, AR: University of Arizona Press, pp. 64–84.

Mason, Ian. (2012) "Text Parameters in Translation: Transitivity and Institutional Cultures," in Venuti (2012b), pp. 399–410.

Mavrogordato, John (trans.) (1951) *The Poems of C. P. Cavafy*, London: Hogarth.

McClatchy, J. D. (ed.) (2002) *Horace, the Odes: New Translations by Contemporary Poets*, Princeton, NJ: Princeton University Press.

McCrum, Robert. (2010) *Globish: How the English Language Became the World's Language*, New York: Norton.

McElduff, Siobhán. (2013) *Roman Theories of Translation*, London and New York: Routledge.

Melley, George, and Michael Wood. (1991) *Paris and the Surrealists*, London: Thames and Hudson.

Melnick, David. (1983) *Men in Aida, Book One*, Berkeley: Tuumba Press.

Mendelsohn, Daniel (trans.) (2012) *C. P. Cavafy: Complete Poems*, New York: Knopf.

Merrill, Christi. (2013) "Postcolonial Translation: The Politics of Language as Ethical Praxis," in Carmen Millán and Francesca Bartrina (eds.) *Routledge Handbook of Translation Studies*, London and New York: Routledge, pp. 159–72.

Merrill, James. (2001) *Collected Poems*, ed. J. D. McClatchy and Stephen Yenser, New York: Knopf.

Meschonnic, Henri. (1999) *Poetique du traduire*, Lagrasse: Verdier.

———. (2003) "Texts on Translation," trans. Anthony Pym, *Target* 15/2: 337–53.

Michals, Duane. (1978) *Homage to Cavafy: Ten Poems by Constantine Cavafy, Ten Photographs by Duane Michals*, Danbury, CT: Addison House.

Mikics, David. (2010) *A New Handbook of Literary Terms*, New Haven, CT: Yale University Press.

Mikkelson, Holly. (1994) *The Interpreter's Rx*, San Diego, CA: ACEBO.

Mitchell, Stephen. (trans.) (2004) *Gilgamesh: A New English Version*, New York: Free Press.

Moi, Toril. (2010) "The Adultress Wife," *London Review of Books* 32/3 (11 February): 3–6.

Molan, Peter D. (1987) "Sinbad the Sailor: A Commentary on the Ethics of Violence," *Journal of the American Oriental Society* 98: 237–47.

Moretti, Franco. (2000) "Conjectures on World Literature," *New Left Review* n.s. 1 (January/ February): 54–68.

Mossop, Brian. (2014) *Revising and Editing for Translators*, 3rd ed., London and New York: Routledge.

Muir, Willa and Edwin (trans.) (1952) "The Metamorphosis," in *Selected Short Stories of Franz Kafka*, New York: Modern Library, pp. 19–89.

Mukarovský, Jan. (1964) "Standard Language and Poetic Language," in Paul L. Garvin (ed. and trans.) *A Prague School Reader on Esthetics, Literary Structure, and Style*, Washington DC: Georgetown University Press, pp. 17–30.

Munday, Jeremy. (2007) "Translation and Ideology: A Textual Approach," *The Translator* 13/2: 195–217.

———. (2014) "Text Analysis and Translation," in Sandra Bermann and Catherine Porter (eds.) *A Companion to Translation Studies*, Malden, MA: Wiley Blackwell, pp. 69–81.

———. (2016) *Introducing Translation Studies: Theories and Applications*, 4th ed., London and New York: Routledge.

Nabokov, Vladimir. (1955) "Problems of Translation: *Onegin* in English," in Venuti (2012b), pp. 113–25.

Nehamas, Alexander. (1983) "Memory, Pleasure and Poetry: The Grammar of the Self in the Writing of Cavafy," *Journal of Modern Greek Studies* 1/2: 295–319.

Neubert, Albrecht, and Gregory Shreve. (1992) *Translation as Text*, Kent, OH: Kent State University Press.

Newman, Francis J. (1861) "The Unlearned Public is the Rightful Judge of Taste," in Robinson (1997b), pp. 255–7.

Nida, Eugene. (1964) "Principles of Correspondence," in Venuti (2012b), pp. 141–55.

Nida, Eugene and Charles Taber. (1969) *The Theory and Practice of Translation*, Leiden: Brill.

Nietzsche, Friedrich. (1882) "Translations," trans. Walter Kaufmann, in Venuti (2012b), pp. 67–8.

Nikolaou, Paschalis. (2006) "Notes on Translating the Self," in Eugenia Loffredo and Manuela Perteghella (eds.) *Translation and Creativity: Perspectives on Creative Writing and Translation Studies*, London and New York: Continuum, pp. 19–32.

Niranjana, Tejaswini. (1992) *Siting Translation: History, Post-Structuralism, and the Colonial Context*, Berkeley and Los Angeles: University of California Press.

Nord, Christiane. (1997) *Translating as a Purposeful Activity: Functionalist Approaches Explained*, Manchester: St Jerome.

———. (2005) "Making Otherness Accessible: Functionality and Skopos in the Translation of New Testament Texts," *Meta* 50/3: 868–80.

Nornes, Abé Mark. (2007) *Cinema Babel: Translating Global Cinema*, Minneapolis, MN: University of Minnesota Press.

Offord, Derek. (1996) *Using Russian: A Guide to Comparative Usage*, Cambridge: Cambridge University Press.

Olohan, Maeve. (2004) *Introducing Corpora in Translation Studies*, London and New York: Routledge.

Oring, Elliott. (ed.) (1986) *Folk Groups and Folklore Genres: An Introduction*, Logan, UT: Utah State University Press.

Oseki-Dépré, Inès. (1999) *Théories et pratiques de la traduction littéraire*, Paris: Armand Colin.

Oustinoff. Michaël. (2001) *Bilinguisme d'écriture et auto-traduction: Julien Green, Samuel Beckett, Vladimir Nabokov*, Paris: L'Harmattan.

Palumbo, Giuseppe. (2009) *Key Terms in Translation Studies*, London: Continuum.

Pamuk, Orhan. (2002) *The Black Book*, trans. Güneli Gün, London: Faber.

———. (2006) *The Black Book*, trans. Maureen Freely, New York: Vintage.

Panikkar, Raimon. (1988) "What is Comparative Philosophy Comparing?" in Gerald James Larson and Eliot Deutsch (eds.) *Interpreting Across Boundaries, New Essays in Comparative Philosophy*, Princeton, NJ: Princeton University Press, pp. 116–36.

Papanikolaou, Dimitris. (2005) "'Words That Tell and Hide': Revisiting C. P. Cavafy's Closets," *Journal of Modern Greek Studies* 23/2: 235–60.

Paravidino, Fausto. (2013) *Still Life in Ditch*, trans. Ilaria Papini, New York: Hanging Loose.

Pasolini, Pier Paolo. (dir.) (1974) *Il fiore delle mille e una notte: Arabian Nights*, United Artists.

Pavis, Patrice. (1992) *Theatre at the Crossroads of Culture*, trans. Loren Kruger, London and New York: Routledge.

Peden, Margaret Sayers. (1989) "Building a Translation, The Reconstruction Business: Poem 145 of Sor Juana Inés de la Cruz," in Schulte and Biguenet (1989), pp. 13–27.

Pérez González, Luis. (2006) "Fansubbing Anime: Insights into the Butterfly Effect of Globalisation on Audiovisual Translation," *Perspectives* 14/4: 260–77.

Peverati, Costanza. (2008) Review of Colina (2003), *The Interpreter and Translator Trainer* 2/2: 253–61.

Pöchhacker, Franz. (2010) "Interpreting," in Gambier and van Doorslaer (2010), pp. 153–7.

Pound, Ezra. (1929) "Guido's Relations," in Venuti (2012b), pp. 84–91.

Powys Mathers, Edward. (ed. and trans.) (1920) *The Garden of Bright Waters: One Hundred and Twenty Asiatic Love Poems*, Oxford: Blackwell.

———. (trans.) (1923) *The Book of the Thousand Nights and One Night. Rendered from the Literal and Complete Version of Dr. J. C. Mardrus*, London: Casanova Society, 16 vols.

Pozzi, Antonia. (2002) *Breath: Poems and Letters*, ed. and trans. Lawrence Venuti. Middletown, CT: Wesleyan University Press.

Pratt, Mary Louise. (1991) "Arts of the Contact Zone," in David Bartholomae and Anthony Petrosky (eds.) *Ways of Reading*, 7th ed., New York: Bedford, pp. 515–30.

Price, Joshua. (2008) "Translating Social Science: Good versus Bad Utopianism," *Target* 20/2: 348–64.

Prins, Yopie. (2005) "Metrical Translations: Nineteenth-Century Homers and the Hexameter Mania," in Bermann and Wood (2005), pp. 229–56.

Pritchard, Robert. (1990) "The Effects of Cultural Schemata on Reading Processing," *Reading Research Quarterly* 25: 273–95.

Pym, Anthony. (1998) *Method in Translation History*, Manchester: St. Jerome.

———. (2003) "Redefining Translation Competence in an Electronic Age: In Defence of a Minimalist Approach," *Meta* 48/4: 481–97.

———. (2012) *On Translator Ethics: Principles for Mediation Between Cultures*, Amsterdam: John Benjamins.

———. (2014) *Exploring Translation Theories*, 2nd ed., London and New York: Routledge.

Quillard, Geneviève. (2006) "Translation and Cultural Mediation: The Case of Advertising in Canada," *Translation and Interpreting Studies* 1/2: 111–46.

Radulescu, Stella Vinitchi. (2011) *I Was Afraid of Vowels . . . Their Paleness*, trans. Luke Hankins, Lubbock, TX: Q Avenue.

Rafael, Vicente L. (1988) *Contracting Colonialism: Translation and Christian Conversion in Tagalog Society Under Early Spanish Rule*, Durham, NC: Duke University Press.

———. (2009) "Translation, American English and the National Insecurities of Empire," in Venuti (2012b), pp. 451–68.

Rambelli, Paolo. (2009) "Pseudotranslation," in Baker and Saldanha (2009), pp. 208–11.

Rappaport, Helen. (2007) "Chekhov in the Theatre: The Role of the Translator in New Versions," in Gunilla Anderman (ed.) *Voices in Translation: Bridging Cultural Divides*, Clevedon: Multilingual Matters, pp. 66–77.

Reiss, Katharina. (1981) "Type, Kind and Individuality of Text: Decision Making in Translation," trans. Susan Kitron, in Venuti (2000), pp. 160–71.

Renkema, Jan. (2004) *Introduction to Discourse Studies*, Amsterdam: John Benjamins.

Richards, Jack, and Theodore Rodgers. (2001) *Approaches and Methods in Language Teaching*, 2nd ed., Cambridge: Cambridge University Press.

Ricks, David. (1993) "Cavafy Translated." *Kampos: Cambridge Papers in Modern Greek* 1: 85–110.

Ricoeur, Paul. (1970) "The Conflict of Interpretations," in *Freud and Philosophy: An Essay in Interpretation*, Denis Savage (trans.), New Haven, CT: Yale University Press, pp. 20–36.

———. (2006) *On Translation*, trans. Eileen Brennan, London and New York: Routledge.

Robinson, Bryan J., Clara I. López Rodríguez and María I. Tercedor Sánchez. (2008) "Neither Born nor Made, but Socially-Constructed: Promoting Interactive Learning in an Online Environment," *TTR: Traduction, terminologie, redaction* 22/2: 95–129.

Robinson, Christopher. (1988) *C. P. Cavafy*, Bristol: Bristol Classical Press.

Robinson, Douglas. (1991) *The Translator's Turn*, Baltimore: Johns Hopkins University Press.

———. (1997a) "Foreignizing Experience: Antoine Berman, *The Experience of the Foreign*," in *What Is Translation? Centrifugal Theories, Critical Interventions*, Kent, OH: Kent State University Press, pp. 81–96.

———. (ed.) (1997b) *Western Translation Theory: From Herodotus to Nietzsche*, 2nd ed., Manchester: St. Jerome, 2002.

———. (2001) *Who Translates? Translator Subjectivities beyond Reason*, Albany, NY: State University of New York Press.

———. (2012) *Becoming a Translator. An Introduction to the Theory and Practice of Translation*, 3rd ed., London and New York: Routledge.

Rodriguez, Richard. (1981) "Aria: A Memoir of a Bilingual Childhood," in Linda Peterson and John Brereton (eds.) *The Norton Reader*, 11th ed., New York: Norton, pp. 492–97.

Rose, Marilyn Gaddis. (1997) *Translation and Literary Criticism: Translation as Analysis*, Manchester: St. Jerome.

———. (ed.) (1981) *Translation Spectrum: Essays in Theory and Practice*, Albany, NY: State University of New York Press, pp. 88–98.

Rosenthal, Mira. (2010) "Revising Anna Świrszczyńska: The Shifting Stance of Czeslaw Miłosz's English Translations," *Canadian Slavic Papers* 52/1–2 (March–June): 59–78.

Różycki, Tomasz. (2007) *The Forgotten Keys*, trans. Mira Rosenthal, Brookline, MA: Zephyr.

Sachperoglou, Evangelos (trans.) (2007) *C. P. Cavafy: The Collected Poems*, ed. Anthony Hirst, Oxford: Oxford University Press.

Said, Edward W. (1978) *Orientalism*, New York: Pantheon.

———. (1990) "Embargoed Literature," in *The Politics of Dispossession: The Struggle for Palestinian Self-Determination, 1969–1994*, New York: Pantheon, pp. 372–8.

Sakai, Naoki. (1997) *Translation and Subjectivity: On "Japan" and Cultural Nationalism*, Minneapolis, MN: University of Minnesota Press.

Saldanha, Gabriela, and Sharon O'Brien. (2014) *Research Methodologies in Translation Studies*, London and New York: Routledge.

Sale, George. (trans.) (1734) *The Koran, commonly called Alkoran of Mohammed*, London: F. Warne, 1887.

Saussy, Haun. (ed.) (2006a) *Comparative Literature in an Age of Globalization*, Baltimore: Johns Hopkins University Press.

———. (2006b) "Exquisite Cadavers Stitched from Fresh Nightmares: Of Memes, Hives, and Selfish Genes," in Saussy (2006), pp. 1–42.

Savery, John R., and Thomas M. Duffy. (1996) "Problem Based Learning: An Instructional Model and Its Constructivist Framework," in Brent G. Wilson (ed.) *Constructivist Learning Environments: Case Studies in Instructional Design*, Englewood Cliffs, NJ: Educational Technology, pp. 135–48.

Savidis, George. (1964) *The C. P. Cavafy Archive: An Initial Informative Report*, Athens: n.p.

———. (1983) "Photographs of C. P. Cavafy, His Family and Home," *Grand Street* 2/3: 127–42.

Schäffner, Christina. (2004) "Review of Kiraly (2000)," *Target* 16/1: 157–62.

Schleiermacher, Friedrich. (1813a) "On the Different Methods of Translating," trans. Douglas Robinson, in Robinson (1997b), pp. 225–37.

———. (1813b) "On the Different Methods of Translating," trans. Susan Bernofsky, in Venuti (2012b), pp. 43–63.

Schulte, Rainer. (ed.) (1994) *Comparative Perspectives: Anthology of Multiple Translations*, New York: American Heritage Custom Publishing.

Schulte, Rainer and John Biguenet. (eds.) (1989) *The Craft of Translation*, Chicago: University of Chicago Press.

———. (eds.) (1992) *Theories of Translation: An Anthology of Essays from Dryden to Derrida*, Chicago: University of Chicago Press.

Scott, Craig. (2001) *Torture as Tort: Comparative Perspectives on the Development of Transnational Human Rights*, Oxford: Hart.

Sedgwick, Eve Kosofsky. (2010) "Cavafy, Proust, and the Queer Little Gods," in Panagiotis Roilos (ed.) *Imagination and Logos: Essays on C. P. Cavafy*, Cambridge, MA: Harvard University Press.

Sells, Michael. (ed. and trans.) (1989) *Desert Tracings: Six Classic Arabian Odes by 'Alqama, Shanfara, Labid, Al-'A'sha and Dhu Al-Rumma*, Middletown, CT: Wesleyan University Press.

———. (ed. and trans.) (1999) *Approaching the Qur'an: The Early Revelations*, Ashland, OR: White Cloud Press.

Shankar, Subramanian. (2012) *Flesh and Fish Blood: Postcolonialism, Translation, and the Vernacular*, Berkeley and Los Angeles: University of California Press.

Shaykh, Hanan al. (1980) *Hikayat Zahra*, Beirut: Al-Adab.

———. (1986) *Story of Zahra*, trans. Peter Ford, New York: Doubleday.

———. (2011) *One Thousand and One Nights: A Retelling*, London: Bloomsbury.

Shillingsburg, Peter. (1996) *Scholarly Editing in the Computer Age: Theory and Practice*. Ann Arbor, MI: University of Michigan Press.

Shreve, Gregory M. (2012) "The Discourses of Translation: An Introduction," in Beverly Adab, Peter A. Schmitt, and Gregory Shreve (eds.) *Discourses of Translation Festschrift in Honour of Christina Schäffner*, Frankfurt: Peter Lang, pp. 39–48.

Shugaar, Antony. (2014) "Translation as a Performing Art," *New York Times*, 27 January. http://opinionator.blogs.nytimes.com/2014/01/27/william-weaver-and-translation-as-a-performing-art/ (accessed 23 January 2016).

Shuman, Amy, and Galit Hasan-Rokem. (2012) "The Poetics of Folklore," in Bendix and Hasan-Rokem (2012), pp. 55–74.

Shuttleword, Mark, and Moira Cowie. (1997) *Dictionary of Translation Studies*, Manchester: St. Jerome.

Simeoni, Daniel. (1998) "The Pivotal Status of the Translator's *Habitus*," *Target* 10/1: 1–39.

———. (2007) "Translation and Society: The Emergence of a Conceptual Relationship," in Paul St-Pierre and Prafulla C. Kar (eds.) *Translation: Reflections, Refractions, Transformations*, Amsterdam: Benjamins, pp. 13–26.

Simon, Sherry. (1992) "The Language of Cultural Difference: Figures of Alterity in Canadian Translation," in Lawrence Venuti (ed.) *Rethinking Translation: Discourse, Subjectivity, Ideology*, London and New York: Routledge, pp. 159–76.

———. (1996) *Gender in Translation: Cultural Identity and the Politics of Transmission*, London and New York: Routledge.

Simons, Margaret A. (1998) *Beauvoir and the Second Sex: Feminism, Race and the Origins of Existentialism*, Lanham, MD: Rowman and Littlefield.

Smith, Barbara Herrnstein. (1968) *Poetic Closure: A Study of How Poems End*, Chicago: University of Chicago Press.

Smith, Lytton Jackson. (2008) "The Translation of Punctuation: An Analysis of Three Poems by C. P. Cavafy," in Karen Van Dyck (ed.) *C. P. Cavafy: The Typography of Desire (Introduction, Course Syllabus, and a Selection of Student Papers)*, Cavafy Forum, University of Michigan 2008, pp. 8–23. http://www.lsa.umich.edu/UMICH/modgreek/Home/_TOPNAV_WTGC/C.P.%20Cavafy%20Forum/The%20Typography%20of%20Desire_web.pdf (accessed 30 December 2015).

Smith, Miles. (1611) "The Translator to the Reader: Preface to the King James Version of the Bible," in Robinson (1997b), pp. 139–46.

Sokel, Walter. (1995) "Kafka and Modernism," in Richard T. Gray (ed.) *Approaches to Teaching Kafka's Short Fiction*, New York: MLA, pp. 21–34.

Spivak, Gayatri Chakravorty. (1983) "The Politics of Translation," in Venuti (2012b), pp. 312–30.

———. (2003) "Crossing Borders," in *Death of a Discipline*, New York: Columbia University Press, pp. 1–24.

———. (2005) "Translating into English," in Bermann and Wood (2005), pp. 94–110.

Stahuljak, Zrinka. (2010) "War, Translation, Transnationalism: Interpreters in and of the War (Croatia, 1991–1992)," in Baker (2010), pp. 393–414.

Steiner, George. (1975a) *After Babel: Aspects of Language and Translation*, 3rd ed., Oxford: Oxford University Press, 1998.

———. (1975b) "The Hermeneutic Motion," in Venuti (2012b), pp. 156–61.

Straus, Nina Pelikan. (1989) "Transforming Franz Kafka's 'Metamorphosis'," *Signs* 14/3 (Spring): 651–67.

Strauss, Claudia. (2006) "The Imaginary," *Anthropological Theory* 6/3: 322–44.

Strauss, Emanuel. (1984) *Dictionary of European Proverbs*, London and New York: Routledge.

Sturge, Kate. (1997) "Translation Strategies in Ethnography," *The Translator* 3: 21–38.

———. (2007) *Representing Others: Translation, Ethnography and the Museum*, Manchester: St. Jerome.

Tageldin, Shaden M. (2011) *Disarming Words: Empire and the Seductions of Translation in Egypt*, Berkeley and Los Angeles: University of California Press.

———. (2012) "Proxidistant Reading: Teaching the Arab *Nahdah* in US Comparative Literary Studies," *Journal of Arabic Literature* 43/2–3: 227–68.

———. (2014) "Untranslatability," *ACLA Report on the State of the Discipline 2014–2015*, 3 March. http://stateofthediscipline.acla.org/entry/untranslatability (accessed 2 January 2016).

Tagore, Rabindranath. (2001) "Presidential Address at the Bengali Literary Convention of North India, 3 March 1923," trans. Swapan Chakravorty, in Sisir Kumar Das and Sukanta Chaudhuri (eds.) *Rabindranath Tagore: Selected Writings on Literature and Language*, New Delhi: Oxford University Press, pp. 310–19.

Tahtawi, Rifaʻa Rafiʻ al. (2004) *An Imam in Paris: Account of a Stay in France by an Egyptian Cleric, 1826–1831 (Takhlis al-Ibriz fi Talkhis Bariz aw al-Diwan al-Nafis bi-Iwan Baris)*, trans. Daniel L. Newman, London: Saqi, pp. 173–89.

Taruskin, Richard. (1995) *Text and Act: Essays on Music and Performance*, Oxford: Oxford University Press.

Tatar, Maria. (1987) *The Hard Facts of the Grimms' Fairy Tales*, Princeton, NJ: Princeton University Press.

Taylor, Christopher. (2009) "Pedagogical Tools for the Training of Subtitlers," in Díaz Cintas and Anderman (2009), pp. 214–28.

Taylor, Diana. (2003) *The Archive and the Repertoire: Performing Cultural Memory in the Americas*, Durham, NC: Duke University Press.

Theoharis, Theoharis C. (trans.) (2001) *Before Time Could Change Them: The Complete Poems of Constantine P. Cavafy*, New York: Harcourt.

Thiong'o, Ngũgĩ wa. (2009) *Something Torn and New: An African Renaissance*, New York: Basic Civitas.

Thomas, D. M. (1985) "He Loved Three Things Alone . . .," in Anna Akhmatova, *You Will Hear Thunder*, ed. and trans. D. M. Thomas, Athens, OH: Ohio University Press, p. 42.

Thompson, Stith. (1955–1958) *Motif-Index of Folk-Literature: A Classification of Narrative Elements in Folktales, Ballads, Myths, Fables, Mediaeval Romances, Exempla, Fabliaux, Jest-Books, and Local Legends*, rev. ed., Bloomington, IN: Indiana University Press, 6 vols.

Thuesen, Peter. (1999) *In Discordance with the Scriptures: American Protestant Battles over Translating the Bible*, Oxford: Oxford University Press.

Toelken, Barre. (1996) *The Dynamics of Folklore, Revised and Expanded Edition*, Logan, UT: Utah State University Press.

———. (1998) "The Yellowman Tapes, 1966–1997," *Journal of American Folklore* 111/442 (Fall): 381–91.

Tognini-Bonelli, Elena. (2001) *Corpus Linguistics at Work*, Amsterdam: John Benjamins.

Torres, Gerald, and Kathryn Milun. (1990) "Translating Yonnondio by Precedent and Evidence: The Mashpee Indian Case," *Duke Law Review* 39/4: 625–59.

Toury, Gideon. (1978) "The Nature and Role of Norms in Translation," in Venuti (2012b), pp. 168–81.

———. (1995) *Descriptive Translation Studies and Beyond*, rev. ed., Amsterdam: John Benjamins, 2012.

Tribe, Keith. (2007) "Talcott Parsons as Translator of Max Weber's Basic Sociological Categories," *History of European Ideas* 33/2: 212–33.

Trivedi, Harish. (2006) "On Our Own Time. On Our Own Terms: Translation in India," in Theo Hermans (ed.) *Translating Others*, Manchester: St. Jerome, vol. 1, pp. 102–19.

Tymoczko, Maria. (1999) "Postcolonial Writing and Literary Translation," in Bassnett and Trivedi (1999), pp. 19–40.

———. (2010) "Western Metaphorical Discourses Implicit in Translation Studies," in James St. André (ed.) *Thinking through Translation with Metaphors*, London and New York: Routledge, pp. 109–43.

Tyulenev, Sergey. (2012) *Applying Luhmann to Translation Studies: Translation in Society*, London and New York: Routledge.

Upton, Carole-Anne. (ed.) (2000) *Moving Target: Theatre Translation and Cultural Relocation*, Manchester: St. Jerome.

Uther, Hans-Jörg. (2008) "Tale Type," in Donald Haase (ed.) *The Greenwood Encyclopedia of Folktales and Fairy Tales*, Westport, CT: Greenwood, vol. 3, pp. 937–42.

Vaidyanathan, Siva. (2001) *Copyrights and Copywrongs: The Rise of Intellectual Property and How It Threatens Creativity*, New York: New York University Press.

Valéry, Paul. (1962) "Historical Fact," trans. Denise Folloit, in *The Outlook for Intelligence*, ed. Jackson Mathews Princeton, NJ: Princeton University Press, pp. 118–29.

Van Lier, Leo. (1996) *Interaction in the Language Curriculum: Awareness, Autonomy and Authenticity*, London: Longman.

Venuti, Lawrence. (1995) *The Translator's Invisibility: A History of Translation*, 2nd ed., London and New York: Routledge, 2008.

———. (1998) *The Scandals of Translation: Towards an Ethics of Difference*, London and New York: Routledge.

———. (ed.) (2000) *The Translation Studies Reader*, 1st ed., London and New York: Routledge.

———. (2001) "Introduction," *Critical Inquiry* 27/2: 169–73.

———. (2005) "Local Contingencies: Translation and National Identities," in Bermann and Wood (2005), pp. 177–202.

———. (2010) "Translation, Empiricism, Ethics," in *Profession 2010*, New York: MLA, pp. 72–81.

———. (2012a) "Genealogies of Translation Theory: Jerome," in Venuti (2012a), pp. 483–502.

———. (ed.) (2012b) *The Translation Studies Reader*, 3rd ed., London and New York: Routledge.

———. (2013) *Translation Changes Everything: Theory and Practice*, London and New York: Routledge.

Vermeer, Hans. (1989) "Skopos and Commission in Translation Theory," trans. Andrew Chesterman, in Venuti (2012a), pp. 191–202.

———. (1996) *A Skopos Theory of Translation: Some Arguments For and Against*, Heidelberg: TextconText.

Vinay, Jean-Paul, and Jean Darbelnet. (1995) *Comparative Stylistics of French and English: A Methodology for Translation*, ed. and trans. Juan Sager and Marie-Jo Hamel, Amsterdam: John Benjamins.

Voigt, Ellen Bryant. (1999) *The Flexible Lyric*, Athens, GA: University of Georgia Press.

Von Flotow, Luise. (1997) *Translation and Gender: Translating in the "Era of Feminism"*, Manchester: St. Jerome.

———. (2007) "Gender and Translation," in Kuhiwczak and Littau (2007), pp. 92–105.

———. (2010) "Gender in Translation," in Gambier and van Doorslaer (2010), pp. 129–33.

Vygotsky, Lev. S. (1978) *Mind in Society: The Development of Higher Psychological Processes*, trans. Michael Cole, Cambridge, MA: Harvard University Press.

———. (1981) "The Genesis of Higher Mental Functions," *The Concept of Activity in Soviet Psychology*, ed. and trans. J. V. Wertsch, New York: Sharpe, pp. 144–88.

Wadensjö, Cecilia. (2009) "Community Interpreting," in Baker and Saldanha (2009), pp. 43–8.

Wallerstein, Immanuel. (1981) "Concepts in the Social Sciences: Problems of Translation," in Rose (1981), pp. 88–98.

———. (ed.) (1996) *Open the Social Sciences: Report of the Gulbenkian Commission on the Restructuring of the Social Sciences*, Stanford, CA: Stanford University Press.

Washbourne, Kelly. (2010a) *Manual of Spanish-English Translation*, Upper Saddle River, NJ: Prentice Hall.

———. (2010b). *Manual of Spanish-English Translation. Instructor's Resource Manual*, Upper Saddle River, NJ: Prentice Hall.

———. (2013) "Teaching Literary Translation: Objectives, Epistemologies and Methods for the Workshop," *Translation Review* 86/1: 49–66.

Weaver, William. (1995) "In Other Words: A Translator's Notebook," *New York Times Book Review*, 19 November, pp. 16–18.

Weber, Max. (1947) *The Theory of Social and Economic Organization*, ed. Talcott Parsons, trans. A. M. Henderson and Talcott Parsons, New York: Oxford University Press.

Weinberger, Eliot, and Octavio Paz. (eds.) (1987) *19 Ways of Looking at Wang Wei: How a Chinese Poem is Translated*, Mount Kisco, NY: Moyer Bell.

West, Kevin. (2010) "Translating the Body: Toward an Erotics of Translation." *Translation and Literature* 19/1: 1–25.

Williams, Jenny, and Andrew Chesterman. (2002) *The Map: A Beginner's Guide to Doing Research in Translation Studies*, Manchester: St. Jerome.

Wilson, William A. (1986) "Documenting Folklore," in Oring (1986), pp. 225–54.

Wolf, Michaela. (2001) "Mapping the Field: Sociological Perspectives on Translation," *International Journal of the Sociology of Language* 207: 1–28.

Yourcenar, Marguerite. (1980) "A Critical Introduction to Cavafy," trans. Richard Howard, *Shenandoah* 32/1: 154–98.

Zetzel, James E. G. (ed. and trans.) (2009) *Cicero: Ten Speeches*, Indianapolis, IN: Hackett.

Zilcosky, John. (2011) "Kafka's Poetics of Indeterminacy: On Trauma, Hysteria, and Simulation at the Fin de Siècle," *Monatshefte* 103/3 (Fall): 344–59.

Zipes, Jack. (1988) *The Brothers Grimm: From Enchanted Forests to the Modern World*, London and New York: Routledge.

Index